British or American English?

Speakers of British and American English display some striking differences in their use of grammar. In this detailed survey, John Algeo considers questions such as:

*Who lives *on a street*, and who lives *in a street*?
*Who *takes a bath*, and who *has a bath*?
*Who says *Neither do I*, and who says *Nor do I*?
*After "thank you", who says *Not at all* and who says *You're welcome*?
*Whose team *are* on the ball, and whose team *is*?

Containing extensive quotations from real-life English on both sides of the Atlantic, collected over the past twenty years, this is a clear and highly organized guide to the differences – and the similarities – in the grammar of British and American speakers. Written for those with no prior knowledge of linguistics, it shows how these grammatical differences are linked mainly to particular words, and provides an accessible account of contemporary English as it is actually used.

JOHN ALGEO is Professor Emeritus in the Department of English, University of Georgia, Athens. His previous posts include Fulbright Senior Research Scholar, University College London (1986–7), Guggenheim Fellow (1986–7), and University of Georgia Alumni Foundation Distinguished Professor (1988–94). Over the past forty years he has contributed papers to a wide variety of books and journals, including 91 book reviews.

STUDIES IN ENGLISH LANGUAGE

The aim of this series is to provide a framework for original studies of English, both present-day and past. All books are based securely on empirical research, and represent theoretical and descriptive contributions to our knowledge of national varieties of English, both written and spoken. The series covers a broad range of topics and approaches, including syntax, phonology, grammar, vocabulary, discourse, pragmatics and sociolinguistics, and is aimed at an international readership.

Already published in this series:

Christian Mair
Infinitival Complement Clauses in English: a Study of Syntax in Discourse

Charles F. Meyer
Apposition in Contemporary English

Jan Firbas
Functional Sentence Perspective in Written and Spoken Communication

Izchak M. Schlesinger
Cognitive Space and Linguistic Case

Katie Wales
Personal Pronouns in Present-day English

Laura Wright
The Development of Standard English, 1300–1800: Theories, Descriptions, Conflicts

Charles F. Meyer
English Corpus Linguistics: Theory and Practice

Stephen J. Nagle and Sara L. Sanders (eds.)
English in the Southern United States

Anne Curzan
Gender Shifts in the History of English

Kingsley Bolton
Chinese Englishes

Irma Taavitsainen and Päivi Pahta (eds.)
Medical and Scientific Writing in Late Medieval English

Elizabeth Gordon, Lyle Campbell, Jennifer Hay, Margaret Maclagan, Andrea Sudbury and Peter Trudgill
New Zealand English: Its Origins and Evolution

Raymond Hickey (ed.)
Legacies of Colonial English

Merja Kytö, Mats Rydén and Erik Smitterberg (eds.)
Nineteenth Century English: Stability and Change

British or American English?

A Handbook of Word and Grammar Patterns

JOHN ALGEO
University of Georgia

CAMBRIDGE UNIVERSITY PRESS
Cambridge, New York, Melbourne, Madrid, Cape Town, Singapore, São Paulo

Cambridge University Press
The Edinburgh Building, Cambridge CB2 2RU, UK

Published in the United States of America by Cambridge University Press, New York

www.cambridge.org
Information on this title: www.cambridge.org/9780521379939

First published 2006

Printed in the United Kingdom at the University Press, Cambridge

A catalogue record for this publication is available from the British Library

ISBN-13 978-0-521-37137-7 hardback
ISBN-10 0-521-37137-6 hardback

ISBN-13 978-0-521-37993-9 paperback
ISBN-10 0-521-37993-8 paperback

Contents

Preface

The study on which this book is based began about forty years ago as a casual interest in the subject engendered by Thomas Pyles's history textbook, *The Origins and Development of the English Language* (now in its fifth revised edition, Algeo and Pyles 2004). It was focused during a year (1986–7) the author spent in the Survey of English Usage at University College London as a Fulbright Senior Research Scholar and a Guggenheim Fellow. In those days, the Survey was only beginning to be converted into electronic form, so at first research involved hunting through paper slips and copying information by hand. Later, as the Survey was computerized, electronic searches became possible, initially only at the Survey office and later through a CD anywhere.

The present study later benefited from the collection of citations made by Allen Walker Read for a historical dictionary of British lexical items. My wife, Adele, and I then set out to supplement Read's files with citations we collected from more recent material than he had used, including citations for grammatical as well as lexical matters. Our own corpus of British citations is now about three million words in size. That is not large for a contemporary data file, but it consists entirely of citations that we had reason to suspect exemplified British use.

Work on this book was delayed by a variety of other duties to which its author had fallen heir. It is now presented, with painful awareness of its limitations, but, as the French are fond of saying, *faute de mieux*. Undoubtedly, British and American English are grammatically different in ways not reported here. And some of the grammatical differences reported here may be less certain than this book suggests because of difficulties in identifying and substantiating those differences or because of the misapprehension of the author. Nevertheless, I hope that it will be helpful in pinpointing various areas of structural difference between the two major national varieties of the language.

Acknowledgments

The debts owed for help in producing this book are more than the author can pay. The greatest debt for a labor of love is to his wife, Adele Silbereisen Algeo, who has assisted him in this, as in all other activities during the nearly fifty years of their married life. In particular, she has been the major collector of British citations that compose the corpus from which most of the illustrative quotations have been taken. She has also critiqued and proofed the text of the book at every stage of its production.

Gratitude is also due to a succession of editors at the Cambridge University Press who have, with kind hearts and gentle words, tolerated a succession of delays in the book's preparation. Likewise gratitude is due to the Cambridge University Press for permission to use the Cambridge International Corpus, without which statements of relative frequency in British and American use would be far more intuitional and far less data-based than they are.

I am indebted to a variety of scholarly studies, both general and specific, for their insights into British-American differences. These are cited in the text of this book and listed in the bibliography of scholarly works at the end. I am particularly indebted to the works by Randolph Quirk, Sidney Greenbaum, Geoffrey Leech, and Jan Svartvik (1985), Michael Swan (1995), and Pam Peters (2004). For existing scholarship that has not been cited here, I can only say "mea culpa, mea culpa, mea maxima culpa."

Individuals who, over the years, have kindly sent Adele and me quotations that have been entered into our corpus include notably Catherine M. Algeo, Thomas Algeo, L. R. N. Ashley, Carmen Acevedo Butcher, Ronald Butters, Tom Creswell, Charles Clay Doyle, Virginia McDavid, Michael Montgomery, and Susan Wright Sigalas.

Finally, and in a sense initially, I am grateful for the support of the John Simon Guggenheim Memorial Foundation and the Fulbright Senior Research Scholar Program for support at the Survey of English Usage, University of London, during the academic year 1986–7, when the project was begun, and to the now departed Sidney Greenbaum, who as Quain Professor of English Language and Literature invited me to the Survey.

Introduction

British and American as national varieties

There are many varieties of English other than British (here the English of the United Kingdom) and American (here the English of the United States). All of those other varieties are intrinsically just as worthy of study and use as British and American. But these two varieties are the ones spoken by most native speakers of English and studied by most foreign learners. They have a special status as the two principal national varieties of the language simply because there is more material available in them than in any other variety.

British is the form of English now used in the country whence all other forms of English have ultimately derived. But present-day British is not the origin of any other variety of the language; rather it and all the other varieties are equally descendant from a form of English spoken in the British Isles in earlier times. In some respects, present-day British is closer to the common ancestral form of the present-day varieties than is American or other varieties; but in other respects the reverse is true, and American, for instance, preserves older uses that became obsolete in British use. To mistake present-day British for the ancestor of all other forms of English is a logical and factual error.

The focus of this study is on how contemporary British English differs from American. That is, in comparing two varieties of a language, it is convenient to take one as the basis for comparison and to describe the other by contrast with it. This study takes American as its basis and describes British in relation to that basis. The reason for this approach is that American has more native speakers than British and is rapidly becoming the dominant form of English in non-native countries other perhaps than those of Western Europe. Much European established academic bias favors British as a model; but evolving popular culture is biased toward American. This widespread dissemination of the American variety makes it a reasonable basis for describing British.

Differences between British and American

The most obvious difference between British and American is in the "tune" of the language, that is, the intonation that accompanies sentences. When a Briton or an American talks, they identify themselves primarily by the tunes of their respective varieties. In singing, the prose tune is overridden by the musical tune, making it much harder to distinguish British and American singers.

Other pronunciation differences exist in stress patterns and in consonant and vowel articulation and distribution. Those differences have been described in fine detail. Vocabulary differences have been very widely noted between the two varieties, and they are fairly extensive, although also often subtler than most lists of supposed equivalences account for. Popular awareness probably centers more on lexical differences than on any other sort, partly perhaps because they are the easiest for the layperson to notice. Subtle differences of national style also exist, but have been but little and only incidentally noted (Algeo 1989, Heacock and Cassidy 1998).

Grammatical differences have been treated, but mainly by individual scholarly studies focused on particular grammatical matters. Extensive and comprehensive treatment is rare. Popular writers on grammar are aware that British and American differ in their morphosyntax but tend to be sketchy about the details. Anthony Burgess (1992), who is one of the linguistically best informed men of letters, settled on a few verb forms as illustrations. The grammatical differences between the two principal national varieties of the language are, however, manifold. Some general treatments of British-American grammatical differences, from various standpoints, are those by Randolph Quirk et al. (1985), John Algeo (1988), Michael Swan (1995), Douglas Biber et al. (1999), Rodney Huddleston and Geoffrey Pullum (2002), Gunnel Tottie (2002, 146–78), Peter Trudgill and Jean Hannah (2002), and Pam Peters (2004).

Although many, few of the grammatical differences between British and American are great enough to produce confusion, and most are not stable because the two varieties are constantly influencing each other, with borrowing both ways across the Atlantic and nowadays via the Internet. When a use is said to be British, that statement does not necessarily mean that it is the only or even the main British use or that the use does not occur in American also, but only that the use is attested in British sources and is more typical of British than of American English.

The basis of this study

A distinction is often drawn between intuition and data as the basis for statements about language. That dichotomy, like most others, is false. Intuition is needed to identify matters to comment on, and data is (or, as the reader prefers, are) needed to substantiate intuition. My wife and I have spent twenty years gathering citations of what intuition told us were British uses. Then I set out to substantiate those intuitions by consulting corpora of data. In most cases, our intuitions proved correct, and the corpora yielded statistics to support our hunches. In some cases, however, what intuition told us was a Briticism turned out to be nothing of the sort, but instead just to be a rare or peculiar use – rare and peculiar in both British and American English. And in a few cases, we were spectacularly wrong. Linguistic intuition is invaluable but unreliable.

Corpus data is likewise invaluable, but it has its own unreliability. The statistics from any corpus should be used with care and reservations, especially in comparing statistics from different corpora or even statistics derived from the same corpus but in different ways. A bit of folk wisdom has it that there are three kinds of lies: lies, damned lies, and statistics. The problems with statistics based on language corpora include the fact that two corpora may not be comparable because they are of different sizes or because they are composed of different kinds of texts. Academic printed texts and conversational oral texts will have strikingly different characteristics.

The way one phrases a search in a corpus can also produce different results; for example, if the search engine is sensitive to capitalization, asking for examples and statistics of a form with a lower-case initial letter may produce rather different results than a query asking for the same information of the same form, but with an upper-case initial letter. In this study, capitalization was taken into consideration when it seemed potentially influential, but not otherwise.

Moreover, many grammatical items are difficult to find in a corpus unless it has been extensively and accurately tagged, and few corpora, especially the larger ones, have the sort of tagging that would make grammatical searches easy. Instead, one must come up with ways of asking the corpus about instances of something that its search engine can find and that will give at least implicit, albeit incomplete, information about grammatical structures. Thus if one wants information about the form of negation in sentences with indefinite direct objects (*They had no money*) versus those with definite direct objects (*They didn't have the money needed*), barring sophisticated grammatical tagging, it is necessary to ask about particular constructions (such as those just cited) and extrapolate a generalization from them. This study generally eschews such broad extrapolation, but some was unavoidable.

Finally, however, one relies on whatever is available. For the entries in this study, such evidence as was convenient to extract from corpora has been cited. But when that evidence was not readily available, intuition was still used. Any entry with no substantiating evidence is an intuitional guess, as far as its Britishness is concerned. In those, as well as other, cases it is advisable to keep in mind the wise words of Oliver Cromwell to the General Assembly of the Church of Scotland: "I beseech you, in the bowels of Christ, think it possible you may be mistaken." The author intones those words as a mantra.

Sources of comparative statistics and citations

Statistics

In the body of this work, several corpora have been used and are cited by name, but the one most used, especially for comparative statistics, is the Cambridge International Corpus (CIC). Statistics from it are sometimes cited as ratios or percentages; in those cases, the base number is of a size to make such form of citation appropriate and easy to follow. CIC statistics are also sometimes cited by an arcane abbreviation: "iptmw," that is, "instances per ten million words," which is the way the CIC reports frequencies from its nearly two hundred million words. The accompanying table shows the composition of this great corpus and the relative sizes of its component parts. As can be seen, the British corpus totals 101.9 million words, of which 83 percent are written texts and 17 percent spoken texts; the American corpus totals 96.1 million words, of which 77 percent are written texts and 23 percent spoken texts.

CAMBRIDGE INTERNATIONAL CORPUS

corpus group	*corpus name*	*million words*	*number of cites*	*contents*
British written	BRNEWS25	25.0	60224	mixed newspapers 1988 – June 2000
	BRWRIT2	25.4	26915	fiction, nonfiction & magazines etc.
	BNCWRIT1	25.1	901	British National Corpus part 1 (1979–1994)
	ACAD_BR	9.2	1260	British academic journals & nonfiction
		84.7		
British spoken	BRSPOK2	7.1	1652	spoken (lexicography) incl. Cancode/Brtrans
	BNCSPOK	10.1	911	British National Corpus spoken (1980–1994)
		17.2		
American written	AMNEWS25	25.0	45026	mixed newspapers 1979–1998
	AMNW01_2	22.0	23042	newspapers 2001
	AMWRIT2	23.8	28453	fiction, nonfiction & magazines etc.
	ACAD_AM	3.6	41	American academic journals & nonfiction
		74.4		
American spoken	AMLEXI	6.2	764	spoken (lexicography) incl. Naec/Amspok
	AMSPPROF	1.9	17	spoken professional (lexicography)
	AMTV	13.6	60881	TV & radio (lexicography & research)
		21.7		

In consulting the CIC, all textual categories were weighted equally, even though only 17 percent of British texts and 23 percent of American texts are spoken versus written, and 11 percent of British written texts and 5 percent of American written texts are academic versus general. That equal weighting emphasizes disproportionately the fewer spoken over written texts and academic over general writing. Different weightings would very likely have produced at least somewhat different results.

Because the focus of this study is not on speech versus writing or academic versus general style, and because British and American are treated alike in this respect, ignoring the differences in text types probably does not greatly affect the general conclusions concerning British versus American use. Thus a statement such as "*daren't* is 13.9 times more frequent in British than in American" refers to a combination of spoken and written texts in both varieties, although it is in the nature of things that contractions are more frequent in speech than in writing. That, however, is not the concern of this study.

The CIC is especially useful for a statistical comparison of British and American because of its large size and because it has roughly comparable samples of British and American texts. As mentioned above, statistics from it are often cited in terms of "instances per ten million words" (iptmw). When some form or construction is cited as occurring X times more or less often in one variety than in the other, or in percentages, the basis for that comparison seemed adequate, and that style of comparison easier to understand.

Citations

In keeping with the focus on British English mentioned above, all of the illustrative citations are of British use. Most of them are drawn from a corpus of British examples compiled by Adele and John Algeo over a period of some twenty years. That corpus consists of British citations gathered because they were suspected to contain characteristically British features, chiefly lexical but also some grammatical ones. Most of the citations are from newspapers or popular fiction. The corpus is stored electronically in word-processor format.

Illustrative quotations are generally limited to one for each entry. In many cases the files that underlie this study contain a great many more, but space was not available for them. Several of the chapters depend heavily on prior studies by the author and draw both examples and exposition from articles reporting those studies.

The sources cited are heavily in the genre of mystery novels and other light fiction, chosen because the initial reading was for lexical purposes, and those genres have a rich store of colloquialisms and informal language (in which British-American differences are most pronounced) whereas serious fiction contains fewer such items.

British fiction that has been adapted for American readers provides a useful source to document the words and expressions that publishers change for the American market. In the case of the *Harry Potter* books, a website (www.hp-lexicon.org/) provides a list of such changes. Quotations from these books in this work note the American adaptation when it was recorded on that site.

Many of the quotations cited here were computerized by graduate assistants at the University of Georgia. They sometimes made mistakes in transcribing a quotation that suggest the quotation's use was at variance with their own native use; such mistakes are occasionally noted as evidence for the Britishness of a particular form.

Examples cited from publicly available corpora are identified appropriately. Those cited from the Survey of English Usage (SEU) have corpus identification numbers preceded by either "s" for spoken or "w" for written.

Conventions and organization of this study

Illustrative quotations are abridged when that can be done without distortion or losing needed context. Matter omitted in the middle of a quotation is indicated by ellipsis points; matter omitted at the beginning of a quotation is indicated only if the retained matter does not begin with a capital letter; matter omitted at the end of a quotation is not indicated.

In the illustrative quotations, periodical headlines have arbitrarily been printed with initial capital letters for each word, as a device to facilitate their recognition.

The abbreviation "iptmw," which is widely used, has been explained above as meaning "instances per ten million words" in the CIC texts. An asterisk before a construction (as in **go sane*) means that the construction is impossible in normal use. A question mark before a construction (as in ?*They dared their friends solve the puzzle*) means that the construction is of doubtful or disputed possibility in normal use. Cross-references from one chapter to another use the symbol §; thus § 2.2.2.3 means "chapter 2 section 2.2.3". Abbreviations of titles of dictionaries, grammars, and corpora are explained in the bibliographies of scholarly works and of citation sources.

Studies and dictionaries are cited either by title abbreviations (e.g., *CGEL*), which are identified in the bibliography, or by author and year (e.g., Peters 2004). Citation sources are cited by date and author (e.g., 1977 Dexter) and short title, if necessary (e.g., 1937 Innes, *Hamlet*) or by periodical date and title (e.g., 2003 June 12 *Times* 20/2; for location in a periodical, "2 4/2–3" means "section 2, page 4, columns 2 to 3").

In headwords and glosses to them, general terms representing contextual elements are italicized, e.g., **pressurize** *someone* means that the verb *pressurize* takes a personal object.

A comment that a construction is "rare" means that the Algeo corpus contains few examples, often only one, and that CIC has no or very few instances of it. Such constructions are included because they illustrate a pattern. The term "common-core English" designates usage common to the two varieties, British and American, and not differing significantly between them.

Of the seventeen following chapters, the first ten deal with parts of speech, and the final seven with matters of syntax or phrase and clause constructions. Because the verb is central to English grammatical constructions, it is considered in Chapter 1. Thereafter, the elements of the noun phrase are taken up: determiners, nouns, pronouns, and adjectives. Adverbs and qualifiers (i.e., adverbs of degree) follow, succeeded by prepositions and conjunctions, with the highly miscellaneous category of interjections coming last in the chapters on parts of speech.

In the chapters on syntactic constructions, no effort is made to treat all matters of English syntax, most of which vary little between British and American use. Instead, chapters have been devoted to those relatively few syntactic matters that do show significant differences between the two national varieties: complementation (*agree [on] a plan*), mandative constructions (*insisted he was/be there*), expanded predicates (*have/take a bath*), concord (*the team have/has won*), propredicates (*I haven't finished but I could [do]*), tag questions (*he would, wouldn't he?*), and other constructions, such as focusing (*it's right tasty, is Webster's*).

I

Parts of Speech

1 Verbs

1.1 Derivation

British has some verbs lacking or comparatively rare in American, many of which are denominal.

bath Bathe: In CIC British texts, *bathe* is 5 or 6 times more frequent than *bath* as a verb, whereas the verb *bath* is very rare in American use, *bathe* occurring about 40 times more often. **1.** *intransitive* Wash oneself in a (bath) tub <We must all **bath** twice a day.> 1990 Aug. 13 *Times* 10/2. **2.** *transitive* Wash (someone) in a (bath) tub <He got her to **bath** herself.> 1992 Dexter 292. Note: In common-core English use, transitive *bathe* also means "apply water or other liquid to something to clean or soothe it," but in British English it does not usually mean "wash someone in a bath," for which *bath* is used; that difference in meaning explains the following: <"Is it all right" she asked. "Not gone gangrenous, has it? I can't see very well." [¶] I assured her it wasn't gangrenous, that I'd bathe it and that it would be better left exposed. [¶] She misunderstood or pretended to. "A bath," she said. "I haven't had a bath for two years. I need someone to get me out. You'll **bath** me."> 1991 Green 40.

beast Behave like a beast: The verbal use of *beast* is very rare. < . . . provost sergeants appear at work at 8am and don't stop shouting, bullying and **beasting** until they clock off at 4.30.> 1995 Aug. 28 *Independent* 2 7/5.

bin Trash; junk; put into a bin "trash can": The noun *bin* is not used in American English of a container for trash, so no corresponding verb exists. <Junk mail? Don't **bin** it, enjoy it.> 1990 Aug. 20 *Evening Standard* 22/3–4.

burgle Burglarize: *Burgle* is frequent in British use; CIC has no tokens of British *burglarize*. Both forms are used in American, but *burglarize* is about 20 times more frequent than *burgle*. Of a random CIC sample of 250 tokens of British *burgle*, 96 were active and 154 were passive; of the active uses, 57 had places as their objects, 3 had persons, 11 had things (*burgle a radio*), abstractions (*burgle a victory*), or were indeterminate, and 25 were intransitive. Of the passive uses, 1 applied to a thing, 56 to places, and 97 to persons. Thus the verb is more likely to be passive than active, and when active to take a noun of place as its object, but when passive to have a personal noun as subject. <But if they **burgle** a country house, they can be miles away in minutes.> 1994 Sept. *Tatler* 147/1. <People over 60 who are **burgled** are more likely to die or be moved into residential care.> 2003 June 26 *Guardian* international ed. 8/7.

cellar *wine* Stock *wine* in a cellar: This use is rare though recorded in both *NODE* and *MW*. < . . . we have not been in the habit of **cellaring** Rhone reds.> 1987 July *Illustrated London News* 70/3.

chair Carry on the shoulders of a group as an acclamation: This use is identified as British in *MW* and *NODE*. <And the choir themselves were **being chaired** round the cricket pitch – > 1988 Trollope 217.

cheek Be cheeky [impudent] toward: CIC has 0.6 iptmw of the verb in British texts and none in American texts. <Thersites was not a traitor, but a rank officer in the Iliad, who got a bloody nose for **cheeking** other officers.> 1998 Jan. 3 *Times* Metro 17/2. Cf. § 5.2 CHEEKY.

pressurize *someone* Pressure *someone*: CIC American tokens of *pressurize* outnumber British by 2 to 1, but of all the American tokens, only 3 have personal objects; on the other hand, two-thirds of the British tokens have personal objects, with which American would use the verb *pressure*. <She could have arranged to meet her lover . . . to **pressurize** him into marriage.> 2003 James 342.

sculpture Sculpt: CIC has 4.5 times as many tokens of *sculpt* as of the verb *sculpture* in British texts, but 7.5 times as many in American texts. Although *sculpt* is the usual verb in common-core English, *to sculpture* is relatively more frequent in British. <Even tiny plastic chocks of Lego can be agglomerated to make a **sculptured** figure.> 1991 Apr. 25, *Evening Standard* 23/3.

slob CIC has 0.6 iptmw of this verb in British texts and none in American. <She [Camilla] . . . can go home to Wiltshire and **slob** in front of the television without the butler spying on her.> 2004 Dec. 15 *Daily Telegraph* 18/6.

treble Triple: CIC has about 1.3 times as many *treble* as *triple* in British texts, and 18 times as many *triple* as *treble* in American texts. < . . . the figure could easily be doubled or **trebled**.> 1989 July 28 *Times* 2/1.

workshop ***a play*** Perform *a play* for the purpose of critiquing and improving it: This use is rare (it is in *NODE*, but not *MW*). <*Yasmin* was written by Simon Beaufoy . . . and nobody can question the nobility of his motives in "**workshopping**" it first with the Muslim community in northern England.> 2005 Jan. 14 *Daily Telegraph* 33/1–2.

1.2 Form

1.2.1 Principal parts

The inflected forms of verbs show some variation, with the irregular *-t* forms used more in British than they are in American (Johansson 1979, 205–6; *LGSWE* 396;

Peters 2004, 173). Conversely, however, British favors the regular preterit and participle of some verbs ending in *t* for which American often uses unchanged irregular forms. In the following list, verbs are listed under their dictionary-entry form, with their preterits and past participles following. If the second two principal parts are identical, only one is given.

awake/awoke/awoken In CIC, *wake (up)* is 6 times more frequent than *awake* in British texts, and 9 times more in American texts. The present tense is comparatively rare in both varieties, but the preterit is frequent in both (1.3 times more frequent in British than in American texts); the participle is 3.9 times more frequent in British than in American texts. <Hopefully the tsunami has **awoken** the true spirit of human compassion the world over.> 2005 Jan. 9 *Sunday Times* 3 1/6.

beat/beat/beaten Beat/beat: CIC has 270.2 iptmw of the participle *beaten* in British texts and 179.8 in American texts. < . . . months of dreary slog, only to find . . . that the other chap had **beaten** you to it.> 1982 Simpson 111. Cf. § 5.1.3 *beaten-up*.

bet/betted Bet/bet: *Betted* is rare in British use (0.5 iptmw), but non-occurring in American (CIC). <Every woman in England had **betted** on him [Derby winner My-Love].> 1994 Freeling 99.

bid/bidded This is a rare variant of *bid/bid*, not in *NODE*. < . . . the prices are **bidded** up all the time.> 1987 June 8 *Evening Standard* 24/6.

broadcast/broadcast Broadcast/broadcasted: CIC has no tokens of *broadcasted* in British texts and 0.6 iptmw in American texts. <He **broadcast** this afternoon.> 1971 Mortimer 34.

burn/burnt Burn/burned: Of 501 tokens in the American *Miami Herald*, 95 percent were *burned* and 5 percent *burnt*; of 277 tokens in the British *Guardian*, 56 percent were *burned* and 44 percent were *burnt*. Thus although both national varieties prefer the regular form, the American preference for it is significantly stronger (Hundt 1998, 24). CIC has about equal numbers of the two forms in British texts, but 11 times more tokens of *burned* than *burnt* in American texts. <Moving past the **burnt**-out garage . . . she saw that he was working in Mrs. Clutton's garden.> 2003 James 292.

burst/burst Burst/bursted: *MW* lists *bursted* as an option, but there are no examples in CIC. < . . . there had also been damage from a **burst** pipe.> 1989 Autumn *Illustrated London News* 74/2.

bust/bust Bust/busted: CIC has 9.2 iptmw of *busted* in British texts and 32 in American texts. < . . . it was the ending of the Cold War that **bust** his business.> 1989 July 29 *Spectator* 22/3.

catch/catched *nonstandard for* Catch/caught: CIC has 0.8 iptmw of *catched* in British texts and none in American texts. <Harry gets **catched**, quietly.> 1987 Oliver 200–1.

cost/costed Estimate the cost of: CIC has 6.3 iptmw of *costed* in British texts and 0.2 in American texts. <The Alliance planned to channel £500,000 to

the inner city in a carefully **costed** programme.> 1987 May 28 *Hampstead Advertiser* 7/6.

dive/dived Dive/dove: CIC has 70 times as many tokens of *dived* as of *dove* in British texts, but only 1.6 times as many in American texts.

dream/dreamt Dream/dreamed: Of 167 tokens in the American *Miami Herald*, 95 percent were *dreamed* and 5 percent *dreamt*; of 104 tokens in the British *Guardian*, 69 percent were *dreamed* and 31 percent were *dreamt* (Hundt 1998, 24). CIC has twice as many tokens of *dreamed* as of *dreamt* in British texts but nearly 13 times as many in American texts. <I **dreamt** mixed-up dreams.> 1991 Bishop 138.

dwell/dwelt Dwell/dwelled: CIC has *dwelt* 14 times more often than *dwelled* in British texts but only 1.3 times more often in American texts. Past forms are 3 times more frequent in British than in American texts. <Danny's . . . mind **dwelt** lovingly now on those accumulated spondulicks ["money"].> 1993 Dexter 195.

eat/ate/eaten The British preterit is typically /ɛt/, the American /et/. In American, /ɛt/ is nonstandard.

fit/fitted Fit/fit: In American use, the preterit and participle are *fit*, except in certain contexts, such as *The tailor* ***fitted*** *him with a new suit* and *They fitted (out) the ship with new equipment*. CIC has more than 7 times as many tokens of *fitted* in British as in American texts. <There were houses . . . that **fitted** the description.> 1994 Symons 145. < . . . it [a coat] had been reduced by 50 per cent and, what's more, **fitted** perfectly.> 2003 July 8 *Times* T2 13/1.

forecast/forecast Forecast/forecasted: *Forecasted* has only minority use in common-core English, but CIC has it 5 times more often in American than in British texts. < . . . he would suffer bouts of the "depression" he **forecast** after his resignation.> 2004 Dec. 17 *Independent* 6/2.

forget/forgot/forgotten Forget/forgot: *NODE* labels the participle *forgot* "chiefly US," and CIC has nearly twice as many tokens of *forgotten* in British as in American texts. In American, participial *forgot* is particularly likely to be used in perfect verb phrases (*we must have forgot*), but not as a subject complement or in the passive voice (**the inventor is / has been forgot*). In the following, however, American could have *forgot* as well as *forgotten*: <They must have **forgotten** to send it.> 1994 Sept. *Tatler* 100/3.

get/got Get/got/gotten *or* got: CIC has 32 times as many tokens of *gotten* in American as in British texts, in which the form is sometimes dialectal and occasionally used interchangeably with *got*: *Haven't you gotten your key?* = "Don't you have your key?" American uses both participles, but often in different senses: *got* typically for static senses like "possess" in *I've got it* = "I have it" and "be required" in *I've got to go* = "I must go"; and *gotten*, typically for dynamic senses like "acquire" in *I've gotten it* = "I have received it" and "be permitted" in *I've gotten to go* = "I have become able to go." The American use of *gotten* is more common in conversation than in written registers (*LGSWE* 398). The following examples show British *got* in a variety of senses, all involving a dynamic change of state, for which American would typically have *gotten*. American use fluctuates, however, in contexts where either *got* or *gotten* can occur without difference in meaning: *He hasn't got/gotten beyond the beginner's stage* (Gilman 1994, 482). In other contexts, however, with a possible semantic contrast, the two forms are used differently: *I've got a cold* = "I have a cold"; *I've gotten a cold* = "I've caught a cold." **A.** *transitive* **1**. Acquire <And what have we **got**? . . . just more unnecessary bills through our letterbox.> 2005 Jan. 14 *Daily Telegraph* 28/3–4. **2**. Cause (someone/something) to become/come <Ron obviously realised that he'd **got** Harry into trouble.> 1999 Rowling 9 (*US ed.* gotten). **3**. Procure <A typical high street price is about 50p to 60p . . . , but they [strawberries] can be **got** for half that.> 1985 June 13 *Times* 3/3. **4**. Produce <The duty of the pilots was to get results. They hadn't **got** them.> 1940 Shute 26. **5**. Receive <Had the match been played, he says, Mrs T would have been invited – "and she would have **got** a good game".> 1986 Oct. 11 *Times* 16/1. **6**. Succeed in causing (someone) to come <Once they'd **got** him in for questioning they'd twig that the late Helen Appleyard wasn't our Jenny.> 1985 Bingham 42. **7**. Succeed in obtaining <If Mrs-Duggins-what-does *had* answered the door she'd have **got** a good look at her.> 1985 Bingham 159. **– get back** Reacquire possession of <I had **got** the mortgage **back**.> SEU w8-1.227. **B.** *intransitive* **1**. Become; come to be <I've **got** quite used to it.> 1987 May 7 *Evening Standard* 35/1. **2**. Succeed in going <Some have **got** no farther than the entrance.> 1988 Mar. *Illustrated London News* 27/3. **– get along/on without/with** Succeed in living without/with <. . . he had **got along without** women for quite a long time.> SEU w16-7.312. < . . . he had liked Colonel Garrett, had **got on** well **with** him.> SEU w16-8.296. **– get away with** Succeed in avoiding undesired consequences from <We've **got away with** it.> 1985 Mortimer 271. **– get in the habit** Acquire the habit <He had **got in the habit** over the years.> SEU w16-7.37. **– get into** **1**. Enter <I was very relieved . . . to get five CSEs. If I hadn't, I wouldn't have **got into** sixth form.> 1994 Oct. 5 *Evening Standard* 12/1. **2**. Become involved with < . . . how on earth had she **got into** this mess?> 1987 Mar. 22 *Sunday Times* 4/7. **– get out/round** Become known <Somehow word had **got round** among the nannies of England.> SEU w16-3.34. <I should have thought word of your U. D. I. plans could easily have **got out**.> 1985 Mann 118. **– get round** Get around <Until now this problem has been **got round**.> 1988 Apr. 10 *Sunday Telegraph* 35/2. **– get round to** Get around to <. . . dividend would have been limited, even if Ethical Financial had **got round to** paying one.> 2005 Jan. 14 *Daily Telegraph* 40/5. **– get through** Succeed in finishing (with) < . . . in my experience you've scarcely **got** half-way **through** [serving a group], when those to whom you dished out first are already crying for seconds.> 1987 Dec. *Illustrated London News* 68/1. **– get to** Come to <I have **got to** know a lot of songs from jazz records.> 1985 July 16 *Times* 10/6. **– get up to** Achieve < . . . mastering this season's trends is simple – once you have **got up to** speed with the new looks.> 2005 Jan. 14 *Daily Telegraph* 27/2.

hang/hung/hanged *or* **hung** In CIC texts, *hung* and *hanged* are used in similar proportions in both British and American texts, with *hung* 5 to 6 times more frequent than *hanged*. In news reports, however, British favors *hanged*, whereas American favors *hung* (*LGSWE* 397). <A boy of two **hanged** himself while playing.> 1994 Sept. 30 *Daily Telegraph* 11/5.

hew/hewed/hewn Hew/hewed: CIC has more than twice as many tokens of *hewn* in British as in American texts. Conversely, American uses participial *hewed* slightly more than twice as often as British does. <The last film . . . has rough-**hewn** Geordie Jimmy Nail in the lead.> 1987 Mar. 13 *Evening Standard* 31/5.

lean/leant Lean/leaned: In CIC, 23 percent of the British and less than 1 percent of the American past forms are *leant*. <Harry **leant** further over the banisters.> 2003 Rowling 73 (*US ed.* leaned).

leap/leapt Leap/leaped: In CIC, 80 percent of the British past forms are *leapt* and only 32 percent of the American. <Two cocker spaniels **leapt** out.> 1962 Lodge 70.

learn/learnt Learn/learned: Of 3104 tokens in the American *Miami Herald*, all were *learned* and none were *learnt*; of 1259 tokens in the British *Guardian*, 78 percent were *learned* and 22 percent were *learnt* (Hundt 1998, 24). In CIC, 34 percent of the British past forms are *learnt* and less than 1 percent of the American. <I **learnt** that traffic humps are not only damaging ambulances and fire engines but are also slowing them down.> 2004 Jan. 4 *Sunday Times* 13/6.

light/lit Light/lighted: In CIC, 83 percent of the British past forms are *lit* and 77 percent of the American. < . . . the blue touch paper was **lit** on July 14.> 1989 July 20 *Midweek* 19/3. Cf. SPOTLIGHT below.

mow/mowed/mown Mow/mowed: In CIC, *mown* occurs in British texts 33 times more often than in American texts; *mowed* occurs in American texts 2.3 times more often than in British texts. <During the hols The Man had got a patch of grass **mown** up behind the stables.> 1983 Dickinson 47.

prove/proved Prove/proved/proven: In one study of 424 tokens of the past participle in the American *Miami Herald*, 65 percent were *proven* and 35 percent *proved*; of 548 tokens in the British *Guardian*, 20 percent were *proven* and 80 percent were *proved* (Hundt 1998, 28). In CIC, *proven* occurs 2.4 times more often in American than in British texts. <From the beginning she had **proved** herself to be a tireless church worker.> 1995 Charles 58.

quit/quitted Quit/quit: Four British dictionaries (*CED*, *CIDE*, *LDEL*, *NODE*) give *quitted* as the preterit, with *quit* as a variant, three calling the latter (chiefly) American. *MW* lists "*quit* also *quitted*." CIC has 36 times more tokens of *quitted* in British texts than in American.

saw/sawed/sawn Saw/sawed: CIC has nearly 6 times as many tokens of *sawn* in British texts as in American. < . . . the keys to one of the ballot boxes were lost and it had to be **sawn** open.> 1987 July *Illustrated London News*

21/2. – **sawn-off shotgun** Sawed-off shotgun <So long as it doesn't involve a balaclava and a **sawn-off shotgun.**> 1995 Jones 49.

sew/sewed/sewn Sew/sewed: CIC has nearly half again as many tokens of *sewn* in British texts as in American. < . . . when they organize anything they get it **sewn** up from A to Z.> 1954 Ellis 118.

shave/shaved/shaven Shave/shaved: CIC has twice as many tokens of *shaven* in British texts as in American. <Sam Langford drove his Jag slowly . . . stopping to ask **shaven**, surly youths the way to the British Legion Hall.> 1991 Critchley 177–8.

shine/shone Shine/shined: CIC has 3 times as many tokens of *shone* in British texts as in American and nearly 4 times as many tokens of *shined* in American texts as in British. American *shone* usually rimes with *own* rather than with *on*. <A single chandelier **shone** feebly.> 1991 Green 25.

shit/shat *or* **shitted** Shit/shit: CIC has more than 3 times as many tokens of *shat* in British texts as in American. It has 0.4 iptmw of *shitted* in British texts and none in American. <My only choice was to smile while you **shat** on me.> 1992 Walters 37. <That **shitted** *them* up.> 1995 Bowker 24.

short-cut/short-cutted Shortcut/shortcut: This form is rare. <He **short-cutted** across the grass towards them.> 1985 Price 212.

smell/smelt *or* **smelled** Smell/smelled: In CIC, the two past forms, *smelt* and *smelled*, occur with similar frequency in British texts, but in American texts, *smelled* is nearly 21 times more frequent. <The air **smelt**, a sour-sweet stink.> 2003 James 74.

sneak/sneaked Sneak/snuck *or* sneaked: In CIC, *snuck* is about 3.4 times more frequent in American than in British texts. < . . . other junk mail artistes **sneaked** up on consumers.> 1989 Aug. 3 *Guardian* 25/1.

speed/sped *or* **speeded** In CIC, *sped* is the more frequent form in both varieties, in British by 67 percent and in American by 77 percent. *NODE* identifies *sped* with the sense "moved quickly" and *speeded* with the senses "traveled faster than the legal limit," "did something more quickly," and "caused something to happen more quickly." <The driver hooted furiously as his car **sped** past the side road.> 1993 Smith 124. < . . . it was going so slowly . . . but by the time I realised, it was too late, he had **speeded** up.> 1992 Green 68.

spell/spelt Spell/spelled: In CIC, British texts use *spelt* more than half again as often as *spelled*; American texts use *spelled* 136 times more often than *spelt*. < . . . it is still unwise to say the word **spelt** p-i-g.> 1988 July *In Britain* 26/3–4.

spill/spilt *or* **spilled** Spill/spilled: In CIC, British texts use *spilt* rather than *spilled* about 32 percent of the time; American texts use it about 2 percent of the time. <Magdalena had **spilt** a few drops of tea into his breakfast marmalade.> 1969 Amis 25.

spin/span/spun Spin/spun: *Span* as the preterit of *spin* is labeled "archaic" in both British and American dictionaries, yet it has some rare use in current

British. <Two teenage friends were killed . . . when their car **span** out of control in torrential rain.> 2000 Dec. 14 *Times* 11/1.

spit/spat *or* **spit** In CIC, British texts use *spat* more than half again as often as American texts do. It is primarily a written form in both national varieties, but almost exclusively so in American. <[American resident in London about her child:] . . . he'd say, 'She **spat** at me.' Can you imagine kids saying that in America?> 1990 Critchfield 74.

spoil/spoilt Spoil/spoiled: In CIC, British texts use *spoilt* in 54 percent of the tokens, and American texts use *spoiled* in 95 percent. <She **spoilt** this spasm of marital solidarity.> 1985 Barnard 24. – **spoilt for choice, be** Have too many options <There were, he calculated, eleven different buttons which he might press. He was **spoilt for choice**.> 1993 Greenwood 35.

spotlight/spotlit Spotlight/spotlighted: CIC British texts have the two past forms about equally; American texts have only *spotlighted*. < . . . the odd **spotlit** bit of Wedgewood.> 1979 Cooper 227.

spring/sprang *or* **sprung** Although *sprung* is labeled American by *NODE*, in CIC it is used in British texts in 45 percent of the incidences and in American texts in 47 percent, so there is only a small, probably insignificant difference.

stave/stove Stave/staved: *Stove* is a rare form in both national varieties; *staved* is about a third more frequent in CIC American texts than in British. <You mean . . . he just killed her, **stove** her head in afterward, and left her.> 1979 Snow 86.

stink/stank *or* **stunk/stunk** In CIC, *stank* accounts for 85 percent of the forms in British texts, and *stunk* accounts for 52 percent in American texts.

strive/strove/striven Strive/strived: In CIC, British uses *strove* about twice as often and *striven* 6 times as often as American does; American uses *strived* about half again as often as British does. <Troy . . . **strove** to think of something perceptive and intelligent to say.> 1987 Graham 112. <Joshua had once **striven** hard for political promotion.> 1991 Critchley 4.

tread/trod *or* **treaded/trodden** *or* **trod** In CIC, British texts use *trod* and *trodden* respectively nearly 4 and 14 times more often than American texts do. The verb in all its forms is more than twice as frequent in British as in American. <Someone **trod** on her foot.> 1992 Granger 3. < . . . powder was **trodden** deep into the carpet.> 1994 Symons 187.

wake/woke/woken The verb is, on the whole, about a third more frequent in British than in American CIC texts. However, *woken* is nearly 10 times more frequent in British. <Most companies and advertisers have not yet **woken** up to it.> 1996 Aug. 6 *Times* 27/8.

wet/wet *or* **wetted** *Wetted* is more than 3 times as frequent in CIC British texts as in American. < . . . at last we got the flock moving – but not one of them **wetted** its feet, for the mob split to skirt the pool on either side.> 1987 Nov. 8 *Manchester Guardian Weekly* 29/1.

write/wrote/written *or* **writ** *Writ* is an archaic past participle still used for effect occasionally but nearly twice as often in British as in American CIC texts. <They must be kicking themselves and wishing they'd never **writ** those letters.> 1987 July 5 ITV morning talk show.

1.2.2 Contraction

The basic rules for contraction in British and American are the same, but their applications differ somewhat.

1.2.2.1 Contraction involving *have*

Unlike the uncontracted verb *have* (cf. § 1.4.1 below), the contraction *'ve* differs in frequency between the two varieties. The LOB and Brown corpora (Hofland and Johansson 1982, 36) have 1.3 times as many tokens of *'ve* in British as in American; a 1000-item sample of the CIC corpus has 1.58 times as many in British. In both national varieties, the overwhelming use of *'ve* is as an auxiliary (British 96.5 percent, American 99.2 percent). But it is more than 5 times as frequent in main-verb use in British (1.1 percent versus American 0.2 percent). The remaining percentages are indeterminate because of interruptions, syntactic inconsistency or incoherence, etc.

When one of the personal-pronoun subjects *I*, *you*, *we*, or *they* is followed by *have* and *not* (e.g., *I* + *have* + *not*), two patterns of contraction exist: contraction of the verb with the subject (e.g., *I've not*) and contraction of *not* with the verb (e.g., *I haven't*). The second pattern is more frequent in common-core English; however, it is only 2.5 times more frequent than the first pattern in British but is almost 26 times more frequent in American. Thus the pattern *I've not* is a statistical Briticism. <**We've not** seen any evidence of copy-cat crimes being committed.> 1987 Feb. 8 BBC2 "Did You See . . . ?"

The past tense *had* is rarer, but its use is similar. The second pattern (e.g., *he hadn't*) is the norm in common-core English but is nearly 20 times more frequent than the first pattern (e.g., *he'd not*) in British English and nearly 140 times more frequent in American. <**I'd not** heard the story before.> 1987 Mar. 30 *Evening Standard* 24/1.

1.2.2.1.1 As a main verb

've Have: In CIC, British uses *'ve a* more than 7 times as often as American does, and *'ve no* close to 11 times more often than American does. <Mum, I**'ve** a boil on my bum.> 1999 Mar. 21 *Sunday Times* Magazine 14/3.

've not Don't have: CIC has 1.4 iptmw of *'ve not the/a/any* in British texts and none in American texts. <He knew bloody well I**'ve not** the faintest idea.> 1982 Lynn and Jay 123.

'd Had: CIC has 8.6 iptmw of *'d a* and 6.9 of *'d no* in British texts; it has none of *'d a* and 0.2 of *'d no* in American texts. <Maybe they**'d** a better map.> 1986 Knox 48.

'd not Didn't have: The construction is rare. < . . . sitting there like he'**d not** a care in the world.> 1997 popular fiction CIC.

've to Have to: This form is 9 times more frequent in CIC British texts (8.2 iptmw) than in American (0.9). <I've got a supervision tomorrow, and I'**ve to** turn in two thousand words on Cowper.> 1985 Benedictus 90–1.

'd to Had to: CIC has 6.2 iptmw of this form in British texts and none in American texts. < . . . **I'd to** hand wash and boil for six children, my husband and myself.> 1987 May 10 (Scotland) *Sunday Post* 33/2.

In British use, *not* sometimes contracts with *have*, whereas American use strongly favors its contraction with the auxiliary *do*.

haven't Don't have: Cf. *CamGEL* 112. The British texts of CIC have 6 times as many tokens of *don't have a* as of *haven't a* and 10 times as many tokens of *don't have any* as of *haven't any*, thus confirming the observation of the lexicographer Paul Beale: "Apparently quite unremarked has been the substitution of . . . 'We don't have . . .' for the former Brit. usage . . . We **haven't** any. . . . It seems to me that the 'do' formation is almost universal in what passes for Standard English nowadays" (1995 Dec. 6 personal letter). Nevertheless, the *do*-less forms are still characteristically British because CIC American texts have a ratio of 55:1 for *don't have a* versus *haven't a* and of 60:1 for *don't have any* versus *haven't any*. < . . . they **haven't** a clue what it means.> 2003 June 28 *Times* Weekend 9/2.

hadn't Didn't have: CIC has 6.2 iptmw of *hadn't a* and 1.5 of *hadn't any* in British texts; it has 1.4 of *hadn't a* and 0.4 of *hadn't any* in American texts. <As far as I know he **hadn't** any enemies.> 2003 James 176.

haven't to Don't have to: CIC has 0.4 iptmw of this rare form in British texts and none in American texts. <I **haven't to** read it all.> *CamGEL* 112.

hadn't to Didn't have to: CIC has 0.3 iptmw of *hadn't to* in British texts and none in American texts. <I wish it **hadn't to** happen.> 1997 popular fiction CIC.

1.2.2.1.2 As an auxiliary

The auxiliary *have* contracts with its subject in both British and American provided the sentence is positive: *We've done that*; but when it is negated by *not*, *have* usually contracts only in British: *We've not done that*; whereas in American, *not* contracts with *have*: *We haven't done that*. However, British may use an unstressed but uncontracted *have* in the phrase *have got*: *She hăs got a cold*; whereas American normally uses only stressed *have*: *She hás got a cold* or contracted *have*: *She's got a cold* (cf. § 1.4.1).

've/'s not Haven't/hasn't: In CIC this construction is about 3 times more frequent in British than in American texts. <I'**ve not** read it.> 1992 Dexter 28.

've/'s not got Don't/doesn't have: CIC has 23.2 iptmw in British texts and 0.3 in American texts. <**I've not got** a breath pack.> 1986 Aug. 27 *Times* 10/5.

'd not Hadn't: In CIC this construction is about 4 times more frequent in British than in American texts. <**I'd not** heard the story before.> 1987 Mar. 30 *Evening Standard* 24/1.

'd not got Didn't have: CIC has only 0.2 iptmw of this rare construction in British texts and none in American texts. <She**'d not got** anything much laid on for next day.> 1989 Dickinson 85.

Have also contracts in common-core colloquial English with a preceding modal, notably *must* and the preterit modals *could(n't)*, *might*, *should(n't)*, and *would(n't)* or *'d*. That contraction is often represented as *'ve* in CIC British printed matter (in 73.1 iptmw) but not in American, in which the frequent contracted pronunciation is not usually represented in standard writing. The contraction is also represented as *of* in both national varieties in nonstandard spelling.

<We **should've** given it out.> 1971 Mortimer 67. <. . . you'd think he'd 've made some kind of effort, wouldn't you?> 1985 Bingham 138.

1.2.2.2 Contraction involving *be*

When a personal-pronoun subject is followed by a present-tense form of *be* and *not* (e.g., *he* + *is* + *not*), two patterns of contraction exist: contraction of the verb with the subject (e.g., *he's not*) and contraction of *not* with the verb (e.g., *he isn't*). The first pattern is more frequent in common-core English; however, it is 20 times more frequent than the second pattern in British and only 10 times more frequent in American. <**You're not** telling me she wasn't hot stuff.> 1991 Jan. 26 *Daily Telegraph* Weekend 1/4.

ain't The term is often taken as a shibboleth of the uneducated; but among certain groups and areas, educated speakers use it informally, as they have since the eighteenth century (Gilman 1994). CIC has twice as many American tokens as British, but more British uses appear to be in otherwise standard-English contexts. <[Jeffrey Archer to his wife, who is conducting the interview:] I wouldn't say more to any other interviewer and you **ain't** getting it out of me on the record, young lady.> 1989 Sept. 9 *Times* 33/7.

aren't I At one time some Americans supposed this to be a Briticism, but it was naturalized long ago in much American use (Gilman 1994). However, CIC has about 1.3 times as many British tokens as American. <Why **aren't** I satisfied?> 1995 Lodge 22. Cf. § 16.2.3 for its use as a tag question.

int, in't Isn't: CIC has 3.9 iptmw of this form in British texts and none in American. A variant of the form is frequent as part of the tag question *innit* "isn't it" (cf. § 16.2.3). <[Yorkshire man:] Aye, . . . and there's summat else – why **in't** Boycott captain?> 1985 Ebdon 145.

Is X not? Isn't X? The negative interrogative pattern of forms of *be* followed by a personal pronoun subject and uncontracted *not* is nearly twice as common in CIC British texts as in American. <**Is** she **not**?> 1989 Nicholson 90.

there's not There isn't: CIC British texts have 3 times as many tokens of *there's not* as of *there isn't*; American texts have only 1.3 times as many. < . . . **there's not** an agenda.> 1986 Oct. 11 TV news.

'tis; 'tisn't Contraction of *it* with a following *is*, "formerly common in prose, now poet., arch., dial., or colloq." (*OED*), still turns up as a stylistic feature. CIC has no tokens in either British or American, but it is probably more frequent in British. <**'Tisn't** often an editor dares disagree with his proprietor.> 1987 Apr. 1 *Evening Standard* 6/3. <And bring the cream jug. **'Tis** over on the dresser.> 1992 Granger 8.

Contraction with *who*, either interrogative or relative, is more frequent with *is* than with *are*, and is primarily a British feature. Thus, CIC British texts have 319.0 iptmw of *who's* and 5.2 of *who're*; American texts have 8.6 of *who's* (mainly in headline style or citing the titles of programs, films, etc.) and none of *who're*.

who's <. . . it' s not just an old tart talking **who's** getting elbowed off the street by young scrubbers.> 1980 Kavanagh 91.

1.2.2.3 Contraction involving modals

For the functions of modals, see § 1.4.4.

cannot, can not; can't ([ka:nt] in standard British English; /kænt/ in standard American): *Can't* is more frequent than *cannot* in common-core English: nearly twice as frequent in British, but nearly 3 times as frequent in American. The open spelling *can not* is nearly 6 times more frequent in British than in American.

daren't; dare not In CIC, *daren't* is 13.9 times more frequent in British than in American; *dare not* is 2.3 times more frequent in British than in American. < . . . the English Department **dared not** give tenure to a man who publicly admitted to not having read *Hamlet*.> 1975 Lodge 136. <You . . . **daren't** use the phone to find out.> 1992 Dexter 39.

mayn't The contraction of the negative with *may*, although rare in British (*CGEL* 11.8n), is more so in American. CIC has 2.2 iptmw of *mayn't* in British texts and none in American. The monosyllabic pronunciation of *mayn't* ([meɪnt]) is apparently more common than the disyllabic one in British; as far as the word is said at all in American, it would usually have two syllables. <He **mayn't** have believed his life would actually be in danger.> 1989 Underwood 115.

mightn't This form is 10 times more frequent in British than in American. <It **mightn't** have been one of the people I mentioned at all.> 1984 Gilbert 166.

mustn't The contraction is more than 5 times as frequent in CIC British texts as in American. Uncontracted *must not* is only about twice as frequent. <I **mustn't** keep you.> 1987 Oliver 18.

needn't; need not *Needn't* and *need not* are each twice as frequent in British as in American. **1**. Do(es)n't have to <He **needn't** eat it, then.> 1988 Lodge 233. **2. needn't/need not have** Didn't have to <I **needn't have** bothered, need I?> 1986 Dec. 20 BBC1 *Bergerac*. **3**. Better not <You **needn't** think you're dossing there.> 1991 Graham 137.

ought not to; oughtn't to Uncontracted *ought not* is more frequent than contracted *oughtn't* in common-core English, about one-fourth more frequent in British than in American. Another notable difference, however, is in its complementation. *Ought* is usually followed by a marked infinitive (e.g., *ought to try*) in common-core English; the negative, however, is followed by an unmarked infinitive (e.g., *oughtn't* or *ought not try*) in 10 percent of CIC British tokens, but in about 20 percent of the American tokens. Also, American uses *ought* about 89 percent as often as British does, but its negative only about 74 percent as often. The reason for that difference is probably the fact that American prefers *shouldn't* as a negative, using it 1.3 times as often as British does. <Well, you bloody well **oughtn't to** be.> 1969 Amis 207.

shalln't This is a rare form. <I **shalln't** try to be a mother.> 1979 Price 177.

shan't *Shan't*, although rare everywhere, is more used in Britain than in the US (*CGEL* 3.23). It is 17.9 times more frequent in CIC British texts than in American, whereas *shall not* is only about 3.6 times more frequent. **1**. With the first person for both simple and emphatic futurity. <I'm sure I **shan't**.> 2003 James 236. **2**. With the second or third person for determination. <Well, this one **shan't** happen.> 1931 Benson 13.

usen't to Didn't use to: Because of the normal pronunciation [ju:stu] the spelling of *use(d) to* is highly variable, even in standard edited texts (Gilman 1994). The *OED* has no tokens of *usedn't*, which might be expected. CIC has no tokens of *use(d)n't* with or without the *d*. In CIC, the negative of *used to* is rare, but *used not to* occurs 11 times more often in British than in American texts, and *didn't use(d) to* occurs 1.39 times more often in American than in British texts. <They **usen't to** take Laura?> 1991 Dickinson 269.

will = 'll The contraction *'ll* is 1.39 times more frequent in British than in American. Although it is normal after pronouns in common-core English, it is less usual, at least in writing, after other forms, especially in American. <. . . one of you lot**'ll** have to buy me another drink to console me.> 1985 Clark 157.

will not = 'll not Won't: In British CIC texts, *'ll not* occurs once for every 36 tokens of *won't*, but in American, once for every 346 tokens. <They**'ll not** be able to set foot outside their gates without being hounded.> 1992 Walters 97.

would have = 'd've Such double contractions are normal in common-core English, but seem more often represented in British writing than in American.

CIC has 4.8 iptmw of *'d've* in British texts and none in American. <Most uncommon, **I'd've** said.> 1988 Mortimer 206.

would not = 'd not In CIC, *'d not* (representing both *would not* and *had not*) occurs 4 times as often in British texts as in American. <**I'd not** touch them as a lass.> 1991 Glaister 53.

1.2.3 Ellipsis

The copula and verbs of motion may be omitted in certain constructions.

be *omitted* <The next thing that happened [**was (that)**] the black lad had crossed a good ball, fifty-fifty between the keeper and Graham.> 1976 Raphael 200. <Smoking [**is**] absolutely out.> 1986 Oct. 7 *Times* 15/7. <[Lady Elizabeth Anson, cousin of the Queen:] Normally I would stay on until 4am or 5am when the last guests were leaving and the plates [**were**] being stacked up.> 1991 Mar. 2 *Daily Express* 14/3.

go/come/return <Let's [**go**] to our beds.> 1977 Barnard 41. <I'll be twenty minutes late [**coming**] in, there's something I have to do.> 1988 Stoppard 24. < . . . large numbers of Iraqi soldiers allowed [**to return**] home from the front line are refusing to go back to their posts.> 1991 Feb. 3 *Sunday Times* 2/4.

1.3 Verb phrases

"Verb phrase" here refers to a simple verb or combinations of a main verb and auxiliaries.

1.3.1 Present tense

A passive present tense is sometimes used in British to report a generally current situation, for which American would use the present progressive, the present perfect, or a future tense.

<Anthony Caro . . . **is made** a knight.> 1987 June 18 *Hampstead Advertiser* 12/1–2. <*The Missionaries* **is published** on May 3.> 1988 Apr. *Illustrated London News* 85/3. <A discount plan . . . **is launched** today.> 1988 Sept. 15 *Times* 3/7.

British also uses the active present tense with future meaning in contexts where American would favor an overtly marked future form or a progressive.

<We had to miss an invitation. . . . So we **make** it another time.> 1976 Bradbury 23. <This summer he **moves** just three miles away.> 1989 Aug. 13 *Sunday Times* Magazine 42/4.

In contrast to the British preference for perfect tenses (cf. § 1.3.4 below), a simple present may occur where a present perfect might be expected.

<It's some years since we actually met.> 1985 Bingham 52.

1.3.2 Progressive aspect

According to a corpus-based study (*LGSWE* 462), American uses the progressive aspect more than British does by a ratio of approximately 4:3. American preference for the progressive is strongest in conversation.

Progressive forms are not usual with stative verbs (that is, those verbs that indicate a state or condition rather than an action: *She had* [stative] *a cold but was treating* [dynamic] *it*). However, some British examples exemplify such use, in which cases the verb expresses a process.

<Breeches **are being** popular among hill-walkers.> 1988 Sept. 3 *Times* 59/1. <Let's **be seeing** you. Soon.> 1989 Daniel 86. <It **is looking** crazy for any man without an income even to contemplate supporting a family.> 1989 Sept. 2 *Spectator* 9/1.

The juxtaposition of two tokens of *be*, as in the progressive passive (*be being*), is not frequent in British: CIC has 6.2 iptmw in British texts, but that is more than twice as many as in American (2.8).

<Collins . . . is now understood to **be being courted** for a major position.> 1996 July 24 *Times* 22/6.

1.3.3 Future time

English has two main verb signals of future time: (1) *will* or *shall* (the modal future) and (2) *be going to* (the periphrastic future). In general, British favors *will* or *shall*, and American *be going to*, notably in American conversation and fiction (*LGSWE* 488). The *be going to* future is more recent and is still expanding in both varieties (Mair 1997). Benedikt Szmrecsanyi (2003) has identified the following differences in corpora of the two national varieties (parenthesized statistics are from CIC for comparison):

1. *Shall* is rare in both varieties, but is more frequent in British than in American (in CIC, 6 times more frequent after personal pronouns).
2. The enclitic *'ll* is more frequent in British than in American (in CIC, nearly 1.4 times more frequent).
3. *Be going to*, on the other hand, is more frequent in American than in British, especially in informal style (in CIC, nearly 2.3 times more frequent).
4. The negative contraction *won't* is more frequent in British than in American (in CIC, on the contrary, it is more than 1.5 times more frequent in American).

5. The negative enclitic *'ll not*, although rare in British, is not used at all in American (CIC American texts have 5.4 iptmw, but British have 32.9).
6. A negated form of *be going to*, e.g., *I'm not going to*, is more frequent in American than in British (more than 2 times as frequent).
7. *Be going to*, however, is relatively more frequent than *will* or *shall* in British English in subordinate clauses, compared with main clauses, but less so in American, and is especially more frequent in conditional *if*-clauses.

British also uses the modal future perfect for events in the past, especially probable ones. Thus *will have left* is the equivalent of "(have) (probably) left."

<I think he**'ll have killed** himself.> 1982 Brett 122. <[with reference to the speed of driving:] 'What car were you in?' [¶] 'My Jag.' [¶] 'Then you **won't have been hanging** about, will you?'> 1988 Ashford 25.

Another use of the modal future is as a polite circumlocution instead of a simple present tense.

<What was that one about loose talk? . . . You**'ll know** the one I mean.> 1989 Burden 115.

1.3.4 Perfect aspect

According to a corpus-based study (*LGSWE* 462), British uses the perfect aspect more than does American by a ratio of approximately 4:3. British preference for the perfect is strongest in news media.

British normally uses the perfect in the environment of adverbs like *already*, *ever*, *just*, and *yet* (*CGEL* 4.22n; *CamGEL* 146n, 713; Swan 1995, 563) and adverbial clauses introduced by the temporal conjunction *since* (*CamGEL* 697), as well as in contexts where the verb can be considered as referring to either a simple past action (preterit) or one with relevance to the present (perfect): *I returned the book* versus *I've returned the book* (Swan 1995, 423). American has a tendency to use the simple preterit in such cases, although the perfect is also acceptable.

<He pulls open the hamburger bun and there indeed is the worm coiled neatly on top of the meat . . . . Everyone agrees that he **has had** a narrow escape.> 1988 May *Illustrated London News* 19/4.

The difference is, however, perhaps not so great as is often supposed. In CIC, the sequences *have had*, *has had*, and *had had* occur only about 1.7 times more often in British than in American. Moreover, American seldom shares a British use of the perfect with reference to a specific past time (*CGEL* 4.23n).

<Look, the bike**'s been invented** in 1890.> 1987 May 31 *Sunday Times* Magazine 76/1. <Sharapova also tried to play down the significance of the vocal

tic which **has** already **got** her into trouble on her first visit to England.> 2003 June 25 *Guardian* international ed. 22/2.

The perfect form *have got* is used in common-core English in the present-tense sense "have" and *have got to* similarly in the sense "must." In both cases, *have* may be (and usually is) contracted: *I've got a cold* and *He's got to go*. The constructions are, however, on average about 1.5 times more frequent in British. The constructions are also similarly used in the past perfect with past-tense sense: *I had got a cold* and *He had got to go*. Such use is rare in American, which uses instead *had* and *had to*. British uses *had/'d got* about 15 times more than American, and *had/'d got to* about 20 times more.

<The park-demon **hadn't got** a body of its own.> 1983 Dickinson 140. <**I'd** still **got** the hots for her, **hadn't** I? I was jealous. Knew she**'d got** somebody else, didn't I?> 1987 Hart 101.

British is especially more likely to use the past perfect where it is logically called for, to denote an action or state that existed prior to some other past action or state. There is nothing un-American about the tense in the following: <Mrs Derrick was astounded that all this **had been going** on under her nose and she **hadn't had** a clue about it.> 1986 Oct. 12 *Sunday Times* 52/1–2. Yet American would be more likely to use *was going on* and *didn't have*. The American preference for a nonperfect form is shown by the first two citations below, in which American typists substituted a preterit for a past perfect; such errors show the natural preference of the typist.

<The days when he **had felt** that the cops were one of the great obstacles to civilized progress were long past.> 1976 Hill 193. <Simeon seemed to find the news less catastrophic than she **had expected**.> 1985 Mortimer 151. <But you **hadn't** really **got** to know Mrs Norris.> 1998 Rowling 111 (*US ed.* haven't got).

In the following examples, the past perfect is not clearly appropriate by the usual interpretation that it signals an action or state anterior to some other action or state. Instead, a simple preterit form seems appropriate. The British preference for the past perfect appears to have produced it even when the context does not suggest it.

<Amy came in and stared at me until I **had noticed** the dirty sweater and holed jeans she had exchanged for her earlier get-up.> 1969 Amis 52. <I'd said – or meant – I'd be there as usual on Saturday, but I **hadn't gone**.> 1989 Burden 76.

British uses the past perfect and especially the *would* perfect for an unrealized circumstance in the present or future, for which a common-core option preferred in American is a nonperfect form. "If my mother **had been** alive, she **would have been** 80 next year. (OR If my mother **were** alive, she **would be** . . .) / It

would have been nice to go to Australia this winter, but there's no way we can do it. (OR It **would be** nice . . .) / If my mother hadn't knocked my father off his bicycle thirty years ago, I **wouldn't have been** here now. (OR . . . I **wouldn't be** here now.)" (Swan 1995, 248).

1.3.5 Voice

The passive voice has some distinctive uses in British English.

be let (to) ***do something*** Be allowed to *do something*: The theoretical passive of *let someone do something* is *someone is let do something*, but that is marginal in American use, in which *someone is allowed to do something* is more idiomatic. CIC has pre-1900 examples in British with a marked infinitive: <I . . . hope I shall **be let to** work.> 1854 Dickens, *Hard Times*. Later examples with an unmarked infinitive are <. . . the younger children **were let** sleep on.> 1891 Hardy, *Tess of the D'Urbervilles*, and <Would he expect to **be let** bring that woman back with him?> 1995 Joseph O'Connor, *Desperados*.

Ditransitive verbs have two objects: indirect and direct: *They gave me this watch*. Such verbs have two possible passive forms: one with the active indirect object as the passive subject: *I was given this watch*, and another with the active direct object as the passive subject: *This watch was given me* (*CGEL* 2.21). American English is less likely than British to have the second construction.

<It was told **me** in confidence.> 1985 Mortimer 231.

British English uses the passive verb *be drowned* as a semantic equivalent of the intransitive *drown*: *He* ***(was) drowned*** *while trying to swim across a river* (Swan 1995, 166). American journalism is reported as conventionally using intransitive *drown* for accidental drowning and the passive of transitive *drown* for intentional drowning: *He* ***was drowned*** *by his kidnappers* (Gilman 1994, 373). However, any context in which transitive *drown* is implied permits the passive, whether or not intention is involved, for example, *The rising waters drowned him* might underlie *He* ***was drowned***. Consequently, the semantic distinction may be difficult to draw. CIC British texts have 4 times as many tokens of *was/were drowned* without a following *by* phrase as do American.

A British idiom for "become unwell" is the passive (*be*) *taken ill*, rather than the active *took ill* (with 15 tokens of the former versus 2 tokens of the latter in the *OED*, and 9.3 versus 1.7 iptmw in CIC British texts). This construction is not a normal passive; *He was taken ill* has no corresponding active **Someone/something took him ill*. Rather, *be taken* in this use is a verb passive in form but functioning as a copula with a limited range of adjective complements. British uses either verb form with *sick* instead of *ill* only occasionally (0.5 iptmw); American seldom uses the idiom in any form, having only 1.6 iptmw of *taken/took sick/ill*.

1.3.6 Imperative

The first person plural imperative is marked by *let's* in common-core English. CIC has 2.4 times as many tokens of *let's* in American texts as in British (cf. also *LGSWE* 1118). For *let us not* and *let's not* cf. § 1.3.8.

1.3.7 Sequence of tenses

Sequencing of tenses occurs notably in reported speech: *She **says** they **are** happy* versus *She **said** they **were** happy*, and in conditions: *If it **rains**, we **will stay** home* versus *If it **had rained**, we **would have stayed** home*. That is, the tense of the verb in the reporting clause or the condition clause attracts the verb of the report or result into a harmonious tense. An exception is the statement of timeless truth or of current events, for which a present tense may be used, even following a past tense. Tenses may be sequenced in some other contexts also.

British, especially reportorial use, strongly favors tense sequencing, even in cases of timeless truth and current events. American is more likely to break the sequence.

<She **said** that there **was** nothing in the Bible that **had** anything to do with ordination as we **knew** it today.> 1986 Oct. 6 *Times* 18/2.

The tendency to sequence tenses is so strong that occasionally a following verb may be put in the past even when the preceding verb is not past or no condition for sequencing tenses exists.

< . . . we **can**not **be** surprised if they [prisoners] **are** already **planning** their next crime before they **came** out.> 1987 June 18 *Times* 3/5.

Sometimes, both verbs are put in the past, even when the context is clearly present, as in the following naïve speech.

<Mind, nowadays you **couldn't tell** whether they **were** a boy or girl.> 1987 Apr. 13 elderly lady in a London Post Office line to her neighbor about a small child wandering around.

A different sort of tense-sequence rule is that for catenative verbs, in which, if the first verb is perfect, a following infinitive is not perfect: *They could have refused to come*. But, perhaps because of tense sequencing under other circumstances, infinitives sometimes appear also as perfects.

<Anyway, we **would have refused to have been** on the same bill as Sting.> 1989 Sept. 4 *Evening Standard* 30/3.

1.3.8 Operators

The operator is a verb (the auxiliaries *be*, *do*, *have*, or one of the modals) that inverts with the subject in *yes-no* questions (*Are you there?*) and other environments calling for subject-verb inversion, that *not* can follow or contract with in negations (*You are not / aren't there*), and that carries the nuclear accent in emphatic statements (*You áre there*). In common-core English the copula *be* also functions as an operator, as in the preceding examples. In British, the main verb *have* can similarly function as an operator: *I hadn't any*; American generally uses *do* with *have*: *I didn't have any* (*CGEL* 2.49; 3.21, 34; 10.55; 11.5, 15; Swan 1995, 231, 355). Operator use of the main verb *have* applies also to the combination *have to*, as in *Have we to get up early tomorrow?* That use is said to be somewhat old-fashioned British (*CGEL* 3.48), but it is hardly imaginable in American.

have (main verb as operator) 1. have + *subject* <Nor **had** he an ounce of curiosity.> 1989 Bainbridge 31. <**Had** he any looks in those days?> 1991 Mar. 17 *Sunday Times* 1 23/1. **2. haven't** <I **haven't** a clue where she is.> 1993 Smith 176. **3. have not** <The village cricket team **has not** enough players for the match.> 1988 Brookes and Fraenkel 5.

have to As noted above, the *have* of *have to* is not generally used as an operator, especially in American English, perhaps because *have to* is regarded as a single item, as its pronunciation "hafta" suggests, and therefore speakers resist treating its two parts as separate syntactical words that can be separated by other words. For that reason, also, there is resistance to inserting adverbial modifiers between *have* and *to*, especially in American English. A comparison of CIC British and American academic texts suggests that British is about 1.5 times more likely to separate *have* and *to* by an adverb. <The fact that he **had**, unlike his predecessors, **to** fight an election to get the job is an indication that there were doubts from the beginning.> 1986 Aug. 25 *Times* 1/2. To take a specific comparative example, of the two expressions, *have still to* and *still have to*, CIC British texts consist of 27 percent *have still to*, and American texts of only 2 percent. <. . . he wanted to end the receivership but some legal problems **had** still **to** be sorted out.> 1986 May 21 *Sun* 2.

The stressed auxiliary *do* can also be used to emphasize a positive imperative, especially in British, where it is often judged to be more characteristic of female than of male speech (*CGEL* 11.30, which cites as an example ***Do** have some more tea*).

<**Do meet** Mark Hasper, our director.> 1987 Bradbury 93.

The inclusive imperative with *let's* can also take the emphatic *do*, but in the negative a difference between British and American arises: *don't let's* is 7 times more frequent in British than in American, and *let's don't* is 4.5 times more frequent than *don't let's* in American, but is not represented in the British CIC texts.

<**Don't let's** talk about it any more.> 1962 Lodge 202.

Do let's not has no representation in CIC, but occurs:

<**Do let's not** chitter-chatter on the green, Caldicott.> 1985 Bingham 100.

The construction *let X not* is used without *do* support (i.e., *don't let X*) chiefly in the first person plural and then primarily with contraction: *let's not*, especially in American English. CIC American texts have almost 2 times as many tokens of *let's not* as British texts do; and British texts have more than 1.5 times as many tokens of *let us not* as American texts do. Third-person pronouns or *me*, instead of *us*, in this construction are rare, especially in American English.

<. . . **let** him **not** think that we have a long way to go.> 1987 Mar. 18 *Evening Standard* 35/1.

Exceptionally, other verbs sometimes behave like operators, particularly in being followed by *not*, but also with subject inversion in questions. This use is about twice as frequent in British as in American, though it is not common in either.

<What **think** you of Rowntree Mackintosh?> 1987 May 10 (Scotland) *Sunday Post* 7/4. <On balance, he **thought not**.> 1991 Critchley 195.

1.4 Functions

1.4.1 Have

Have occurs with somewhat similar frequency in the two national varieties. Although the LOB and Brown corpora (Hofland and Johansson 1982, 501) have about 1.16 times more tokens of *have* in British than in American, the larger CIC corpus has about 1.03 times more tokens of *have* in American. The uses of *have* seem, however, to be different in the two varieties. In a 500-item sample from CIC British corpus, 53 percent of the *have* forms are auxiliaries in function, 34 percent are main verbs, 11 percent are the semi-auxiliary *have to*, and 2 percent are indeterminate. In a similar sample from CIC American corpus, 42 percent are auxiliaries, 43 percent are main verbs, 14 percent are *have to*, and 1 percent are indeterminate. Among the reasons for the larger use of *have* as an auxiliary in British may be the stronger British preference for perfect verb forms over American simple preterits and the British preference for *have got* (in which *have* is an auxiliary) over American simple *have* (as a main verb). For the contraction *'ve*, cf. § 1.2.2.1.2 above.

have and *have got* British English has traditionally made a distinction between *have* and *have got*, using *have* for habitual or repeated events or states and *have got* for single events or states. Thus, *They have appointments on Mondays, don't they?* versus *They have got an appointment today, haven't they?* In the following citation, presumably the first clause is about a general situation (there is never a bin-end sale), and the second clause is about a present-time situation (the inexpensive wines are currently available): <Majestic Wine **does not have** a bin-end sale,

but they **have got** two ridiculously good-value sparkling wines.> 1998 Jan. 3 *Times Magazine* 65/2.

American does not make this distinction, giving rise to such jokes as this supposed conversation: an American to an English woman: "Do you have children?" English woman: "Not oftener than every nine months" (Andersen 1972, 857). The British distinction, however, seems no longer to be rigorously observed.

British uses *have/has got* 2.7 times more frequently than American does and *had got* 9.7 times more frequently. British uses the contracted forms *'ve/'s got* 1.8 times more frequently than American and *'d got* 26.6 times more frequently. In both national varieties, as a main verb, *have* is far more frequent than *have got*, particularly in American. However also in both, the contracted form *'ve got* is more frequent than simple *'ve* as a main verb.

A corpus-based study (*LGSWE* 216; also Johansson 1979, 206–7) of the three interrogative forms exemplified by *Do you have any . . .* , *Have you any . . .* , and *Have you got any . . .* shows American preference for the first of those options and British preference for the last two. In CIC, *do you have any* is overwhelmingly the most frequent option in American texts with comparatively few tokens of the other two options. In CIC British texts, *do you have any* and *have you got any* are of about equal frequency, and *have you any* occurs about three quarters as often as either of the other two options. In the preterit, both varieties strongly favor *did you have?* with only a few examples of *had you got?* in British and none in American.

With negation, the favorite form in British is *have no*, which (at 621.8 iptmw) is more than twice as frequent as its closest British rival, *don't/doesn't have*. The latter is the favorite form in American (at 1495 iptmw), where it is more than twice as frequent as *have no*. A distant third in both varieties is *haven't/hasn't got*, which is 2.3 times more frequent in British (at 63.4 iptmw) than in American. An even more distant fourth is *'ve/'s not got*, which is 77 times more frequent in British (at 23.2 iptmw) than in American. CIC has a few tokens of *'d not got* in British texts and none in American. Fifth in line is *have/has not got*, which is 8 times more frequent in British (at 14.5 iptmw) than in American. The preterit *had not got* is even rarer, with 5.1 iptmw in British texts and none in American. Another corpus-based study (*LGSWE* 161) presents evidence that *have no* is used before indefinite objects, as in *They have no idea*, and that *do not have* is used in American before definite objects, as in *They do not have the answer*, but *have not got* in British, as in *They have not got the answer*.

In the sense "must," *have/has to* is overwhelmingly favored over *have/has got to* in common-core English. The latter option is, however, about a third more frequent in British than in American. And the contracted forms *'ve/'s got to* are much more frequent in both varieties than the full form, especially in British. The contracted form *'ve to* is rare in both varieties, but is more frequent in British.

have/has got Have/had; 've/'s got <We **have got** defibrillators in offices and one-stop shops.> 2005 Jan. 14 *Daily Telegraph* 14/8.

had got <It [the wall] **had got** safety notices and postcards and a map of London taped to it.> 1989 Nicholson 19.

've/'s got <He'**s got** a bit of previous form ["criminal record"], I know.> 2001 Mortimer 188.

'd got <Because he hadn't got the opportunity in Poland he'**d got** here!> 2000 Granger 335.

have/has got? Do have: <'**Have** you **got** your own chapel?' [¶] 'I do.' [¶] Laverne was baffled by this Americanism. 'I didn't ask to marry you. I asked if you'd got a chapel.'> 1995 Bowker 130. *Do* is also used as the operator with main verb *have* in British English. <Do you work? **Do** you **have** children?> 1986 Oct. sign in the London West Hampstead Post Office.

had got? <. . . how on earth **had** she **got** into this mess?> 1987 Mar. 22 *Sunday Times* 4/7.

have/has/had? <**Had** he any enemies . . . ?> 2003 James 195.

have/has no <I **have no** problem with them.> 2003 June 20 *Times* 40/4.

haven't/hasn't got <I **haven't got** siblings.> 2003 James 178.

hadn't got <. . . he worked, illegally of course – he **hadn't got** any papers.> 1991 Dickinson 275.

've/'s not got <You'**ve not got** t'nous [the brains] you were born with.> 1985 Byatt 164.

'd not got <She'**d not got** anything much laid on for next day.> 1989 Dickinson 85.

have/has not got <If you . . . **have not got** your card, are you going to be detained?> 2004 Dec. 13 *Times* 21/4.

had not got <To his dismay Sam realized that he **had not got** an answer to this.> 1955 Tolkien 216.

have/has got to Have to; 've got to; must <**Have** we **got to** wait till Tuesday before making a start?> 1940 Shute 140.

had got to <He **had got to** go out . . . He **had got to** be alone and he **had got to** be on the move.> 1984 Gilbert 184.

've/'s got to <Not that you'**ve got to** be that old to have grandchildren – there must be some grannies under thirty.> (American typist wrote "you have to be" for "you've got to be") 1991 Dickinson 11.

'd got to < . . . he was told he'**d got to** wait for two or three days.> 1991 Feb. 3 *Sunday Times* 2/4.

have to? In questions (***Have you to** attend lectures?*), *have* is not favored as an operator in either British or American, but it is more often used in British (Johansson 1979, 209).

haven't got to Don't have to: This form is not very frequent in British use (about 4.4 iptmw), but it is very rare in American. <We **haven't got to** do anything yet!> 2003 Rowling 617.

have had The perfect *have had* or *had had* is used in British English in the sense of acquisition: "have/had received." For this sense, American prefers *have/had gotten*.

've had Have gotten <[of invitations:] She's just sent out – oh, you**'ve had** yours.> 1994 Dickinson 187.

'd had Had gotten <. . . they said they**'d had** one bid already.> 1987 May 27 *Punch* 34/3.

1.4.2 Been

been Come <Has the telly-man **been** yet? I meant to ask you yesterday?> 1977 Dexter 82.

been and (gone and) This expression, which is a quasi-adverbial modifier of perfect-aspect verbs, with the sense "despite what might be expected or what is advisable," has three variants. **1. gone and** This common-core variant is nearly 3 times as frequent in CIC British texts as in American. <Now he'd **gone and** overshot the entrance.> 1993 Mason 4. **2. been and** British English has another such pseudo coordination using *been and*, which may be used alone or followed by *gone and* (*CGEL* 13.98n). *Been and* may have the sense of "finally," as in the following citation. <Well [we] have **been and** done it and our . . . e-mail address is . . . .> 2004 June 14 personal e-mail. **3. been and gone and** <'Well, it's like this, dad,' said Peregrine, 'I've **been and gone and** shot a professor.' [¶] Mr Clyde-Browne's eyes bulged in his head. 'I'm not hearing right,' he muttered, 'It's those fucking Mogadons. You've **been and gone** . . . Where the hell did you pick up that vulgar expression?'> 1982 Sharpe 206.

1.4.3 Participles and gerunds

Present participles occasionally appear in British where past participles might be expected in common-core English.

owing Owed; due (to one) <You haven't any holiday **owing**?> 1992 Walters 198.

preached, being Preached <I've heard many sermons **being preached** on that event.> 1989 Sept. 24 sermon in the Camberley Baptist church.

stuffing with Stuffed with <Heads full of letters and diaries and heaven knows what scribblings that they imagine the place [a library] must be **stuffing with**.> 1983 Innes 26.

On the other hand, the following citation of *sat* has the reverse.

sat Sitting <I remember spending three days once **sat** in a tree.> 1987 June 17 *Times* 23/6.

disappeared, be The construction *is disappeared* is rare, but is represented in CIC also. <Queen Bess herself was thrilled with the invention [a flushing lavatory] and had one installed in Richmond Palace. It **is** long **disappeared**.> 1988 Feb. *Illustrated London News* 28/3.

The following citation contains an active gerund without a subject, *paying*, where other constructions might be expected: *your paying*, *being paid*, *payment*.

<"Please, Kate, just give me a few more days. . . . I'll pay extra." [¶] "It's not just the money," I said hurriedly, "although I could do with **paying** for these two days."> 1992 Green 30.

1.4.4 Modals

The marginal modals like *dare* and *need* are very rare and practically confined to British English (*LGSWE* 484). For modals like *would* and *should* in adverbial phrases, cf. § 6.1 I + *MODAL* + *VERB OF OPINION*.

can *Can have*, when used to question possibilities, as in ***Can** they **have** missed the bus*? is more often *could have* in American (*CGEL* 11.13).

dare *Dare* without *to* is British, rare, and mainly negative as in *dare not*, *daren't* or interrogative as in *dare I?* (Peters 2004, 139). In American, its modal use is rare (Johansson 1979, 208). CIC has 5 times as many tokens of *dare I?* in British texts as in American. <**Dare we** say it, he's a bit of a drug-crazed, boring git ["contemptible person"].> 1995 Sept. 6–13 *Time Out* 38/1.

may *May* is used in British English in expressions of unrealized possibility in the past, for which American (and most British usage) would require *might* (Swan 1995, 325; 1990 Howard, 176). <. . . if they had been left to their own devices without interference from outside influences they **may** well **be sitting** down right now and planning just how to get that title back.> 1986 Oct. 1 *Times* 42/8.

must *Must* is somewhat more frequent in British than in American, by about 1.7 times in CIC. It has several uses that are common-core English, but are more characteristic of British than of American. **1**. To express necessity, certainty, or obligation; have to (Swan 1995, 343–5). < . . . he felt he had done nothing for which he **must** climb down.> 1987 Jan. 16 *Times* 12/2. **2**. In the negative, to express what is not allowed or reasonable; can't (Swan 1995, 344). <Now you've got false teeth, . . . you **mustn't** expect to eat toffee.> 1969 Rendell 120.

need (not) (Don't) have to: The modal use of *need*, although uncommon in British English, is even more so in American (*CGEL* 3.42; Johansson 1979, 207–8). It occurs primarily in negative contexts. <Mrs Haines **need not** then have been embarrassed in any way.> 1989 Aug. 29 *Times* 15/3.

ought to Should: In CIC, *ought* is about 1.13 times more frequent in British than in American, but *ought* immediately followed by *to* is about 1.08 times more frequent in American, perhaps because in American, *ought* is more likely to be affirmative than either negative (cf. § 1.2.2.3) or interrogative (Johansson 1979, 211). In a corpus study of fiction (*LGSWE* 218), interrogative *ought to* was rare in British fiction, but wholly lacking in American, which uses *should* instead. <**Ought** you **to** have been listening?> 2003 James 101.

shall In pronunciation, British *shall* is often weakly stressed with a reduced [ə] vowel, whereas American *shall*, when it occurs, is typically strongly stressed with a full [æ] vowel. In CIC, ***shall*** approaches a frequency in British 5 times that of American. American use of *shall* is greatest in academic discourse and is generally restricted to a few formal contexts: (1) in legalistic language to express a mandative sense: *Minority groups* ***shall*** *receive preferential consideration*, (2) in a suggestion that seeks the agreement of the addressee but also implies the speaker's preference: ***Shall*** *we leave now?* and (3) rarely in a strong expression of determination: *I* ***shall*** *return!* The greater British frequency of *shall* is due to the infrequency in American of a number of its British uses, for example, its use for simple futurity with the first person and its volitional use with the second and third persons (*CGEL* 4.42, 11.13), albeit that is not now majority use (Peters 2004, 495). An example of such older British use is the following, which shows simple futurity in *shan't* and volition in *shall* with the third person but in *won't* with the first person: <I **shan't** raise a finger against her, if she behaves. But she ***shall*** ring the bell, and I ***won't*** be dictated to, and I ***won't*** be called Lulu.> 1931 Benson 110. Such a clear traditional distinction in the use of *shall* and *will* is hard to find nowadays, and indeed the rule stating it has been declared to be invalid (*CamGEL* 195). **1**. For future time, *shall* is relatively frequent in British use with the first person, whereas *will* is used with the second and third person. <. . . passive drinking . . . **will** be the next target on the list of liberties we **shall** be robbed of.> 1993 Feb. 13 *Spectator* 41/2. **2**. Volitional *shall* is used with the first person when asking about the will of the addressee (*CGEL* 11.13). This type of use is shared by American, but the pragmatics often differ. <**Shall** we call it a night? I'm keeping you up.> 1983 Dickinson 63. **3**. *Shall* may be used with the second and third persons with an implication of determination by the speaker. <Every time some terrible accident occurs . . . , everyone agrees that we must learn lessons from it so that it **shall** never happen again.> 1987 Mar. 28 *Daily Mail* 6/1. **4**. First-person *shall* is occasionally used in a strongly emphatic sense, like the American sense (3) above. <[A:] You must please yourself, dear. [B:] Bernard: I **shall**! I bloody **shall**!> 1974 Potter 174. **5**. *Shall* is also used, exceptionally, with the second and third persons for simple futurity. Note the inconsistent use of *will* and *shall* in apparently the same sense: <The buffet **will** open in about 5 minutes. A further announcement **shall** be made.> 1987 announcement over the PA system on a train.

should *Should* is significantly much more frequent in British than in American, by 1.4 times in CIC. Its greater British frequency is due to several factors. The British use of *should* in mandative constructions is a factor (cf. § 12), as are various other particular conditions (Swan 1995, 252, 345, 518–9, 542), including a preference for first-person *should* in the main clause of a conditional sentence (*CGEL* 14.23): *If I had been at home last night, I* ***should*** *have heard the noise*. The rare abbreviation *shd* is also more British than American: <Translate into Argentinian if you **shd** wish.> 1989 Oct. 26 *London Review of Books* 8/3.

The putative meaning of *should* (that is, signaling that an action has an assumed reality) is more frequent in British than in American (*CGEL* 3.39n; 4.64; 14.25; 16.30): *I regret that he* ***should*** *be so stubborn.* <Robert Barrow's have installed certain machines for those ladies who need them once a month on the 2nd and 4th floors. Please feel free to use them if the case **should** arise.> 1990 Mar. 22 notice in a women's toilet at a brokerage house, London.

British uses of *should* are particularly common with the first person, where American would more often have *would*. In CIC, British percentages of *I should* versus *I would* are 28 versus 72; American are 13 versus 87. <**I should** think she'll get a good talking to.> 1987 Oliver 73. (Cf. § 6.1 I + *MODAL* + *VERB OF OPINION*.)

used to 1. Neither American nor British favors *used* as an operator, although British is somewhat less averse to it than is American (Johansson 1979, 209). In CIC, it is about 1.3 times more frequent in British than in American. 2. The negative of *used to* generally requires *do* as an operator in American, whereas it can itself serve as an operator in British. When the *do* operator is used in British, the form *didn't used to* has greater acceptance than it does in American (Gilman 1994, 933–4; Johansson 1979, 209). In CIC, *used not to* is 3.25 times more frequent in British than in American. <I **used not to** dream.> 1987 Bawden 187. Cf. also § 1.2.2.3. USEN'T TO. 3. Although rare in British English, *used* without *to* occurs. <I wish you would trust me, as you **used**.> 1954 Tolkien 43.

will In CIC, the verb *will* occurs 1.14 times more often in American than in British texts, but following a personal pronoun subject, it is very slightly more frequent in British.

would In CIC, *would* is used about equally in British and American, but some uses seem more characteristic of British. 1. Supercilious *would* "A comment on the annoyingly typical" (*LDEL*). <. . . the rain came in sharp windy gusts, blowing as it does on the streets of Brussels. Well, it **would** be the same rain, **wouldn**'t it, blown by the same west wind.> 1994 Freeling 4. 2. Polite *would* "Used . . . to soften direct statement" (*LDEL*). <When **would** they want to come?> 1985 Clark 135. 3. Contingent *would* <He [G. B. Shaw] was a vegetarian most of his life. 'God help us if he **would** ever eat a beef-steak,' opined Mrs Patrick Campbell.> 1984 Smith 217. 4. *I would(n't) have thought* <**I'd have thought** you a fool if you had.> 1983 Brooke-Taylor 78. <**I wouldn't have thought** so.> 1989 Dickinson 115.

1.4.5 Subjunctive

The subjunctive in English is not an inflected form of the verb, but a cover term for certain uses of the uninflected base or present form of the verb (*be*, *go*), and of the preterit (*was* or *were*, *went*) and past perfect forms (*had been*, *had gone*). Those uses are as follows.

(1) The present subjunctive is used in mandative constructions: *It is necessary that he be/go there*. This use had become rare in British English, surviving mainly in formal and legalistic styles and generally replaced by a modal form (*It is necessary that he should be/go there*) or more recently by an indicative form (*It is necessary that he is/goes there*), for which see § 12. The use of the mandative subjunctive has, however, been revived in British use, doubtless through American influence (*CGEL* 3.59; 10.55n; 16.30, 32).
(2) The present subjunctive is also used in certain traditional formulas or constructions, such as *God save the Queen!* and *Lord help us*. Such use is formal and old-fashioned (*CGEL* 3.60).
(3) The present subjunctive also has an obsolescent use in conditional and concessive clauses: *If this be treason*, . . . and, in American English, a current use in clauses introduced by *lest*: . . . *lest he be/go there* (*CGEL* 3.61, 15.48).
(4) The preterit subjunctive is used in conditions contrary to fact at the present time: *If he were/was here now, we could ask him*. In such use, the invariant form *were* is traditional for all persons and numbers, but in British use especially, *was* and *were* are both used in their usual agreement pattern with the subject. A less common option is the indicative as in <In America Neil Jordan's new film, Mona Lisa, is doing business as if it **is** the only movie in town.> 1986 Sept. 6 *Times* 16/5.
(5) The past perfect subjunctive is similarly used in conditions contrary to fact at past times: *If he had been here yesterday, we could have asked him*.

The latter two subjunctives use back-shifting of the verb forms to indicate an unreal state: the preterit in present time, and the past perfect in past time.

Characteristically British uses of these forms follow.

1.4.5.1 Preterit subjunctive with subject concord

In common-core English, *was* is sometimes used with first and third person subjects in conditions contrary to fact, where traditional use calls for *were*. But that use seems to be more prevalent in edited British English than in edited American English. This introduction of subject concord into subjunctive use is one indication that the subjunctive is marginal in the system. That is, the traditional subjunctive is being assimilated to the concord pattern of indicative verbs, leaving only past time shift as a mark of subjunctiveness.

was *counterfactual subjunctive* <Does he [Prince Charles] seriously believe that if the A Team **was** taken off television, the people in Brixton market would start taking old ladies across the road tomorrow?> 1988 Sept. 25 *Manchester Guardian Weekly* 24/3. <"Are you Canadian or American?" he [Jeffrey Archer] asked. [¶] "American." [¶] "I'd keep rather quiet if I **was** you."> 1990 Critchfield 290. <We have solved the problem by bunging an 's at the end of the phrase, as though it **was** a single word.> 1990 Howard 67.

1.4.5.2 Preterit subjunctive form in past time

The preterit subjunctive *were* is used for counterfactual conditions in present time, traditionally without subject concord. British English, however, sometimes uses *were* with third person singular subjects for past time in constructions that traditionally call for the indicative. Thus in the following citation <Sometimes he wondered if it **were** worth it.> 1927 Firth 58, the condition is an open one: "he" does not know about the worthiness of "it," but is wondering. Traditionally the construction would be expected to be *Sometimes he wondered if it was worth it*. Through their departure from traditional use, these constructions attest the marginality of the preterit subjunctive.

These pseudo subjunctive uses are primarily in clauses introduced by *if*, which is often a signal for a counter-factual condition, as in *If I were you. . . .* This occurrence of *if* seems to trigger the form *were*, even when it is traditionally inappropriate. Other subordinating conjunctions with a similar effect are *unless* and *whether or not*. Pseudo subjunctives are part of standard, especially British, English, because they occur in a variety of edited uses. They do, however, indicate the marginal status of the past subjunctive in present-day English.

were *pseudo subjunctive* <But the joke, if it **were** a joke, came too late.> 1985 Mortimer 12. <Now if ever there **were** a gilt-edged education for a girl, then that is it.> 1994 Oct. 4 *Daily Telegraph* 25/3.

1.4.5.3 Past perfect subjunctive form in present time

The past perfect subjunctive is rare. The following use of the form is inappropriate because the time reference is present, not past. The final clause would traditionally be *if he were here now*. The past perfect is generally more frequent in British use than in American, but here it is used in a context where it is traditionally inappropriate.

had been *past perfect for preterit* <I think Neil would have counted me a friend – and I promise you he would have answered if he**'d been** here now.> 1972 Price 94.

1.4.5.4 Anomalous present subjunctive forms

Pseudo subjunctives exist also for *be*. In the following, instead of *be*, one might expect *should be* or an indicative form. Because the mandative subjunctive, recently introduced back into British use by American examples, has those options (*We insist he be / should be / is here*), *be* has apparently been extended to contexts that are not mandative.

<Housing chairman Alan Woods said that it was a national disgrace that the flats **be** left empty when their [sic] were people sleeping rough outside.> 1987 Apr. 16 *Hampstead Advertiser* 1/2.

Some constructions seem to misinterpret the subjunctive *be* in a mandative construction as an infinitive and consequently introduce the infinitive marker *to*.

<Hilary Torrance suggested that a letter from the parents **to be** sent to County Hall.> SEU w.6.4c.13.

The subjunctive is a marginal form in common-core English, so variations from its traditional use are found in American as well as in British. But British seems to have variations of the sort illustrated here with greater frequency in edited use.

1.4.6 Verb adjunct

Because of the freedom with which verbs and nouns shift use, it is sometimes not possible to say whether the first element in a compound is a noun (as in § 3.3.1.1) or a verb adjunct.

backing track Back-up recorded music as background for a singer or soloist <He did the **backing tracks** when the groups weren't good enough to do them themselves.> 1994 Walters 46.

close season Closed season; a time of the year when certain sporting events are not held <Marigold spends the **close season** on yachts with Albanian or Greek flags on them.> 1989 Daniel 46.

dialling tone Dial tone <The **dialling tone** changed to a sardonic whine.> 1993 Stallwood 277.

draining board Drain board <He approves the logical placing of double sink and **draining-board**.> 1994 Symons 2.

driving <Do you have your **driving licence** and log book, sir?> 1992 Green 180. <Alice could see his smeary wet red face reflected in the **driving mirror**.> 1989 Trollope 7. <And it was she . . . who got into the **driving seat**.> 1972 Rendell 89.

extending ladder Extension ladder <Hung on the wall was an **extending ladder**.> 1992 Green 166.

hijack bus Hijacked <Pupils And Nuns In **Hijack Bus**> 1988 Sept. 14 *Times* 1/2.

kidnap <Tears Of Joy As **Kidnap Girl** Is Found Safe> 1990 Aug. 15 *Daily Telegraph* 1/7–8. <**Kidnap Man** Shot> 1986 May 21 *Sun* 16.

pay bed < . . . people can pay for their health care, through private clinics or NHS **pay beds**.> 1987 June 5 *Evening Standard* 7/1.

paying-in slip Deposit slip <. . . a **paying-in slip** at the back of his cheque book.> 1988 Trollope 161–2.

pre-pay card <Hundreds of thousands of people are expected to switch to the [Transport for London] **pre-pay** Oyster **card**.> 2004 Jan 5 *Times* 4/5–6.

punch bag; punchball Punching bag <He used her as his personal **punch bag** whenever he was drunk.> 1992 Walters 30. <Harry . . . had served as Dudley's first **punchball.**> 2003 Rowling 15 (*US ed.* punching bag).

rushed job Rush job <It's a **rushed job.**> 1993 Cleeves 57.

sailing boat Sail boat "*chief Brit.* a boat propelled by sails" (*NODE*).

signalling failure Signal failure <The . . . [train's] late arrival, ". . . was due to a **signalling failure** near Tring".> 1995 Lodge 37.

skimmed milk Skim milk <Long life **skimmed milk** with non milk fat> 1996 label on a milk container.

sniff youth <**Sniff Youth** Found Dead> 1986 Aug. 29 (Newcastle) *Evening Chronicle* 1/2.

soured cream Sour cream <Serve hot with a dollop of creme fraiche, **soured cream** or yoghurt.> 1989 Aug. 2 *Evening Standard* 31/6.

sparking plug Spark plug <. . . there is no obvious legitimate purpose in carrying the shattered top of a **sparking plug** in one's pocket.> 1987 Dec. *Illustrated London News* 20/1.

stab girl/victim <**Stab Girl** Cathy To Go Home Soon / Schoolgirl **stab victim** Catherine Humphrey may be allowed home next week.> 1987 Feb. 3 *Evening Standard* 3/5.

washing line Clothesline <In the last cottage garden, a rubber sheet blew on the **washing line.**> 1989 Trollope 198.

2 Determiners

2.1 Definite article

2.1.1 Definite article versus no determiner

2.1.1.1 With nouns of time

British English may use *the* in certain expressions of time where American English would have no determiner.

all the ***afternoon/morning/evening*** All afternoon/morning/evening: The forms without *the* are common-core English. CIC has 5.9 iptmw with *the* in British texts but none in contemporary American use. <I slept **all the afternoon.**> 1970 Johnson 18.

all the day long All day long: The definite article is optional in British use (*CGEL* 8.63n). CIC has 0.3 iptmw of the phrase with *the* in British texts and none in American.

the ***month*** The implication of this construction, without any posthead modifier, is "this month of some implied year." In a random sample of 150 tokens of *January* in CIC British texts, 6 were preceded by *the*; a similar American sample had none. <A settlement . . . was proposed by the MPs in **the June**, before the legal costs had started to mount.> 1986 Oct. 19 *Sunday Times* 1/2.

the ***date*** **of** ***a month***; ***month*** **the** ***date*** *Month date*: See § 17.4.

in the night At night: CIC has nearly twice as many British tokens of *in the night* as American; *at night* is nearly 6 times as frequent as *in the night* in British texts, but nearly 10 times as frequent in American. < . . . he gets up **in the night** for [his child].> 1993 Neel 70.

the once Once: The adverbial use of *the once* is about 14 times more frequent in British than in American. <Well, just **the once.**> 1989 Rendell 31. Cf. § 6.1 ONCE.

the ***weekday*** In British English, the definite article *the* is sometimes used with days of the week to imply "this day of that particular week." Although regarded by some as nonstandard, this construction is popular (*CGEL* 5.67n). The construction is generally the object of the preposition *on*, although other prepositions also occur. <He and his lady wife walked the dog . . . on **the Saturday**, and on **the Sunday** morning they put the dog in kennels.> 1991 Neel 210. <By **the Saturday** afternoon he was back.> 1993 Feb. 13 *Daily Telegraph* 11/2.

at the weekends On the weekend; on weekends: *At the weekends* and *on the weekend* have similar frequencies in British, and *on weekends* is twice as frequent as either of them. In American *on the weekend* and *on weekends* have similar frequencies, and *at the weekends* is very rare. <Getting out the barbie and ghetto blaster then popping some nice cold tubes **at the weekends**.> 1996 Graham 157.

all the year All year: CIC shows that both British and American prefer this expression without the definite article, but the American preference is much stronger. CIC has 7.8 iptmw of *all the year* and 63.8 of *all year* in British texts (8 times as many). It has 0.5 of *all the year* and 49.1 of *all year* in American texts (98 times as many). Cf. also § 5.4 ALL (THE) YEAR ROUND.

over the *cardinal number* years Over *cardinal number* years < . . . it was well over **the** five **years** since he had followed his doctor's advice and given it [smoking] up.> 1987 Amis 3.

2.1.1.2 With nouns of place

The use of *the* with names of lands has become variable, with a tendency away from *the*. Until recently, *the Congo, the Sudan*, and *the Ukraine* were normal in both British and American; now, however, *the*-less forms are normal or frequent. Lands that, at least until recently, sometimes had the definite article in British use, but rarely American, are the following:

the Argentine Argentina <1959 *Evening Standard* 31 Dec. 8/6, I am home from **the Argentine**.> *OED* s.v. *the* a. 3.b.

the Gambia <I hear they have very cheap packages to **the Gambia** in January.> 1988 Lodge 62.

the Lebanon <He has helped . . . to evacuate **the Lebanon**.> 1987 Oct. *Illustrated London News* 28/2.

the Yemen <1981 *Church Times* 6 Nov. 14/5 The Hoopoo had nested in his walls when he was in **the Yemen**.> *OED* s.v. *the* a. 3.b.

The names of certain streets and roads are also sometimes preceded by *the*:

the A + *number* *A* designates a major road (other than a motorway); an American analog is *US* (as in *US1*). However, the designation for *A*-roads regularly includes the definite article; that for *US*-roads does not. < . . . the Grade One-listed building . . . lies close to **the A1**.> 2005 Jan. 23 *Sunday Telegraph* (Web ed.).

the Broadway <A Jack Russell terrier crossed **the Broadway** looking neither to its left nor right.> 1991 Critchley 168.

the Earl's Court Road <They acquired a small flat in **the Earl's Court Road.**> 1980 Archer 86.

the High Street: If *high street* is a generic term for the principle street of a town, it normally takes a determiner, as does its American analog, *main street*: *They do their shopping on the high/main street*. But if it is the proper name of a street, no determiner would be expected in American use: *They do their shopping on Main Street*. However, it is not always possible to tell from the linguistic context or the capitalization whether the term is generic or proper in British use. <St Michael's Church of England School was in **the High Street**.> 2002 Smith 17.

the King's Road <Pedalling to work along **the King's Road** . . . .> 1987 Sept. *Illustrated London News* 16/1.

the M + *number* *M* designates a multilane, restricted-access road; an American analog is *I* (for interstate highway, as in *I75*). However, the designation for *M*-roads regularly includes the definite article; that for *I*-roads does not. < . . . a diesel tanker ran into the back of a queue of slow-moving traffic on **the M61**.> 1987 Nov. 8 *Manchester Guardian Weekly* 4/4.

the Tottenham Court Road < . . . Kentucky Fried Chicken sold in **the Tottenham Court Road**.> 1987 Aug. *Illustrated London News* 34/3.

The names of some other places or institutions may also take *the* in British use:

the Grammar As a generic, *grammar school* [in England, a prestigious secondary school] would take a determiner. The following use, however, appears to be a clipping of a proper name. <Peter . . . was . . . having a tough time at **the Grammar**.> 1980 Drabble 20.

the Medway Town <However in **the Medway Town** it is still possible to purchase 2 and 3 bedroom properties for under £35,000.> 1986 Dec. 4 *Midweek* 30/3.

the munitions <They evacuated everyone . . . . I was working in **the munitions** at the time and it caused quite a scare.> 1989 Quinton 9–10.

2.1.1.3 With personal names and titles

The definite article is used before personal names and titles under certain circumstances in English (*CGEL* 5.64, 66), but the following are exceptional:

<He twisted his neck to contemplate the exhibit which **the Merkalova** had cast on the bed and then straightened it to observe the more compelling exhibit of **the Merkalova** herself.> 1937 Innes, *Hamlet* 149. <Mr Tucker and Sir Ronald sat down with **the Mr and Mrs Thatcher** to discuss the lastest poll findings.> 1987 June 13 *Times* 28/4.

In the following instances, use of *the* before title and name is normal in British, but less so in American:

the Prince N <**The Prince** Edward was received by Her Majesty's Lord-Lieutenant for the City of Glasgow.> 1990 Aug. 13 *Times* 12/2.

the Rev N <Protestant rector **the Rev** Timothy Kinahan . . . > 1993 Feb. 12 *Sun* 2/3.

2.1.1.4 With other nominals

A number of other miscellaneous examples show *the* in British use where American would have nothing:

at the back of In back of; behind < . . . a used car lot **at the back of** Shire Hall.> 1990 Rowlands 172.

the cricket The cricket game <1961 *New Statesman* 10 Feb. 210/3 It all began with la Starkie clutching her brandy in front of the Tavern at Lord's with her back to **the cricket**.> *OED* s.v. *la*.

the emotion <James Munro, who is involved in a victim support scheme in south-east London, has to fight his way through layers of **the emotion** before he can explain his work to solitary elderly women.> 1987 Nov. *Illustrated London News* 75/3.

the falafel <In designer flats they talked, over **the falafel**, of financing a film . . . and getting divorced.> 1987 Bradbury 15.

the half of it CIC has 3.4 iptmw in British texts and 1.3 in American. <Nobody heard him. . . . Mrs. Hannigan had, but she didn't pretend to understand **the half of it**.> 1987 Mar. 2 *London Daily News* 17/3.

the most of This sequence is common after *make*, but not otherwise. <As you succumb to once-a-year foodie treats this Christmas, spare a thought for the unsung professionals who have spent **the most of** the past year sampling them.> 1997 Dec. 13 *Times* Weekend 10/1.

the moths <There isn't anything of value there unless you count the Mothers' Union banner . . . which incidentally I've promised to repair. It's got **the moths** in it, or something.> 1975 Price 123.

the one son <She had **the one son**.> 1979 Snow 15.

the pumps In the following description of a small garage, there has been no prior mention of pumps. <The garage stood on a corner . . . . Just **the two pumps**.> 1987 Hart 14.

the sales < . . . she barges into the crowd like a shopaholic at **the sales**.> 2003 July 15 *Times* T2 7/3. – **in the sale(s)** On sale <It was so gorgeous that I would have bought it even if it hadn't been **in the sale**.> 2003 July 8 *Times* T2 13/1.

the social services < . . . public spending on **the social services** has been cut.> 1988 May *Illustrated London News* 7/3.

the television <Once, politicians got on **the television** only to talk about an Issue.> 1987 Nov. *Illustrated London News* 98/1.

all over the town CIC British texts have 5 times as many tokens without *the* as with *the*, but American texts have none with *the*. <Why, 'tis **all over the town**, Miss.> 1981 Lemarchand 16.

the welfare <Scrounging on **the welfare**.> 1985 Mortimer 320–1.

if the worst comes to the worst CIC has no British tokens of *worse comes to worst* and no American tokens of *the worst comes to the worst*. <Think carefully about each option so that, **if the worst comes to the worst**, you will be prepared.> 1989 BNC.

2.1.2 Definite article versus indefinite article

The following postdeterminers frequently follow *the* in British.

the occasional The closest American equivalent is *an occasional*, but American might also have the adverb *occasionally*, as in "blizzards, freezing winds, and occasionally earthquakes" instead of "blizzards, freezing winds and the occasional earthquake." In CIC, *the occasional* is more than twice as frequent in British texts as in American. <After they [child visitors] have gone, I find sticky fingerprints everywhere, . . . not to mention **the occasional** breakage.> 1998 Jan. 3 *Times* Weekend 30/1.

the odd An occasional: American has no simple equivalent to this collocation; *an odd* is likely to suggest "a strange." In CIC, *the odd*, as a sequence, is nearly 6 times as frequent in British texts as in American. <I can recall **the odd** fishfinger or beefburger for high tea.> 2003 Nov. 12 *Times* T2 3/2. Cf. § 2.5.2 THE ODD.

the sporadic A sporadic < . . . there were actually poppies bobbing at the verges. Even **the sporadic** cornflower.> 1989 July 18 *Times* 14/6.

Other constructions using *the* in British are either set collocations or syntactic structures.

off/on/to the boil Expressions with *the boil* are more than 20 times as frequent in British CIC texts as in American; expressions with *a boil* are more than 9 times as frequent in American as in British. <His play went **off the boil**.> 1991 Feb. 2 *Times* 23/3. <It is instructive to see what sets local loyalties **on the boil**.> 1991 Feb. 9 *Telegraph* Weekend Magazine 8/1.

the clergyman's <His father had **the clergyman's** interest in Darwinism.> 1988 Oct. *Illustrated London News* 59/1–2.

the day A day <If I could have an animal head on my body for **the day** I'd be a cat so I could lick my own bits.> 2004 Dec. 8–15 *Time Out* 8/1.

the draw, agree Agree to a draw <Karpov . . . refused to **agree the draw**.> 1986 Oct. 9 *Times* 2/7.

the half hour *Half an hour* is the dominant form in common-core English. CIC American texts have more than 5 times as many tokens of *a half hour* as British texts do. British texts have nearly 4 times as many tokens of *the half hour* as American texts do. < . . . within **the half hour** he was sitting disconsolately in the accident room of the Radcliffe Infirmary.> 1975 Dexter 79.

the hell of a *A hell of a* is the dominant form in common-core English. CIC British texts have some tokens of *the hell of a*; American texts do not. <. . . there's **the hell of a** lot more we need to know.> 1989 Underwood 181.

the market <Smart dresses for this age group are thin on the ground partly because . . . there simply isn't **the market.**> 2003 June 21 *Times* Weekend 9/1.

the power of good, do *one* CIC British texts have 3.3 iptmw of *a power of good* and 0.9 of *the power of good*. Neither option appears in CIC American texts. However, *DARE* has many examples of *a power of* in the sense "a lot of," but labels it chiefly Southern, South Midland, and old fashioned. <I think a little drop of Scotch would **do** me **the power of good.**> 1975 Dexter 29.

the world of good/difference CIC British texts have similar numbers of *the world of good* and *a world of good*; American texts have no tokens of *the world of good*. CIC British texts have 8 times as many tokens of *a world of difference* as of *the world of difference*, but American texts have 14 times as many. <Choosing the right travel insurance can make **the world of difference.**> 1998 June insurance ad poster on a London underground train.

2.1.3 Definite article versus possessive

Occasionally, in both British and American, *the* is used where a possessive pronoun is more appropriate. Among the following examples, only the third (*the machismo*) seems impossible in American (and perhaps unusual in British as well), but these examples are included because they are part of a larger pattern of the use of *the*.

the girl friend <He had arranged to meet **the girl friend** in the evening.> 1940 Shute 28.

the home <[In] Switzerland, . . . every male . . . has to have a semi-automatic rifle in **the home** by law.> 1988 Aug. *Illustrated London News* 27/1–2.

the machismo <Some . . . eager for trouble and anxious to prove **the machismo** . . . swaggered past and made two-fingered gestures to the unheeding police.> 1985 Ebdon 79.

the work <Only something to do with **the work.**> 1940 Shute 37.

2.1.4 Definite article versus demonstrative

for the matter of that For that matter: CIC British texts have 0.3 iptmw of the longer form; American texts have none. < . . . she bore every appearance of being able, at need, to put young people through it still – or elderly people too, **for the matter of that.**> 1983 Innes 63.

on the day CIC has 1.7 times as many tokens of *on the day* in British texts as in American; British texts have 4.3 times as many tokens of *on the day* as of *on that/this day*; American texts have only 2.3 times as many tokens of *on the day* as of *on that/this day*. <Of the four only Roberts was not sent off by the referee **on the day**.> 1987 Nov. 8 *Manchester Guardian Weekly* 30/1. Cf. §§ 2.1.1.1; 8.1 ON (THE) *DAY*.

on the night CIC has 1.7 times as many tokens of *on the night* in British texts as in American; British texts have 7.9 times as many tokens of *on the night* as of *on that/this night*; American texts have only 4.9 times as many tokens of *on the night* as of *on that/this night*. < . . . viewers will be encouraged to pledge money **on the night** [of a BBC1 charity program].> 1988 Feb. *Illustrated London News* 24/4. Cf. § 8.1 ON THE NIGHT.

2.2 Indefinite article

2.2.1 Form of the indefinite article: a/an

For all of the following, majority British use has *a* rather than *an*. However, for all except *historic(al)*, CIC American texts have no tokens of *an* at all. British preference for each form is given in parentheses as the percentage of iptmw for *a* followed by that for *an*.

an hallucination (50/50) < . . . **an hallucination**, nothing more.> 1985 Benedictus 13.

an hilarious (85/15) < . . . **an hilarious** hour with an inspired tutor.> 1993 Feb. 1 *Times* 15/6.

an historic(al) (British 57/43; American 78/22) <Carefree Retirement In **An Historic** Country Mansion> 1987 Aug. *Illustrated London News* 71/1.

an horrendous (70/30) < . . . **an horrendous** blunder.> 1988 Apr. 10 *Sunday Telegraph* 48/1.

an horrific (71/29) < . . . such **an horrific** offence.> 1988 Sept. 6 *Daily Telegraph* 3/5.

an hotel (93/7) <The woman . . . was living with her daughter in **an hotel** for the homeless.> 1987 Jan. 21 *Daily Mail* 2/1.

an Hussar (no CIC tokens) <Nicholas Soames, **an Hussar** and all of sixteen stone, grabbed hold of Worthington Evans.> 1991 Critchley 146.

2.2.2 Indefinite article versus no determiner

2.2.2.1 With mass nouns

Most mass nouns can also be used as count nouns under appropriate circumstances (*much bread* : *a rye bread*). However, some uses of the indefinite article with nouns that are normally mass are distinctively British. Cf. § 3.2.3 for such nouns in plural form.

Many of these constructs seem to be fairly recent. Sidney Greenbaum, who was in the United States from 1968 to 1983, remembered being struck by *a nonsense* on his return to England (Greenbaum 1986, 7). The first example of the count use of *nonsense* in the *OED* is by Evelyn Waugh in 1942, but it doubtless took about a generation to move into frequent use.

In the following entries, the parenthesized figures following the entry form are the British/American iptmw, respectively, of the noun preceded by *a(n)*. Where no figures are given, the number of tokens in both national varieties was too small to make comparison useful.

cheek (3.0/0.1) *Cheek* in the sense "insolent boldness" is usually a mass noun, but can take the indefinite article in British use with the sense "an act of insolent boldness" or, in *have a cheek*, the sense of "nerve, presumption." Other collocations are *got a cheek, a bit of a cheek*, and *What a cheek. Cheek* in all these uses is more British than American, which is likely to prefer other terms, such as *gall, nerve*, or *chutzpah*. <What **a cheek**.> 1995 Stoppard 17.

coffee (24.3/2.9) *Coffee* is usually a mass noun, but may be used as a count in both British and American, as in *I'll have two coffees*, or *a coffee* may refer to a social event at which coffee is served. Each national variety, especially American, prefers *a cup of coffee* for countable use, British by 1.2 times and American by 6.9 times. <Nescafe Gold Blend coffee commercials [featured] courting neighbours who never seem sure whether to share **a coffee** or a bed.> 1993 Feb. 8 *Times* 27/2.

curry (2.7/0, probably reflecting the fact that curry is far more popular in Britain than in America) <Anyway they went out for **a curry**.> 1992 Green 132.

eye liner <I used to spend . . . £14 on **an eyeliner**.> 1995 Sept. *Marie Claire* 245/2.

fly spray *Fly spray*, like mass nouns generally, can be countable in reference to a type of the substance; but here it means a unit (bottle/can) of it. <I've never bought **a flyspray**.> 1990 Aug. 18 *Daily Telegraph* Weekend 5/5.

gingerbread <There were scones and **a gingerbread**.> 1993 Cleeves 95.

gossip (0.6/0.1) <Just in time. Coffee and **a gossip**.> 1990 Hardwick 114.

heroin <The American musician . . . had taken **a heroin**.> 1986 Oct. 9 *Hampstead Advertiser* 7/1.

ice-cream (3.8/1.6) A dish/cone/serving of ice cream <Having consoled myself for my ruined omelette with a *croque-monsieur* and **a** chocolate **ice cream** . . . .> 2000 Caudwell 189. Cf. § 3.2.3.

isolation (1.1/0.3) < . . . if a man in a sensitive job went sick, he was liable to be whisked into **an isolation**.> 1987 Rutherfurd 888.

lasagne <I had a cappuccino and **a lasagne**.> 1987 May 27 *Punch* 38/2.

lettuce (0.8/0) A head of lettuce <Joanna's doing something to **a lettuce**.> 1989 Daniel 49.

mascara (0.5/0) <I used to spend £15 on **a mascara**.> 1995 Sept. *Marie Claire* 245/2.

misery (9.7/0.5) Instead of *make (something) a misery*, American is likely to have *make (something) miserable*. <MPs . . . demand police action against a handful of demonstrators armed with megaphones who are making their working lives **a misery**.> 2003 June 20 *Times* 13/1.

nonsense (11.8/0) – **be a nonsense** Be (a) nonsensical (action). <It was **a** military **nonsense** mounted under political pressure.> 1986 Sherwood, *Mantrap Garden* 110. – **make a nonsense of** ***something*** Make *something* nonsensical. <Does all this **make a nonsense of** the Vienna talks on conventional forces in Europe?> 1990 Jan. 27–Feb. 2 *Economist* 54/2.

persecution <If a health official or a teacher expresses that homosexuality is abnormal or immoral he is subjected to **a** great **persecution**.> 1987 Feb. 10 *Evening Standard* 35/5.

good service (3.7/0.3) <We [a garage] give **a good service**.> 1989 Wainwright 126.

sleep (5.7/0.9) <I understand the doctor wanted you to have **a sleep**.> 1991 Neel 59.

medical training <If . . . she'd had **a medical training** . . . , she'd have a better chance of being competent.> 1991 Greenwood 78.

wood < . . . my husband . . . turned round to see a huge pile of **a** sawn **wood** already done by his elderly mother-in-law.> 1987 May 27 *Punch* 14/3–15/1.

2.2.2.2 With days of the week

on a ***day of the week*** The alternative to *on a Sunday* is *on Sundays* (*on Sunday* is very frequent but may refer either to Sundays generally or to a particular Sunday). In CIC, British texts prefer *on a Sunday* by 1.3 times, and American texts prefer *on Sundays* by 1.8 times. The other days of the week follow generally the same pattern. <In the old days . . . we got paid weekly **on a Thursday**.> 1999 Mar. 21 *Sunday Times* 10/7.

2.2.2.3 With plural nouns

An unusual construction is *a* with a plural noun as head. In the following cases, the noun head logically refers to "a building housing . . . ," and the implied reference to a building doubtless favors the indefinite article in British use.

a Council Offices < . . . the Council first built **a** dramatic new **Council Offices**.> ca. 1988 (exact date n/a) *In Britain*, 18/2.

a public baths <It was . . . a lousy description, admittedly, of **a public baths**.> 1991 Feb. 26 *Times* 14/1.

2.2.3 Indefinite article versus possessive

a lip <Wilcox curled **a lip**. 'Nancy boys?'> (An American clerk, in copying this citation from the original, mistyped "his lip.") 1988 Lodge 114.

2.3 Possessive construction

A possessive pronoun or occasionally a possessive noun phrase is used as a determiner in British English where American would have other options.

2.3.1 Possessive versus definite article

One of the most characteristically British constructions of this type is *in their [large numbers]*, for which the American analog would be *by/in the [large numbers]*. In CIC, 60 percent of the British tokens of such constructions have *their*; 99 percent of the American tokens have *the*. Cf. § 8.1 IN THEIR *LARGE NUMBERS*.

dozens <. . . one of those mass-produced plaster ornaments to be seen **in their dozens** at every motorway junction garden centre.> 1989 Rendell 44.
droves <. . . they flocked here **in their droves**.> 1998 Joss 31.
hordes <. . . the office workers started scurrying home **in their hordes**.> 1987 Fraser 26.
hundreds <Residents . . . turned out **in their hundreds** to welcome the Prince.> 1998 June 19 *Times* 5/5.
hundreds of thousands <Sikhs have suffered and died **in their hundreds of thousands**.> 1999 Mar. 24 *Independent* Review 5/3.
millions <They subscribe **in their millions** to women's magazines.> 1967 Frost and Jay 112.
scores <Labour voters and MPs will be encouraged to turn up **in their scores**.> 2004 Jan. 2 *Times* 25/2.
tens of thousands <Blacks and whites [in South Africa] came together **in their tens of thousands**.> 1989 Sept. 13 ITV news.
thousands <Party workers . . . quit the conference hall **in their thousands**.> 1992 Critchley 32.

A rare construction also has a British possessive corresponding with *the* in common-core English use.

make their most of Make the most of <The Sandinistas have **made their most of** both qualities.> 1985 June 14 *Times* 15/1.

2.3.2 Possessive versus indefinite article

one's bit of fun In CIC British texts, fewer than 3 percent of *bit of fun* have a possessive; most of the rest have the indefinite article; all of the American texts have the indefinite article. <Your mother's only having **her bit of fun**.> (An American clerk, in copying this citation from the original, mistyped "a bit of.") 1985 Mortimer 264.

2.3.3 Possessive versus no determiner

A characteristic of colloquial British is the use of *our* with a given name. In American, this construction would normally imply a contrast between two particular persons of the same name, an implication not made in the British use.

our *Name* <For them she's "**our Maggie**" – a term of endearment as insulting in its way as "that bloody woman," since nobody, but nobody, would ever have dreamed of calling Churchill "**our Winnie**."> 1990 Hazleton 110. <**Our** Kenny told me all about it. . . . He's a cousin of mine.> 2000 Granger 237.

2.4 No determiner versus some determiner

British English has no determiner with some nouns for which American English would require one, either definite or indefinite depending on the context, or else a plural noun.

2.4.1 In collocations

Some of these constructions occur in particular collocations. Most of these nouns are normally countable.

to boiling point Of tokens of *boiling point* following a preposition, CIC British texts have 14 percent without a determiner, and American texts have 3 percent. < . . . processed white bread . . . is usually enough to bring any modern self-respecting whole-foodie **to boiling point**.> 1986 Sept. 24 *Times* 15/3.

at/in/out of college The expressions *at, in*, and *out of college* occur in American English, but in general senses such as "attending a college" and "finished with college education." Senses like "located at/in the college" and "away from the college building" take a determiner in American use. <Mr Knellie had had his lunch and gone **out of college**.> 1956 Lewis 47. <Dr. Alan Hardinge decided that Monday evening to stay **in college**.> 1992 Dexter 202. <"Is she there . . . ?" [¶] "No, not **at college**. Can I take a message?"> 1993 Smith 182.

on condition (that) CIC British texts have 3 times as many tokens of *on condition that* as of *on the condition that*; American texts are about evenly divided between the two. <Lawrence had been awarded a Fellowship by All Souls **on condition** he wrote a history of the Arab Revolt.> 1988 Nov. *In Britain* 36/3.

at dead of night CIC British texts are about evenly divided between *at dead of night* and *in the dead of the night*; American texts have only the latter. < . . . there is just no evidence that the Bank of England is dumping French francs and Danish kroner, **at dead of night**, on the Tokyo market.> 1993 Feb. 13 *Spectator* 14/2.

devil there is The devil there is <If there was a dead body around, you know, it would be another matter. But **devil there is** – unless it has been stuffed up a chimney.> 1983 Innes 38.

down at heel CIC has 0.7 iptmw of *down at heel* in British texts and none in American; it has 0.7 iptmw of *down at the heels* (plural) in American texts and none in British. <Teesside, then as now a **down at heel** seaside resort.> 1990 BNC.

in future The collocation *in future* "from now on" contrasts with *in the future*, which has either the same sense or means "at some time in the future" (*CGEL* 8.59n). CIC has 80 iptmw of adverbial *in future* in British texts and 3.6 in American. <Put me in a taxi, tell me not to be a naughty girl **in future** and send me home?> 1991 Grant-Adamson 219.

on holiday *Holiday* in the sense "a period away from home or work for travel or relaxation" is a Briticism. CIC has 136.7 iptmw of *on holiday* in British texts and 6.8 in American. The ICE-GB corpus has 27 tokens of *holiday* in British constructions as the head of a noun phrase without a determiner (*It's the second Monday that we get back from Easter holiday*). In 22 of those tokens, *holiday* is the object of the preposition *on* (*You're going* **on holiday**). In American use, *on vacation* is possible, but primarily in a general sense (*We'll be on vacation in July*); in a specific sense (*We're taking the family on a vacation to Alaska*), the determiner is likely. < . . . an actress who is believed to have gone **on holiday** to Spain.> 1993 Feb. 13 *Daily Telegraph* 1/6–7.

(in/to/into/out of) hospital British uses *hospital* without a determiner after certain prepositions of location (*CGEL* 5.44) but also as the direct object after verbs implying motion from or to a hospital (*leave* and rarely *attend*). CIC has 143.4 iptmw of adverbial *in hospital* in British texts and 9.1 in American texts. It has 25.3 iptmw of *in the hospital* in British texts and 74.3 in American. < . . . they didn't send for an ambulance to take him **to hospital**.> 1966 Priestley 122. <I had been **out of hospital** for six weeks.> 1985 June 2 *Sunday Telegraph* 11/2. < . . . she was taken **into hospital**.> 1986 Aug. 29 (Newcastle) *Evening Chronicle* 12/4. < . . . where would I hide a knife **in hospital**?> 1991 Green 184. <She . . . received a telephone call to **attend hospital**.> 1991 Feb. 20 *Times* 4/5. <. . . the Department of Environment bans the use of Housing Corporation money to provide supported housing for people **leaving hospital**.> 1994 Sept. 12 *Guardian* 20/5.

on hunger strike Although *on strike* is idiomatic in American English, *on hunger strike* is less so. CIC has 2.3 iptmw of it in British texts and 1.0 in American; it has 0.2 of *on a hunger strike* in British texts and 2.8 in American. <The Rev Jesse Jackson has gone **on hunger strike**.> 1993 Feb. 17 *Times* 11/8.

for/at interview *also* **after/refused interview** CIC has 6.4 iptmw of *for interview* and 1.8 of *at interview* in British texts and 0.1 of the former and none of the latter in American. <Many graduates are made to feel ashamed of a

2.2 **at interview**.> 1993 Feb. 13 *Spectator* 21/3. <St Benedict's . . . invited him **for interview**.> 1999 Mar. 22 *Times* 15/3. < . . . he had been **refused interview**.> 1999 Mar. 22 *Times* 15/3. <If, **after interview**, you still feel he's not right, I will accept it.> 1999 Mar. 22 *Times* 15/3.

a bit of ladies man Something of a ladies man <Stephenson, known as "**a bit of ladies man**", may be travelling with another woman.> 1986 Sept. 4 *Daily Telegraph* 40/5.

on look-out On the lookout <He and a white accomplice, who was **on look-out** outside the victim's home escaped with two suitcases.> 1987 Apr. 8 *Daily Telegraph* 32/4.

on mortgage CIC has 0.4 iptmw of *mortgage* without a determiner in British texts and none in American. **1**. With a mortgage; mortgaged <The big advantage of buying a home **on mortgage** is that it provides a roof over your head while you pay for it.> 1986 Oct. 4 *Times* 32/1. **2**. In a mortgage <She had about £50,000 **on mortgage**, which was far too high in relation to her salary.> 1991 Neel 219.

next day In random CIC samples of *next day*, British had 42 tokens out of 250 without a determiner and American had only 1. <. . . he thought he'd better speak to his aunt and uncle about getting to King's Cross station **next day**.> 1997 Rowling 67 (*US ed.* the next day).

next moment In CIC samples, 11 percent of the British tokens of *next moment* were without a determiner; none of the American were. <**Next moment**, Professor Dumbledore was there.> 1999 Rowling 120 (*US ed.* A moment later). <**Next moment** – > 1999 Rowling 227 (*US ed.* Then again).

on offer Available: This collocation, although parallel to several other common-core English ones (*on display, on sale, on view*), is a Briticism. In CIC, it is 42 times more frequent in British texts than in American. <There is still time to apply for one of the 45 MSC scholarships **on offer**.> 1986 Sept. 23 *Guardian* 12/8.

pound a minute This use is rare. <And his standard charge is **pound a minute**.> 1985 Price 146.

at source In CIC, *at the source* is of approximately equal frequency in British and American; *at source* is 27.3 times more frequent in British than in American. <BT could . . . deal with the problem **at source**.> 1991 Mar. 10 *Sunday Times* Magazine 3/3.

at/on/to/*etc.* table In CIC texts, *at/on table* without a determiner is 7 times more frequent in British than in American. <It was the presence of the head of the order which cast a blight **over** High **Table**.> 1977 Barnard 100. <. . . send them [muffins] very quickly **to table**.> 1983 Brooke-Taylor 104. <[Barbara Cartland:] One day . . . there were thirteen **at table**.> 1990 Critchfield 296. <I dined **on** High **Table**.> 2000 Caudwell 322.

to/at/out of/leave university *University* is much like *hospital* and *college* with respect to its use without determiners, typically after certain prepositions of location or verbs of motion. In American use, however, whereas *college* can be so used in general statements (*When she finishes high school, she's going to college*) but not specific ones (*She's going to the college by train*), *university* and *hospital* usually have a determiner in all cases. In CIC texts, *university* in such constructions is 17 times more likely to be without a determiner in British than in American. <I haven't the slightest regret about **leaving university**.> 1986 Aug. 19 *Times* 8/3. <Raymond dropped **out of university** last year.> 1988 Lodge 238. <Something strange happened to Joanne **at university**.> 2002 Smith 89. <Today, of course, she would have gone **to university**.> 2003 James 10.

2.4.2 With count nouns

In British English, a number of count nouns, in addition to those exemplified above, are exceptionally used without determiners. Cf. § 3.2.4.

accusation <. . . he can blether on about **accusation** of dishonesty.> 1986 Sept. 15 *Times* 12/7.

-ache (*CGEL* 5.49n) See BACKACHE, EARACHE, STOMACHACHE, TOOTHACHE below.

allotment The term *allotment* is not used in this sense in American, but if it were, a determiner would be expected. <He's up on **allotment** today. . . . A little plot of land . . . like an extra garden where people grow vegetables.> 1991 Glaister 28–9.

backache In CIC British texts *backache* has no determiner in about 71 percent of its occurrences; in American texts in about 50 percent. <Many people who work in offices get **backache** because they do not sit at their desks properly.> *CIDE*.

ball The term *good ball* is used mainly in sports reporting, often as an exclamation; in CIC British texts, approximately 3 uses out of 5 have no determiner. American texts have very few such uses. <Wasps' international wings . . . showed what they can do when good **ball** comes their way.> 1989 Feb. 19 *Manchester Guardian Weekly* 32/3.

bog <I became stuck in **bog** only twice.> 1993 Feb. 13 *Daily Telegraph* Weekend 2/8.

break CIC has 8 British tokens without a determiner to 22 with *the* in the constructions *in/during ____ break*. It has no comparable American examples without *the*. < . . . phone me in first **break**.> 1988 Stoppard 22.

breaking point In CIC British texts, this expression is 10 times more likely to be used without a determiner than with one; in American texts, it is 15 times more likely to be used with a determiner than without one. <Relatives go on looking after them [the elderly] through and beyond **breaking point**.> 1988 Sept. 18 *Sunday Telegraph* 3/3.

bursting point In CIC British texts, this expression is 17 times more likely to be used without a determiner than with one; in American texts, *bursting* *point* does not occur. <. . . stands that were packed to **bursting point**.> 2000 Rowling 427 (*US ed.* the bursting point).

car bomb <. . . Ian Gow's death by **car bomb**.> 1991 Critchley 193.

carriageway Highway: In CIC British texts, about 4 percent of the tokens of *carriageway* are without a determiner. <A contra-flow will be in operation on the A2 Bexleyheath affecting westbound **carriageway** between Danson interchange and the borough boundary.> 1987 Mar. 25 *Evening Standard* 5/1.

certificate <We did it [*Paradise Lost*] for higher **certificate**.> 1975 Dexter 90.

century In CIC British texts, about 10 percent of the phrase *of (the) last century* are without the determiner; in American texts, none are. <. . . a magazine of last **century**.> 1988 Nov. *In Britain* 16/1.

in chambers In CIC, the phrase is nearly 5 times more frequent in British texts than in American; it usually refers to a law office in British, but to a judge's office in American. <Let's have a woman **in Chambers**.> 1971 Mortimer 72.

chapter <'I understand the new dean is sworn to restore proper Catholic worship to the cathedral.' [¶] 'What do **chapter** think of that?' . . . [¶] 'In general, they're against anything which lengthens the services.'> 1993 Greenwood 66.

collision In CIC British texts, a determiner is 2 times more likely than not before the noun of the phrase *in collision*; in American texts, it is 9 times more likely. <. . . her official Jaguar . . . was in **collision** with a police car.> 1993 Feb. 3 *Times* 4/1–2.

common room <. . . the assistant masters emerged from **common room** and took charge.> 1959 Innes 25.

concussion In CIC British texts, 84 percent of the uses of *concussion* are without a determiner; in American texts, 81 percent have a determiner. <I thought it was **concussion**.> 1992 Walters 251.

contract In CIC British texts, 59.5 percent of the phrases *of contract* have a determiner; in American texts, 76 percent do. <I am suing the Strand Theatre for termination of **contract**.> 1989 July 27 *Evening Standard* 31/2.

control <. . . in room 10 you have to sit well up in bed to see the screen and **control** is manual.> 1987 July *Illustrated London News* 72/4.

convoy In CIC British texts, 66 percent of the phrases *in convoy* have a determiner; in American texts, 96 percent do. <I'd like to hear . . . why his ship wasn't in **convoy**.> 1940 Shute 27.

diet <. . . many obese girls . . . have ruined themselves with bad **diet**.> 1991 Feb. 16 *Weekend Telegraph* 7/1–2.

diocese In CIC British texts, when *diocese* is preceded by a proper place name (e.g., *Canterbury, London, Rochester*), 60 percent of its tokens have no determiner; in American texts, 97 percent have one. <In other dioceses, . . . the congregations may then be more worryingly low than even those in London **diocese**.> 1990 Aug. 21 *Times* 9/3.

doorsteps <I suppose you'd better come in then, rather than stand there nattering on **doorsteps**.> 1994 Freeling 105.

drink See § 3.2.4.

driver <By 1902 the self-propelled forty-two-inch mower with saddle for **driver** was being used by Cadburys.> 1984 Smith 147.

earache In CIC British texts *earache* has no determiner in about 71 percent of its occurrences; in American texts in about 43 percent. <When I was a child I used to get terrible **earache**(s).> *CIDE.*

exchange of contract <[comment on gazumping:] If at any time before **exchange of contract** someone makes a higher offer to the agent he is duty bound to take his principal's instructions.> 1987 Apr. 10 *Evening Standard* 45/1.

favourite In CIC British texts *favourite* is used after forms of *be* without a determiner in 8.2 iptmw; in American texts, *favorite* is not so used. <Miss Jo Richardson . . . is **favourite** to hold the cabinet post if Labour wins the election.> 1987 Apr. 8 *Daily Telegraph* 4/5.

fire In CIC British texts, the phrase *with (an) open fire* has no determiner in about 22 percent of its occurrences; in American texts that phrase does not occur. <That red room with open **fire** flanked by lion statues . . . is classic bourgeois.> 1987 Feb. 2 *Evening Standard* 24/3, 25/1.

flu In CIC British texts *flu* has no determiner in 88.5 percent of its occurrences, and in American texts in 63 percent. <He's got **flu**.> 1998 Rowling 96 (*US ed.* the flu).

freezing point In CIC British texts, *freezing point* has no determiner in 73 percent of its occurrences; in American texts it always has *the.* <From the moment they [strawberries] are picked . . . they are kept at just above **freezing point**.> 1987 June 20 *Times* 13/7.

gas service <Turn off the whole supply at the meter and call **gas service**.> 1980s poster of instructions on leaking gas.

golf-course <. . . the local Inspector who played such a steady game on **golf-course**.> 1949 Tey 17.

grant < . . . the Arts Council may intervene and make reasonable access for broadcasters a condition of **grant**.> 1988 Sept. *Illustrated London News* 64/3.

grounds In the sense "area of land used for a particular purpose," *ground(s)* may be either singular or plural: *parade ground(s)*. But when it is unmodified, it is usually plural and takes a determiner: *the grounds.* British, however, sometimes has *grounds* without a determiner especially when it is the object of a preposition. CIC has 1.7 iptmw of *in/from grounds* in British texts and none in American texts. <In spite of policing measures taken in **grounds**, . . . the Government says there are still too many incidents of violent hooliganism in **grounds**.> 1989 Mar. 5 *Manchester Guardian Weekly* 31/1.

hall CIC has 2.8 iptmw of *in hall(s)* in British texts and none in American texts. <Like many students spending their first year in **halls**. . . .> 1994 Oct. 3–9 *Big Issue* 16/3.

head office In CIC British texts *head office* has a determiner in 58 percent of its occurrences; in American texts in 89 percent. <. . . the JVC showroom had closed some years ago, presumably without telling **head office**. I wrote to **head office**.> 1989 July 31 *Times* 12/2.

home *From home* is normal in many uses in common-core English, but in *remove a child from home* it appears to be a British social-work idiom. < . . . a child who has been abused . . . should be removed from **home**.> 1991 Feb. 24 *Sunday Times* Magazine 58/1.

hornbeam British often uses terms for trees in the singular without a determiner. CIC British texts have 3.7 iptmw of singular *hornbeam*, with no determiner in 79 percent of the tokens, and no tokens of plural *hornbeams*; American texts have no tokens of the singular and 0.2 iptmw of the plural. <Here oaks vie with **hornbeam**.> 2003 July 12 *Times* Weekend 1/4.

house CIC has 0.2 iptmw of *share house* in British texts and none in American texts. It has forms of *move house* in 19.3 iptmw in British texts and none in American, which uses the verb *move* alone in this sense. <. . . her demanding . . . mother, with whom she shared **house**.> 1979 Dexter 27–8. <He had moved **house**.> 1989 Rendell 36.

honeymoon CIC British texts have 57 percent of *on honeymoon* with a determiner, and American texts have 96 percent; British texts have 63 percent of *from honeymoon* with a determiner, and American texts 100 percent. <. . . the lovers got back from **honeymoon**.> 1993 Feb. 1 *Times* 12/4.

jug Prison <Unfortunate chaps who look after homicidal maniacs in **jug**.> 1973 Innes 32.

kettle CIC British texts have 0.3 iptmw of *put kettle* without a determiner and 13.0 with a determiner (*put the kettle on*, etc.); American texts have none without a determiner, and 0.7 with *the*. Quite apart from the use of determiners, it is apparent that British people put kettles on a good deal more than Americans do. <Go and put **kettle** on.> 1987 Feb. 9 ITV *Coronation Street*.

line < . . . the traffic had to filter into single **line**.> 1975 Dexter 165.

manner <The papers require to be signed and sworn . . . in similar **manner**.> SEU w.7.10.14.

mortgage CIC has 0.4 iptmw of *on mortgage* in British texts and none in American. <She had about £50,000 on **mortgage**.> 1991 Neel 219.

moustache <He is a big man . . . with bushy sideboards and RAF-style **moustache**.> 1988 Lodge 70.

newsreel <The vulnerability of the crew . . . was all too obvious in the cuts taken from wartime **newsreel**.> 1989 Sept. 7 *Times* 13/6.

party conference CIC British texts have *party conference* without a determiner in about 2.5 percent of its occurrences, but no American use of the analogous *political convention* is without a determiner. <His speech . . . was adequate, but too serious – more suited to **party conference**.> 1993 Feb. 13 *Daily Telegraph* 11/3.

off plan <. . . half of the 252 homes . . . have been sold **off plan**.> 2000 Jan. 19 *Times* 27/2–3.

plant <**Plant** tends to be better used, and teaching staff are deployed less luxuriantly.> 1987 Dec. 20 *Manchester Guardian* 6/2.

post Mail: Although the expressions are rare, CIC British texts have equal numbers of *by (the) first/second post*, with and without the determiner; American texts have neither (with the analog *mail*). <The eleven pounds, etc., came by second **post**.> 1985 Townsend 65.

post Job: CIC British texts have 11 times as many tokens of *in post* in the sense "in office" or "on the job" as American texts do. <You're hoping that . . . there might be someone still **in post** who knew her.> 2001 James 319.

practice <The task force was established . . . to spread best **practice** among schools.> 1999 Mar. 19 *Times* 43/6.

race <. . . the only point in taking part in **race** was to win.> 1999 Mar. 16 *Independent* Review 4/6.

radar screen <It [an airplane] . . . disappeared from **radar screen**.> 1989 Aug. 4 BBC1 news.

record, on *On record* "recorded" is common-core English, although it is 2.7 times more frequent than *on the record* in CIC British texts and only 1.5 times so in American. <I'm not making a bet on this election because the odds are probably the meanest **on record**.> 1987 June 5 *Evening Standard* 6/4. In the following citation, *on record* means "on a phonograph record," in which sense, a determiner would be expected in American. <I don't even think I've heard it **on record**, though I did see *Rosenkavalier* in Amsterdam.> 1993 Smith 60–1.

roll <Autumn Term . . . begins today with 330 girls on **roll**.> 1986 Sept. 6 *Times* 17/3.

saddle See DRIVER.

send up <. . . this 1850 pantomine is played perfectly straight. Any attempt at **send up** would ruin the inherent humour of the piece.> 1987 Feb. 5 *Hampstead Advertiser* 2/4.

shot Camera shot: CIC British texts have 0.8 iptmw of *in shot* and 0.4 of *out of shot*; American texts have none. <Henry, get out of the way, you're in **shot**.> 1987 Bradbury 135.

spring CIC has *in (the) spring* without a determiner in 40 percent of the British tokens, and in 21 percent of the American. <. . . in **spring** I did the Season and curtseyed to Her Majesty and the Duke.> 1991 Barnard 61.

standard <Shell have put great emphasis on **standard** of service.> 1987 Jan. 29 *Deptford & Peckham Mercury* 8/4.

stomachache CIC British texts have 5 times as many tokens of *stomachache* without a determiner as American texts do. American texts have 3 times as many tokens of *a stomachache* as British texts do. <. . . the orange juice was giving him **stomachache**.> 1988 Taylor 158.

system <Mr Bill Phillips . . . will oversee new management information **system**.> 1987 Feb. 26 *Hampstead Advertiser* 6/2.

term CIC has 11.3 iptmw of the phrase *of term* in British texts and none in American texts with the sense "a division of the school year." < . . . the last

Herbology lesson of **term** was cancelled.> 1998 Rowling 147 (*US ed.* the term).

toothache In CIC British texts, *toothache* has no determiner in 72 percent of the tokens; in American texts, it has a determiner in 83 percent of the tokens. <People get **toothache** in Tangiers.> 1988 Apr. 10 *Sunday Telegraph* 17/1.

train <. . . a frantic Kennedy took **train** to Gatwick in order to fly north.> 1989 Feb. 19 *Manchester Guardian Weekly* 27/5.

uproar CIC has 1.7 iptmw of *cause uproar* and 2.9 of *in uproar* in British texts; it has neither in American texts. <Mr Clinton risks further alienating the military, already in **uproar** over the issue of homosexuals.> 1993 Feb. 15 *Daily Mail* 10/4–5.

value CIC has 1.5 iptmw of *be + value* and 12.9 of *be + good value* in British texts; it has 0.5 and 0.2 respectively in American texts. <. . . the admirable book by Robert Sommers called *The US Open-Golf's Ultimate Challenge* . . . is wonderful **value** at £12.95.> 1987 Dec. 20 *Manchester Guardian* 31/4.

window, out of CIC shows that *out of the window* is the overwhelmingly dominant form in common-core English, but *out of window* is 5 times more common in British than in American. <I noticed Jamie's head sticking **out of window** one floor below.> 1997 fiction CIC.

A number of nouns of this category denote articles of clothing, and they tend to collocate with the verb *wear* or the preposition *in*, being in that respect like the nouns of § 2.4.1.

boiler suit; balaclava <Eyre, . . . dressed in **boiler suit** and **balaclava**, was confronted by the young policeman in the darkness.> 1987 June 20 *Times* 2/4.

cap; muffler <Green . . . had found him there, wearing woollen **cap** and **muffler**.> 1985 Clark 129.

suit; trilby <. . . more conservatively dressed in dark **suit** and **trilby**.> 1987 Feb. 20 *Guardian* 3/2.

uniform Combinations like common-core *in uniform* and British *wear uniform* (1.7 iptmw in CIC British texts and none in American) have no determiner. When *uniform* has no determiner but another modifier after *in*, such as *in school/full/military/army/police uniform*, CIC British texts have more than twice as many tokens as American texts do. < . . . he took delivery of a bag . . . from a man in airline **uniform**.> 1986 Sept. 16 *Times* 1/2. <Louise . . . wondered whether Soppy would ever wear **uniform** again.> 1989 Dickinson 80.

2.4.3 With proper or quasi-proper nouns

Some items of this general category are proper names (such as that of the former royal vessel *Britannia*) or are quasi-proper names, that is, common nouns or noun phrases that serve, in a particular context, to identify their referents uniquely.

The latter are often capitalized in recognition of their proper-like function. They also may (and in American usually do) take a definite determiner, typically *the*.

Big Bang A 1986 change in Stock Exchange practices <. . . the redevelopment of the City after **Big Bang** offers a chance to make ample amends.> 1988 May *Illustrated London News* 40/1.

Britannia <In the morning there will be a sail past by Dutch and British yachts before Her Majesty The Queen and Prince Philip in **Britannia**.> 1988 June *In Britain* 20/1.

Cabinet CIC British texts have more than 9 times as many tokens of *in Cabinet* without a determiner as American texts do. <This analysis was accepted in **cabinet**.> 1989 Dec. 23–1990 Jan. 4 *Economist* 61/2.

casualty The emergency room; ER: CIC British texts have about 3.8 iptmw of *in casualty* and 0.5 of *in the casualty department*. <A woman of 79 with peritonitis was kept in **casualty** for four hours.> 1987 Feb. 19 *Hampstead Advertiser* 1/2.

Cathedral <You weren't in **Cathedral** on Saturday, were you, Bert?> 1984 Gilbert 118.

Central Office This term is very frequent as a proper noun in CIC British texts, but has no CIC American tokens. <He will take over responsibility for running **Central Office**.> 1986 Sept. 6 *Times* 1/7.

Cosmos <Nothing happens in **Cosmos** except interactions.> 1987 Feb. 1 lecture in London.

Council <If **Council** invite you to take the chair, . . . it will be because they are going to make me Vice-Chancellor.> 1980 Archer 183–4.

Court <A College porter . . . directed him to his rooms in Third **Court**.> 1976 Raphael 16.

government <. . . some MPs believe last weeks reshuffle . . . will make a privacy law more attractive within **government**.> 2003 June 16 *Guardian* 1/4.

Grand Lodge <**Grand Lodge** has . . . put out a video.> 1988 May *Illustrated London News* 23/1.

Hall In British use, *Hall* after a preposition is often without a determiner; in American use, rarely. <'One hell of a chap,' remarked an undergraduate queueing for lunch outside **Hall**.> 1988 Nov. *In Britain* 36/1.

Labour Party <Mr Chenery was appointed to these posts by Westminster South **Labour Party**.> 1987 May 27 *Evening Standard* 2/1.

London Underground <The letter of thanks to **London Underground** must surely have been a send up?> 1987 Feb. 2 *Evening Standard* 29/1.

National Service, on In the army <After leaving school each of them spent eighteen months **on National Service**.> 1979 Dexter 94.

public institutions A CIC sample has the following tokens of the names of public institutions without/with a determiner. British: *Waterloo Station* 22/1; *Salisbury Cathedral* 25/0; *Birmingham Airport* 11/0; *Bristol Zoo* 7/0; *Manchester City Council* 15/0; *Liverpool Football Club* 12/0. American: *Pennsylvania Station* 10/1; *National Cathedral* 4/22; *San Francisco Airport* 2/6; *San Diego Zoo*

0/39; *New York City Council* 0/12; *Pacific Coast League* 0/18. Only with train stations does American practice agree with British (Swan 1995, 68).

reception The reception desk; the reception lobby/area <Back in **Reception**, Mrs Stapleton is at her diplomatic best dealing with a family of seven who have arrived two and a half hours early.> 1988 Apr. *In Britain* 11/3.

Senate <I don't remember it coming up at that meeting of **Senate**.> 1988 Lodge, *Nice Work* 85.

Star Chamber <Cecil Parkinson, recently promoted to head of **Star Chamber** . . . will get one of the important jobs.> 1988 Aug. *Illustrated London News* 16/1.

synod The General Synod of the Church of England <. . . 20 per cent of the members of **synod**.> 1993 Feb. 27 *Times* 15/3.

2.4.4 With mass nouns

air CIC British texts have more than 3 times as many tokens of *off the air* as of *off air*, but American texts have none of the latter and 4 times as many of the former as British does. <He seemed rather to have discharged the weapon warningly and wrathfully in **air**.> 1983 Innes 89. <Anne and Nick [broadcasters] went off **air** for their summer break.> 1994 Oct. 5 *Evening Standard* 61/1.

cabling < . . . a fire burnt through **cabling** [in a hovercraft].> 1986 Aug. 25 *Times* 1/7.

commission <. . . how do we know we are being sold the right product and they are not simply telling us to take it to get **commission**?> 2005 Jan. 15 *Daily Telegraph* 10/6.

honour <Maurice . . . is sent down on a thin pretext for the sake of college **honour**.> 1987 Nov. *Illustrated London News* 89/1.

play The cricket game: CIC has 1.4 iptmw of *start of play* in British texts and 0.1 in American. <If we left at once, we could be back for the start of **play**.> 1985 Bingham 78.

2.4.5 With predicate nouns

Some nouns without determiners are used as subject complements, equivalent to adjectives. This construction is unexceptional in British English, but rare in American.

champion Great <'I've got some [chips] in, would you like them for your tea with a couple of sausages?' . . . [¶] 'Yes, that'd be **champion**.'> 1995 Jones 73.

necessity Necessary <. . . it was agreed that it would be **necessity** for the Foundation to continue to receive a certain amount.> 2004 Jan. minutes from a financial meeting, London.

wizard Expert <She appears to be **wizard** at the job.> 1986 Sept. 15 *Times* 12/1.

2.5 Predeterminers and postdeterminers

2.5.1 Predeterminers

A noun phrase or pronoun followed by *of* and a determiner, if there is one, may signify a quantity or quality of the following noun. One of those, namely *various of*, as in *Candidates came from* ***various of the*** *schools*, is listed without comment in *MW*, but has a usage note in *NODE* commenting that "it is sometimes regarded as incorrect" in British use.

all (of) Common-core English strongly prefers *all the* to *all of the*, but that preference is somewhat stronger in British than in American. Of the two options, *all the* predominates in CIC British texts by 96 percent and in American by 89 percent. The pattern with other determiners, such as *these* and *those*, is similar. <He was standing in front of an estate agent's window, studying **all the** cards with house details.> 2000 Granger 295. Cf. BOTH (OF) below.

a bit of + *count noun* Something/somewhat of: CIC British texts have this construction 5 times more often than American texts do. < . . . on weekend evenings when they aren't having **a bit of** a "do" themselves, they are probably round at their friends' houses for dinner.> 2003 June 21 *Times* Weekend 1/2.

a bit of + *mass noun* Some; a little: CIC British texts have this construction nearly 4 times more often than American texts do. <I'd fancy **a bit of** that.> 2002 Feb. 19 poster ad on an underground train. – **a blind bit of** <I'll tell him what I think of him – not that it'll do **a blind bit of** good.> 1991 Dickinson 188.

both (of) Common-core English preference is strongly for *both the* over *both of the*, also when the determiner is a possessive pronoun (*my, our, your, his, her, its, their*). But with the demonstratives *those* and *these* and the relative *whose*, the frequency of these forms in CIC is more complex. Both national varieties have a preference for *both of those* over *both those*, British only slightly (by 51 percent) and American somewhat more (68 percent). Similarly, both prefer *both of whose* over *both whose* (although the first option is quite rare, in the 0.2 to 0.6 iptmw range); CIC British texts have no tokens of *both whose*, and American texts prefer *both of whose* by 2.5 to 1. For *both (of) these*, however, the two national varieties differ. CIC British texts prefer *both these* by 58 percent; American texts prefer *both of these* by 64 percent. In the American Michigan Corpus, *both of these* is 3 times more frequent than *both these*. <Today, melde . . . is known as "Fat-hen" in Britain and as "Lambs-quarter" in America. . . . **Both** these names refer to its farm food value.> (an American typist substituted *both of* in copying) 1965 Aug. 29 *Observer* 22/3. Cf. ALL (OF) above.

bunch of This quantifier is nearly twice as frequent in American as in British CIC texts. When applied to a group of people, it is usually disparaging in the BNC, according to Pam Peters (2004, 83). The following citations illustrate the disparaging use: <. . . a **bunch of** Sloanes [upper middle-class, snobbish young people who frequent fashionable Sloane Square] and show-offs in lavish restaurants.> 1991 Feb. 13 *Daily Mail* 7/3–4. < . . . she makes the rest of them [other models] look like a **bunch of** trannies [= transvestites].> 2003 July 13 *Times* Style 58/2.

but Only: The predeterminer use of *but* in phrases like the following is twice as frequent in CIC British texts as in American. <I am **but** a crooked, amoral, ill-educated, clapped out old drunk.> 1989 Daniel 66.

close on Close to; nearly *before expressions of duration*: CIC British texts have about 4.4 iptmw, but American texts only about 0.1. <We were left in the bar to study the menus for **close on** an hour.> 1989 July 25 *Evening Standard* 31/1.

a couple of Both British and American use *couple of*, British slightly (about 1.0 times) more than American in CIC texts. American also uses *couple* alone, as in *a couple samples* and *the first couple chapters* (Gilman 1994, 303–4; Peters 2004, 131). – **a good couple of** CIC has 11 times as many tokens of this expanded form in British texts as in American. <For **a good couple of** years there've been any number of whispers about a possible "hostile" takeover of Christie's.> 1987 Feb. 2 *Evening Standard* 6/1.

ever such CIC British texts have 6.3 iptmw of *ever such a*; American texts have 0.4. <**Ever such** a mess she made.> 1980 Sharpe 223.

half CIC British texts have nearly twice as many tokens of *half a (n)* as American texts do. American texts have somewhat more tokens of *a half* than British texts. With *pint*, British uses both *half a pint* and *a half pint*, but with other nouns: *half a dozen, half an hour*, etc., British prefers *half* as a predeterminer, whereas American uses it more freely as a postdeterminer: *a half dozen, a half hour*, etc. (Peters 2004, 239). <But the sport did not take on, and only **half a** century later was it introduced in its present form.> 1987 Sept. *Illustrated London News* 40/1.

lashings of CIC British texts have 4.8 iptmw of *lashings of*; American texts have 0.2. <Her . . . lips glistened under **lashings of** lip-gloss.> 1994 Oct. 5 *Evening Standard* 3/2.

a load of CIC British texts have 86.4 iptmw of *a load of*; American texts have 12.4. <Well, that was **a load of** rubbish.> 1983 Radley 140.

near Nearly <John Braine began to talk, the voice **near** a parody of the gravelly "trouble oop at t' mill" Yorkshireman of *Room at the Top*.> 1986 Oct. 30 *Times* 18/3–4.

no less CIC has 1.67 times as many tokens of *no less a* in British as in American texts. < . . . **no less** a personage than the 51-year-old Duke of Kent fell foul of the clampers.> 1987 Mar. 26 *Evening Standard* 6/2.

quite The form *quite* is more British than American; CIC has nearly 3 times as many tokens in British as in American texts. As a predeterminer before nouns in the combinations *quite a* and *quite the*, it is about 1.7 times more frequent in British than in American CIC texts. When its predeterminer sense is evaluative, *quite* is common-core English: *quite a bore, quite a genius, quite the* *hero*. In these uses, it is semantically equivalent to the adjective *real*: *a real bore*. Other senses, however, such as "completely" or "a lot of" or "just" or "only," seem to be British. <. . . half a dozen people have probably brought men-servants – some **quite** strangers to the Scamnum staff.> 1937 Innes, *Hamlet* 111. <It might be **quite** fun.> 1959 Innes 5. <I've known him, of course, since he was **quite** a lad.> 1988 Mortimer 202. And even in common-core uses, colloquial American would be more likely to use a different construction. Thus for British *That's **quite** a bike*, American might have *That's some bike* (Swan 1995, 547). When *quite* is in predeterminer position before an adjective-noun construction, it is equivalent to the qualifier use of *quite* (§ 7.1): *quite a tall building* = *a quite tall building*.

rather CIC has more than 3 times as many tokens of *rather a* in British as in American texts. <It is all **rather** a mess.> 1995 Aug. 29 *Evening Standard* 8/1.

right the way Right; all the way: CIC has 12.7 iptmw of *right the way* in British texts and none in American texts. <I tailed them **right the way** down to the stream.> 1991 Grant-Adamson 78–9.

a spot of Some / a little: CIC has 8.4 times as many tokens of *a spot of* in British texts as in American. <And then a chap . . . called out to ask me if I'd like **a spot of** fishing before dinner.> 2000 Caudwell 143.

such + another CIC has twice as many tokens of *such another* in British texts as in American, and a few more tokens of *another such* in American than in British. <Twenty-one years before . . . he had commanded just **such another** trawler.> 1940 Shute 72.

2.5.2 Postdeterminers

(a) further An additional: CIC has nearly 6 times as many tokens of *a further* in British texts as in American. If a noun follows, *a further* can also be paraphrased as *another*; if a number follows, the paraphrase can also be *[number] more*, as in the entry for (AN)OTHER *NUMBER* below; if a following noun is one of measurement, such as *hour*, either paraphrase is possible, with retention of the article in the second case (*an hour more*). <On October 4 a **further** 50 people were injured.> 1987 Nov. *Illustrated London News* 14/2–3. <A **further** patrol car had arrived.> 1993 Graham 141.

the (*rarely* **an**) **odd** CIC has nearly 6 times as many tokens of *the odd* in British texts as in American. **1**. An occasional; a . . . occasionally: <I don't mind the **odd** ticket but I haven't got time to hang around getting the car unclamped.> 1993 Smith 167 **2**. Some; a . . . or so (*an approximate number or amount*) < We've simply got to get the **odd** bob together.> 1993 Greenwood 172. Cf. § 2.1.2 THE ODD.

(an)other *number* *Number* more: CIC has 1.6 times as many tokens of expressions like *another six* in British texts as in American. Conversely, it has 1.6 times as many tokens of expressions like *six more* in American texts as in British.

<. . . **another five** companies . . . make material for the suits.> 1990 Aug. 23 *Times* 4/1.

plural number* more** When the number before *more* is plural (*hundreds, thousands, millions*), the American preference for the *number more* construction is even stronger (2.7 times as frequent as in CIC British texts). However, American also has an alternative construction in such cases: *costing* ***hundreds of more *workers their jobs; the lives of* ***thousands of more*** *Americans;* ***millions of more*** *customers come onto our networks.* This alternative is rare in American, but is not attested in CIC British texts, which have only the construction without *of.* <We're taking on **hundreds more** staff to keep stations spick and span. We're putting in **hundreds more** litter bins.> 1990 Aug. 14 London poster on tube trains.

one or other CIC has 49 times as many tokens of *one or other* in British texts as in American. American prefers *one or another* and *one or the other*, both of which are more frequent in American than in British. <. . . children . . . who are unloved, beaten and abused by **one or other** parent.> 1990 Aug. 19 *Sunday Times* Books. 2/2. Cf. § 4.6.

3 Nouns

3.1 Derivation

The derivation of words of one part of speech from those of another is universal. In Modern English, it has been common to make such derivation without an overt signal in the stem of the word, but rather merely by shifting it to a new part of speech. This is a common feature of English, but the particular items so shifted may be characteristic of one or the other variety of the language.

3.1.1 From verbs

Some British nouns are derived from verbs.

3.1.1.1 By simple functional shift

The derivation may be a simple shift of the function of a verb form to noun use by analogy with many others of that type in English, for example, *to strike* is to *a strike* as *to go slow* is to *a go-slow*.

barrack Jeering: *MW* does not enter the noun but labels the verb chiefly British. <1949 P. Newton *High Country Days* 46 The other four, full of noisy **barrack**, were playing pitch and toss with a set of old horse shoes.> *OED* s.v. *barrack* n.

bathe Swim: *MW* labels it British. <Tomorrow a **bathe** in the cold north sea.> 1991 Greenwood 11.

brush Brushing (of the hair): CIC has 2.4 iptmw of the noun in collocation with *hair* in British texts and 0.8 iptmw in American texts. "Your hair wants a good **brush**" (Swan 1995, 615).

capsize CIC has 1.1 iptmw of *a/the capsize* in British texts and none in American. <Increasing the metacentric height of the intact ro-ro would do little to make her safer against **capsize**.> 1987 June 15 *Times* 11/3.

carry-on Carrying-on: *MW* labels it British. CIC has a few British tokens. <If she told him about the **carry-on** at Monk's Mead he would become masculine and protective and make a huge chivalrous fuss.> 1986 Sherwood 76.

cheat CIC has 3.5 times as many tokens of *a cheat* in British texts as in American, and equal proportions of the two senses "act of deception" and "deceiver." <It was a bit of a **cheat** having Gerry to play for House as he wasn't really.> 1994 Dickinson 29.

chuck Rejection: *NODE* labels the sense "Brit. dated." <I suppose this is a **chuck**.> 2003 James 126.

clean Cleaning: *NODE* labels it chiefly British. <If the ultimate spring **clean** is going on around you it's not something you can fail to notice. 2003 Nov. 8 *Times* 7/8.

clearout Auction sell-off <The **clearout** will finance a continuing programme of restoration.> 1994 Oct. 5 *Times* 18/3.

cover Coverage: *MW* labels it British. <. . . an estimated one in three of American executives has insurance **cover** against abduction.> 1988 Sept. 15 *Times* 6/1.

cuddle CIC has 7.4 iptmw of *a cuddle* in British texts and 0.3 in American. <A kiss and a **cuddle**.> 1994 Sept. 28–Oct. 5 *Time Out* 178/1.

delve Act of delving; exploration: CIC has 0.1 iptmw in British texts and none in American. <Ask him what makes him tick – I was going for a psychological **delve** here.> 1989 Sept. 8 *Evening Standard* 44/3.

distort The use is rare. <. . . on shortwave radio . . . voices . . . have a slight **distort**.> 1988 Stoppard 1.

do *NODE* labels this sense chiefly British. <I expect the wedding'll be a posh **do**. Marquees and all that?> 1987 Graham 88.

draw Drawing; a chance selection of names to select a prize winner <Enter our Free Prize **Draw** and you could win up to £50,000.> 1999 Mar. 10 sign in Barclays Bank, Swiss Cottage branch, London.

drink Drinking; excessive consumption of alcohol: This use of *drink* is found also in American English; nevertheless the British use seems more frequent and wider in its contexts. <**Drink** had made George sentimental.> 1969 Rendell 12–3.

dust Dusting <This could do with a good **dust**.> 1989 Sept. 5 BBC1 *EastEnders*.

feed Feeding; the action of feeding a baby at regular intervals; *also metaphorical* <She taught herself all about . . . formula **feeds**.> 2001 Drabble 172.

fire, hire and Hiring and firing <Heads are now having to take serious notice of their governors, who do have the power of **hire and fire**.> 1990 Aug. 20 *Times* 25/1–2.

fly past Flyby, flyover: *MW* labels it chiefly British. <There will then be a **fly past** by a Hurricane and a Spitfire fighter.> 1985 May 24 *Times* 2/7.

go In some contexts it is difficult to distinguish the following first two senses of *go*. **1**. A turn; an opportunity to do or use something <I had a **go** on Nigel's racing bike.> 1985 Townsend 61. **2**. An attempt; a try <Christine had said to

try and get that green stain off the marble and he had had a **go** with soap and water but unsuccessfully.> 1989 Rendell 14. **3.** An attack, often verbal: *NODE* labels this sense chiefly British. <This year, they had a **go** at Jewish protesters and Western journalists trying to cover their demonstration.> 1987 Dec. 20 *Manchester Guardian* 10/4. – **in one go** All at once: CIC has 18.6 iptmw in British texts and 0.7 in American. <. . . he'd swallowed a bottle of hot Butterbeer **in one go**.> 1999 Rowling 316 (*US ed.* in one gulp). – **on the go** CIC has 11.9 iptmw of various senses in British texts and 7.3 in American. <Celia climbed the stairs; she was fully awake now and Arabella would almost certainly have a pot of tea **on the go**.> 1988 Taylor 36.

go-slow Slowdown: *MW* labels it British. <I think they've got a sort of strike or **go-slow**.> 1992 Granger 32.

graze CIC has 0.6 iptmw of *a graze* in British texts and 0.2 in American. <I have a **graze** on my leg which I will cover with plasters.> 1995 Aug. 30 *Daily Telegraph* 21/5.

hire Rental: *MW* labels it British. Cf. § 3.3.1.1. <AGS Vehicle **Hire**> 1999 March 20 sign on the side of a truck.

hold-ups Hose with an elastic top <. . . delicate black lace tights and **hold-ups**.> 1994 Sept. 25 *Sunday Times* Magazine 64/3.

kidnap Kidnapping <Fear of **kidnap** is . . . strong among the international business community.> 1988 Sept. 15 *Times* 6/1.

laugh "*informal* a cause for derision or merriment" (*LDEL*). <. . . she's probably the sort of person it'd be a **laugh** to have a few drinks with of an evening.> 1995 Sept. 6–13 *Time Out* 20/2.

lie-down Rest; nap: *NODE* labels it "chiefly Brit." <I thought you'd gone for a **lie-down**.> 1998 Taylor 87.

lie-in Time spent in bed past the usual hour of rising: *NODE* labels it "chiefly Brit." <Having a **lie in**, dear? So sorry to disturb you on a Sunday morning.> 1992 Green 114.

listen CIC has 7.0 iptmw of *listen* as a noun in British texts and 4.5 in American. <. . . take the LP . . . home for a **listen**.> 1987 May 29 *Evening Standard* 28/2.

look-in Consideration, chance: CIC has 3.4 iptmw in British texts and none in American. <An opponent wouldn't have got a **look in**.> 1989 Williams 190.

look (a)round <Go there and have a **look round**.> 1986 Sherwood 3.

meet Meeting, assignation <The **meet** at the pool came unstuck this morning. We have to consider you blown as our joe. The Russians must consider you blown as their sleeper.> 1988 Stoppard 10.

moan Complaint: CIC has 0.5 iptmw of *have a moan* in British texts and none in American. <Blast the Navy. . . . They've always got a **moan**.> 1940 Shute 23.

nose round <. . . there's no reason why we shouldn't . . . have a thorough **nose round**.> 1985 Bingham 83.

overspend <. . . he expected a £1.5 million **overspend** by the end of the financial year.> 1994 Sept. 20 *Times* 6/2.

picket Picketing <In Liverpool, another mass **picket** is planned for this morning.> 1988 Sept. 15 *Times* 2/3.

prune Pruning <Needs a good **prune**, doesn't it [a tree]?> 1986 Oct. 12 *Sunday Times* Magazine 46/4.

read CIC has about 1.5 times as many tokens of *a read* in British texts as in American. **1.** Something that is read <What's a good **read** this year?> 1989 July 22 *Times* 40/1. **2.** "*chiefly British* : a period of reading <it was a night . . . for a **read** and a long sleep . . . .>" (*MW*). <. . . a relaxed holiday **read** spread over several days.> 1995 Mar. 22 *Financial Times* p n/a.

read-through <. . . a thorough **read-through** of the paper.> 1969 Amis 23.

rebuild Rebuilding <. . . this process of decay, collapse, and **rebuild** created large mounds that we call 'tells'.> 1996 Knight and Lomas 82–3.

refit CIC has 1.4 iptmw of *a refit* in British texts and none in American. <In a **refit** costing £110 million the 18-year-old ship gets new engines.> 1987 Apr. 9 *Times* 9/4–6.

re-mark Remarking; reevaluation <. . . the board . . . has stuck by its judgment through three **re-marks**.> 1996 Aug. 6 *Times* 2/5.

rethink Instance of rethinking; a reconsideration: CIC has 6.6 iptmw of *a re(-)think* in British texts and 0.2 in American. <Provident has had a **re-think** and offered to continue insuring her.> 2003 July 9 *Times* 29/5.

revolve <*Exclusive* [a play] had rather a wobbly start because we have an amazing set . . . that revolves on two levels in two directions. . . . By Manchester, they'd mastered the **revolve**.> 1989 Sept. 9 *Times* 33/1.

rise (in salary) Raise: *MW* labels it chiefly British. <Unofficial action by some members demanding a £64-a-week **rise** led to further disruption on the Tube.> 1989 Autumn *Illustrated London News* 11/2.

roll-up *NODE* labels the sense "hand-rolled cigarette" "Brit. informal." <[Emma] Thompson lights a **roll-up**. . . . She draws on the ciggie.> 1995 Sept. 6–13 *Time Out* 21/2.

sail past <. . . there will be a **sail past** by Dutch and British yachts before Her Majesty.> 1988 June *In Britain*, 20/1.

sell Disappointment because of being oversold <Hawaii's a bit of a **sell** as far as tit goes.> 1991 Lodge 244.

shoot Shooting party <This is the first formal **shoot** of the season.> 1989 Quinton 237.

shop Shopping <Tomorrow I shall have to do a big **shop**.> 1992 Charles 105.

sift <. . . he had a good **sift** through his brown leather executive case.> 1987 May 19 *Times* 22/7.

sit CIC has 1.4 iptmw of *a sit* in British texts and none in American. <A **sit** on the beach.> 1953 Mortimer 49.

sit down Rest <Cecily reckoned she was due for a **sit-down**.> 1998 Joss 148.

sleep A period of sleeping: CIC has 6.3 iptmw of *a sleep* in British texts and 4.5 in American <I told him to have a **sleep**.> 1991 Green 301.

spend Amount of money spent; expenditure; income <The average **spend** per bottle was a miserly £3.89.> 2003 June 21 *Times* Weekend 1/1.

surround "*Chiefly Brit* a border" (*CED*). CIC has 25 times as many tokens in British texts as in American. <I planted it in a terracotta pot and it made a wonderful **surround** for a *Deutzia rosea*.> 1994 Oct. 1 *Times* Weekend 11/2.

take-away Takeout: *MW* labels the sense chiefly British. <Why don't I pick up something at the **take-away** for both of us?> 1990 Rowlands 142.

take-up CIC has 6.9 iptmw in British texts and 0.2 in American. <. . . **take-up** of services had dropped noticeably.> 1994 Sept. 27 *Guardian* 2/5.

undershoot <The figures and the likely **undershoot** this year suggest that buoyant tax revenues will continue through into the next financial year.> 1987 Jan. 20 *Guardian* 1/4.

walkabout *NODE* labels it chiefly British. CIC has 6.9 iptmw in British texts and 0.7 in American. <But she [Camilla] is not obliged . . . to shake the hands of hundreds of people on **walkabouts**.> 2004 Dec. 15 *Daily Telegraph* 18/6.

wander (round) Act of wandering (around) <. . . a leisurely **wander** among the tombstones.> 2001 Lodge 232.

wash An instance of washing oneself <He went upstairs for a **wash**.> 1994 Freeling 83.

weed Weeding <The approach to the front step and garage could do with a **weed**.> 1996 Graham 48.

whip round Collection of money for a charitable purpose: *MW* labels it chiefly British. < . . . the passengers all chipped in when a "**whip round**" was organized by the crew.> 1987 Apr. 23 *Times* 2/6.

work-to-rule A labor protest that slows down work by adhering punctiliously to work rules: *NODE* labels it chiefly British. CIC has 0.8 iptmw of the noun and 0.4 of the verb in British texts, and 0.4 of the phrase as a modifier in American texts. < . . . an additional cause of serious delay . . . a **work-to-rule** by air traffic controllers.> 1991 Lodge 4.

3.1.1.2 By affixation

Other nouns are formed by adding affixes to a verb to form a related noun. One frequent affix in this use is the suffix *-ing*. It is sometimes difficult to be sure whether the stem to which that suffix is added is a verb or a noun (§ 3.1.2).

barracking Jeering <Once in the House, women have to survive the public school humour and **barracking** and the unsocial hours.> 1993 Feb. 1 *Times* 12/1.

fitting Fit (of shoes): CIC has 26.9 iptmw of all noun senses of *fitting* in British texts and 8.8 in American. <Size eight . . . and a narrow **fitting**. I never realised what dainty feet he had.> 1992 Walters 115.

parting Part in the hair <. . . the pin-thin scrupulous **parting** – not a single hair straying to the wrong side.> 1993 Graham 151.

turning Turn (off or onto a road) <Uncle Vernon would take a sharp **turning** and drive in the opposite direction for a while.> 1997 Rowling 35 (*US ed.* turn).

Another type of deverbal noun is that derived from a verb-particle combination, with the agent suffix *-er* (as well as the plural ending *-s*) infixed.

handers-out <We'll need some more **handers-out** . . . . Len and I can't do it all.> 1985 Gilbert 104.

pullers-back <A tenant [at Smithfield meat market] cannot stock his stall without paying "**pullers-back**". . . . **Pullers-back** take the meat off the lorries.> 1988 June *Illustrated London News* 70/1.

3.1.2 From other nouns

The suffix *-ing* (§ 3.1.1.2) can also be added to a noun, and the resulting construction is typically a collective mass noun (although both *guttering* and *gutterings* are attested).

cabling Cables: CIC has 20.1 iptmw in British texts and 1.6 in American. < . . . pollutants such as asbestos and polychlorinated biphenyls in the electrical **cabling**.> 2003 Nov. 13 *Times* 3/2.

chippings Chips: CIC has 5.1 iptmw in British texts and none in American. < . . . **chippings** of stone flew.> 1993 Graham 71.

curtaining Curtains: CIC has 0.6 iptmw in British texts and none in American. <Di's also done the upholstery and **curtaining**.> 1992 Walters 80.

fencing Fence: CIC has 32.9 iptmw in British texts and 24.2 in American. <The expense . . . to sell it [wood] to furniture dealers, or **fencing** designers . . . would always be considerable.> 1992 Dexter 109.

guttering(s) Gutters: CIC has 6.6 iptmw in British texts and 0.5 in American. <He secured the top of the ladder to the **gutterings**.> 1999 Dexter 237.

piping Pipes <There were also numerous lengths of . . . **piping** lieing around.> 1992 Walters 79.

schooling School <Kristina – still only eighteen – was in her last year of **schooling**.> 1992 Dexter 168.

shelving Shelves <. . . she noticed . . . the white **shelving** of a kitchen unit.> 1992 Dexter 85.

tiling Tiles: CIC has 8.9 iptmw in British texts and 1.2 in American. <A circular bath . . . sat like a giant shell, surrounded by walls of expensive **tiling**.> 1992 Green 127.

towelling Towels: CIC has 7.1 iptmw in British texts and none of *toweling* in American. <She taught herself all about . . . birth weights, . . . and **terry towelling**.> 2001 Drabble 172.

troughing Troughs, gutters: CIC has 0.2 iptmw in British texts and none in American. < . . . he used to anchor the top of his ladder to the **troughing**.> 1999 Dexter 355.

For two of the preceding forms, context is crucial. *Schooling* and *shelving* as general collective nouns are common also in American, as in *She was a self-made woman, without benefit of formal schooling* and *The library is running out of shelving for its collection*. However, in the specific sense of the citations above, "her last year of schooling" and "the white shelving of a [particular] kitchen unit," the *-ing* forms would be less expected than "her last year of school" and "the white shelves."

Another productive suffix is *-er(s)*, which began as public-school and Oxbridge slang, added usually to the first syllable of a word. The best and only widely known of the forms in America is *soccer* (from *association football*), though most Americans would be unaware of its origin.

brekker(s) <. . . a kindly gent could rise from his bed, . . . step into the shower and enjoy a good hosing-down before **brekkers**.> 1991 Feb. 7 *Midweek* 5/1.

champers Champagne: CIC has 1.7 iptmw in British texts and none in American. <They'd drunk a bottle of far-from-vintage champers.> 1994 Dexter 188.

Duggers <This is my colleague Douglas C. Douglass, known to one and all as **Duggers**.> 2001 Lodge 55.

ethnickers Ethnic garments <What do they wear? Wampum beads and **ethnickers**?> 1993 Graham 295.

fresher Freshman: CIC has 1.6 iptmw of *freshers* in British texts and 0.3 in American (news reports of the schooling of Prince William). <Oxford University JCR ["Junior Common Room"] distributed **Freshers'** Handbooks this summer.> 2003 Nov. 11 *Times* 6/4.

gratters Congrats < . . . congratulations became *gratters*.> 1989 Honey 49.

rugger Rugby: CIC has 4.4 iptmw in British texts and none in American. <He looked more like a professional **rugger** player than a lawyer.> 1997 James 145.

shockers <In American English shock absorbers are known colloquially as 'shocks', whereas in Britain they are often called '**shockers**'.> 1982 Trudgill 29.

starkers Stark naked: CIC has 1.1 iptmw in British texts and none in American. <Do they dance **starkers** under the moon?> 1993 Graham 294.

Another suffix:

nuddy, in the In the nude: <I had to do battle with the old dragon in the **nuddy**.> 1992 Walters 207.

3.1.3 From adjectives and adverbs

Chinese Restaurant with Chinese food to go: *NODE* labels it British. <Joyce had said would he mind terribly . . . getting something from the Indian or **Chinese** for his supper.> 1989 Graham 305.

illegal An illegal or undercover agent: Recorded in the *OED* s.v. *illegal* B.2. < . . . a network of "**illegals**", spymasters working under cover away from Cuban embassies.> 1988 Sept. 18 *Sunday Telegraph* 5/3.

Indian Restaurant with Indian food to go: *NODE* labels it British. See CHINESE.

medical Medical examination <I had to have two very thorough **medicals**: heart, lungs, blood pressure, Aids, everything.> 1990 Aug. 17 *Evening Standard* 24/1–2.

speciality Specialty: CIC has 57.8 iptmw of *speciality* in British texts and 2.6 in American. It has 11.2 iptmw of *specialty* in British texts and 111.5 in American. <IBM . . . was rated the leader . . . in every area of their **speciality**.> 1993 Jan. 16 *Economist* 24/3.

An instance of conversion from an adjective, with the addition of the suffix *-s* (as in *apologetics* or *athletics*) is *electrics* "the system of electrical connections in a house or vehicle":

electrics Electrical system: CIC has 11.3 iptmw in British texts and 1.5 in American. <. . . the coroner did say a lot of fatherly things about getting properly qualified workmen to mess around with gas and **electrics**.> 1994 Dickinson 231.

Nouns from adverbs are fewer.

abroad "*Br informal* places outside one's country" (*LDEL*). <On balance, **abroad** has probably done the Englishman more good than harm, and the fact that some six hundred million now speak his lingo bears eloquent testimony to the peripatetic restlessness of his forebears; even as it makes him one of the world's worst linguists.> 1984 Smith 12.

3.2 Form

3.2.1 Plural for singular count noun

In some cases, British English uses the plural form of a count noun for which American customarily uses the singular.

ban(n)isters The *OED* says the word is usually in the plural; *MW* has no statement about plural use. *BBI*-97 enters for *banister* "to slide down a – (BE also has *to slide down the bannisters*)." In CIC, the single *n* spelling is favored in both varieties, slightly more in American. Singular and plural forms are about equal in British texts; American texts favor the singular by almost 4 to 1.

baths *plural in form, plural or singular in construction* A place with bathing facilities or a swimming pool: *MW* labels the sense and plural form British. <. . . a lousy description, admittedly, of a public **baths**.> 1991 Feb. 26 *Times* 14/1.

classes CIC British texts slightly favor *classes*, and American texts *class*. The British *chattering classes*, meaning "liberal intellectuals," was widely misunderstood in America as referring to media people. <Her [Margaret Thatcher's] humor comes out mean and cutting, like her taunting of liberal critics as "moaning minnies" or "the **chattering classes**." 1990 Hazleton 108. <The **chattering classes**, as sociable Hampstead folk are sometimes known, are as fond of writing letters as they are of holding forth about the evils of Thatcherism at dinner parties.> 1990 Aug. 15 *Daily Telegraph* 15/3. <Just as some Asian homes keep a bottle of Heinz tomato ketchup on the table as a Western status symbol, today no card-carrying member of the **chattering classes** would be without their prominently displayed bottle of extra-virgin [olive oil].> 1999 Mar. 20 *Times* Weekend 6/1. Other classes identified by British journalism are the *banner-bearing classes, landowning classes, lower classes, lower-middle classes, middle classes, monied classes, scoundrel classes, scribbling classes, taxi-driving classes, The Times letter-writing classes, upper classes*, and *working classes*.

favours, do *someone* In CIC, both British and American favor the singular, but British does so by only 2.4 times, whereas American does so by 4.3 times. <We are doing them no **favours**.> 2003 Nov. 12 *Times* T2 3/3.

flies Fly; trouser opening at the crotch: *NODE* says "Brit. often *flies*." <. . . black woollen breeches tied with a drawstring at the top . . . there's none of that nonsense about wrestling with your **flies** – a quick tug of the drawstring is all that's needed.> 2003 Nov. 11 *Times* T2 13/2–3.

(football) pool(s) In CIC British texts, the plural is about 40 times more frequent than the singular, both usually in collocation with *win*. American texts have neither. <Perhaps he's won the **pools**.> 1992 Walters 2.

holidays Vacation: *NODE* labels the sense "extended period of recreation" chiefly British and adds that the form is often plural. Note the singular agreement of *that* in the citation. <There was a short cricket tour that **holidays**.> 1994 Dickinson 17.

impressions Both British and American CIC texts favor singular *first impression* over plural *first impressions*, but British by only 1.5 times and American by 2.6 times. <She appeared, on first **impressions**, a decided cut or two above her horticultural spouse.> 1992 Dexter 120.

innings CIC British texts have 118.3 iptmw of plural-form *innings* and 1.1 of singular-form *inning* (mainly in reference to American baseball); American texts have 90.7 of the plural form and 109.7 of the singular. **1.** Plural in form, but singular in concord, a cricket term for the time at bat of a player or team: In American use, an *inning* is a part of a baseball game during which the teams have their turns at bat. < . . . coming off the cricket field after a successful **innings**.> 1994 Dickinson 138. **2**. Also metaphorical, the period during which anything lasts <Surely the word "bloody" has had a long enough theatrical **innings** (how old is Pygmalion?) not to cause a laugh when used quite naturally in an extremely well-written emotional scene.> 1935 Nov. 28 *Oxford Magazine* 222/2. – **a good innings** A long, satisfying life or career <[Name] has died. . . . At 93 he has had **a good innings**.> 2004 May 31 private letter from East Sussex.

kennels *NODE* observes that the term is usually plural; *MW* makes no such observation. CIC has approximately equal numbers of singular and plural in British texts, but 2.75 times as many singular as plural forms in American texts. In nominal use, *kennels* usually takes a determiner (sometimes singular), unless it is the object of prepositions like *in* and *into*. <It is a **kennels**, a boardinghouse for dogs.> 1989 Drabble 197. < . . . on the Sunday morning they put the dog in **kennels**.> 1991 Neel 210.

maths Math: CIC British texts have 112.3 iptmw of *maths* and 4.2 of *math*; American texts have 363.3 of *math* and only a scattering of the plural form. <I'd always thought anyone doing your type of job had to be good at **maths**.> 1993 Mason 11.

moustaches The *OED* has two subsenses for *moustache*: "1. The hair which grows upon the upper lip of men. a. The hair on both sides of the upper lip taken to form a single moustache . . . . b. The hair covering either side of the upper lip; one half of a 'pair of moustaches'." American English, in addition to spelling and pronunciation differences for *mustache*, uses primarily only the first subsense. CIC British texts have 44.2 iptmw of *moustache* and 7.2 of *moustaches*; American texts have 35.5 of *mustache/moustache* and 2.9 of the plural, most referring to mustaches on different persons. <"What lovely **moustaches**, nurse," said Lettice, unable to think of a more suitable comment [on being shown a picture of the nurse's brother].> 1942 Thirkell 23.

nights, at At night: CIC British texts have 4.7 iptmw of *at nights* and American texts have 0.5; they have almost exactly the same iptmw (291.0) of the singular. <*The Times*'s lawyers sleep easy **at nights**.> 1994 Oct. 1 *Times* Weekend 5/3.

qualifications *usually plural* "a pass of an examination or an official completion of a course, especially one conferring status as a recognized practitioner of a profession or activity" (*NODE*), a sense not used in American. <A student who wanted to study history at Oxford University would continue to take a specialised A-level course, while others might acquire a wider variety of **qualifications**.> 1994 Sept. 22 *Times* 4/3.

roadworks Road repair: *NODE* labels the sense British. In CIC British texts, the plural is 22 times more frequent than the singular. <**Road works** on the A217.> 1987 Feb. 24 *Evening Standard* 5/6.

stables *pl. in form, sing. in construction* A stable: CIC British texts have 0.6 iptmw of *a stables*. <He trained racehorses for a friend at a **stables** outside Johannesburg.> 1994 Sept. 30 *Daily Telegraph* 27/3.

standards, by any In CIC British texts, the plural is 3 times more frequent than the singular in this phrase; in American texts, the singular is 2.5 times more frequent than the plural. <. . . he was a lovely baby, **by any standards**.> 1991 Dickinson 8.

thoughts, on second In CIC British texts, the plural is 8 times more frequent than the singular in this phrase; in American texts, the singular is 3 times more frequent than the plural. <I might work it up into a sermon. **On second thoughts**, perhaps not.> 2001 James 148.

(traffic) lights (Traffic) light: In CIC British texts the plural is 7.8 times more frequent than the singular; in American texts the plural is also more frequent, but only by 1.4 times. The American plurals, however, generally refer to multiple sets of traffic lights at different intersections, whereas the British plurals generally refer to the lights of one set. < . . . at the bottom of the road there was a lorry waiting at the **traffic lights**.> 1998 Sayers and Walsh 187.

3.2.2 Singular count noun for plural

Nouns listed here can be used with a determiner like *a/an*. Cf. § 3.2.4.

accommodation CIC British texts have 511.0 iptmw of *accommodation* and 8.5 of *accommodations*; American texts have 48.8 of *accommodation* and 88.1 of *accommodations*. <Sir John Chadwick . . . gave her two days to leave her **accommodation**.> 1998 Jan. 6 *Times* 3/4.

Bakewell tart <The more humble queue . . . for cold cuts and **Bakewell tart**.> 1992 Critchley 32.

barrack CIC British texts have nearly 9 times as many tokens of *barracks* as of *barrack*; American texts have nearly 17 times as many. *MW* notes "usually used in plural in all senses." <The dormitory was a long, dark, bare, **barrack**-like room.> 1985 Mortimer 31.

birch Birch trees <Here . . . little silver **birch** struggle up to reach the light.> 2003 July 12 *Times* Weekend 1/4.

boot <Riding **boot**? Well, . . . anyone who rides seriously would need a **boot**.> 1988 May *In Britain* 14/3.

brace Orthodontic appliance: *MW* indicates that in this sense the noun is plural; *NODE* has it singular. <. . . they wanted me to carry on with my **brace**. You know, they're dentists.> 2000 Rowling 353 (*US ed.* braces).

chop In CIC British texts, the plural *pork chops* is 1.5 times more frequent than the singular; in American texts, it is 2.7 times. <Harry nodded and tried to keep eating his **chop**.> 2003 Rowling 110 (*US ed.* chops).

eel worm <It was full of insects too: leather jackets and chafer grubs; pea thrips and **eel worm**.> 1993 Graham 34.

final *MW* says of the deciding event in a contest "usually used in plural"; *NODE* makes no such comment. <If this week's "grand **final**" . . . was anything to go

by, the entire concept of piano competitions may as well be written off. . . . In the **final**, however, he had clearly sensed that a slick performance would go down a treat.> 1994 Sept. 30 *Daily Telegraph* 23/4.

firework American use avoids the singular, using instead the plural or singular terms for particular varieties of fireworks: firecracker, sparkler, pinwheel, etc. CIC British texts have 4.6 iptmw of the singular *a firework*; American texts have 0.2. <It was November the fifth [Guy Fawkes Day]; the neighbours thought it was a **firework**.> 1987 Oliver 190.

fruit-machine <. . . bars blessedly free from juke-box and **fruit-machine**.> 1996 Dexter 24.

gear, changing Shifting gears: CIC British texts have 15 times as many tokens of *gear* as of *gears* in this construction; American texts have no singulars. <**Changing gear** without a clutch.> 1999 Mar. 13 *Times* Magazine 41.

ground Grounds; sports area < . . . plans to install extra seating at the Kenilworth Road end of the **ground** would enable the club to accommodate away supporters.> 1990 Aug. 17 *Daily Telegraph* 30/1.

handicap <Fragile X syndrome . . . causes mental **handicap** and behaviour problems.> 1991 Feb. 16 *Daily Telegraph* 9/3.

head or tail, make Make heads or tails: CIC British texts have only the singular; American texts have only the plural. <I, an innumerate, cannot **make head or tail** of them [figures].> 1992 Apr. 5 BNC.

heel, down at CIC British texts have only *down at heel*; American texts have only *down at the heels*. < . . . nothing on her feet but an old **down-at-heel** pair of court shoes.> 1996 Neel 7–8.

juke-box See FRUIT-MACHINE.

minute *MW* labels the noun sense "record of the proceedings of a meeting" as plural; *NODE* does not. <No **minute** of this gathering has ever been made public.> 2003 Nov. 7 *Daily Express* 40/2.

motorway <Ministers were cutting the ribbon to open small new stretches of **motorway**.> 1987 Bradbury 12.

pickle, Branston The singular is the only form attested in CIC British texts; the term does not occur in American texts. In a sample of CIC texts, the simple term *pickle* occurs in this mass-like use in 42 percent of the British tokens and in 8 percent of the American. <Major sent Gummer out to the kitchen in search of **Branston pickle**.> 1992 Critchley 164.

reception Reception rooms: *NODE* labels the full term British and comments "(chiefly in commercial use) a room in a private house suitable for entertaining visitors." Neither the full term nor the clipping are used in American. <What did we want with five bedrooms and three **reception**?> 1992 Granger 83.

saving of, a A savings of: CIC British texts have 5.3 iptmw of the singular and no plurals; American texts have 0.5 of the singular and 3.4 of the plural.

snipe CIC British texts have some tokens of plural *snipe*; American texts have none. <There are also Dartford and grasshopper warblers, **snipe**, curlews and otters.> 2005 Jan. 23 *Sunday Telegraph* http://www.telegraph.co.uk/.

track <. . . privately-owned carriages are pulled by BR locos [British Rail locomotives] on public **track**.> 1987 Mar. 25 *Evening Standard* 2/5.

uniform In the construction *in MODIFIER uniform(s)*, CIC British texts have 3 times as many tokens of *uniform* as of *uniforms*; American texts have approximately the same number of singular and plural forms. <Malfoy, Crabbe and Goyle resembled nothing so much as three gigantic slugs squeezed into Hogwarts **uniform**.> 2003 Rowling 761 (*US ed.* uniforms).

wood In the construction *to the wood(s)*, CIC British texts have 2.5 times as many tokens of *wood* as of *woods*; American texts are the reverse, with 2.5 times as many *woods* as of *wood*. <And [tell them] not to let the badger out. . . . He's not well enough to go back to the **wood** yet, poor thing.> 2000 Aird 177.

A particular construction in which British often has a singular noun where American tends to have a plural is the pattern *type(s) of* ____ (Johansson 1979, 212). This construction involves general nouns like *class, kind, sort, type*, and *variety*.

class of <. . . the élite who could be described as "a nice **class of person**."> 1986 Brett 12.

kind(s) of <In every crowded alley were the roughest **kinds of pickpocket**.> 1998 Winchester 3.

sort(s) of Pam Peters (2004, 507–8) found that *sort(s) of* is usually, but not invariably, followed by a plural noun and is more common in British than in American, which prefers *kind of*. <. . . it ought . . . to give an impression not unlike a tabby cat, or certain **sorts of lizard**.> 1989 Sept. 14 *Daily Telegraph* 20/6.

type(s) of <There are three **types of child trust fund**: those using cash deposits, share-based funds, and stakeholder plans.> 2005 Jan. 15 *Daily Telegraph* B 4/1.

varieties of The plural rather than the singular *variety* seems likely to be followed by a singular noun. <Norfolk has . . . **varieties of terrier, herring, plover**, and **jacket**.> 1994 Sept. 24 *Spectator* 24/3.

3.2.3 Plural for mass noun

Some words that are normally mass nouns are used in British English as count nouns and therefore have a plural. Cf. § 2.2.2.1 for such nouns with the indefinite article. This construction has distinguished precedents, one of which is the King James version of Isaiah 64.6: "All our **righteousnesses** are as filthy ragges." In the following entries, the figures following the entry forms are the percentages of plural forms in British/American in CIC. They show that for these forms, the plural is more frequent in British.

attendances (12/0) <We notice a peak in **attendances** that other museums don't experience.> 1991 Feb. 17 *Sunday Times* Magazine 15/1.

brains (19/14) <Hamilton . . . described the Princess of Wales as "a very lucky woman with not many **brains**."> 1987 Feb. 24 *Evening Standard* 6/1.

cauliflowers (21/0) < . . . **cauliflowers** [cost] 25p–50p each.> 1989 July 28 *Times* 6/6–7.

envies (1/0) <I thought I detected a touch of the **envies** back there.> 1989 Quinton 239.

excitements (3/1) <. . . after the initial **excitements** the Scrolls have left things pretty much where they were.> 1987 Oct. 25 *Sunday Telegraph* 18/8.

ice creams (11/1) Ice cream; ice cream cones <Carrie . . . asks Ralph to go with the children to buy **ice-creams**.> 2001 Lodge 241. Cf. § 2.2.2.1.

ices (1/0) <I'm going for ice creams. . . . you can't have an afternoon at the beach without **ices**.> 1998 Taylor 11.

insurances (1/0) <Extended **insurances** can cost up to £230 for five years' cover.> 1993 Feb. 7 *Sunday Times* 5 4/8.

lettuces (13/3) <Then she looked at the kitchen, . . . the trug ["basket"] of **lettuces** on the table.> 1993 Trollope 16.

newses (0/0) This unusual plural is a shortening of *news programs* or the like. <I crash out and watch the first 10 minutes of one of the **newses**.> 1993 Feb. 7 *Sunday Times* Magazine 58/4.

nonsenses (1/0) <I simply wanted to draw attention to the **nonsenses** in Labour's policies.> 1992 Critchley 124.

overheads (20/2) Overhead; overhead expenses <The coffee-pushers will argue that their **overheads** are higher.> 2005 Jan. 14 *Daily Telegraph* 24/4.

toasts Plural *toasts* "toasted slices of bread" is 3 times more frequent in CIC British texts than in American. <Baked Blackcurrant **Toasts** [slices of bread baked with a blackcurrant topping]> 1989 Aug. 2 *Evening Standard* 31.

wallpapers (7/2) <Spring sunlight lit up the house so beautifully that nobody remembered it needed a coat of paint and new **wallpapers**.> 1934 Travers 161.

weathers (1/0) In all weather <He sits out there all **weathers** now.> 1985 Mortimer 317.

yoghurts (10/2) <. . . the firm makes ingredients for frozen desserts, **yoghurts**, and ice creams.> 1995 Sept. 4 *Daily Telegraph* 27/3.

3.2.4 Mass noun for plural

Some otherwise plural nouns are used as mass nouns. Cf. §§ 2.4.2; 3.2.2.

art and craft *Arts and crafts* is usually plural in both British and American, but CIC has 2.9 iptmw of singular *art and craft*, whereas American has 0.4.

<. . . students who took **art and craft.**> 1989 Sept. 10 *Sunday Telegraph* 7/1.

beetroot The American equivalent, *beet*, is a count noun. <There's good pickled **beetroot.**> 1989 June *In Britain* 16/2.

benefit Benefits; welfare (payments) <. . . a bed-ridden woman who receives invalidity **benefit.**> 1996 Aug. 14 *Daily Telegraph* 13/8.

blossom < . . . children and their mums . . . are paid £2 a kilogram for [elderflower] **blossom** collected in the lanes and fields.> 2003 July 12 *Times* Weekend 7/3.

cloud <The weather is poor with **cloud** and bad visibility.> 1989 Sept. 9 *Times* 1/5.

dog-biscuit <. . . laying in an immense stock of **dog-biscuit**, because he said it didn't go mouldy as fast as human food.> 1994 Dickinson 31.

drink <And why should he keep spiked **drink** ready? . . . What a fool to accept **drink** at all.> 1990 Hardwick 104.

egg <We'll buy potatoes and eggs and have a bit of a fry up. **Egg** and chips.> 1998 Trollope 55.

finance <. . . as long as I have been in academic life, colleges have been grumbling about **finance.**> 1987 May 14 *Evening Standard* 7/4–5.

moth <Fraud appears everywhere once you've got it – like **moth.**> 1993 Neel 183.

potato <. . . dishing great mounds of mashed **potato** on to everyone's plates.> 2003 Rowling 143 (*US ed.* potatoes).

spirit < . . . a unit is either half a pint of beer, one small glass of wine, or one measure of **spirit.**> 1999 Mar. 20 *Times* Weekend 6/6.

sport British uses the singular *sport* as a mass noun denoting sports in general; American uses the plural *sports* for that sense. <He is a bit of a loner and no good at **sport.**> 1998 Jan. 3 *Times* Vision 5/4.

tax <It suddenly must find an extra £8,000 a year in **tax.**> 2003 June 28 *Times* Weekend 1/3.

water cannon <Use of CS gas and **water cannon** was advocated yesterday by a leading authority on the police as a better way of breaking up disorderly crowds than traditional methods.> 1989 July 19 *Times* 7/1.

3.2.5 Plural formation

Several plural formations are notable. When a noun consists of more than one word, the position of the plural marking suffix *-s* may be variable.

courts martial Its grammar as noun-plus-adjective is sometimes masked by hyphenating it as *court-martial* and favoring the alternative plural, *court-martials*. Dictionaries record both plurals. <Uncle Johnny said you'd done loads of **courts martial.**> 1987 Feb. 16 ITV *Rumpole of the Bailey*.

gins and tonics The common expression *a gin and tonic* suggests that the compound is taken as a lexical, not a grammatical unit, in which case *gin and tonics* is the expected plural. CIC has 0.1 iptmw of *gins and tonics* in British texts and none in American. <The landlord had once told her that if anyone ordered "**gins and tonics**" instead of the universal "gin and tonics" – he really *was* a don.> 1975 Dexter 65.

Lords Justices of Appeal In this case, both nouns are made plural. <Sir John . . . as one of 31 **Lords Justices of Appeal** earns £134,551 a year.> 1998 Jan. 6 *Times* 3/4.

Words that are loans from other languages may keep their foreign plurals, more characteristically so in British English than in American. In particular, nouns borrowed from Latin may have either native or Latin plurals: singular *persona*, plurals *personas* or *personae*. Preference for native or Latin plural forms varies considerably among nouns; however a national preference is also apparent (Peters 1999, a study based on 129 questionnaires). British respondents were more inclined to use Latin plurals than Americans (or Australians). Notable was a British preference for *formulae* over *formulas* (86 to 14 percent), whereas American preference was the reverse (21 to 79 percent). The American preference may be influenced by the fact that *formula* is an American term for a milk or milk substitute food for infants, for which only the native plural is normal. A reverse preference exists for the plurals of *syllabus*: British preferring *syllabuses* by 62 to 38 percent, and Americans *syllabi* by 64 to 36 percent.

appendices In CIC texts, both national varieties prefer *appendices* over *appendixes*, British by 90 to 10 percent, American by 75 to 25 percent.

bureaux In CIC texts, British prefers *bureaux* over *bureaus* by 94 to 6 percent; American, *bureaus* by 98 to 2 percent. <Their disappointment is revealed by the National Association of Citizens Advice **Bureaux**.> 1989 Sept. 12 *Daily Telegraph* 10/8.

milieux In CIC texts, British prefers *milieux* over *milieus* by 84 to 16 percent; American, *milieus* by 67 to 33 percent.

stadia In CIC texts, both national varieties prefer *stadiums* over *stadia*, British by 58 to 42 percent, American by 99 to 1 percent. < . . . with all-seater **stadia**, . . . the better off are being attracted to football as they have not been in the past.> 1995 Sept. 9 *Times* Magazine 30/3.

Some nouns have unchanged plurals, depending on a variety of circumstances, which differ between British and American use.

birch < . . . little silver **birch** struggle up to reach the light.> 2003 July 12 *Times* Weekend 1/4.

duck Words for animals considered as game sometimes have unchanged plurals (*CGEL* 5.87), a use that seems more widespread in British than in American. <. . . men grumble because they are no longer allowed to shoot things – unless, indeed, there are **duck** around.> 1983 Innes 54.

flight The unchanged plural of *flight* seems exceptional, and may be by association with birds considered as game. <. . . three **flight** of duck came over – a vast assemblage of seven hundred birds or more.> 1985 Ebdon 161–2.

foot (+ *adjective*) "The plurals *feet* and *foot* both occur between a number and an adjective. . . . In present-day American printed use, *feet* is more common than *foot*, and is prescribed in many handbooks. *Foot* seems to be more frequent in British English" (Gilman 1994, 455–6). A comparison of two corpora (Peters 2004, 213–4) reports that in expressions like *six foot/feet tall*, although *feet* is the major choice in both varieties, British has twice as many tokens of *foot* as does American. <Give them a month and Hagrid'll have them **twenty-foot-high**.> 2000 Rowling 478 (*US ed.* twenty feet high).

pound In citing cost or income, an unchanged plural is possible for this unit of British currency. <[a waitress in Bradford:] And [the salary was] just seven pound a week.> 1990 Critchfield 217.

quid Pound <. . . you can sit down to a main course for three **quid**.> 2003 Dec. *Square* 41/1.

stone Fourteen pounds <. . . he was at least four **stone** lighter than Burns.> 1992 Critchley 175.

Conversely, in some cases, British has the normal plural where an unchanged plural might be expected.

feet + high/tall + *noun* "In hyphenated adjectives used before a noun, *foot* is the only possible form . . . *a six-foot-tall man*" (Kahn and Ilson 1985); "the plural *foot* . . . regularly occurs (and *feet* does not) between a number and noun. . . . the 15-foot high statue" (Gilman 1994). Yet *feet* is attested in some, probably divergent British use. <I could have looked in at the pub . . . with its 130-**feet**-tall chimney.> 1988 Apr. *In Britain* 14/1–2.

Some nouns ending in *-f* have a plural in *-ves*. This morphological variation goes back to a phonetic variation in Old English but has been preserved in a number of nouns and even extended to a few for which it is an innovation. For the most part British and American treat these nouns alike, for example *loaf/loaves* is the common-core norm. But a comparative study of British and American corpora (Peters 2004, 198) has shown differences of at least 10 percent for the following nouns (percentages cited are for the *-ves* forms). For comparison, CIC percentages are given in parentheses. The differences between them and Peters's figures are sometimes striking, but may be explained by differences in the corpus samples and by the fact that the total occurrences are sometimes few, so a small difference in numbers can produce a large difference in percentage. Cf. also POOVES below.

dwarves British 17 percent vs. American 4 percent (CIC 37 vs. 15 percent). This noun did not participate in the Old English *f/v* alternation. The oldest example of *dwarves* in the OED is from 1818; the popularity of the form may be due to its adoption by J. R. R. Tolkien.

hooves British 82 percent vs. American 66 percent (CIC 80 vs. 84 percent).

scarves British 97 percent vs. American 76 percent (CIC 93 vs. 91 percent). Like *dwarves*, this is an analogical form, *scarf* itself being a sixteenth-century word with the plural *scarves* dating only from the eighteenth century.

turves British 45 percent (CIC 29 percent) vs. American no occurrences of a plural. This plural is also not of Old English provenience but dates from the thirteenth century.

A few special cases warrant notice.

overall *Overall(s)* may have different meanings in British ("a protective smock worn over other clothing") and American ("heavy-cloth trousers with a bib and shoulder straps") that affect the word's grammar. British use is as a normal count noun, and it has the usual plural denoting more than one item of the same kind. American use of *overalls* is as a summation plural, like *trousers*. <He was a mournful-looking man . . . wearing a beige-coloured working **overall**.> 1983 Dexter 149.

pee "Since the decimalization of British currency and the introduction of the abbreviation **p**, as in *10p*, . . . the abbreviation has tended to replace *pence* in speech, as in *4p* [pi:]" (*CED* s.v. *pence*). <All right, clever clogs, you owe me sixty **pee**.> 1993 Mason 8.

pence *Pennies* is the plural for coins; *pence* is used for prices, sometimes as a singular, as in *That'll be three pounds and one* ***pence****, please* (Swan 1995, 523). <The cost is still thirty **pence**.> 1985 Bingham 9.

pooves *Poof* (perhaps from French *pouffe* "puff") is not used in American, but is a derogatory Briticism for "effeminate man; male homosexual" with the usual plural *poofs*. There is also, however, a variant singular *poove*, plural *pooves*, as well as a verb *poove* "to act like a poof." The singular *poove* may be a backformation from the plural *pooves*, itself formed by analogy with plurals from Old English that voice final fricatives (*hoof, hooves*), and the verb similarly by analogy with denominal verbs like *prove* from *proof*. < . . . a lot of **pooves** don't form these establishments [i.e., living together as spouses]> 1988 Amis 256.

3.3 Function

3.3.1 Noun adjuncts

Noun adjuncts (of which *noun adjunct* is an example) have been common in English throughout its history. However, certain uses are characteristic of British English. Although not limited to newspaper style, noun adjuncts are characteristic of journalese and are rife in British newspaper headlines. The British vogue for noun adjuncts as a concise method of expression in headlines has doubtless promoted their use in ordinary prose as well.

3.3.1.1 Singular noun adjuncts

It has been traditional in English for a noun adjunct to be singular, even if its referent is logically plural: a *book list* customarily has more than one book on it. That pattern is followed by many constructs that are characteristically British.

In some cases, it is difficult or impossible to say whether the initial item in a combination is a noun or a verb adjunct (§ 1.4.6). When a noun adjunct is used with various head nouns, even though only one may be illustrated in the following list, only the adjunct is used as the lemma here; when a particular combination of noun adjunct and head noun is notable, both words are used as the lemma.

British and American may also differ with respect to which item in a combination is the head and which is the adjunct, for example, British *Leeds town centre* and American *downtown Atlanta*, as in <Every Saturday we'd go into **Leeds town centre**.> 1987 Nov. *Illustrated London News* 84/3. The pattern *City-name city centre* occurs in CIC British texts at 8.6 iptmw; the pattern *downtown City-name* occurs in American texts at 181.7 iptmw.

alleyman A criminal who stalks alleys looking for women victims <The **Alleyman** was finally brought to book.> 1987 June 3 *Sun* 4/6.

barrack room In nominal use, *barracks* is usually plural. But as a noun adjunct, it is usually singular. The *OED* records *barrack-field*, *-flat*, *-life*, *-master*, *-rat*, *-room* (often used as a compound noun adjunct), *-school*, *-shed*, *-square*, *-wing*, and *-yard*. American noun-adjunct use, on the other hand, tends to the plural, as in *barracks bag*. <Even an old **barrack room** bruiser like Nicholas Winterton . . . had some kind words for the Government.> 1993 Feb. 4 *Daily Telegraph* 2/6.

blaze <**Blaze Boys** Die> 1987 Feb. 1 *Daily Mail* 18/1. <Children Saved As **Blaze Mother** Dies> 1987 Mar. 10 *Evening Standard* 13/3–6.

centre party Central party <. . . there may well be 6,179 normally loyal Tories in the constituency ready to lodge a protest vote with the **centre party**.> 1993 Feb. 27 *Times* 15/1–2.

check Checked <. . . immaculate as ever in **check trousers**.> 1996 Aug. 4 *Sunday Times* 3 8/2. Among many other similar compounds are *check cap, check cloth, check gingham, check jacket, check-patterned sports coat, check shirt, check suit, check tablecloth*, and *check waistcoat*.

Christ fantasy A fantasy that one will die and be resurrected <**Christ Fantasy** Of Death Leap Man> 1988 Sept. 6 *Daily Telegraph* 4/2.

coma <A tragic **coma boy** showed the first signs of life yesterday.> 1986 Aug. 23 *Daily Mirror* 5/4.

consultant <Anthony Fry – **Consultant Psychiatrist**> 1987 Oct. 25 *Sunday Telegraph* 31/4.

cookery book Cook book <I started buying a few antiquarian **cookery books**.> 1989 Sept. 10 *Sunday Telegraph* 42/5.

danger man 1. A man committed to taking chances <Harrison Birtwistle may not look like an obvious **Danger Man**.> 1987 Mar. 26 *Evening Standard* 31/4.

2. A man who is dangerous <'**Danger Man**' Alert In Mass Killer Hunt> 1986 Sept. 4 *Daily Telegraph* 1/7–8.

drink A frequent collocation is *drink-driving*, for which American would have *DUI* (*driving under the influence*) or *DWI* (*driving while intoxicated*). <The report proposes a lowering of the **drink-drive** limit.> 1991 Feb. 20 *Times* 1/4. Other combinations have other probable American equivalents: *drink bill/bottle/shop* might be *liquor bill/bottle/store*; *drink driver* might be *drunk driver* or *driver over the limit*; *drink problem* might be *drinking problem*.

drug <Police Not To Charge **Drug Man**'s Mother> 1986 Aug. 30 *Times* 4/7–8.

entry <The flow of people into the building is checked by **entry phone**.> 1994 Oct. 3–9 *Big Issue* 24/3.

exam <Worried **Exam Girl** Died From Anxiety> 1987 June 20 *Times* 2/3.

fire girl <**Fire Girl** Fights For Life> 1986 Aug. 29 (Newcastle) *Evening Chronicle* 1/4.

founder member Founding member <Mr. Carter was a **founder member** of the community.> 1993 Graham 10–1.

hire Rental: *Hire purchase* is American *(buying on the) installment plan*. <**Hire purchase** and other forms of borrowing have shot up by more than four times since 1982.> 1991 Mar. 2 *Daily Express* 40/3. Other compounds with this adjunct in the American sense "rental" are *hire boat, hire car, hire clubs* (golf), *hire culture, hire firm, hire papers*, and *hire shop*.

holiday <. . . a **holiday father** marooned with his family five miles from the nearest telephone.> 1975 Price 24.

horror hospital Hospital whose closing caused "horror stories" <Row Over **Horror Hospital**> 1987 Feb. 19 *Hampstead Advertiser* 1/1.

kidnap <Tears Of Joy As **Kidnap Girl** Is Found Safe> 1990 Aug. 15 *Daily Telegraph* 1/7–8.

knife man Attempted rapist who laid down his knife <**Knife Man**'s Mistake Saved A Nurse> ca. 1980s *Evening Standard*, 11/2–5.

murder <**Murder Girl** Was Bank Job Grass> 1993 Smith 131. In the foregoing, *murder* is the equivalent of "murdered"; in the following, of "murder-site": *murder house* and *murder monastery*.

nurse training Nurse's training; training as a nurse < . . . during my **nurse training** the beds had been covered identically.> 1991 Green 226.

pedigree dog Pedigreed dog <Last week . . . he found a **pedigree dog** – *and* got a reward.> 1987 Oliver 77.

pot plant Potted plant <Broderick Bode, 49, was . . . strangled by a **pot plant**.> 2003 Rowling 482 (*US ed.* potted-plant).

£ twenty-thousand earnings Earnings of £20,000; a £20,000 income <They are the young men . . . who have set their sights on **£20,000 earnings** this year.> 1989 Aug. 27 *Sunday Telegraph* 2/6.

rabies <£2m Or We Free **Rabies Dogs**> 1989 Sept. 2 *Sun* p. n/a. <**Rabies Woman** Is Dead> 1986 Aug. 30 *Times* 1/2.

rape husband Husband charged with the rape of his wife <**Rape Husbands** 'Must Not Be Identified'> 1991 Jan. 29 *Daily Telegraph* 5/1.

removal van Moving van <. . . the **removal vans** went in.> 1993 Graham 365.

safari <Two wildlife rangers are to be charged with the murder of **safari girl** Julie Ward.> 1991 Feb. 13 *Daily Mail* 2/6. Also *safari woman*.

saleroom Salesroom < . . . there is a complete range of different types of shop to buy from – department stores, . . . auction **salerooms**.> 1988 Brookes and Fraenkel 70.

shock In the late 1980s and early 1990s, the adjunct *shock* "shocking" had voguish use on both sides of the Atlantic. British examples: <Liberal Democrats voted last night to decriminalise the use of cannabis in a **shock decision**.> 1994 Sept. 20 *Times* 1/1. Also *shock choice, shock confession*, and *shock vote*.

skirting board <Harry heard something scuttling behind the **skirting board**.> 2003 Rowling 59 (*US ed.* baseboard).

sport <The gym at Swiss Cottage **sport centre** will be out of action for at least a month.> 1987 Feb. 19 *Hampstead Advertiser* 7/4.

suicide <**Suicide Stepfather** Murders Daughter> 2003 July 9 *Times* 5/8.

Sunday working Working on Sundays <**Sunday working** . . . would become a condition of employment.> 1989 Aug. 29 *Times* 15/2. Cf. WEEKEND WORKING below.

thatch cottage Thatched cottage < . . . the house was a beauty, a totally rebuilt **thatch cottage**.> 1989 Burden 127.

trim, chrome- Chrome-trimmed <. . . here beneath the flyover of London's Westway the gipsies park **chrome-trim** caravans on concrete.> 1987 Aug. *Illustrated London News* 48/1.

weekend working Working on weekends <They are the young men prepared to turn a blind eye to union rules on **weekend working**.> 1989 Aug. 27 *Sunday Telegraph* 2/6. Cf. SUNDAY WORKING above.

youth continental Member of a youth team from the continent of Europe <Of the **youth continentals** at Ryhope this week, names worth noting include Sergio Esclusa and Angel Nebreda, of Barcelona.> 1990 Aug. 17 *Daily Telegraph* 30/6.

3.3.1.1.1 Multiple noun adjuncts

Multiple noun adjuncts, although often thought to be typical of American use, are not unknown in British. Such sequences of two or more noun adjuncts are sometimes difficult to interpret, specifically to analyze for their internal constituent structure. For example, is a *management information system* (see below) a system of management information (i.e., information about management) or an information system for management (i.e., information about various matters for management to use)? Such multiple adjuncts are frequent.

car blaze boy A boy burnt in a fire inside a car <**Car Blaze Boy**> 1987 Mar. 19 *Evening Standard* 5/6.

death leap man Man who jumped to his death from a building <Christ Fantasy Of **Death Leap Man**> 1988 Sept. 6 *Daily Telegraph* 4/2.

death-cell man Man on death row <Mercy Plea By **Death-Cell Men**> 1987 Feb. 1 *Daily Mail* 18/1.

drink trade paper <. . . it would be morally wrong to "grass" on customers, reports the **drink trade paper** *Morning Advertiser*.> 1988 Sept. 18 *Sunday Telegraph* 4/8.

drug-plot husband Husband who drugged his second wife to end their marriage <**Drug-plot husband** . . . has found romance again – with his first wife.> 1987 Feb. 23 *Daily Mirror* 5/2.

four hours traffic chaos <Tuesday's Royal's comings and goings caused **four hours traffic chaos** in the West End and beyond.> 1987 Mar. 27 *Evening Standard* 47/1.

high-pay high-profit company; low-pay low-profit concern <. . . it was not the **high-pay high-profit companies** that contributed to our economic decline – it was and is the **low-pay low-profit concerns**.> 1987 June 19 *Times* 16/3–4.

home alone girl Girl left at home by herself while her mother vacationed <**Home Alone Girl**, 11, Left By Mother> 1993 Feb. 13 *Daily Telegraph* 1/6–7.

hunger-strike Baptist minister <Supporters of a **hunger-strike Baptist minister** disrupted a Haringey council meeting when it refused to hear their views on its gay and lesbian policies.> 1987 Feb. 24 *Evening Standard* 5/5.

local development agency scheme <A Whitehall source said last night that the Home Office would "pull the plug" on all **local development agency schemes**.> 1987 Oct. 25 *Sunday Telegraph* 3/6.

low-pay economy <Successive governments contributed to the establishment of a **low-pay economy**.> 1987 June 19 *Times* 16/3–4.

management information system <Mr Bill Phillips . . . will oversee new **management information system**.> 1987 Feb. 26 *Hampstead Advertiser* 6/2.

murder hunt man Man hunted on a charge of murder <**Murder Hunt Man** Gives Up> 1986 Sept. 5 *Times* 1/7.

murder-charge man Man charged with murder <**Murder-Charge Man** Defiant> 1989 July 22 *Times* 9/4–5.

rape ordeal story <British Girl's **Rape Ordeal Story** Shocks A Nation> 1987 Jan. 26 *Daily Mail* 1/4–5.

sex change dad <It tackles the big subjects: cancer, flab, the **sex change dad** who became a mum.> 1989 Aug. 31 *Midweek* 11/1.

three year wait patient <Agony Of **3 Year Wait Patient**> 1986 Sept. 12 *Daily Mirror* 1/1.

two-point-five metre diameter gravity-fed circular ring main <The plan proposes nearly 60 kilometres of **2.5 metre diameter gravity-fed circular ring main**.> 1985 Apr. 24 *Times* 4/4.

US-trip girl <**US-Trip Girl** Loses Her Fight Against Cancer . . . Chelsea, who was sent to the United States for treatment on a brain tumour . . . died early yesterday.> 1995 Aug. 28 *Independent* 4/5–6.

3.3.1.1.2 Nation noun adjuncts

A characteristically British construction is the use of the name of a nation as a noun adjunct in connection with sports teams, particularly cricket and soccer. In all the following examples, American English would have an adjectival form of the nation's name (*Bulgarian, English, Romanian*) or else a prepositional phrase (*for Great Britain*). Cf. § 5.1.2.

Bulgaria <. . . a small model figure wearing **Bulgaria Quidditch robes**.> 2000 Rowling 386.

England <Combat clothing experts . . . are collaborating with Umbro, official manufacturers of the **England strip** [team uniform of a particular color] to devise a high-tech cloth that will give players an advantage.> 1999 Mar. 14 *Sunday Times* 1 8/8. Other tokens: *England bowler, England cap* "player awarded a cap signifying membership on the national team," *England captain, England captaincy, England coach, England cricketer, England fans, England line, England party, England physio* "physiotherapist," *England players, England selectors, England squad, England team*, and *England Women*.

Great Britain < . . . the **Great Britain centre** [soccer player] . . . almost settled the issue a few minutes from the end when he was held inches short.> 1987 Nov. 8 *Manchester Guardian Weekly* 31/5.

Romania <Don't miss the chance to see some of the world's best women athletes in action at Crystal Palace . . . . England Women v **Romania Women**.> 1985 Aug. London tube-station billboard.

The use of a noun denoting a nation in place of the corresponding adjective is not limited to sports, however, but extends to general use as well.

Romania baby couple Couple seeking to adopt a baby from Romania <**Romania Baby Couple** Told To Pay £2500> 1990 Aug. 22 *Evening Standard* 15/1–3.

Spain drugs haul <12 Britons In **Spain Drugs Haul**> 1988 Sept. 3 *Times* 1/2.

Turkey carpet <In the centre of the floor was a blue and red **Turkey carpet**.> 2000 Granger 180.

3.3.1.2 Plural noun adjuncts

Nouns modifying other nouns have generally been in the singular form in English: *pencil sharpener, peanut candy*. Recently, however, British and, to a lesser extent, American have been favoring plural attributive nouns (*CGEL* 17.108–9). Although this new pattern occurs in both varieties, it is most frequent in British (Johansson 1979, 213), and notably in news reports (*LGSWE* 594).

American fluctuating use of the plural adjunct is doubtless due to British influence, which is strong in certain channels, such as reportage. For example, an issue of the *New York Times* (July 3, 2004) had several articles on employment statistics (A1-B3 and B1–3). The texts of these articles used primarily singular adjuncts (*job base, job creation* 3 times, *job figures* 2 times, *job growth* 4 times, *job report, job market* 2 times, *job numbers, job survey*) and only occasionally plural adjuncts (*jobs data, jobs front, jobs survey*). The headlines, however, had a reverse proportion, with only one singular adjunct (on the front page, *Job Growth*) and three plural adjuncts (*Jobs Growth, Jobs Report* 2 times). Headlines and their articles are written by different persons.

In some cases, adjunct nouns may be spelled variably with an apostrophe (*appointments' board, drinks' cabinet, trades' unionist*), so that it might be argued that it is in fact a genitive determiner rather than a noun adjunct. However, the apostrophe spelling is relatively rare and both the syntax and the semantics of the constructions point to the noun-adjunct construction, so the apostrophe is probably just an indication that the writer was subconsciously aware that the plural noun adjunct is a departure from the norm, and thus "corrected" its written form to that of the genitive.

Goods in the sense of "products," "material," or "freight" occurs only in the plural, so there is no possibility of its use as a singular noun adjunct. In its adjunct use, the usual American equivalent is *freight*. Similarly, *Guards*, in the sense of "troops originally to protect the monarch" is normally plural. Although such nouns have no singular, their occurrence as adjuncts provides not only additional tokens of plural noun adjuncts but also reinforces that pattern.

Athletics and *maths* (American *math*, as the short form of *mathematics*) are not plurals at all, their final *-s* being a noun-forming suffix (as also in *astronautics, physics*, etc.). Yet because they have the appearance of plurals, their use as adjuncts also reinforces the plural noun adjunct pattern.

As a collective term for competitive activities of physical skill, *sports* is usually plural in American, but may be singular in British. Its British use as a plural noun adjunct, as in *sports hall*, is therefore noteworthy in this context, even though it would be usually plural also in American, as in *sports arena*.

The part of speech of *thinks* in *thinks bubble* is not clear (it might be a verb). However, it might also be a noun, as in *give it a think*, and an American equivalent might be *thought balloon*.

accounts Accounting department <. . . she has started work . . . in the **accounts department.**> 1995 Aug. 30 *Daily Telegraph* 4/6.

Accommodations <. . . in the Civil Service, by some quirk of official irony, dealing with bombs came under the **Accommodations Officer**.> 1977 Aird 57.

admissions <. . . some **admissions tutors** expect an above-average increase when this summer's results are published next week.> 1996 Aug. 9 *Daily Telegraph* 7/4.

aggregates <They include . . . scrap metal and **aggregates wharves** at Greenwich Reach.> 1994 Sept. 22 *Times* 20/4–5.

Airports <The lounges are run on the FO's behalf by the British **Airports Authority**.> 1987 Jan. 16 *Times* 1/3–4.

animals <I was never much of an **animals person**.> 1994 Sept. *Tatler* 58/1.

antiques <Kate and Piers entered it gingerly, as if venturing into an overstocked **antiques market**.> 2003 James 200. Also *antiques shop*.

appointments <. . . changes to create a supreme court and independent judicial **appointments commission**.> 2003 June 21 *Times* 2/5. Also *appointments advertising, Appointments' Board, Appointments Card, Appointments Department, appointments diary*, and *appointments list*.

Arrears <**Arrears Officer** . . . Do you have the determination, patience, experience and sensitivity to recover rent arrears from former tenants?> 1990 Aug. 20 *Evening Standard* 14/3.

arrivals In CIC, *arrivals hall/lounge* outnumbers *arrival hall/lounge* by 26 to 3 in British texts. *Arrival(s) lobby* is not attested in CIC. <Instead of distributing the luggage among all the carousels in the **arrivals hall**, four or five flights have to share the only one working.> 1996 Aug. 8 *Times* 21/2. Also *arrivals lobby* and *arrivals lounge*.

arts <In 1976 it opened as an **arts venue**.> 1998 Jan. 6 *Times* 17/6. Also *arts centre, arts editor, arts graduate*, and *arts programme*.

assisted places <. . . the **assisted places scheme** . . . subsidises the private school fees of bright children from poorer backgrounds.> 1994 Oct. 3 *Times* 41/6.

athletics <Fame has its price. Ask . . . ITV's **athletics commentator**.> 1995 Aug. 28 *Daily Mail* 43/4. Also *athletics coach* and *athletics team*.

awards <. . . at the **awards' breakfast**, Sigourney told me she started the organisation.> 1988 May *In Britain* 58/2. Also *awards committee* and *awards programme*.

Benedictines <The Grace and Compassion **Benedictines Order** runs six residential homes.> 1989 Aug. 2 *Evening Standard* 3/3.

Benefits <. . . people can . . . pass on information about suspected cheats to **Benefits Agency** staff.> 1996 Aug. 4 *Sunday Times* 1/1.

books <The **books section** is particularly popular.> 1988 Mar. *Illustrated London News* 28/2.

Boroughs Grants <The chairman of the London **Boroughs Grants Committee** warned that voluntary organisations will have to send out redundancy notices by the end of the month.> 1987 Feb. 12 *Evening Standard* 5/1.

brains trust "A few idiomatic differences in colloquial phrases are apparently of recent origin, as are the phrases themselves; thus Mr H. G. Nicholas (in *The American Government*, 1948) follows BBC usage in speaking of Mr Roosevelt's New Deal experts as his '**Brains Trust**,' whereas the form actually *always* used in America was 'Brain Trust' " (Partridge and Clark 1951, 318–19). <Some **Brains Trust** at Reading University.> 1996 Dexter 219.

breeds, rare- <... you can get a very acceptable bacon by post from Heal Farm, a **rare-breeds survival establishment**.> 1988 June *Illustrated London News* 80/4.

bricks-and-mortar <From the end of this year it will be possible for private individuals to own shares in . . . large **bricks-and-mortar investments**.> 1987 Aug. *Illustrated London News* 54/1.

buildings < . . . no charge for building maintenance has been carried to the accounts, and . . . at least £75,000 a year should have been placed to **buildings reserve** ["depreciation"].> 1993 Neel 45.

burns <Mr. McArdle was detained in the **burns unit**.> 1986 Aug. 29 (Newcastle) *Evening Chronicle* 2/7.

careers Although singular *career* may be used as a noun adjunct in American English, other expressions are more likely: *careers advice* might be American *guidance* or *counseling*; *careers office* might be *counseling office* (or in a military context, *recruiting/recruitment office*); *careers adviser/master/officer/teacher* might be *guidance counselor*. <**Careers Advice** [chapter title]> 2003 Rowling 574 (*US ed.* Career Advice). Also *careers brochure, Careers Convention*, and *careers-opportunities booklet*.

chemicals <. . . a career in the oil and **chemicals industry**.> 1983 magazine CIC.

cloaks <Sitting/Dining-Room; Fully Fitted Modern Kitchen; **Cloaks/** Shower **Room**.> 1994 Dexter 51.

comics <Forbidden Planet, the **comics shop**.> 1988 Oct. *Illustrated London News* 18/1–2.

complaints <Studying his **complaints list** is a way of defining why.> 1989 July 20 *Midweek* 6/3.

components <Mr Channon refused to say how many jobs were at risk in the **components industry**.> 1987 Feb. 20 *Guardian* 1/3.

costs collection Bill collection <Mr Parrish has asked me to deal with all **costs collection** matters.> 1995 Jones 40–1.

Counties, Home <Daphne . . . comes to England in 1946, among eccentric **Home Counties relations**.> 1987 July *Illustrated London News* 66/3.

courts <Anti-Smoking Campaigners Prepare **Courts Assault**> 1986 Aug. 21 *Guardian* 2/1–7.

cuttings Clipping <His **cuttings file** bulges with tabloid headlines.> 1987 June 4 *Independent* 8/5. Also *cuttings book*.

damages <If they won, the legal aid fund would be able to claw back from the **damages award** all its outstanding expenses, with nothing or very little left for compensation.> 1987 June 4 *Independent* 1/7.

days, seven <. . . similar Syrian wedding-songs and customs . . . obtain to-day, during the **seven days festivities**, when the bride and bridegroom are represented as a royal couple.> 1908 Mead 16.

deeds <Mr. Ounce replaced the stiff ivory parchment folds in a metal **deeds box** and snapped the lock.> 1989 Graham 265.

departures <Morse . . . stood under the high **Departures Board** and noted the time of the next train.> 1996 Dexter 209. Also *Departures Concourse* and *Departures Lounge*.

Descriptions, Trade(s) <A picture, surely in breach of the **Trades Descriptions Act**, showed bikini-clad girls running across a golden beach.> 1983 Mann 14.

dominoes <He . . . adopted the name of a chap in his father's **dominoes team**.> 1995 Aug. 28 *Daily Mail* 20/3.

drinks <He had held the obligatory farewell **drinks party** before luncheon.> 2003 James 31. Also *drinks allowance, drinks-bar, drinks cabinet, drinks cans, drinks company, drinks cupboard, drinks dispenser, drinks industry, drinks-list, drinks machine, drinksmaker, drinks manufacturer, drinks market, drinks order, drinks table, drinks trade, drinks tray, drinks trolley*, and *drinks writer*.

drugs <Meanwhile, the politicians make a meal out of the problem because at the wrong end of the **drugs ladder** [range of drug problems] there are dreadful social problems and major criminality.> 2000 Jan. 18 *Times* 17/3. Also *drugs baron, drugs bill, drugs Briton, drugs company, drugs don, drugs economy, drugs haul, Drugs Intelligence Unit, drugs market, drugs menace, drugs officer, drugs overdose, drugs problem, drugs raid, drugs ring, drugs-smuggler, drugs smuggling, drugs squad, drugs test, drugs trade*, and *drugs trafficking*.

earnings <. . . it is likely your house will increase in value much more quickly than your **earnings power**.> 1987 July *Illustrated London News* 63/4.

engagements <At first they did not even appear in the Prime Minister's **engagements diary**.> 1987 June 13 *Times* 28/4.

entertainments <The first 10 years of his working life were spent on board the Queen Mary as the ship's **entertainments purser**.> 1995 Aug. 30 *Daily Telegraph* 13/3–4. Also *entertainments industry*.

exams <. . . the biggest shake-up of the **exams system** for 50 years.> 2004 Dec. 17 *Independent* 7/1.

expenses <. . . the [European] Parliament . . . last month voted itself an **expenses regime** that would send an English district councillor to jail.> 1999 Mar. 17 *Times* 20/4. Also *expenses cheque, expenses claim*, and *expenses fiddle*.

ex-pensions < . . . we'll have to start recruiting **ex-pensions salesmen**.> 1994 Sept. 21 *Times* 16/2.

families, happy <The secretarial assistant was today at the heart of a **happy families scene** at the Highland estate and looked perfectly at home among the Royal Family.> 1995 Aug. 29 *Evening Standard* 3/3.

fares <London commuters face swingeing **fares increases** of up to four times the rate of inflation.> 1994 Sept. 15 *Evening Standard* 7/1. Also *fares rises*.

features <"I was absolutely furious at first," **features editor** Richard Williams admits.> 1987 Feb. 16 *Evening Standard* 6/2.

feeds <If you need larger quantities of fertilizer, then go to an agricultural **feeds merchant**.> 2003 June 21 *Times* Weekend 13/4.

fees <Among the other papers in Grunte's personal file was a letter from the Commons' **fees office**, the department responsible for the payment of MPs' salaries and expenses.> 1991 Critchley 19.

finals <Its [Oxford University's] **finals students** are required to traipse to their exams in lounge suits, white ties and scratchy gowns.> 1994 Sept. 27 *Evening Standard* 28/6. Also *finals papers*.

fines <The unit **fines system** also aims to fine on the basis of better information.> 1989 Aug. 4 *Times* 5/2.

fixtures <Their names positively don't appear on the school **fixtures list**.> 1985 Bingham 121.

forces <Theoretically they [contact lenses] were supplied only to **forces personnel**.> 1987 Mar. 9 *Evening Standard* 29/3.

Galleries <. . . the recent item in the diary of your newspaper about myself and the Royal Fine Art and Museum and **Galleries Commissions** encouraging freer movement of art treasures across EEC boundaries is more than usually absurd.> 1986 Sept. 10 *Times* 13/5.

games <The **games field** is the place where all classes can cooperate.> 1990 Aug. 16 *Times* 11/6. Also *games afternoon, games cupboard, games facilities, games player, games room, games staff, games table*, and *games teacher*.

gays and lesbians <. . . the **gays and lesbians issue** is costing us dear amongst the pensioners.> 1987 May 11 *Evening Standard* 24/5.

gilts <. . . a huge booming industry generating pop-star-scale salaries for Eurobond and **gilts traders**.> 1990 Critchfield 141.

goodies <They tend to have been the bad boys at school, not the **goodies swots**.> 1986 Oct. 26 *Sunday Times* 48/6.

goods Freight <. . . **goods vehicles**, oil tankers and military transport littered the highway like the giant carcasses of animals hunted down in the night.> 1991 Feb. 1 *Times* 1/3. Also *goods access, goods entrance, goods lift, goods train, goods waggon*, and *goods yard*.

Grants Committee <Take, for example, the Universities Funding Council, which replaces the University **Grants Committee**.> 1987 Dec. 20 *Manchester Guardian* 6/4.

greetings card <. . . she . . . collects and sells a huge range of paper ephemera from **greetings cards** to small purse calendars.> 1988 Dec. *In Britain* 26/2.

groundnuts Peanut <We use best quality fresh fish fried in pure **groundnuts oil**.> 2000 sign at Big Bite Fish & Chips Shop on Walm Lane, Willesden Green, London.

Guards officer <. . . men who looked like retired **Guards officers** and probably were.> 1992 Granger 52.

highways <. . . **highways chairman** Corbett Singleton.> 1994 Oct. 3 *Evening Standard* 20/4. Also *Highways Act*.

holidaymakers, working <Tens of thousands of men and women under 30 from the Commonwealth are to be allowed to work full-time in professional jobs under an overhaul of the two-year **working holidaymakers scheme**.> 2003 June 21 *Times* 2/6.

ideas <Being on television, though, is nothing compared with the terror of a *Tatler* **ideas meeting**.> 1999 Mar. 13 *Times* Magazine 9/3.

improvements <And top of the **improvements list** is the swimming-pool.> 1989 July 29 *Times* 5 1/1.

incomes policy <Mr Kinnock made an oblique but not insignificant hint to what used to be called an **incomes policy**.> 1986 Oct. 1 *Times* 13/2.

infants <Derek's wife would be away running a course for **infants teachers**.> 1998 Joss 14.

interests, special <. . . a succession of policy climbdowns . . . have signalled to **special interests groups** that this is a government well worth standing up to.> 1993 Feb. 13 *Daily Telegraph* 10/1–2.

islands <Her income of £8,500 is bumped up with a £500-a-year **islands allowance**.> 1986 Oct. 16 *Times* 40/2.

jobs <**Jobs Offer** / Tens of thousands of men and women under 30 from the Commonwealth are to be allowed to work full-time in professional jobs.> 2003 June 21 *Times* 2/6. Also *jobs list, jobs market, jobs programme, jobs scheme, jobs search*, and *jobs shortfall*.

lettings Rental <It is quite normal for **lettings agents** to handle the routine management.> 1986 Winter *For Sale Magazine* 56/2.

machines, cigarette vending <Don had his own **cigarette vending machines business**.> 1989 June *In Britain* 11/4–12/1.

materials <. . . **materials suppliers** who reap a healthy harvest from spending on building and repairs.> 1987 May 10 (Scotland) *Sunday Post* 7/4.

maths <What is he, after all? An ex-**maths teacher**.> 1990 Hardwick 38.

meals < . . . up until this week at least one [new school] didn't even have a proper **meals service** arranged.> 1989 Sept. 13 *Times* 15/3–4.

meetings <Enquiries about the meeting should be sent to the **Meetings Secretary**.> 1988 first circular Autumn meeting, Linguistics Association of Great Britain.

men, three- <Ballesteros, who captains the **three-men** Spanish **team** at St Andrews.> 1986 Sept. 24 *Times* 40/5.

menaces <Gave Barry Kent his **menaces money**.> 1985 Townsend 42.

mergers <Mr Channon . . . will meet Tory backbenchers tonight over **mergers policy**.> 1987 Jan. 20 *Guardian* 1/8.

meths <. . . you might as well take in **meths drinkers** from the streets.> 1980 Drabble 86–7.

metres, 400 <Victory smiles from Britain's 4 × **400 metres team**.> 1989 Aug. 7 *Times* 1/4–8 (caption to picture of four team members). Also *ten metres line*.

minutes, 15 <Most centres will give staff 75 minutes off and it is up [to] the individual whether he takes it all in one go, has 45 minutes for lunch and two **15 minutes breaks** or has several short breaks.> 2003 July 10 *Times* Appointments 4/3.

Monopolies and Mergers <He faces severe criticism over his decision . . . not to refer the bid by BTR . . . to the **Monopolies and Mergers Commission**.> 1987 Jan. 20 *Guardian* 1/8.

Museums <Now it is the silly season, may I recommend a suitable game for **Museums Year**. It is to search the shops attached to museums and tourist attractions for the most irrelevant souvenir.> 1989 Aug. 7 *Times* 13/6.

no-claims <. . . boat owners laying up their craft should . . . review their insurance to take advantage of **no-claims bonuses**.> 1994 Sept. 25 *Sunday Times* 4/5.

obituaries <. . . they were not convinced that these sympathies justified mutilating a copy of the Daily Telegraph – least of all its **obituaries page**.> 1991 Feb. 9 *Daily Telegraph* 13/5.

opportunities, careers- <I wrote a **careers-opportunities booklet**.> 1990 Aug. 21 *Times* 25/6.

opportunities, equal <The Armed Forces are **Equal Opportunities Employers**.> 1987 Oct. 25 *Sunday Telegraph* 2/3. Also *equal opportunities manager*.

outpatients <. . . the introduction of appointment times in hospital **outpatients departments** should raise a cheer.> 1989 Feb. 12 *Manchester Guardian Weekly* 12/4.

palaces <. . . families could wait ten years on the council housing list to fulfil the dream of a nice modern purpose-built flat somewhere like the **palaces estate**.> 1991 Grant-Adamson 112.

paratroops <He's wearing a scruffy salt-and-pepper tweed suit and a **paratroops tie**.> 1989 Daniel 109.

parcels <**Parcels Office** . . . **Parcels Point**> 1986 Oct. signs in Euston Station, London.

passes, A level <Its schools have about as much chance of topping the **A level passes league** as the driver of a family saloon has of winning the Monaco Grand Prix.> 1987 Sept. *Illustrated London News* 86/2.

payments <Outdated **payments rules** mean, for example, that the cost to the Royal Mail of delivering letters sent from Moscow is not fully borne by the Russian authorities.> 1992 Nov. 7 *Economist* 73/2.

pensions <If you are in the dark about the whereabouts of some of your **pensions money**, contact the **Pensions Tracing Registry**.> 1995 newspaper CIC.

phones <There will be no formal talks to end the **phones dispute** until the strikers go back to work, British Telecom said today.> 1987 Jan. 28 *Evening Standard* 2/4.

pinnacles, eight- <Here is rustic England at its best, a little **eight-pinnacles church**, a war memorial, a maypole.> 1938 Crawford 18.

places, assisted <Delegates at Blackpool this week may cheer pledges to scrap the **assisted places scheme** that subsidises the private school fees of bright children from poorer backgrounds.> 1994 Oct. 3 *Times* 41/6.

plates, printing <The prestigious Rolls-Royce car . . . looks set to be overtaken this year by the sharp acceleration of profits from the group's more mundane **printing plates business**.> 1987 Feb. 23 *Evening Standard* 41/1.

points <. . . a "tariff system" . . . would give a single **points total** for progression to higher education.> 1994 Sept. 22 *Times* 4/3. Also *points victory*.

pools < . . . rises and falls in tone informed viewers, with heads down over their **pools coupons**, which team had won even before the visitors' score was given.> 1995 Aug. 28 *Independent* 10/1. Also *pools win* and *pools winners*.

profits <The **profits performance** was achieved despite a 14pc increase in the price of milk.> 1995 newspaper CIC.

railways <Michael Meacher, shadow transport secretary, said he would ask the **railways inspectorate division** of the Health and Safety Executive to review safety procedures.> 1995 Sept. 4 *Daily Telegraph* 5/1.

rates <The unpopularity of the domestic **rates system** in Scotland came about because of its unfairness.> 1986 Dec. 10 *Times* 4/7.

real-terms <William Hague will also commit the Conservatives to **real-terms increases** in health spending.> 2000 Jan. 18 *Times* 1/2.

records <This licence is not valid until it is initialled and properly stamped by the officer issuing it at a post office or the National TV Licence **Records Office**.> 1987 May 18 TV license.

removals <. . . the Gilbert twins: one of them a housing agent; the other a **removals man**. Sell some property – and recommend a highly reputable and efficient **removals firm**.> 1983 Dexter 153.

roads protest Truck-driver strike <Although senior figures in the industry tried to deter drivers from staging a **roads protest**, they said that the action was "inevitable".> 1999 Mar. 19 *Times* 2/1–2.

runners-up <Win . . . One Of These **Runners-Up Prizes**.> 1991 Jan. 31 *Midweek* back cover.

scenes-of-crime officer <Indeed it was . . . the dreams . . . of the hardened **Scenes-of-Crime Officers**, that would be haunted by the sight of so much blood.> 1996 Dexter 52.

schools <My prize was for writing a **schools booklet**.> 1991 Feb. 9 *Daily Telegraph* Weekend 3/7. Also *Schools Council, schools crossing warden, post-schools director of education, schools drama, Schools Minister, schools problem, schools programme, schools system*, and *schools year*.

seconds <Their [Royal Doulton's] smaller **seconds shop** sells genuine seconds from all the group's companies at reduced prices.> 1989 June *In Britain* 40/3.

secrets <Britain has no Freedom of Information Act. What it does have is the Official **Secrets Act** of 1911, which makes it an offence for government officers

to give or receive official information.> 1989 Feb. 12 *Manchester Guardian Weekly* 20/1. Also *secrets bill.*

securities <. . . the banks were wondering whether to go nap on the great new business of **securities trading** in London.> 1989 Apr. 1 *Spectator* 25/2.

services <. . . we are looking for a Public **Services Officer** to patrol a designated area of the Borough.> 1990 Aug. 20 *Evening Standard* 14/1. Also *services rationalisation.*

ships <Mr Ray, . . . director of a **ships instrument repair business**, said he had a premonition.> 1987 Mar. 9 *Evening Standard* 1/5.

signals <Antoine Lurot drifted into estate agency after completing . . . French national service with a **signals parachute regiment**.> 1986 Winter *For Sale Magazine* 28/3.

sittings <The backlash that has developed against the 12-month-old change in the **sittings hours** of the Commons is more to do with the convenience of MPs than with the effectiveness of Parliament.> 2004 Jan. 5 *Times* 8/7.

skills <**Skills shortages** . . . are having a profound effect on the training, career development and influence of personnel managers.> 1990 Aug. 21 *Times* 25/1.

sounds <Prices . . . include VAT, Car Tax, front/rear seat belts and **sounds system**.> 1989 Aug. 28 *Daily Telegraph* 7.

sports <And there's a supermarket and restaurants and **sports halls**.> 2001 Lodge 40. Also *sports centre.*

standards, trading <My local **trading standards officer** informs me that terms such as "traditional" are not legally defined.> 1994 Sept. 22 *Times* 19/5.

stores <I left the **stores man** wondering if it was him or me who was mad.> 1991 nonfiction CIC.

students <It is a chance for students . . . of involving themselves in the **Students Union** in a more positive way than simply going to the Union Bar for a drink.> 1991 Mar. *UCL News* (University College London magazine) 11/1.

sweets Candy (shop/stand) <I was regularly given the job of paying the takings from my grandmother's **sweets kiosk**, into the bank.> 1999 Mar. 21 *Sunday Times* News Review 4/4.

swings <Wexford's car . . . was parked [near] a children's playground. . . . [¶] The men who had come to search for him stood about in groups, some in the **swings field**.> 1972 Rendell 10–11.

talks <George Mitchell, the former US senator . . . is chairing the **talks process**.> 1997 newspaper CIC.

thinks bubble Thought balloon <. . . we fell silent for a minute or two. The **thinks bubbles** over our heads filled up.> 2001 Lodge 252.

tours <. . . we got your address from the **tours manager** – the coach company fellow.> 1974 Price 131.

towns <. . . all self employed **towns people**, working from home, should pay no rates, at least on their work premises or garages.> 1987 Feb. 13 *Evening Standard* 9/1.

trades <. . . she's an . . . active **trades' unionist**.> 1992 Walters 67. Also *Trades Descriptions Act*, *trades union*, and *trades unionism*.

under-fives <Special play-groups and **under-fives clinics** for "homeless" children have been set up in hotel basements and church halls.> 1987 Mar. 18 *Guardian* 25/4.

universities <. . . the **Universities Funding Council** . . . replaces the University Grants Committee.> 1987 Dec. 20 *Manchester Guardian* 6/4–5.

utilities <I picked up a hammer . . . from the tool-box in the **utilities cupboard**.> 1969 Amis 152.

wages <. . . his total **wages bill** was still a mere £15 a week.> 1984 Smith 116.

weapons <. . . someone sold Downing Street duff goods about Iraq's **weapons programme** last year.> 2003 June 20 *Times* 22/5. Also *weapons policy*.

weights <". . . *lift*, you're not waving goodbye to your mum, you know." The dark-haired instructor loomed menacingly over Loretta as she lay on her back in a corner of the **weights room**.> 1993 Smith 41.

works <My favourite memories are of our **works outings**.> 1998 Jan. 3 *Times* Magazine 18/4. Also *works access*, *works party*, *works schedule*, and *works yard*.

3.3.2 Object of preposition for noun adjunct

In a few cases, British English has the structure *noun*^{1} *of noun*^{2} for the structure *noun*^{2} *noun*^{1}.

Captain of Games Team captain <He became **Captain of Games** in my house [at Eton].> 1994 Dickinson 15.

hall of residence Residence hall <They . . . went off together . . . towards the **hall of residence**.> 1993 Neel 123.

3.3.3 Individual and collective meanings

Some nouns refer either to individuals who are part of a collection or to the collection as a whole. Cf. § 2.4.2.

crew Crew members <The presence of British air **crew** as prisoners of war in Baghdad means the RAF Benevolent Fund is having second thoughts.> 1991 Feb. 11 *Daily Telegraph* 17/1.

police Policemen: In common-core English, the plural noun *police* normally has a collective sense "the police force." That rule, however, has occasional exceptions in British use. <In the subsequent brawl . . . four **police** were injured.> 1987 Nov. *Illustrated London News* 78/1.

staff Staff members <. . . she is looking for office premises and . . . hopes to employ two **staff**.> 1994 Oct. 3 *Evening Standard* 14/3. Cf. § 14.1.

3.4 Names and titles

3.4.1 Personal names

A difference in the treatment of personal given names is in the use of initials. British tends to reduce all given (or Christian) names to initials, as in *J. R. R. Tolkien* or *J. K. Rowling*. That pattern is clear from bibliographies, reference lists, and other formal lists of names in British sources. American, on the other hand, tends to favor a full first name and middle initial (*CGEL* 5.66), as in *Harry S. Truman*.

British use of a double-barreled surname is sometimes mistaken by Americans for a middle name followed by surname, as in the case of Andrew Lloyd Webber. The double-barreled surname was largely unknown in America until recent times, when it was adopted on an ad hoc basis by couples who combined their surnames as a statement of the equality of the sexes. There is, however, not much evidence that such combined names will be handed on through the succeeding generations. The British motivation was often to combine one surname with another of a more prominent, related family. An example is the novelist and politician Edward Bulwer-Lytton, who was the son of William Bulwer and Elizabeth Lytton, but adopted the surname Bulwer-Lytton in 1843 when he inherited the Lytton family estate at Knebworth.

A practice once common in both countries, in correspondence and in certain social situations, was the familiar use of a man's surname in place of his given name by his equals or superiors. This practice is said to have arisen out of public school practice in England; in America it was known particularly in a military context. It is now rare in American use and is doubtless less frequent in England than formerly.

<Dear **Rogers**, [¶] I was interested to meet you last Tuesday and would have liked to talk longer.> 1983 Dickinson 13.

In America it is, or once was, common to pass on a father's full name to a son, usually the first-born son. In such cases, suffixes were used to distinguish the generations: *Sr.* for the parent and *Jr.* for the offspring. In the case of later successive generations bearing the same name, roman numerical suffixes were used: *III, IV*, etc. The practice is now rare. A distinctively British custom is the use after the surname of *major* and *minor* for, respectively, an older and younger brother in the same public school, often although not always capitalized.

<It was by this odd closeness to Dobbs **minor** that I had been able to recall that a Dobbs **major** must have existed.> 1983 Dickinson 13.

3.4.2 Titles

The use of occupational titles as a name title, as in *Secretary of State Colin Powell* and *Prime Minister Tony Blair* is more characteristic of American than of

British use (*CamGEL* 520). Social titles, however, are more used in British than American. The parenthesised figures are those of British/American iptmw in CIC texts.

ma'am (57.4/22.8) <'Would you care to lead in to lunch now, **ma'am**?' inquired someone politely. 'I don't think quite yet,' replied Her Majesty.> 1989 March *In Britain* 37/3.

madam (38.3/7.2) <"Would you stop calling me **madam**, Sergeant, and suggest whom I could see regarding a criminal matter?" [¶] "No need to get shirty, **madam**," he said.> 1992 Green 21.

Miss (1135.7/331.2) <[young girl to teacher:] I saw it in a magazine. Honest, **Miss**. Honest.> 1989 Aug. 30 *Guardian* 38/2–3.

Mr (6438.1/3555.2) **1:** British newspapers have a greater tendency than their American counterparts to use titles for persons. <**Mr** [Graham] Greene, whose first play this was, probes the spiritual consequences of an affair between a married, 45-year-old psychology lecturer and a 17-year-old Roman Catholic orphan.> 1987 Nov. 8 *Manchester Guardian Weekly* 25/4. **2:** The general titles of *Mr.*, *Mrs.*, and *Miss* have less prestige in American use than professional titles like *Prof.* and *Dr.* <[Hagrid writes:] Dear **Mr** Dumbledore, . . .> 1997 Rowling 43 (*US ed.* Professor).

Sir (1460.6/142.1); **sir** (435.8/126.8) **1.** A general term of address, used formerly between upper-class social equals or by inferiors to superiors <. . . the only people now aware of the distinction between the classes are the upper class; the rest of us are confident the whole thing has been abolished. "I don't have to call *you* '**Sir**' do I?" says the party worker to the Cabinet Minister, the waiter to the famous playwright, the train driver to the chairman of a nationalized industry, the gamekeeper to the scrap metal millionaire.> 1967 Frost and Jay 29. <When I was at Cambridge the split personality role of the college porter was summed up in one sentence when he caught me climbing in illegally late at night. 'What the hell do you think you're doing (pause) **Sir**?'> 1983 Brooke-Taylor 77. **2.** A title of honor for knights and baronets <. . . excuse me, **Sir** Thomas – *Tom* . . . But I'll put the kettle on for a cup of tea while I'm about it.> 1986 Price 65.

3.4.3 Place names

Place-naming patterns in the two countries are also distinct. In the following rhapsody on Englishness, most of the place names (*Broadway* excepted) are characteristically British:

<Broadway and **Moreton-in-Marsh, Bourton-on-the-Water**, where the dog in the pub was called Winston, **Stow-on-the-Wold**, the Swells and the Slaughters – such a glut of thatched streets, tea-rooms and cottage gardens, swans on village streams and manor houses in that bright honey stone: after the busloads

of trippers, the empty village street of **Minster Lovell**, sweet village, freshened things.> 1988 Nov. *In Britain* 48/1–2.

Similarly, the name of Harry Potter's Muggle hometown, **Little Whinging**, Surrey, is unmistakably English, and generally not understood by Americans, who do not use the verb *whinge*.

3.4.4 Institutional names

The personal name of a shop's proprietor may be used for the shop itself. The grammatical significance of this substitution is that a personal nominal is used for an inanimate referent.

<The place she heads for . . . is **Elizabeth King**, the local delicatessen, fishmonger, greengrocer and bakery.> 1998 Jan. 3 *Times* Weekend 4/1. <Turn up to **Navajo Joe** (34 King St, WC2, Covent Garden tube) on Thursday 11 to take part in history's biggest ever tequila slam.> 1999 Mar. 10–17 *Time Out* 7/1.

When a proper name is used for a business, it may be plural, yet when it is followed by a generic term, it may be singular, despite the British tendency toward plural noun adjuncts.

<**Barings'** modest bet on the Far Eastern markets, **Baring Securities**, is now paying off like a fruit-machine, and competitors wonder whether **Barings** may float the securities business as **Hambros** did with **Hambro Life**.> 1989 Apr. 1 *Spectator* 25/2.

When the name of a business firm is that of its proprietor, the proprietor's name may be followed by an explanatory appositive, the head of which is a plural noun identifying the sort of workers characteristic of the business.

<. . . a group operating under the umbrella of **Richard Ellis the builders** announces its plans for . . . developments in central London.> 1987 Aug. *Illustrated London News* 54/2. <. . . a spokesman for **Barnard Marcus, the London estate agents**.> 1989 July 30 *Sunday Times* A 9/8.

3.5 Genitive constructions

3.5.1 Enclitic **'s** *and periphrastic* **of**

The two main forms of the genitive construction are (1) that with the grammatical enclitic *'s* (originally an inflectional suffix) and (2) that with the periphrastic *of*. Anette Rosenbach (2002) has studied the frequency of the two forms historically and the factors that affect their choice in present-day English.

Reports of differences between British and American English in their use of the two constructions have been contradictory. Rosenbach (40, 45–6) points to an unpublished 1980 Oslo thesis and also to a study by Marianne Hundt (1998a), both showing that American is more likely than British to use *'s* genitives with inanimate possessors, but also to a study by Magnus Ljung (1997) showing that the opposite is true in texts from the British *Independent* newspaper and the American *New York Times* and *Time* magazine. Rosenbach's own study (166) indicates that *'s* with inanimate possessors is more frequent among Americans and younger British than among older British speakers; she therefore concludes that the *'s* genitive is extending its domain into British English from American influence. In that case, a smaller proportion of inanimate *'s* genitives would be a characteristic of conservative British usage. However, until the discrepancy between this conclusion and Ljung's findings has been resolved, the question must be regarded as open.

One possible explanation suggested by Ljung is that the difference is correlated with formality (*of* being more formal with inanimates than *'s*). Ljung cites Douglas Biber (1987) in support of the greater formality of American written news texts over their British counterparts in the matter of abstraction (as measured by the number of nominalizations and prepositions). Biber's study, however, shows a complex of differences in style that he suggests amounts to a greater adherence to stylistic prescriptions in British than in American texts. In that case, one might expect inanimate genitives with *of* rather than *'s* in British, as according closer with prescriptions.

3.5.2 Shopkeeper's *versus* shop

British English has a preference for designating a place of business with the genitive of the term for its shopkeeper (or the term for the shopkeeper alone), whereas American prefers a term for the store.

baker's (shop) Bakery <They seem to be staring at the world through plate-glass, like a child in the **baker's** unable to decide between a caramel slice and a fondant fancy.> 2001 May 10 *London Review of Books* 39/3.

chemist's (shop) Pharmacy; drug store <Perhaps one of you could drop this prescription in at the **chemist's**.> 1986 Hardwick 90.

confectioner's (shop) Candy store <Laverne stepped out of a **confectioner's** in Low Petergate.> 1995 Bowker 29.

(green)grocer's Grocery; supermarket <. . . saw me at the **grocer's** with a long list.> 1985 Townsend 306. <. . . there's a **greengrocer's** in West End Lane that's even open on Sundays.> 1989 Sept. 13 *Evening Standard* 29/1.

ironmonger's Hardware store <Shout if there's an **ironmonger's**.> 1986 Gash 212.

newsagent's (shop) Newsstand <Loretta . . . remembered that the **newsagent's shop** was in the opposite direction.> 1993 Smith 45.

tobacconist's (shop/store) Cigar store <The two youths . . . started shopping for knives in a **tobacconist's store**.> 1997 Dec. 12 *Evening Standard* 5/1.

Sometimes, however, the shop term may lack the genitive apostrophe or even the *s*.

<The **ironmongers** . . . have sold out to yet another boutique.> 1989 Mar. 19 *Manchester Guardian Weekly* 23/2. <. . . **confectioners, tobacconists** and **newsagents**, specialist food shops and traditional hardware shops [will be] among the losers over the next five years.> 1989 Aug. 28 *Daily Telegraph* 3/2–3. <Sam Langford drove his Jag slowly past chip shops, launderettes and tired **greengrocers**.> 1991 Critchley 177. <In the end his mother fixed him up with a job in a Cambridge **ironmongers**.> 1993 Feb. 27 *Times* Saturday Review 46/5. <Family doctors will be able to set up lunch-hour surgeries in high street **chemists** under radical proposals to be announced by the Government this month.> 1999 Mar. 13 *Times* 1/4.

<Anyway in the **newsagent**, I happened to glance at some of those, er . . . you know, those things they have in there.> 1986 Brett 69. <In the main street were a supermarket and a fishmonger's, a dairy, a bakery, and a very basic **greengrocer**.> 1989 Graham 82. < . . . a long street of shops: supermarket, **chemist**, video shop, off-licence, wine bar, Chinese takeaway, Italian restaurant.> 1991 Barnard 146. <He sat like a lumpy Guy Fawkes in the doorway of a **tobacconist** in Southampton.> 1992 Walters 67. <Dolphin Square has its own shopping arcade, including an off-licence, a **dry cleaner**, a **hairdresser**, a **newsagent**, a **chemist** and a **grocer**.> 1993 Feb. 7 *Sunday Times* 2 7/4.

The lack of a genitive sign extends also to proper names for shops, although practice is inconsistent.

<**Fortnum's** or **Claridge's** or **Rolls Royce** or **White's** or **Harrods** aren't going to sue for a few hundred pounds.> 1967 Frost and Jay 192. <The battle between Yorkshire grocer **Hillards** and its would-be owner **Tesco** is descending into the realm of knocking copy. [¶] 'Quite untrue, quite ridiculous,' splutters **Hillard's** chairman Peter Hartley as he decries the **Tesco** arguments.> 1987 Apr. 4 *Daily Mail* 37/5. <The nylon cord . . . was of a type readily obtainable in . . . all branches of **Woolworths**.> 1983 Radley 28. <Imagine never prowling round **Woolworth's**.> 1985 Cannell 9.

4 Pronouns

4.1 Personal

In the first person, the use of *me* as a nonstandard form of *my* is doubtless the result of vowel reduction under low stress, with consequent confusion or merger of the vowels in the two words.

me My <Patrick, **me** boyo, we've had our break.> 1989 Quinton 37.
meself Myself: CIC has 7.8 iptmw in British texts, principally speech, but also written representations of speech, and only 0.5 in American texts. <I'd put **meself** in an old people's home just for the peace and quiet.> 1990 Critchfield (quoting TV's *EastEnders*) 83.

CGEL (6.18n) reports two uses of the first person plural that are British rather than American. (1) The "royal *we*" is said to be "virtually obsolete . . . traditionally used by a monarch, as in the following examples, both famous dicta by Queen Victoria: / *We* are not interested in the possibilities of defeat. / *We* are not amused." (2) A nonstandard use of plural *us* for singular *me* is exemplified by "Lend ***us*** a fiver." This use is also reported by Michael Swan (1995, 432): "In very informal British speech, *us* is quite often used instead of *me* (especially as an indirect object) / *Give* ***us*** *a kiss, love*." The contraction of *us* to *'s* in such constructions is an additional British feature. For the use of *our* with personal names, see § 2.3.3.

us Me <'Give'**s** a fag' said one [small boy].> 1995 June 8 *London Review of Books* 8/4. <Auditions are this morning. Pack **us** a pickle sandwich. I'm off to London.> 2003 July 4 *Times* T2 2/2.

Since the loss of the second person singular/plural distinction that *thou* and *ye* represented in earlier English, the language has been trying to fill the lacuna, generally by taking the originally plural *you* as a singular and constructing new plurals based on it. America has *youse*, a typically Northern, urban form and *you 'uns*, a Southern Mountain rural form – both uneducated. It also has *y'all*, a standard Southern form, which, though regionally marked, is socially unrestricted in Southern dialect and is a phonological variant of the universally standard *you all*. It tends to be used as a pronoun of solidarity to indicate that the speaker considers those so addressed as forming a community with the speaker. Hence it would not be used where formality or social distance is appropriate. A more recent colloquial form is *you guys*, applied to males, females, or mixed groups; it is younger generation in use but widespread in the United States and has spread to British use as well (Wales 1996, 73).

In addition to various dialect forms, some similar to those used in America (Wales 1996, 73), British has *you lot*, which is affectively marked: it often indicates annoyance or disdain or impatience with the referents. Occasionally, it is an affectionate form, although even then tinged with a tone of condescension. Because of their difference in emotional tone, the new British and American plural pronouns are by no means equivalent.

you lot CIC has 22.8 iptmw in British texts, principally speech, but also written representations of speech, and only 0.5 in American texts. <[student:] 'What about you? Are you writing anything?' [teacher:] 'No, not really,' I said. 'I've been too busy with **you lot**.'> 2001 Lodge 306.

A variant of *you lot* is *your lot*, which makes the form into a syntactically normal noun phrase.

your lot CIC has 5.8 iptmw in British texts, principally speech, but also written representations of speech. Some of the tokens, however, are noun phrases (e.g., "You have thrown in your lot with the forces of evil") so the actual number of pronoun uses is smaller. American uses are all of noun phrases. <**Your lot** [the police] frightened him off!> 1992 Granger 135.

Another variant is *you chaps*, which is a friendly option, close to American *you guys* in tone, though not in the typical age of its users. It is also rare and old-fashioned.

you chaps CIC has 1.3 iptmw in British texts, principally speech, but also fictional representations of speech. It has no American tokens. <**You chaps** don't believe in that.> 1988 Stoppard 70.

The following examples of abnormal gender concord of third-person pronouns are exceptional.

he It (a car): Personification of cars is not unusual, though feminine rather than masculine, and the object form is often contracted (*'er, 'im*). <Yes, I parked **him** [a car] outside the chip shop, and when I came out again, beggar me, **he**'d [the car had] gone!> 1994 Sept. 16 *Times* 39/1.

it They; he or she: Singular to agree with *one*, although plural *they* is frequent in such constructions; the neuter for a human referent is odd. <One in six **employers** said that **it** was not hiring any graduates this year and

almost 40 per cent had openings for 25 people or fewer.> 2003 July 16 *Times* 9/2.

its His: The neuter pronoun suggests a lack of human identity in the adolescents, who are thereby identified as objects rather than persons. <. . . social workers on shift work worry their guts out in case some runty adolescent with manipulative skills persuades another runty adolecent [sic] to stick a safety pin through **its** nostril.> 1989 July 21 *Punch* 43/2.

In common-core English, *it* is "used with many verbs and prepositions as a meaningless object <*run for* ~> <*footed* ~ *back to camp*>" (*LDEL*)). Particular tokens of this use, however, are variety-specific.

<Crookshanks [a cat] leapt lightly from the basket . . . and sprang onto Ron's knees. . . . [¶] 'Get out of **it**!'> 1999 Rowling 62 (*US ed.* Get out of here!).

The contraction of *it* with forms of *be* (*'tis, 'twas*) is called "now poet., arch., dial., or colloq." in the *OED*. CIC has 39.8 British iptmw of *'tis* and 17.9 of *'twas*, principally in written texts, especially literary ones, but also academic texts, where the forms generally occur in literary quotations. It has only 8.1 American iptmw of *'tis* and 1.4 of *'twas*. An example of its British dialect use follows.

<Why, **'tis** all over the town, Miss. . . . **'Twas** Bert Luke, the milkman, knocked [woke] me up.> 1981 Lemarchand 16.

The contraction is, however, sometimes a stylistic affectation in standard use.

<**'Tisn't** often an editor dares disagree with his proprietor.> 1987 Apr. 1 *Evening Standard* 6/3.

Pronoun order differs somewhat between British and American.

CIC has 287.2 iptmw of *them all* in British texts and 171 in American texts. It is preferred by 2 to 1 over *all of them* in British texts, but by only 1.2 to 1 in American texts.

<What's the matter with **them all** tonight?> 1940 Shute 89.

When two objects (direct and indirect) follow a verb, the indirect object comes before the direct object (*give the students a test*), unless it is preceded by a preposition, when it comes after the direct object (*give a test to the students*). When both objects are pronouns, those options are still available (*give them it* or *give it to them*), although American prefers the second as avoiding two sequential pronoun objects (indirect + direct), which is more typically British. A search in ICE-GB for the function-category combination "indirect object realized as a pronoun" followed immediately by "direct object realized as a pronoun" results in 110 examples, such as *Connie hadn't told* ***them that***.

<So – what are you going to do with it? Give **me it** back?> 1990 Hardwick 100.

However, British also uses the reverse order for two sequential pronoun objects (direct + indirect), as in *give it them* without a preposition (*CGEL* 10.17n, 18.38n; *CamGEL* 248n). This construction is foreign to American use. It seems to occur with a limited number of verbs, of which *give* is the most frequent.

<How I love hearing you talk Italian. . . . Will you teach **it me**?> 1931 Benson 154. <Made my will. . . . Show **it you**, if you like.> 1940 Shute 146. <Skynner finally got the order to give **them me** this morning.> 1995 Harris 240.

If the indirect object is a noun, but the direct object is a pronoun, as in *I gave **Kim it***, the prepositional option *I gave **it to Kim*** is generally favored, the first option being "inadmissible for most speakers, especially in AmE" (*CamGEL* 310).

Standard British English does not use the ethical dative (also called "dative of interest or advantage," Wales 1996, 88), as in such colloquial and lyrical American examples as *We've elected **us** a President, and now we're stuck with him* and *I'm gonna cry **me** a river*.

A noun phrase functioning as the direct object of a phrasal verb (verb and adverbial particle) can be ordered either before or after the particle: *send the letter off* or *send off the letter*. However, a pronoun in that function normally is ordered only before the particle: *send it off* but not **send off it*. Occasionally, however, the exceptional order occurs.

<Sylvia had **rung up me** . . . about booking for a meal.> 1992 spoken text CIC.

4.2 Impersonal

One in an impersonal sense is frequent in British use; it is less common in American, in which it is perceived as formal or mannered. The typical American options are *you* or various paraphrases. The line between a genuinely impersonal sense and self-reference (see below) is often difficult to draw, but some uses are genuinely impersonal in intention.

<"**One** doesn't say such things," you are told.> 1990 Hazleton 25.

The uses and history of impersonal *one* have been treated by Anne Seaton (2005) with evidence that the *one . . . he/him/his* construction, which had been common–core English, fell out of British after the seventeenth century but continues in American. In British use, *one* is repeated for coreference (*CGEL* 6.56; 10.50; 19.51): ***One** cannot control **one's** temper easily if **one** is discussing a matter over which **one** has feelings of guilt*. American prefers *he/him/his* for subsequent references (Johansson 1979, 198; Swan 1995, 394). Or, at least, American used to prefer the masculine pronoun in that use. Recent sensitivity to gender neutrality has promoted alternative expressions, including sometimes *one*, although Americans as a whole are uncomfortable with it.

<Nor is it difficult to drown **oneself** with a millstone round **one's** neck – if **one**'s intent on leaving behind **one** as much mystery and anxiety as possible.> 1959 Innes 49.

The impersonal use of *one* shades into a personal, first-person use that is characteristic of upper-class and intellectual usage, especially British, but very rare in American (Swan 1995, 394). Even in British English, this self-reference is often regarded amusedly or satirically. L. R. N. Ashley (personal letter, 27 June, 1990) noted such British response: "I like the Londoner who described *one* as 'the first person singular in Kensington and Chelsea.'"

<He [Sir John Tooley, General Director of the Royal Opera House] refers to himself as "**one**" (as in "**one's** parents used to take **one** to the opera when **one** was a child").> 1987 Feb. 12 *Evening Standard* 29/2. <Did Roy Jenkins really say, after winning the Oxford chancellorship at the weekend: "**One** is immensely pleased"? [¶] **One** can believe it. Mr Jenkins has long looked and sounded like a duke.> 1987 Mar. 16 *Evening Standard* 9/1. <On November 24th the queen made a rare appeal for sympathy, dubbing 1992 an *annus horribilis* (the *Sun's* translation: "**One**'s bum year").> 1992 Nov. 28 *Economist* 63/1.

4.3 Demonstrative

The basic semantic distinction between the demonstratives *this* and *that* is nearness versus distance. But nearness and distance are matters of perception rather than of physical measurement. American English thus tends to use *this* in contexts where British prefers *that*. Michael Swan (1995, 41 and 581) observes this/that national difference with respect to telephone language, in which Britons ask *Who is that?* and Americans *Who is this?* John Kahn and Robert Ilson (1985, 630) also comment that in many contexts it is possible to use either *this* or *that*, e.g., *This/That is true* and *This/That is the problem*; they also note that some people (presumably British) object "often with surprising strength of feeling" to *this*. (On *that* with a propredicate, cf. § 15.2.)

Extended forms of the demonstratives are *these ones* and *those ones*. Curiously, the only token of *these ones* in the text of the *OED* is in a 1934 citation (s.v. *jinx* v.) from the American writer J. T. Farrell. There are no tokens of *those ones*. CIC, however, has 7.2 iptmw of *these ones* in British, chiefly spoken, texts and 0.6 in American texts. On the other hand, it has 4.8 iptmw of *those ones* in British, also chiefly spoken, texts and 3.2 in American texts. It appears that *these ones* is more characteristic of British than of American English, but that the frequency of *those ones* is closer in the two national varieties.

<There are family photographs all over the house, and **these ones** are Susan's favourites.> 1993 Feb. 13 *Telegraph* magazine 66/1.

4.4 Relative

In standard English, *as* is used as a relative pronoun when it is preceded by *such* or *same* (Gilman 1994, 122: *such poor things as are our own* and *the same people as objected*). Otherwise, relative *as* is marginal, though it has both nonstandard and formulaic use in British. Some British uses appear to be jocularly Dickensian, especially in the formula *though X says it as shouldn't*. On one academic occasion (in April 1987), that formula was volunteered as an example of colloquial speech by Prof. John Honey: "He's a good lad, though I'm his father who says it **as** shouldn't."

as That, who <My friend has got some info **as'll** open your eyes all right.> 1972 Rendell 112–3. <'E's [He is] brother-in-law to one of the ambulance men **as** came.> 1981 Lemarchand 16.

Whose as a relative pronoun was relatively late in developing. An earlier option was *that* (or still earlier Anglo-Saxon *þe*) followed by a genitive personal pronoun, an option still occasionally used in standard English.

that + *genitive pronoun* Whose <[actor Simon Callow:] William Rees-Mogg is the kind of person **that** just **his** [whose very] existence depresses one.> 1990 Critchfield 306.

The use of *what* as a relative pronoun in place of *which, who*, or *that* is nonstandard in both British and American. It is sometimes used as a literary signal of nonstandard use, as in the following citation from a British soap. However, it is more common in conversation than the relative *as* (*LGSWE* 609).

what Which; that; who <I've got a mate turning up next week **what** owes me; then I'll be quids in.> 1986 Dec. BBC1 *EastEnders*.

In accord with the British tendency to treat collective nouns as animate plurals that take plural verb concord (cf. § 14), British also is more likely than American to use *who* as a relative with collective nouns.

who *with a collective noun as antecedent* That <But it was a subdued group **who** headed back to the fireside.> 1998 Rowling 52 (*US ed.* that).

In common-core English, a relative pronoun other than the subject may be lacking in a restrictive clause, thus *This is the book [which/that] I bought* but *This is the book which/that was sold*. British has some subjectless relative clauses that seem less likely in American use, such as the following.

< . . . how many people do you know **[who/that]** live in a baronial pile complete with butler?> 1991 Feb. 25 *Ms London* 10/3. <There was a letter [**which/that**] came from him the other day, wasn't there?> 1992 Granger 11.

Because objective case forms in English are limited to the first- and third-person personal pronouns and *who(m)*, it is inevitable that confusion in their use should arise on both sides of the Atlantic. Such common-core confusion can often be explained by the syntagmatic environment of the word. Occasionally, such a use emerges that is noteworthy, such as the following use of hypercorrect *whom*, illustrating that the quality papers also fumble: <Sylvia [Plath] and Ted [Hughes]. Even those **whom** have not so much as glanced at a stanza of their oeuvres have a powerful reaction to their names.> 2003 Nov. 8 *Times* 31/1.

The relative pronouns *which* and *that* have variable uses (Gilman 1994, 894–5). In descriptive (i.e., nonrestrictive) relative clauses, *which* is normal: *"Hamlet," which I saw last night* . . . but **"Hamlet," that I saw last night*. . . . On the other hand, either pronoun is normal in restrictive relative clauses: *the play that/which I saw last night* . . . . Writers who recommend usage often aim for a neater complementarity and therefore recommend the sole or primary use of *that* in restrictive clauses to balance the use of *which* in descriptive clauses. The facts, however, are otherwise, as Ward Gilman has shown.

Nevertheless, it is possible that the recommendations of usage writers have been more effective in American than in British English. Or it may be that American is in this respect more conservative than British because *that* is older as a relative than *which*. In any case, restrictive *which* is more frequent in British than American. British news uses restrictive *which* 3 times more often than American news does; and in conversation, American uses restrictive *that* about twice as often as British does (*LGSWE* 616).

<We were both members of a club **which** meets in Caroline Dupayne's flat.> 2003 James 362.

Paul Heacock and Carol-June Cassidy (1998, 95) report their experience in adapting a British dictionary to an American version:

> We noted a number of words and phrases that were perfectly acceptable in American English, but which were used with such abandon in British English that they in fact marked the text as being British. Words like *which*. . . . Americans very often use *that* to introduce restrictive clauses. Writers and speakers of British English use *which* to introduce just about any clause they want to, restrictive or nonrestrictive. So in CIDE [*Cambridge International Dictionary of English*] the definition for *gold*, for instance, reads "a soft, yellow, heavy, metallic element **which** is quite rare and very valuable," whereas in CDAE [*Cambridge Dictionary of American English*] it's "a soft, yellow metal that is highly valued."

4.5 Interrogative

The use of *how?* in the sense "what?" occurs in both British and American. The *OED* documents the interrogative use from 1382 and the exclamatory use from even earlier, and calls both archaic, but has examples of *How do you mean* from Sheridan (1777), Thackeray (1849), and Wodehouse (1942). In the expression *What/How do you mean*, CIC British texts use *How* in 10.9 percent of the tokens; American texts use it in 3.9 percent.

<**How** d'you mean?> 2003 James 201.

4.6 Indefinite

For indefinite pronouns referring to persons, English has a choice between compounds with *-body* (*anybody, everybody, nobody, somebody*) and with *-one* (*anyone, everyone, no one, someone*). One study (*LGSWE* 352) reports that, in fictional texts, British strongly prefers the compounds in *-one* over those in *-body* (*anyone* 4:1, *everyone* 2.3:1, *no-one* nearly 2:1, *someone* 3:1) and that American is more equally divided, with a slight preference (11:9) for *anyone*, *everyone*, and *someone*, but a reverse preference (11:9) for *nobody*. CIC texts, however, show little overall difference between British and American preference for forms with *-one* over those with *-body*: 1.79 to 1.73, respectively, nor are there striking differences for any of the individual compounds with *any-*, *every-*, *no-*, or *some-*.

The *OED* has 483 tokens of *one or other* in its text and only 28 tokens of *one or another*. CIC British texts have 24.5 iptmw of *one or other*, nearly 6 times as many as of *one or another*. American texts have only 0.5 iptmw of *one or other*, but more than 12 times that many of *one or another*. Cf. § 2.5.2 ONE OR OTHER.

<And ahead of me along the road were three cottages, no doubt once tied to **one or other** of the various farms in the area.> 1991 Barnard 196.

Several distinctively British forms exist among indefinite pronouns. Most of them are marginal, being limited stylistically or regionally.

a bit A little; something: The form *bit*, in all of its uses, is half again as frequent in the British LOB corpus as in the American Brown corpus (Hofland and Johansson 1982, 478). CIC has 2.7 times as many tokens of *a bit* in British texts as in American. <. . . you still put by **a bit** each week to ensure you could pay for a decent funeral.> 2003 James 12.

fuck all Nothing at all: CIC British texts have 2.7 iptmw of this expression, most in this sense; American texts have none in this sense. <He knows **fuck all** about it.> 1989 Drabble 176.

no-one *spelling variant* No one: In the BNC, *no-one* outranks *no one* by 3:2 (Peters 2004, 375); the hyphenated spelling is rare and nonstandard in American. CIC shows the same difference in national preference, although not the same British preference for *no-one*. It has, in British written texts, 645.5 iptmw of *no one*, 149.1 of *no-one*, and 2.5 of *noone*, and in American written texts, 849.3 iptmw of *no one*, 3.2 of *no-one*, and .03 of *noone*. Thus both national varieties prefer *no one*, but British has *no-one* as a strong alternative and *noone* as a weak option. American hardly uses the other two forms at all.

nowt *Northern form of* naught; nothing: CIC British texts have 28.2 iptmw of this form; American texts have none. <. . . the three monkeys were see **nowt**, hear **nowt**, and say **nowt**.> 1988 Ashford 40.

summat *Northern form of* somewhat; something: CIC British texts have 49.4 iptmw of this form; American texts have none. <Do you want to know **summat** else?> 1981 Dexter 130.

4.7 Expletive

The two main expletive pronouns are *it* and *there*. Certain uses of expletive *it* are common-core English, such as <. . . **it** was not done to ask him questions.> 1986 Dec. 9 *Times* 12/2. The only thing slightly British about that clause is the use of *done* in the sense "socially acceptable." But other uses, in which *it* can be replaced by *there*, are characteristically British.

it There (or a paraphrase with the notional subject as grammatical subject) <[speaker from Leeds:] Aye, . . . it's quiet enough now but **it** were quite a do at weekend round Chapeltown.> 1985 Ebdon 145. <[Eddie, twenty-one, of Liverpool:] **It**'s no one's to blame.> 1990 Critchfield 208. <[cartoon of two elderly ladies scraping ice off a TV:] Keep scraping – **it**'s the weather forecast in a minute.> 1991 Feb. 5 *Daily Telegraph* 1/7.

Verb concord with expletive *there* is variable in both British and American, so it is hard to identify a distinctive use in either variety. The following examples show variation from alternative patterns.

there 1. *with a singular verb and a plural noun* <. . . **there was families** at the pit who traced their connection with coal back to the last century.> 1989 Sept. 7 *Midweek* 32/1. 2. *with a singular verb and a singular quantifier for a plural noun* <**There is a further five bedrooms and a second bathroom.**> 1986 Aug. 21 *Hampstead Advertiser* 40/2. 3. *with a plural verb and a plural noun of measurement* <In London, for instance, **there have been three inches of rainfall** this month.> 1987 June 22 *Times* 1/4.

A colloquial and dialect construction consists of the expletive *there's* followed by an adjective, a subject and verb, and an optional complement to the adjective (*There's sorry I am to hear it*), which is the equivalent of the subject and verb followed by the adjective and its complement (*I am sorry to hear it*). The construction focuses the adjective.

there's <You two had a lot on your minds, but **there's glad** I am I remembered.> 1987 Oliver 217.

An unusual construction is illustrated by expletive *that* in the following example, for which *there* could be substituted.

that There <But Malloch is positively an *Ober-Gott*. Better brain. . . . [¶] But that's not all **that**'s to Malloch.> 1937 Innes, *Hamlet* 182.

A catch-phrase pattern is *there* PRONOUN *BE*, as in *there you are* and *there it is* (*OED* s.v. *there* adv. 16). This catch phrase comments on a state of affairs regarded as inevitable and therefore to be accepted: <c 1921 D. H. Lawrence *Mr. Noon* viii, in *Mod. Lover* (1934) 266 It's just like him – but **there you are**. Those that won't be ruled can't be schooled.> *OED* s.v. *rule* v. 1b. Or it is used in presenting someone with something desired or calling attention to a completed matter: <1925 J. Metcalfe *Smoking Leg* 26 **There you are**, old horse; don't say I never did you a good turn> *OED* s.v. *horse*, n. 4. The American equivalent might be *Here you are*. Cf. § 6.1 THERE WE/YOU ARE.

<"But **there one is**, alone. . . . Well, **there it is**," with which philosophy she went down to breakfast.> 1942 Thirkell 5.

4.8 Case

British and American do not differ substantively in their use of subject and object case forms of pronouns. In both national varieties, the prescribed forms are often more honored in the breach (Gilman 1994, s.v. *pronouns* and the other lemma cited there). How acceptable the following proscribed forms are in actual use varies according to the form. Some are normal in both British and American; others would be rare in standard use in either variety. But use of the objective form of pronouns where the nominative is prescribed seems to be more accepted in Britain than in America, where copyediting often corrects that use.

The norm in both varieties favors the object form in *It's me* and *She's as tall as me*. As Michael Swan (1995, 435–6) observed, the subject form is "extremely formal" and "is usually considered over-correct (especially in British English)." Fewer British voices than American ones are raised in protest against such forms.

<Most of his friends were older than **him**.> 1986 May 21 *Sun* 8. <They were as puzzled as **me**.> 1989 July 21 *Private Eye* 13 (a letter from Ivan Fallon, deputy editor of the *Sunday Times*).

Other constructions, however, are less normal. Katie Wales (1996, 100) cites British use of the objective form of pronouns, under certain circumstances, even in the subject function. Other examples:

<"Only **us** can save this country!" perorated an excited lady delegate, making one glad the Liberals were not yet running the nation's schools.> 1989 Sept. 14 *Daily Telegraph* 38/7. <Asked if he had tried to keep his marriage vows . . . [Prince Charles] replied: 'Yes, . . . until it became irretrievably broken down – **us** both having tried'.> 1994 June 30 *Evening Standard* p n/a.

Use of the subject form where the object form is prescribed is less frequent and largely restricted to particular contexts: especially when *I* follows a coordinating conjunction or when a personal pronoun is next to a word like *who*, which attracts the pronoun into the subject form.

<Everything Comes To **He** Who Waits.> 1987 Mar. 2 *London Daily News* 4.

5 Adjectives

British and American use of adjectives shows little systematic variation between the two varieties. Most of the differences are associated with particular lexical forms.

5.1 Derivation

The adjectival use of other parts of speech, with or without derivational affixes, is common in English. Some particular examples, however, are indicative of Britishness.

5.1.1 From nouns + -ed

British and American differ in their use of the suffix *-ed* to form adjectival modifiers from nominals. British uses certain forms that American does not, such as *booted*. But differences between British and American use of individual items are less significant than the apparent over-all more frequent British use of the pattern. There are, to be sure, exceptions such as *teenage(d)*. In CIC, 1 percent of the British tokens are *teenaged* and 99 percent are *teenage*, whereas 4 percent of the American tokens are *teenaged* and 96 percent are *teenage*. It would be difficult to ascertain the frequency of all denominal *-ed* forms in the two varieties, but on the whole it seems to be greater in British.

aged ***number*** For this construction, American might have simply the number, e.g., *20*, or such expansions of it as *20 years old* or *20 years of age* or even *age 20*, depending on the syntactic use of the construction. **1**. As an appositive: *Number* (years old, years of age), age *number* < . . . the would-be robber hit Mr Paul Harry, **aged** 23, over the head with his gun and made off.> 1989 July 28 *Times* 2/2. **2**. As a subject complement: *Number* (years old, years of age) <His father was on the staff of the castle and he was **aged** 13 at the time.> 1989 Aug. 29 *Times* 15/4. 3. As a complement of *described as*: *Number* (years old, years of age) <The raider is described as **aged** about 30.> 1987 Feb. 5

Hampstead Advertiser 7/5. **4**. As a post-head modifier: Of *number* (years old, years of age), of age *number* <The pair **aged** about 40 entered by the unlocked back door.> 1993 Feb. 3 *Times* 4/7. **5**. As an adverbial: At *number* (years old, years of age), at age *number* <Rudolf Hess, Hitler's former deputy, died **aged** 93.> 1987 Oct. *Illustrated London News* 20/2.

Other predominantly British *noun* + *-ed* adjectives are the following, some of which have no precise American equivalent:

alarmed Protected with an alarm <Spotted on a swanky, burglar-proofed BMW in a London street: "This car **alarmed** by Mike Wells car stereo systems."> 1989 Aug. 10 *Times* 12/1.

badged Decorated in a way indicating status: CIC has 2.0 iptmw in British texts and 0.4 in American texts. <Bruno Lazlo's office was . . . plumply furnished and **badged** with the symbols of mild success in the film business.> 1976 Raphael 154.

bedded, double/two- With two beds: CIC has no American tokens. <The master bedroom is a **double bedded** room.> 1988 Sept. *In Britain* 46/3. <I was back in the **two-bedded** room.> 1995 Lodge 11.

bedroom(ed), ***number-*** *Number* bedroom: With the numbers *one, two*, and *three*, CIC British texts have 43.5 iptmw of *number(-)bedroom* and 13.9 of *number(-)bedroomed*; American texts have only *number bedroom* (58.7 iptmw). <Roger and Jennifer Crawford lived . . . in a modern four-**bedroomed** house.> 2003 James 52.

bibbed overalls Overalls (American overalls usually have a bib, so the combination would be redundant.) <The one in the **bibbed overalls**.> 1989 Wainwright 137.

booted With a car trunk; having space at the rear of a car to carry luggage or other things <. . . the next generation Ford Escort, and its **booted** sister model, the Orion.> 1990 Aug. 24 *Times* 33/1.

branded Brand name: CIC has 18.6 iptmw of *brand name* in British texts and 44.7 in American texts. It has 68.4 iptmw of *branded* in all senses (including "with a brand name") in British texts and 34.0 in American texts. <**Branded** Label Fashion / Less than Half Price> 1990 Aug. 23, sign outside clothing shop, Green Street, Oxford.

breeze-blocked Cement block <Inside the **breeze-blocked** houses, the sparse furniture and personal belongings have been left untouched.> 1986 Aug. 30 *Times* 1/4.

bricked <. . . she walked slowly . . . before arriving at a row of two-storey, yellow-**bricked**, newish properties.> 1992 Dexter 85.

buttoned <Barbara . . . was lying on one of the twin **buttoned** chesterfields.> 1976 Raphael 260.

capped, flat- <Every Sunday more than 17 million fans watch actor Richard Wilson, left, play **flat-capped** moaning groaner Meldrew.> 1993 Feb. 12 *Sun* 11/2.

ceilinged, low-/high- CIC has 5.8 iptmw of *low-* or *high-ceilinged* in British texts and 3.2 in American texts. <The **low-ceilinged** living-room would have been a good setting for a more fey, more folk-tale-type figure than Freya.> 1985 Mann 24.

corded CIC has 3.1 iptmw of *corded* (in various senses) in British texts and 1.1 in American texts. <. . . a convenient convertible **corded**/cordless model [iron].> 1989 Aug. 5 *Times* Review 41/4.

crewed (Of a bus) with a driver and a conductor; (of a boat) with a crew: CIC has 21 tokens of *crewed* as an attributive adjective in a random sample of a thousand British texts, and 2 tokens in a similar sample of American texts. <There may still be scope for **crewed** buses in the centre.> 1987 Feb. 18 *Evening Standard* 31/6. <Sometimes six to 10 people hire a **crewed** boat for three days.> 1987 Feb. 23 *Evening Standard* 19/3–4.

flagged Flagstone: CIC has 24 tokens of *flagged* in the sense "paved with flagstones" in a random sample of a thousand British texts, and 19 tokens of *flagstone* as an attributive adjective. It had no such tokens of *flagged* and 14 of *flagstone* in similar American texts. <Access to the dustbins was by a **flagged** path.> 1987 Hart 77.

footed, left-/right- CIC has 8.0 iptmw of *left-* or *right-footed* in British texts and 0.7 in American texts. < . . . when a shipload of desperately needed footwear arrived it was discovered that the hold was filled with **left-footed** boots.> 1983 Brooke-Taylor 113.

garaged, double- With double garages < . . . the powerful commercial developer wanting to build **double-garaged** executive houses . . . gets the planning permission.> 1989 Aug. 13 *Sunday Times* Magazine 43/4.

gravelled Gravel: CIC British texts have 3.1 iptmw of *gravelled*; American texts have 0.6 of *graveled*. <A **gravelled** drive ran up one side of a curved lawn and down the other.> 1980 Sharpe 70.

haired, golden- CIC has 2.2 iptmw in British texts and 1.0 in American texts.

headed, swollen- Big-headed: CIC has 0.2 iptmw of *swollen-headed* in the sense "conceited" in British texts and 0.4 of *big-headed* in the same sense in American texts.

holed Holey; with holes in them <I had noticed the dirty sweater and **holed** jeans.> 1969 Amis 52.

iced Ice (water); cold (drink): CIC has 1.4 iptmw of *iced water* and 0.8 of *ice water* in British texts and none of *iced water* and 6.0 of *ice water* in American texts. <Nor do I always relish American drinking habits with meals: . . . **iced** water and weak coffee.> 1991 Feb. 16 *Daily Telegraph* Weekend 7/3.

lavatoried, *number-* *Number*-bathroom <. . . the five-bedroomed, **four-lavatoried**, neo-Georgian house.> 1988 Lodge 160.

lensed <Hardinge took a pair of half-**lensed** spectacles from their case.> 1992 Dexter 172.

minded, bloody- Uncooperative: CIC has 3.5 iptmw in British texts and 0.8 in American. However, the American sense is "inclined to violence or bloodshed."

<. . . the boatmen were being "**bloody minded**" and didn't see why they should pay the government anything for the right to fish.> 1989 July 22 *Times* 53/3–4.

nosed, snub- CIC has 1.5 iptmw in British texts and 0.6 in American. In addition, all British tokens except one refer to facial features; all American tokens refer to revolvers.

parqueted Parquet <He left the cadet at the urn and came across the **parqueted** floor.> 1987 Hart 45.

patterned, check- <He . . . thought he recognized someone . . . dressed in grey flannels and a **check-patterned** sports coat.> 1981 Dexter 95.

polo-necked Turtleneck <Barbara, wearing . . . a white **polo-necked** sweater, was lying on one of the . . . chesterfields.> 1976 Raphael 260.

receipted <We have a system where drivers are not paid for the trip unless they can produce a **receipted** document signed at the proper waste-tipping site.> 1988 Dec. 30 *Independent* 3.

resourced <The . . . medical and scientific fronts are seriously under-**resourced** and under-manned.> 1986 Dec. 10 *Times* 14/7.

roomed, *number*- *Number*-room: With the numbers *one, two*, and *three*, CIC has 1.4 iptmw of *number-roomed* and 6.7 of *number-room* in British texts. It has no tokens of *number-roomed* and 18.4 of *number-room* in American texts. <They . . . moved together into a one-**roomed** flat in their second year.> 1990 Byatt 11.

sized, similar- Similar-size; of similar size: CIC has 1.3 iptmw of *similar-sized* in British texts and 1.0 tokens in American texts. *Similar size* is used attributively in 7 percent of its British occurrences and in 12 percent of its American ones. <And because the houses are often freehold, there are none of the service charges associated with **similar-sized** flats.> 1987 Mar. 11 *Evening Standard* 21/3.

springed, sagging- With sagging springs <Nonie Anholt sat down on a **sagging-springed** sofa.> 1985 Mann 49.

storeyed, *number*- *Number*-story: Forms like *three-stor(e)y* are dominant in both varieties. However, CIC has 2.0 iptmw of the *-ed* form in British texts and none in American texts. <The amalgamation . . . had the advantage of giving the Shaws a well-appointed, three-**storied** house in a smart part of Dublin.> 1988 Holroyd 28.

suited, *x-type* In an *x-type* suit <The visitor . . . will within encounter a number of three-piece **suited** figures . . . talking loudly about money.> 1987 Apr. 6 *Guardian* 12/2.

tarmacked CIC has 1.3 iptmw of *tarmacked* in British texts and none in American texts, which use forms like *tarmac road*. <Dalgliesh drove down a **tarmacked** drive so narrow that two cars would have difficulty in passing.> 2003 James 14.

terraced (house) Row house: CIC British texts have 12.4 iptmw of *terraced house* and none of *row house*; American texts have 0.3 of *terraced house* (in fiction set in England) and 5.3 of *row house*. <She was . . . born in a two-storey **terraced** house in a narrow street in Stepney.> 2003 James 49.

turfed Sodded: CIC has no American tokens of *turfed* "covered with turf" and no British tokens of *sodded* "covered with sod." <Fully fitted kitchens with fridge freezer, . . . **turfed** lawns, garage and security system.> 1988 Apr. 10 *Sunday Telegraph* 41/6.

unstepped Without steps; on the same level <Exhibition continues / For **unstepped** access please retrace your route past the entrance and follow signage> 2002 Feb. 18 sign at Hayward Gallery, South Bank, London.

waisted CIC has 1.6 iptmw of *waisted* "having a waist" in British texts and none in American texts. <. . . looking like a schoolmaster in his **waisted**, off-the-peg suits, Neil Kinnock grabs every opportunity to be snapped in his weekend wear.> 1987 June 1 *Evening Standard* 26/2.

wheeled, *number-* *Number*-wheel: For combinations of *two, three*, or *four* with *wheel(ed)*, CIC British texts have 27 percent with *wheeled*; American texts have 13 percent. <Beside him was a mother with a swaddled baby in a three-**wheeled** pram.> 2003 James 23.

zipped Provided with a zipper: CIC has 40 tokens of this meaning in 95 randomly selected examples of the form in British texts and 2 tokens (from a single text about couture) in 95 such American examples. <The cover is **zipped** for easy removal to facilitate cleaning.> 1989 Sept. 7 *Times* 13/6–8.

5.1.2 From place names + -an

The use of adjectival forms of certain place names as attributives of nouns is British. In all the following examples (mainly US state names), American English would have the place names themselves as noun adjuncts (*California, India, Oklahoma, Texas, Virginia*). This British use of adjectives for place-name modifiers is in contrast with the British use of some nation-name noun adjuncts (§ 3.3.1.1.2).

Californian In 154 randomly selected examples of *Californian* from British texts, CIC has 119 tokens in which *California* would be possible in American use. In a similar sample of the same size from American texts, it has 32 tokens of *Californian* in contexts in which *California* would also be possible. <. . . the **Californian** student Jeannie.> 1991 Lodge 55.

Indian ink India ink: CIC has 2.6 iptmw of *Indian ink* in British texts (none in American) and 0.3 of *India ink* in American texts (none in British). <yes, think of a woman in a house of net / that strains the oxygen out of the air / thickening the night to **Indian ink**.> 1995 Stoppard 11.

Oklahoman <He levered trees of 18ft or so into a removal van and drove off into the west as purposefully as any **Oklahoman** pioneer.> 1991 Feb. 9 *Telegraph Weekend Magazine* 51/1.

Serbian Serb: A corpus-based study (Peters 2004, 493) reports adjectival *Serbian* to be more than twice as frequent as *Serb* in British texts, but the reverse in American, in which *Serb* is especially collocated with military and *Serbian* with nonmilitary terms.

Texan <Here in Wimbledon our borough council promises us a hideous **Texan-**style shopping precinct on the site of our town hall.> 1987 May 28 *Evening Standard* 41/4. CIC has no tokens of *Texan-style* but 0.7 iptmw of *Texas(-)style* in American texts. <Fortunately for Britain the Ambassador of the United States at the Court of St James is Mr Henry Catto, a highly respected and very able **Texan** oil millionaire.> 1989 July 19 *Times* 9/6. CIC has no tokens of *Texan millionaire* but 0.2 iptmw of *Texas millionaire* in American texts.

Virginian <. . . Pat Robertson, the other **Virginian** preacher who is vulgar enough to say he will run for President next year.> 1987 Apr. 6 *Guardian* 21/2.

5.1.3 From verbs and predicates

beaten-up Beat-up: CIC has 1.0 iptmw of *beaten-up* and 1.3 of *beat-up* in British texts. It has 0.8 of *beaten-up* and 6.6 of *beat-up* in American texts. <. . . the only way [television] can ensure a character's individuality is to burden him with a tic, deface him with a quirk – . . . Rockford's **beaten-up** trailer.> 1974 Potter 15.

drink-drive CIC has 3.5 iptmw of adjectival *drink-drive* in British texts and none in American. <Eastenders star Pam St Clement says her life has been turned into a nightmare because of her character's **drink-drive** shame in the soap. . . . Pam backs the plot because it highlights **drink-drive** dangers.> 1993 Feb. 12 *Sun* 3/4. Cf § 3.3.1.1 DRINK.

have-a-go hero This use is of an expanded predicate (§ 13) as an adjectival. CIC has 1.8 iptmw in British texts and none in American texts. <Footie boss is **have-a-go hero**> 2004 May 29 sign in Hereford concerning a football manager who foiled a crime.

laden Loaded: CIC has 36.3 iptmw of *laden* in British texts and 20.9 in American texts. <Here, I think fondly of the driver of a police coach **laden** with prisoners who rammed a bit of the Old Bailey.> 1987 Apr. 14 *Evening Standard* 7/2.

lock-up garage Locked garage; garage with a lock <Neville Dupayne has been burnt to death in his Jag in a **lock-up garage** at the museum.> 2003 James 124.

sawn-off Sawed-off: CIC has 5.4 iptmw of *sawn-off* and none of *sawed-off* in British texts. It has none of *sawn-off* and 5.2 of *sawed-off* in American texts. In both cases, the main collocation is with *shotgun*. <Years ago, a good villain would cross the pavement with a **sawn-off** shotgun to rob a bank.> 1994 Sept. *Tatler* 147/1.

shaming Shameful <It's too **shaming** to retire to bed alone before midnight, but really, she's almost had enough.> 2001 Drabble 87.

unladen Unloaded; empty: CIC has 2.1 iptmw in British texts and none in American texts. <This contributed to the accident, and the effect was increased by . . . the fact that the lorry was **unladen**.> 1986 Oct. 11 *Times* 3/6.

5.1.4 From adverbs

all-round All-around: Of the options, CIC British texts have 99 percent *all-round*; American texts have 56 percent. <1958 *New Statesman* 6 Dec. 802/3 An excellent **all-round** performance by the Guildford Repertory Company.> *OED* s.v. *all round* C. Cf. §§ 6.1 ALL-ROUND, ROUND and 8.1 ROUND.

early days In adverbial use, *early days* is well established in British use (§ 6.1). It has little American use as either adjective or adverb. <In spite of the inevitable **early days** hiccups, I think we've done it.> 1989 Sept. 12 *Evening Standard* 29/4.

down for "on the list to enter (e.g., a race or school)" (*LDEL*); American has a similar but distinct use: "being on record <you're down for two tickets>" (*MW*). <My name was **down for** Eton.> 1998 Rowling 73.

on – be on about *something* Go (on and) on about: In CIC British texts, the verb that most often collocates with *on about (something)* is *be*, occurring in hundreds of tokens. The second most frequent is *go* (which is the most frequent in American texts); others in British use include *bang, blather, bleat, dream, drone, gibber, gush, harp, jabber, moan, mope, mumble, nag, prattle, rabbit, rabble, rave, run, scream, spout, start, waffle, wank, whine*, and *yammer*. In CIC American texts, *be on about* occurs in only about 5 tokens. <What are you **on about**?> 1997 Rowling 193 (*US ed.* talking about). **– be on at *someone*** "*Brit. informal* nag or grumble at someone" (*NODE*). <1952 A. Baron *With Hope, Farewell* 94 Well, now the second one**'s on at** him to get married.> *OED* s.v. *on* adv. 11.b. **– not on** "**on** *adj . . . chiefly Br informal* possible, practicable – usu negative *<you can't refuse, it's just **not** ~>*" (*LDEL*). <1975 *Guardian* 20 Jan. 4/3 Reductions in the standard of living were **not on**.> *OED* s.v. *on* adv. 13.f.

5.1.5 From adjectives and nouns + -ish

Adjectives are freely and spontaneously formed by adding *-ish* to adjectives, nouns, and a few other forms.

-ish <It was a **biggish** bit of wooded country, surrounded by a wire fence.> 2001 Lodge 39. Also *1850-ish, 1930ish, bitterish, bluntish, boffinish, C. P. Snow-ish, cheapish, donnish, dullish, earlyish, elevenish, fastish, flattish, fullish, good-ish, grayish, Greek-ish, highish, Kandinsky-ish, largeish, latish, live-ish, longish, lowish, Mod-ish, more-ish, newish, oddish, poorish, quaintish, quietish, Rightish,* *school-dinnerish, sharpish, shortish, Sloaneish, slowish, slummish, smallish, smartish, softish, stuntish, thinnish, Thirties-ish, toughish, yellowish, youngish*, etc.

5.1.6 With the suffix -making

Adjectives are formed with *-making* suffixed chiefly to other adjectives and nouns.

-making <. . . what a **blush-making** time that poor fellow must have had during rehearsals.> 2005 Jan. 14 *Daily Telegraph* 24/4. Also *anxiety-making, cringe-making, giddy-making, mad-making, programme-making, safe-making, shy-making, sick-making, squirm-making*, etc.

5.2 Frequency and collocation

Sometimes the difference between British and American adjectives is in their frequency or collocational probabilities.

away *attributive adjective* Visiting (of a sports team or fan): The sports use of *away* (contrasting with *home*) in reference to a game played on the opponent's grounds is common-core English. But its American use is primarily in collocation with *game*. CIC has 2.5 iptmw of *away game* in American texts and 8.3 in British texts. British use also combines *away* with many other nouns, such as *defeat, defence, enclosure, fan, fixture, form, goal, ground, kit, leg, match, performance, point, record, setback, side, strip, success, supporter, team, ticket, trip, victory*, and *win*. British use of adjectival *away* is both more frequent and wider in collocation than American use. <Luton Town, who tried . . . banning **away fans**, are planning . . . to accommodate **away supporters** at the Oak Road end.> 1990 Aug. 17 *Daily Telegraph* 30/1–2.

bloody *Bloody* is the all-purpose British vulgarism, though it has lost the power to shock that G. B. Shaw relied on for comic effect in *Pygmalion*. A contemporary lexicographer would be unlikely to label its use as "foul language," as the *OED* did; more recent dictionaries call it "slang" or "slightly rude." The word is of grammatical interest for the variety of syntactic functions it fills: adjective, interposed adjective, adverb (§ 6.1), qualifier (§ 7.1), and interjection (§ 10). **1.** *attributive* <. . . many of the **bloody** kids and their parents are Scots or Geordies on their annual hols.> 1989 Mar. 5 *Manchester Guardian Weekly* 5/1. – **Bloody Monday** An October 19, 1987, precipitous drop in the stock market. **2.** *interposed* An interposed word or other structure is one used in the middle of a syntactic structure or set expression (*brand* ***goddam*** *new* or *West* ***by God*** *Virginia*). James McMillan (1980) has treated this phenomenon with both British and American examples. A favorite British interposed word is *bloody*. < . . . and the investigation of a possible crime committed perhaps a year earlier in either Blenheim Park or Wytham Woods or where **bloody** ever . . . was not going to be the number-one priority.> 1992 Dexter 184.

cheeky This adjective is almost 9 times more frequent in CIC British texts than in American ones. <He may be trying to shake off his **cheeky-**chappie image.> 2003 June 19 *Times* 6/4.

cracking nick, in The usual expression in British English is *in good nick*, that is, "in good condition." <The hotel's turn-of-the-century features are, says McCarthy, "**in cracking nick**".> 1994 Sept. 24 *Guardian Weekend* 77/4.

last/next but + ***number*** *ordinal adj. or postdeterminer* (Swan 1995, 101). If we take the *OED*'s evidence as typical, it appears that *last but* and *next but* are used primarily by lexicographers. The text of the *OED* has 11 tokens of *last but* in this use, of which 8 are from *OED* definitions and 1 is in a quoted definition from an eighteenth-century dictionary. Of the 2 remaining tokens, 1 appears to be an invented example: <*Mod*. . . . He is **last but** one in the class> *OED* s.v. *but* C.2. A typical example from a definition is "antepenult . . . Preceding the penult; the **last but** two." By contrast, the *MW* definition of the same term is "the next to the last member of a series; *esp* : the next to the last syllable of a word." *Next but* is similar. Of 7 tokens, 4 are in *OED* definitions and 1 in a quoted definition. A typical definition is "meta . . . Characterized by or relating to (substitution at) two carbon atoms separated by one other in a benzene ring; at a position **next but** one to some (specified) substituent in a benzene ring." The corresponding *MW* definition is "involving substitution at or characterized by two positions in the benzene ring that are separated by one carbon atom."

effing CIC has 2.6 iptmw in British texts and none in American texts. <Double entendres? But that's meant to be the Sun and Mirror's stock in trade. Fleet Street can be a confusing place. I rest my **effing** case.> 1999 Mar. 17 *Evening Standard* 63/5. (Cf. § 7.1.)

obliged ***to do something*** Obligated *to do something*: The adjectival use of *obliged* (usually with an infinitive complement) is much more frequent than *obligated* in British English; in American they are used about equally (Peters 2004, 387). CIC has 170.9 iptmw of *obliged to* and 1.9 of *obligated to* in British texts. It has 37.8 of *obliged to* and 28.7 of *obligated to* in American texts. <. . . as I'm against the Gulf War I'm not morally **obliged** to send food parcels to the troops.> 1991 Feb. 15 *Evening Standard* 25/1.

opposite Across; on the other side, e.g., of the road (Swan 1995, 397). <Uncle Vernon, waving at Mrs Number Seven **opposite**, who was glaring from behind her net curtains.> 2003 Rowling 10 (*US ed.* [deleted]).

proper Complete, real: CIC has 583.9 iptmw in British texts and 359.5 in American texts. <I'm in charge of the case for months, and then Morse here comes along and solves it in a fortnight. Made me look a **proper** Charley, if you ask me.> 1979 Dexter 224.

right *intensifier* Real <I shall look a **right** pig's ear.> 1991 Graham 33. – **right one** "*Brit. informal* a silly or foolish person" (*NODE*). Cf. also § 7 RIGHT.

ruddy *euphemism for* BLOODY: CIC has 21.4 iptmw of *ruddy* in all senses in British texts and 6.0 in American texts. <All right, your kitchen's a **ruddy** marvel.> 2000 Granger 236. (Cf. § 6.1.)

shot of, be/get The common-core expression *be/get shut of* has a British variant with *shot* instead of *shut*. <. . . one can understand why the likes of Labour Women Against War would be annoyed about the Prime Minister and want to be **shot** of him.> 2003 July 14 *Times* 16/1.

soluble Solvable: *Soluble* means "dissolvable" in common-core English; the meaning "solvable" is characteristically British. The word form is more frequent in British: CIC has 25.4 iptmw in British texts and 6.8 in American texts. The American sample contained no tokens with the meaning "solvable"; the British sample contained 16 such tokens, about 6 percent. <Media psychos talk as if "the problem" (such as depression or obesity) is **soluble** by following a particular strategy.> 1988 Sept. 6 *Daily Telegraph* 15/6.

unbeknown Unbeknownst: CIC has 3.0 iptmw of *unbeknown* and 0.9 tokens of *unbeknownst* in British texts, and 1.0 of *unbeknown* and 4.1 of *unbeknownst* in American texts (Cf. Peters 2004, 556).

underhand Underhanded: CIC has 6.1 iptmw of *underhand* and 0.6 of *underhanded* in British texts. It has 1.2 of *underhand* and 3.8 of *underhanded* in American texts.

voluntary work Volunteer work: CIC has 11.0 iptmw of *voluntary work* and 1.0 of *volunteer work* in British texts. It has 0.3 of *voluntary work* and 12.1 of *volunteer work* in American texts. < . . . it was just an argument about her **voluntary work**. She never really had enough time for me.> 1991 Green 84.

5.3 Comparison

5.3.1 Comparison of equivalence

The usual signal of a comparison of equivalence is *as . . . as. . . .* The standard of comparison (the item following the second *as*) is sometimes a catch phrase or proverbial expression.

as thick as a plank This catchphrase has several variations. British *thick* is a synonym for "stupid, dense" hence the pun in the comparison. < . . . she's **as thick as two short planks**.> 1993 Smith 148.

as ***adjective*** **as makes/made no difference** This catchphrase is not common in CIC, being represented by 0.3 iptmw in British texts and 0.1 in American texts. <As far as brain is concerned, . . . he [Bertie Wooster] is **as** near to being null and void **as makes no difference**.> 1984 Smith 262.

as daft as a brush CIC has 0.9 iptmw in British texts and none in American. <You're **as daft as a brush**.> 1995 CIC fiction.

as sick as the manager's proverbial parrot The manager's proverbial parrot, sick or otherwise, is not to be found in the British or American texts of CIC. The allusion is to a game program "Sick as a Parrot," described on the Web page www.machoward.com/saap.html as "the thinking fan's soccer management game." <Both university departments study similar fields in spite of their names and each will be **sick as the manager's proverbial parrot** if they fail to establish dominance on the football pitch.> 1993 Feb 26 *Guardian* 3/2.

5.3.2 Comparative and superlative forms

The way adjectives are compared, by inflection (*-er, -est*) or periphrasis (*more, most*), is primarily correlated with the number of syllables – monosyllables by inflection and polysyllables by periphrasis. Two-syllable adjectives vary both within and somewhat between the two national varieties. The comparison of monosyllabic adjectives does not vary greatly between British and American English according to the LOB and Brown corpora. In both varieties, although there is greater complexity than simple descriptions imply, inflection with *-er* and *-est* is the rule (Fries 1993, 30).

A study by Hans Lindquist (1998) of the 1995 issues of two newspapers, the British *Independent* and the *New York Times*, shows that both British and American favor inflectional comparison for adjectives ending in *-y*: *-er* by percentages in the 80s and *-est* by percentages in the high 90s, but also that the American percentage is slightly higher in both cases.

CIC percentages for the following two adjectives support Lindquist's conclusion:

more healthy In CIC British texts, 91.7 percent of comparative forms of *healthy* are *healthier*, and in American texts 94.7 percent; in British texts 91.8 percent of superlative forms are *healthiest*, and in American texts 93.7 percent. <But it's a bit of healthy blood-letting in order to ensure that the patient becomes **more healthy**.> 1989 Autumn *Illustrated London News* 19/3.

more easy CIC shows that in British English 99.6 percent of both comparative and superlative forms of *easy* are inflectional *easier/easiest*, and in American English 99.7 percent of comparative forms are *easier*, and 100 percent of superlative forms are *easiest*. <Good women find it **more easy** to come through the national party [than through local politics].> 1987 Jan. speech by Ian Twinn, Conservative MP.

Other two-syllable adjectives differ.

commoner In CIC British texts, *more common* is 10 times as frequent as *commoner*, but in American texts, it is 55 time as frequent. So *commoner* is comparatively more common in British.

A number of one-syllable adjectives may also occasionally form periphrastic comparison.

juster The comparative *more just* accounts for 74 percent of British comparative forms of *just* and 86 percent of American forms. Apparently the form *juster* is found to be awkward by all English speakers, but British speakers have a slightly greater tolerance for it. The superlative is too rare for generalizations. <. . . we can make a great advance . . . in a **juster** distribution of the fruits of Labour.> 1990 CIC nonfiction.

more soft In contrast with *just, soft* is generally inflectional in its comparison, as *softer/softest*. The following periphrastic comparative is therefore all the odder, occurring as it does in a series of otherwise inflectional forms. <There [West Riding county districts] the speech sound is warmer, slower and **more soft.**> 1985 Ebdon 156.

most twee *Twee* occurs rarely in American use, sometimes with an explicit acknowledgment of its British identity. It generally resists comparison of any kind, and in particular there are no tokens in CIC of inflected forms **tweer/tweest*, and only a few tokens of analytical comparison. <This year's **most twee** toy is Dozzy, a £60 electronic teddy bear with light-up eyes that goes on sale in the summer.> 1987 Mar. 2 *Evening Standard* 22/7.

The irregular comparison of *old* (*elder, eldest*) is more common in British use than in American (Swan 1995, 9; Peters 2004, 175–6). That is especially the case when the forms are used as attributive modifiers with reference to seniority in a family (*CGEL* 7.76): *my elder sister, his eldest son*. In CIC British texts, 15.8 percent of compared forms of *old* are irregular *elder/eldest*, and in American 9.4 percent.

elder <His **elder** brother was frowning, clearly taking the matter extremely seriously.> 1985 Mortimer 67.

eldest <Vic . . . has frequent rows with his **eldest** son, Raymond.> 1988 Lodge 16.

Double comparison, using both inflectional and periphrastic for the same adjective, occurs occasionally and exceptionally in both national varieties. CIC has 1 British token of *most simplest*, from an orally delivered lecture by an academic. British CIC texts have 0.6 iptmw of *least worst*, half of which are in the collocation *least worst option*. Those particular forms of double comparison have no tokens in CIC American texts.

<A cucumber sandwich is the **most simplest** thing there is and the **most tastiest.**> ca. 1980s TV interview with a butler on *Wogan*. <Brace yourself for the **least worst** imports coming from the States.> 1989 July 23–29 *Sunday Telegraph* magazine 37/1–2. <The licence fee . . . had proved to be "the **least worst** way to pay for the BBC".> 1995 Aug. 28 *Independent* 4/4.

5.4 Adjective order

Noun + adjective

Positioning an adjective modifier after its noun head is a feature of common-core English in certain constructions, such as *time immemorial* and *devil incarnate* (*CGEL* 7.21). Other constructions are characteristically British.

Air Officer Commanding Air Force commanding officer <He would have to see the **Air Officer Commanding** and tell him all about it.> 1940 Shute 27.

decade gone Ten years ago <He bought it a **decade gone**.> 1986 Gash 17.

***weekday* last/next** Last/next *weekday*: A search for the word sequences *Monday* (*Tuesday*, etc.) *next* and *Monday* (*Tuesday*, etc.) *last* in limited samples of CIC produced 13 relevant tokens with *next* and 14 with *last* in British texts. A comparable search in American texts produced only 2 tokens.

all (the) year round All year long: In CIC texts, British prefers *round* to *long* in this construction by 35 to 1; American prefers *long* to *round* by 2 to 1 (and also does not use *the* in this construction, cf. § 2.1.1.1 ALL THE YEAR). < . . . the public can enjoy them **all the year round**.> 1989 July 25 *Evening Standard* 3/2.

***time* spare** *Time* free, *time* to spare, (a) free *time* <. . . whenever I had ten minutes **spare**, I'd pop in somewhere for pens or knickers.> 1990 Aug. 24–30 *Good Times* 5/7.

6 Adverbs

6.1 General

British and American differ somewhat in form, frequency, and use of adverbs. American has certain characteristic uses, such as *some* in *The wound bled* ***some*** and *any* in *That doesn't help us* ***any***. The common-core adverbs *anywhere, everywhere, nowhere*, and *somewhere* have minority American options *anyplace, everyplace, no place* (usually spelled as two words), and *someplace* (*CamGEL* 423).

The aphetic form *most* from *almost* has been used since the sixteenth century. Originally Scottish, it is now limited to American and some British dialects (Burchfield 1996, 504). American nondialectal use is chiefly in spoken English as a modifier of *all, always, any, every*, and compounds of *any* and *every* with *body, one*, and *thing* (*MW* s.v. [5]*most*).

The use of "flat" adverbs, that is, adverbs identical in form with corresponding adjectives (such as *fast*) rather than distinguished by the suffix *-ly*, is said to be particularly widespread in American colloquial use, as opposed to British (*LGSWE* 542). Historically, however, flat adverbs are the older traditional form. The ending *-ly*, which we think of as marking adverbs, is more recent in that function than adverbs like *fast*. Other adverbial uses of adjectives, such as *good, bad*, and *real*, now thought to be characteristic of American (*LGSWE* 542–3; Peters 2004, 62), developed between the fourteenth and eighteenth centuries in Britain.

Other adverbial forms identified as distinctively American include *in back* with reference to the rear seat of a car (Burchfield 1996, 85; Peters 2004, 60–1) and *pretty much* (*LGSWE* 547).

Distinctively British forms are the following:

a bit A little (Swan 1995, 96) <'You revise ["review material for an examination"], I suppose?' [¶] '**A bit**. But I usually watch telly.'> 1977 Dexter 97.

about Around <Drive carefully and slowly when there are pedestrians **about**.> 1996 *Highway Code*, 16. Cf. § 6.5 ABOUT.

actually CIC has more total uses of *actually* in British texts than in American (3625.9 iptmw versus 2406.7). But as Swan (1995, 6, 7, 158) points out, important differences are in context and implication. **1**. Used to break bad news <I'm sorry, Raymond. . . . But we do rather mind, **actually**. There is a significant risk of getting lung cancer from passive smoking, you know.> 1989 Mar. 19 *Manchester Guardian Weekly* 6/2. **2**. Used to confirm or disconfirm expectations <'Miss yer train mate?' asked one of them. [¶] 'Yes, I did **actually**,' replied the newcomer, blushing. There was a general laugh. Someone echoed the '**actually**'.> 1962 Lodge 33. <'Constable, can you kindly tell me what's happened?' [¶] 'I was hoping you'd tell me that, sir, **actually**.'> 1974 Price 24. **3**. Used to identify additional information <"Is it more fun to play pranks on British people or Americans?" [¶] [British comedian Sacha Baron Cohen:] "It depends on the class, **actually**."> 2004 July 15 *New York Times* B 1/1.

additionally *conjunct* In addition: CIC has 46 iptmw in British texts and 37.3 in American texts. <**Additionally** her phone runs on an 'airware' system, powered by a battery box in her hallway.> 1994 Sept. 28–Oct. 5 *Time Out* 29/1–2.

after Used nonstandardly with a progressive verb form instead of a perfect for a recent event, as in *am after attending* "have (just) attended" <See, **I'm just after attending** the post mortem.> 1989 Turnbull 38.

all round All around <The show is bloody good. What it's particularly good at is giving stick **all round**: to Asians who try to be English, to the English who try to be Asian, to the people who try too hard to understand other cultures and to the people who don't try at all.> 1998 Jan. 7 *Evening Standard* 53/2. Cf. §§ 5.1.4 ALL-ROUND and 8.1 ROUND.

along Further on/down: Peters (2004, 30) notes that in the Brown Corpus, *along* in the sense of accompaniment (*They came along with us*) is twice as frequent as any other sense; that is not true in British, in which spatial and other senses predominate. <As we settled into our places, I noticed a young man on the other side of the table and two **along**, slight and decidedly handsome.> 1994 Dickinson 133.

always An expression of inevitability with a progressive verb form, as in *be always going to* "be bound to; be inevitably going to" <It **was always going to** be a hard task in a place like that to find who fired the fatal shots.> 2003 June 28 *Times* 1/1.

and no mistake Make no mistake about that: CIC has 3.3 iptmw in British texts and none in American texts. <But then it was out of the fryin' pan an' into the fire, **an' no mistake**.> 1974 Price 161.

any more In CIC texts, British favors *any more* over *anymore* by 563 to 55.7 iptmw, and American favors *anymore* over *any more* by 450.4 to 283. *Anymore* is generally used in negative or interrogative contexts, but an expanding use in America is in positive statements with the sense "nowadays": "Everybody's cool **anymore**" (*MW*).

any road, anyroad *northern English dialect, but found in general texts* Anyway: CIC has 0.4 iptmw of the solid spelling *anyroad* in British texts and none in American texts. <I don't care where you park, but you can't leave that van here. **Anyroad,** who are you?> 2002 Sept. *Square* 22.

anywhere CIC has 500.3 iptmw of *anywhere* in British texts and 472.9 in American texts; it has no British tokens of *anyplace* and 14.2 in American texts. *Anywhere* is the norm in both national varieties, but *anyplace* is a minority American option, listed from 1916 without comment by *MW*.

apart The word *apart* is more frequent than *aside* in British, and *aside* more frequent in American (Hofland and Johansson 1982, 475; Peters 2004, 50). CIC has 420.6 iptmw of the adverb *apart* in British texts and 347 in American texts. It has 331.3 of the adverb *aside* in British texts and 393 in American texts. **1**. Aside: <Britain's borders (Ireland **apart**) are fixed by cliffs and oceans, not rivers or hedgerows.> 1992 Aug. 1 *Economist* 49/3. **2**. Away, distant (from each other) <Patrick realized with a sudden glow of elation that the shop where he would be getting the nice bread for Jenny and the second-best horn shop known to him could be no more than two minutes' walk **apart**.> 1988 Amis 52. Cf. § 8.1 APART FROM.

as well Also (Swan 1995, 38): CIC has slightly more tokens of *as well* in British texts than in American, and slightly more of *also* in American. <He smoked **as well**.> 1995 June 8 *London Review of Books* 9/1.

a treat Very well: CIC has 34.1 iptmw of *a treat* in all senses in British texts and 13.8 in American texts. CIC has 4.9 iptmw of some form of *work a treat* in British texts and none in American texts. <Actually, this is a tactic I don't strongly disapprove and it worked **a treat** on this occasion.> 1994 Sept. *Tatler* 57/2. Cf. § 11.1.6.2 GO DOWN A TREAT.

at speed At high speed: CIC has 15.2 iptmw of *at speed* and 11.9 of *at high speed* in British texts and 0.2 and 5.8, respectively, in American texts. American presumably favors other expressions for high-speed automotive movement, but when this one is used, the form with *high* is typical. <She was hurled into a stolen car which was then driven **at speed** at two policemen who tried to stop it.> 1987 Mar. 5 *Evening Standard* 5/6.

away On one's way <[to policeman:] 'I'm just **away** home, sir.' The girl stepped off the steps with a flourish at her skirt and walked away quickly into the night.> 1989 Turnbull 39.

awfully, most Very much <Oh I say, ta ["thanks"] **most awfully**.> 1987 Feb. 23 ITV *Rumpole of the Bailey*.

backwards Backward: CIC has 163.9 iptmw of *backwards* and 61 of *backward* (including some adjectival uses) in British texts and 52.3 and 93.2, respectively, in American texts.

been and (gone and) See § 1.4.2.

bleeding The frequency of the form *bleeding* is not greatly different between British and American (111.5 versus 93.9 iptmw), but the intensive use is notable in British texts and extremely rare in American. <Well, that **bleedin'** narrows it down.> 2000 Granger 281.

bloody <Of *course* I'm trying to **bloody** scare you.> 1993 Smith 171. Cf. HELL below and §§ 5.1.1 MINDED, 5.2, 7.1, 10 BLOODY.

bloody well CIC has 15 iptmw of *bloody well* (intensive in use) in British texts and 0.8 in American texts. <"**I bloody well** don't." He didn't say it aggressively but quietly as someone who hears bad news.> 1987 Oliver 85. Cf. §§ 5.2, 7.1.

clean Completely; all the way <It's said you can chop its head off and it will still run **clean** round the fowl yard.> 1983 Innes 69.

close Closely <But the Prime Minister is worried that Parliament does not share her obsession with secrecy and may narrow the focus of the [Official Secrets] Act too **close**.> 1987 June 3 *Evening Standard* 7/1.

close on Nearly <India . . . has been given **close on** £1 billion over the past five years.> 1987 Dec. 20 *Manchester Guardian* 9/1.

close(r) to Close(r) up; up close(r) <**Closer to**, the cottage looked even more decrepit than it had from the car.> 1987 Hart 31. <. . . but **close-to** Harry thought he looked rather weak and foolish.> 2003 Rowling 142 (*US ed.* up close).

come to that For that matter; as far as that goes <. . . Captain Prosser had not seen fit to mention the fact to the police. [¶] Nor, **come to that**, had the two workmen.> 2002 Aird 103. There is also a finite clausal form in <What had Emma been up to after she left Charles Harvey? **If it came to that**, what had Harvey been doing in the hours between two and eight a.m.?> 1991 Critchley 201.

early days Early so that other things might yet happen: CIC has 7.1 iptmw of *it is* (or *it's*) *early days* in British texts and 0.4 in American texts. <They didn't know too much about AIDs at that time; it was **early days**.> 1993 Greenwood 151.

early next Early next year <Paul Hutchins will end his reign as the supremo of British tennis **early next**.> 1987 Feb. 18 *Evening Standard* 52/1.

early on At an early period of time: *MW* (abridging Gilman 1994) comments: "This adverb is sometimes objected to in American writing as an obtrusive Briticism. It is a relative newcomer to the language, having arisen in British English around 1928. It seems to have filled a need, however. It came into frequent use in American English in the late 1960s and is now well established on both sides of the Atlantic in both speech and writing." CIC has 90.8 iptmw in British texts and 110.5 in American texts (both including a few with other senses). This form is therefore an example of a historical Briticism (still perceived as such by some older Americans) that has been fully naturalized statistically into American use. <I realised **early on** that when you do impressions you get people's attention very quickly.> 1994 Sept. 14–21 *Time Out* 21/1. – **earlier on** The *OED* derives *early on* from *earlier on* by backformation, and *earlier on* from *later on* by analogy (*early* 5.b). <Now you mention it,

there was a woman hanging about at the top of the stairs **earlier on**.> 1969 Amis 29.

else Otherwise <*must be coming; they'd have phoned* ***else***> *LDEL*.

endways "Am also *endwise*" (*CIDE*). CIC has 0.2 iptmw of *endways* in British texts and none in American texts; it has no tokens of *endwise* in either national variety. *MW* lists both without comment, but defines the latter by reference to the former. They are both marginal forms.

evening, in the Evenings <evenings . . . *esp. Am* • *What time do you get home evenings* (= in the evening)*?*> *CIDE*.

ever, the moment . . . Whenever; the very moment <. . . they came, it could be guaranteed, **the moment** he **ever** went near the lavatory.> 1987 Bradbury 72. Cf. also ONLY EVER below.

ever so Very much <Ooh, my, thanks **ever so**!> 1990 Rowlands 25. Cf. *LGSWE* 566.

everywhere "everywhere . . . *Am infml* everyplace" (*CIDE*). *Everywhere* is the norm in common-core English. CIC has 1.5 iptmw of *everyplace* in American texts and none in British texts.

fairly British is partial to *fairly* as an emphasizing adverb with the sense "it is no exaggeration to say" (*CGEL* 8.88, 100): "He **fairly** jumped for joy."

firstly First: "Our evidence also suggests that *firstly* is more frequent in British English than in American English" (Gilman 1994, 447). "In practice many different patterns are used: *First*, . . . *second*, . . . *third*; *Firstly*, . . . *secondly*, . . . *thirdly*; . . . (AmE) *First of all*, . . . *second of all*, . . . and numerous others" (Burchfield 1996, 298). ". . . in enumerations, the phrases *first of all* and *last of all* are probably now acceptable variants of *first* and *last* throughout the English-speaking world, but *second of all, third of all* and the like are regarded as Americanisms" (Kahn and Ilson 1985, 239). CIC data supports the foregoing conclusions: the ratios of British to American iptmw of *firstly, secondly*, and *thirdly* are, respectively, 115.5 to 2.2, 181.8 to 56.3, and 51.2 to 7. On the other hand, those of *first of all* and *second of all* are respectively 159.3 to 176.3 and 0.3 to 6.1. There has also been controversy about mixing forms of enumeration: *first, secondly, thirdly*; *first of all, secondly, third*; etc., but ". . . it does appear that consistency in this specific usage has not always had a particularly high priority with good writers" (Gilman 1994, 447).

flaming *emphasizer* <Says Closed, doesn't it? Can't you **flaming** read?> 1974 Potter 93.

forwards Forward: CIC has 151.5 iptmw of *forwards* in British texts and 28.2 in American texts. <Harry darted **forwards** to pick up the letter.> 2003 Rowling 40 (*US ed.* forward).

frigging CIC has 4 iptmw of *frigging* (in all uses) in British texts and 2.2 in American texts. <At least I assume she is. I can't **frigging** see, can I?> 1994 Sept. 28–Oct 5 *Time Out* 8/2.

full on Head on <[In deliberately running down a pedestrian with a car:] 'You hit them **full on**.' [¶] 'Amidships, so to speak?' [¶] 'Between the headlamps,' said Harpe seriously. 'You wouldn't break any glass then.'> 1968 Aird 95.

getting on Nearly; getting on to (with measurements of time or space) <"What's the time?" [¶] "**Getting on** two."> 1989 Dickinson 146.

going on with, to be Temporarily; to start with <We've charged the guy who hit Barton with driving under the influence. Just **to be going on with**, mind you.> 2000 Aird 69–70.

gone Ago <Well, it's 'ome, in't it, Benny? Course my Fred an' me always wanted a place at Southend. And, six months **gone**, whole street thought it was gonna be out on its lug'ole.> 1988 Cannell 88.

half-ways Halfway: CIC has no tokens of *halfways* (solid or hyphenated) in either British or American texts. The *OED*'s only token of the form is the proper name *Mr. Halfways* from C. S. Lewis's 1933 *Pilgrim's Regress* (s.v. *escapist* 2). It seems to be a marginal form made by analogy with other adverbs in *-s*. <And he . . . had no one like that on whom he could **half-ways** depend.> 1984 Price 129.

hell, the bloody In hell: Following a *wh*-word, *the hell* has similar frequencies in British and American (with a somewhat greater frequency in American, 130.0 to British 119.9 iptmw in CIC). The addition of *bloody* makes it British: 7.6 to American 0.3 iptmw. However, *in hell* is favored in American, with about 4.5 versus British 0.8 iptmw. <But he wanted to phone Jaggard again, and ask him what **the bloody hell** was actually happening.> 1986 Price 106.

how Why, how it was that <I was being rather po-faced about the seals being slaughtered. And I asked **how** he [the Secretary of State for Scotland], as a man who had the power to revoke the culling licences, had not done so.> 1987 Nov. *Illustrated London News* 64/2.

I + *modal* + *verb of opinion* Comment clauses of this pattern have a verb of opinion, which is usually *think* or *say* (after *dare*) but may be a negated verb of unbelief (*be surprised, imagine, wonder*). In initial position, such clauses are best interpreted as main clauses followed by noun clauses as direct objects (cf. § 1.4.4 SHOULD, WOULD), but in medial and final position, they are clearly adverbial. Final position is most typical for these clauses. <You'll be old enough, **I daresay**, to remember that militia call-up of lads a few months before war broke out.> 1985 Clark 139. <SIS were always treading on SOE's toes, accidentally on purpose, **I shouldn't be surprised**, and vice versa.> 1985 Taylor 135. <He'll be here presently to have a word with you, **I shouldn't wonder**.> 1987 Aug. 23 ch. 8 Athens GA *Jewel in the Crown* rerun. <Several hundred miles, **I should think**. Getting on a thousand.> 1989 Dickinson 136. <It was a mews house in Kensington, expensive, well above her bracket **I'd have thought**, but what did I know?> 1989 Nicholson 32. <He won't be in till Monday, **I shouldn't think**, but I promised to keep him fully informed.> 1992 Dexter 238.

I + *verb of opinion* In comment clauses of this pattern, the verbs *think* and *suppose* have been reported as somewhat more common in British conversation than in American, whereas *I guess* is almost exclusively American (*LGSWE* 983). The "American" *I guess* is well represented in Chaucer and other pre- and early seventeenth-century texts as *I gesse*, of which the *OED* has 33 examples, as well as 221 examples of the modern spelling *I guess*, most of them British. In CIC, *I think* and *I guess* are predominantly American, with respectively 8713 and 1101.9 iptmw, compared with British 4113.1 and 120.2. However, *I suppose* and *I reckon* are predominantly British, with respectively 588.2 and 85.8 iptmw, compared with American 180.4 and 6.2. *Reckon* in the sense "suppose" is dialectal in American English. <It's just that the Ranulph business is tiresome, **I suppose**.> 1945 Innes 52. <They say he's bent, but everyone's bent nowadays **I reckon**.> 1980 Kavanagh 101. A different picture emerges for the intransitive negative *I don't think* used adverbially in medial or final position. CIC British texts have nearly twice as many of it as American texts do. <"Had she got nice legs?" "Not so nice as the other's, **I don't think**."> 1975 Dexter 100.

if needs be CIC indicates that *if need be* is the usual form in both British and American, with 7.6 and 7.1 iptmw, respectively. However, *if needs be* has 1.8 British and no American tokens. <I'll take him round and introduce him to a few people, **if needs be**.> 1985 Barnard 50.

I'm sure <. . . the vicar's redoubtable housekeeper appeared in the doorway. [¶] 'Excuse me, **I'm sure**,' she said.> 2000 Granger 297.

indeed *emphasizing, often in final position* <However, once you go down the road towards the kind of censorship he envisages you can end up in exceedingly dangerous waters **indeed**.> 1990 Aug. 20 *Evening Standard* 31/5.

in the event *conjunct* As it turned out; as it was; as it happened: The conjunctive use of this expression seems to be about 10 times more frequent in British use than in American. "*Br* when it actually happens or happened <*I was very frightened beforehand but* in the event *I didn't fall*>" (*LDEL* s.v. *event*). Common-core English uses *in the event that* followed by a present tense, referring to a future event. <If the remainder of the magazine had been free from potential libel, this might have been sufficient. **In the event**, we decided it was not.> 1993 Feb. 27 *Times* 15/5.

jolly <'I don't aim to keep you long, gentlemen.' [¶] 'I should **jolly** hope not.'> 1985 Bingham 144. Cf. § 7.1.

just 1. *following an echoic tag question* <'Well, that bleedin' narrows it down,' said Hayes sarcastically. [¶] 'Doesn't it **just**?'> 2000 Granger 281. **2**. Barely <Lennon seems not to have inspired the same level of loathing and comes off rather better, ending the book, **just**, a hero.> 1988 Sept. 25 *Manchester Guardian Weekly* 27/5. The word order is also notable; an expected American version would be "ending the book as a hero, but only barely." **3**. *modifying expressions of time and place* Right: *LGSWE* (547) suggests that before conversational expressions of time and place, British has *just* and American has *right*.

The situation is, however, complex. For example, when *just now* is used in a context of past time, *right* is not possible. So, <You didn't half go it **just now**> 1988 Lodge 168, could not have American *right now*. Indeed the American idiom would be completely different, something like *You didn't hold back just then* [or *a moment ago*]. However, if the context is present time, American *right* for *just* is a likely possibility: <Finally my central heating packed up [*i.e.*, broke down], and it is very cold here **just now**.> 1990 April 4, personal letter from a Londoner. This use is particularly frequent after *a lot on my plate*: <I've got a lot on my plate **just now**.> 1985 Gilbert 133, for which American might have *I've got a lot to do* [or *I'm very busy*] *right now*. Similarly, American *right* may replace British *just* as a modifier of *after* or *before* in <**Just after** nine.> 1989 Quinton 113. <**Just before** they went off for their dirty weekend.> 1984 Brett 70. But American *right* seems less probable than *just* before *then* in <**Just then**, the police constable on duty outside the flat opened the front door to admit Grimes.> 1985 Bingham 19. In combinations of *just* versus *right* before *now, after*, and *before*, CIC has 378.8 iptmw of *just* and 156.5 of *right* in British texts, and 284.3 of *just* and 1146.2 of *right* in American texts. Thus British prefers *just* and American *right* in these combinations. Before *then*, however, both national varieties prefer *right* over *just*, British by 38.8 to 22.2 iptmw and American by 19.6 to 11. Similarly, before the expressions of place *here* and *there*, both British and American prefer *right*, although American does so far more clearly. As modifiers of *here*, CIC has 7.6 iptmw of *just* and 22.4 of *right* in British texts, but 7.9 of *just* and 122.1 of *right* in American texts. As modifiers of *there*, CIC has 17.2 iptmw of *just* and 25.3 of *right* in British texts, but 13 of *just* and 114.7 of *right* in American texts.

just on British dictionaries define this expression before numbers as "exactly." <I followed a police Range-Rover for several miles up the motorway and my speedo read **just on** 70.> 1989 July 21 *Evening Standard* 9/3.

less soon *Opposite of* rather: This use has no examples in CIC for either British or American. <. . . he would **less soon** watch television than, in his own phrase, have a lump of vegetable marrow shoved into his skull instead of a brain.> 1969 Amis 24.

like *nonstandard* As it were; so to say: This use has something in common with the colloquial use of *like* as a meaningless filler (presumably an Americanism originally), but it is older. <1778 F. Burney *Evelina* II. xxiii. 222 Father grew quite uneasy, **like**, for fear of his Lordship's taking offence.> *OED* s.v. *like* adv. 7. <It was a commune **like**, everyone paid something, more if they were in work, and we made **like** improvements.> 1994 Symons 251–2.

like as not, (as) Probably: CIC has 1.6 iptmw in British texts and 0.5 in American texts. The omission of the first *as* is not a distinguishing feature, being found in both varieties. The variant (*as*) *likely as not* is also more frequent in British, but by a smaller proportion (1.5 to 1). <'What happened to Paul

Morris?' asked Morse. [¶] 'Buggered off with Joseph's wife, **like as not**.'> 1979 Dexter 84–5.

mark you *comment clause* (*CGEL* 15.54) This is a rare expression in British, occurring only in some 0.7 iptmw, but not at all in the American texts of CIC. <They aren't dissembling, **mark you**: they haven't a clue themselves what they are going to do.> 1996 Aug. 4 *Sunday Times* 3 4/3.

mind (you) *comment clause* See § 10.

momentarily Although the characteristic American sense of this word is "in a moment; very soon," as in *The plane will be landing momentarily*, its oldest attested and still primary British sense is "for a moment; lasting a brief time." <James was **momentarily** distracted.> 1991 Cleeves 117.

near enough Nearly; almost: The expression, in all uses, is 3 times more frequent in British than in American, and this particular use is unusual in American. <But it might yet amount to the same thing, **near enough**.> 1986 Price 155–6.

near on Nearly: This is rare in British (only 0.2 iptmw of CIC), but does not occur in any CIC American texts. <My last Subaru . . . had clocked up about 50,000 miles when I bought it and **near on** 90,000 when I part-exchanged it.> 1994 Sept. 17 *Times* Weekend 13/1.

never Not by any means <'I'm from Rummidge University. I'm, er, taking part in, that is to say . . . I'm on a kind of educational visit.' [¶] The man freezes in the act of stowing away his wallet. 'You're **never** Vic Wilcox's shadow?'> 1988 Lodge 102.

never ever CIC has 19.5 iptmw in British texts and 7 in American texts. <Believe it or not, but there has **never, ever**, been a lodge called the Goose and Gridiron.> 2004 June *Square* 17/2.

nights, of At night <What d'you say I come and sleep here **of nights**?> 1949 Tey 121.

nobbut *Northern English dialect* Nothing but; only: CIC has 0.7 iptmw in British texts and none in American texts. <He looked a lot like his uncle when he was nobbut a lad.> *NODE*.

none the less Nonetheless: Although the solid spelling is the primary or only entry in most British and almost all American dictionaries, the *OED* text contains 38 tokens of the spaced spelling, 21 of the solid spelling, and 3 of a hyphenated spelling. CIC has 46.9 iptmw of the spaced spelling and 143.9 of the solid spelling in British texts and 3.2 and 189 respectively in American texts. The spaced spelling accounts for nearly a quarter of the British spellings, but for only an insignificant proportion of American spellings. <**None the less**, the guarantee of some degree of subsidy is a victory for Channel 4.> 1989 July 23–9 *Sunday Telegraph* magazine 17/1.

nor Neither <And she is adamant she cannot foresee a day when she will stop spending. [¶] But then once upon a time **nor** could John de Lorean.> 1989 Sept. 11 *Daily Express* 21/6.

northwards Northward: CIC has 21 iptmw of *northwards* and 12.4 of *northward* in British texts, and 1.5 and 24.7 respectively in American texts. <I was driving **northwards** to the ring road so that I could go south from Oxford.> 1978 Jan. 18 *Punch* 97/2.

not a bit of it Not at all: CIC has 6 iptmw of this expression in British texts and 0.2 in American texts. <Given our present circumstances, you might think we would first ask whether there was oil, or gas, or cheap fertiliser on Mars. **Not a bit of it.**> 1976 Aug. 11 *Punch* 207/1.

not before time None too soon: CIC has 3.5 iptmw of *not before time* and 0.4 of *none too soon* in British texts, and none of *not before time* and 0.7 of *none too soon* in American texts. <'So I've been telling her things are clearing up.' [¶] '**Not before time**,' Giles Tancock said.> 1983 Innes 134.

not half The qualifying combination *not half* is both a downtoner and an amplifier. **1**. As a downtoner, it modifies the determiner *enough* (*CGEL* 5.17n): *He hasn't **half** enough money*, and adjectives or verbs (*CGEL* 8.107n): *I'm **not half** satisfied*, i.e., "I am only partially satisfied (or, in fact, I am dissatisfied)." In these uses, it is equivalent to *not enough money by half* and *not satisfied by half*. **2**. It also has use as an amplifier. *I'm **not half** satisfied* can also mean "I am fully satisfied." Similarly, *She doesn't **half** swear* may be "She swears a great deal (that is, fully)." A similar American use is the qualifier in the collocation *not half bad* "very good." In some cases the British order of the expression is unlike anything to be found in American: *It hasn't **half** been cold today*. <You seen that Yamaha he's got? I would**n't half** like a go on that!> 1992 Granger 207. **3**. The expression is also an emphasizer. <A nurse came with cups of tea for both of them. Bridget whispered, 'Old Smurthwaite does**n't half** keep her running.'> 1985 Mortimer 338.

not to worry Don't worry <**Not to worry**. . . . I was just ringing to let her know . . . he's out of the country till next week.> 1993 Smith 176.

now *especially after a tag question* <I don't want wet and mud all over my shop, do I **now**?> 1974 Potter 94.

on Later, afterwards: CIC contains only a few examples of this use in American texts, but a great many in British texts. <It is still owned by a descendant of the founder six or seven generations **on**.> 1989 July 28 *Times* 33/1. <Seven years **on** from that party at No 11, Mr Blunkett again surprised Labour MPs with his brazen self-confidence.> 2004 Dec. 16 *Daily Telegraph* 4/1.

once, the Once <She seemed determined, having met Roper's eye **the once**, not to do it again.> 1987 Hart 161. Cf. § 2.1.1.1 THE ONCE.

only ever Only; always only; merely: CIC has 40.5 iptmw in British texts and 2.8 in American texts. <. . . he **only ever** surmounted the first hurdle.> 1989 Aug. 5 *Times* Review 34/2. <Henry Fowler . . . insisted . . . that *protagonist* is a word that can **only ever** be used in the singular.> 1998 Winchester 30. <He was **only ever** going to be involved in football.> 2005 Jan. 9 *Sunday Times* 4 3/8.

only just Barely: CIC has 113.1 iptmw in British texts and 17.6 in American texts. <Yes he passed, . . . but **only just**.> 1962 Lodge 161.

on the whole For the most part: CIC has 119.4 iptmw of *on the whole* in British texts and 44.4 in American texts. Conversely, it has 70.3 iptmw of *for the most part* in British texts and 128.8 in American texts. <"Do you want to go in, sir?" [¶] "No. No, **on the whole** I think not."> 1949 Tey 111.

perhaps CIC has 3054 iptmw of *perhaps* in British texts and 1698.5 in American texts. Conversely, it has 1342.9 iptmw of *maybe* in British texts and 2327.8 in American texts. British prefers *perhaps*, and American *maybe*.

quite **1**. Very much; completely; fully: CIC has 4761.8 iptmw of *quite* (in all uses) in British texts and 1604.2 in American texts. <Then my wife **quite** likes foreign food.> 2004 Jan. 4 *Sunday Times* Magazine 70/4. **2**. Exactly <**Quite** what she did for the next seventeen years remains far from clear.> 1994 Mark Bevir (British scholar) *Journal of the American Academy of Religion* 62:749. **3**. Fully <. . . the knots . . . had been tied so effectively . . . that Sergeant Forsyte struggled with them for **quite** ten minutes.> 1977 Barnard 80.

rather CIC has 4065.2 iptmw of *rather* (in all uses) in British texts and 2174.2 in American texts. <But we do **rather** mind, actually.> 1989 Mar. 19 *Manchester Guardian Weekly* 6/2.

really <I've **really** no idea, old man.> 1985 Bingham 61.

right enough CIC has 79 iptmw in British texts and 0.5 in American texts. <It was a shell **right enough**.> 1974 Price 137.

rough CIC has 8 iptmw of *sleep rough* and 3.4 of *live rough* in British texts and no American tokens. <. . . the rather harsh conditions under which excavationists work – living fairly "**rough**" on overseas digs is another example.> 1986 Oct. 28 *Times* 37/2. <His explosives were soaked with snow as he wandered around Moscow and slept **rough** at stations.> 1993 Feb. 1 *Times* 8/4.

round Around: CIC has 1408.8 iptmw of adverbial *round* in British texts and 98.4 in American texts. In addition, although the number of senses listed for a word in dictionaries may represent the style of the lexicographer as much as the semantics of the language being described, it is noteworthy that *NODE* has 14 senses or subsenses for the adverb *round* but only 6 for the adverb *around*, whereas *MW* has 1 for *round* and 13 for *around*. <I think I'd like to take a few days' leave, from the months owed to me, which I shall never get **round** to taking.> 1984 Price 20. <Slavin trundled **round** with him a huge 20-inch by 24-inch Polaroid.> 1987 Mar. 12 *Evening Standard* 25/3. <Mrs Figg had recently taken to asking him **round** for tea.> 2003 Rowling 8 (*US ed.* around). Cf. §§ 5.1.4 ALL-ROUND and 8.1 ROUND.

round about Nearby <Larking [a village] shared . . . a doctor with a cluster of small communities **round about**.> 1968 Aird 6.

ruddy well; the ruddy hell CIC has 0.3 iptmw of these expressions in British texts and none in American texts. <'I should **ruddy well** think not,' growled

Hagrid.> 1998 Rowling 46. <. . . who **the ruddy hell** are you?> 2003 Rowling 385. (Cf. § 5.2.)

sideways on CIC has some 15 tokens in British texts and none in American texts. <He had . . . a beaky nose that plunged downwards to meet his tiny oral orifice. If he had a girlfriend he could only have managed to kiss her **sideways on**.> 1992 Green 32.

so So much <The old sweetie would adore it **so**.> 1969 Amis 226.

sort of *adverb of imprecision* British conversational use of this *sort of* is 3 times as frequent as American; on the other hand, the adverbs of imprecision or doubt *kind of, like*, and *maybe* are about 5 times more frequent in American conversation than in British (*LGSWE* 869–70). – **sort of thing** As it were <'How old is she **sort of thing**?' Shirley asked Brian Everthorpe. [¶] 'I dunno. Young.'> 1988 Lodge 107.

specially Especially: *Specially* is less common than *especially* in both British and American English (Peters 2004, 509) but especially in American; CIC has a British ratio of 1:10 versus an American ratio of 1:26. <I helped collect the soiled plates . . . and to stack them in the kitchen ready for the domestic help, who was coming in next morning **specially** to attend to them.> 2001 Lodge 143.

straight away, straightaway Right away: CIC has 14.8 iptmw of *straightaway* (plus 91.7 of *straight away*) in British texts and 5.2 of *straightaway* (plus 3.7 of *straight away*) in American texts. By contrast, CIC has 37.8 iptmw of *right away* in British texts and 117 in American texts. <Better get these ready-prepared meals from M and S into the freezer **straight away**.> 2001 James 112.

straight on Straight ahead: CIC has 31.4 iptmw in British texts and 7.5 in American texts. <**Straight on** for Bakerloo and Jubilee Lines> 1999 Mar. 10 sign in the Baker Street tube station.

surely CIC has 455.0 iptmw in British texts and 200.7 in American. <Nothing that a couple of nice lunches at The Ivy wouldn't put right, **surely**.> 1999 Mar. 17 *Evening Standard* 61/4.

thank you (very much) *emphasizer* <. . . most Britons are, despite everything, well enough pleased, **thank you**, not to be numbered among the foreigners.> 1990 Critchfield 83.

then In all positions, *then* as a linking adverb is nearly twice as frequent in British conversation as in American; on the other hand, *so* in the same use is half again as frequent in American conversation as in British (*LGSWE* 887). A distinctive British use of *then* is in terminal position: <Who's a clever boy, **then**?> 1987 Fraser, *Your* 35. <Well, there you are **then**.> 1988 Mortimer 265. Cf. also THERE WE ARE 1992 below.

there we are *comment clause* CIC has 43.9 iptmw in British texts and 2.3 in American. <"And *The French Lieutenant's Woman*." [¶] "Ah. I'm with you. Saw that at the pictures with the wife . . . Or was it on the box?" [¶] "Well, **there we are** then," said Morse lamely.> 1992 Dexter 6. Cf. § 4.7.

there you are *comment clause* CIC has 91.3 iptmw in British texts and 10.4 in American. <. . . we have got accustomed to the idea . . . that musicals can sound good as well as make sense. But **there you are**.> 1986 Oct. 12 *Sunday Times* 55/8. <[response to the answer of a question:] Well, **there you are**. Learned something anyway.> 1989 Jan. 28 *Mystery: Inspector Morse* ch. 9 San Francisco. Cf. § 4.7.

too right Of course; certainly: CIC has 5.5 iptmw in British texts and none of this use in American texts. <"That's not usual, is it?" [¶] "**Too right** it isn't."> 1985 Taylor 77.

unawares Unaware (Peters 2004, 556): CIC has 11.6 iptmw of *unawares* in British texts and 1.5 in American. <This development took me entirely **unawares**.> 2000 Caudwell 276.

undoubtedly; doubtless; doubtlessly: These three are listed in the order of their frequency in common-core English. American has proportionately a stronger preference for *undoubtedly*, and *doubtless* is proportionately a stronger second choice in British than in American. (Cf. also Peters 2004, 557.) <This body . . . **doubtless** includes a number of wild-eyed cyclists.> 1988 June *Illustrated London News* 7/3.

up (from/on/to) <. . . he had travelled **up from** London on the same train as Tim.> 1989 Quinton 100–1. <He's **up on** allotment today. . . . Same plot he's had since 1934.> 1991 Glaister 28–9. <Though it would be theoretically possible to travel **up to** London and back in the morning, it would be an awful fag.> 2001 Lodge 224.

very <The United States is not, to be sure, part of the Economic Community, but is present in Brussels, **very**, and what does it do there? Spying on us, obviously.> 1994 Freeling 34.

-wards Adverbs in *-wards* are typical of British, the ending *-ward* being preferred in edited American use (*CGEL* I.41; *CamGEL* 615; Swan 1995, 615–16). Cf. BACKWARDS, FORWARDS, NORTHWARDS.

-ways See ENDWAYS, HALF-WAYS. As an option to *-ways* (as in *endways*), *-wise* is primarily American, as it is also in the recent sense of "with regards to" as in *healthwise, moneywise, plotwise*, and *weatherwise* (*CamGEL* 567). It has recent use with phrases, notably on the Internet: <The hostels in London are . . . centrally located, which makes them great **location and staying there wise**. . . . [a British example from a Web site on youth hostels]> (bracketed matter in original) 2005 *American Speech* 80:108.

well and truly This is a legal phrase in common-core English dating from the fifteenth century at least. The *OED* (s.v. *truly* adv. 4.b), however, has a usage note: "now also for colloq. emphasis: decisively, 'good and proper,'" which use is more characteristic of British than of American use. CIC has 21.4 iptmw of *well and truly* in British texts and 1.1 in American texts. <I should think the mechanism's **well and truly** seized up by now.> 1991 Graham 159.

wherefore CIC has 7.9 iptmw of *wherefore* in British texts and 1.6 in American texts. <[receptionist to booking clerk in next room:] There's a lady here to see you, Lynn. [booking clerk, fem., age ca. 35:] **Wherefore**?> (probably a joking use) 1990 Feb. 1 London House (Univ. of London).

while(s), the The whole/entire time <Rooks were . . . producing a great deal of clamour **the while**.> 1983 Innes 131. <. . . she followed the Order of Mass that early Sunday morning, glancing **the whiles** around her at the familiar stations of the cross.> 1992 Dexter 190.

whilst While, meanwhile: CIC has 380.8 iptmw in British texts and 8.8 in American texts. <**Whilst** over the coming months, Central [Television] promises several memorable nights.> 1986 Oct. National Theatre program for *Dalliance* [23].

with it As well; in addition <She is sincere, but funny **with it**.> 2003 June 28 *Times* Weekend 9/2.

you + ***verb of perception*** <But that wasn't quite what I asked, **you see**.> 1977 Barnard 38. <There is a significant risk of getting lung cancer from passive smoking, **you know**.> 1989 Mar. 19 *Manchester Guardian Weekly* 6/2. Cf. § 10 YOU SEE.

6.2 Disjuncts

A syntactic category of adverbials is the disjunct (*CGEL* 8.121–2). Disjuncts are semantically superordinate to the clauses in which they occur. Thus, *It has rained, obviously* = "It is obvious that it has rained"; or *Frankly, this is not working* = "I am frank in saying that this is not working." Disjuncts, as a category, are part of common-core English. But in British, there appear to be a greater propensity to use them and a greater variety of forms with disjunctive function. Most, if not all, of the following can be found also in American. Yet the category as a whole is suggestive of Britishness. CIC shows each of the following to be more frequent in British use than in American (except for *more like*, which is too rare as a disjunct for a judgment of frequency). The British/American iptmw is shown within parentheses after each lemma.

amazingly (62.1/34.2) <**Amazingly** – that is, it amazed me – she smiled with an almost impish good humour.> 1987 Bawden 82.

arguably (71.9/48.5) <He will retire as **arguably** the greatest race horse in the world.> 1986 Oct. TV sports report.

astonishingly (29.4/11.9) <Perhaps, **astonishingly**, she disarmed self-defence.> 1972 Drabble 24.

awkwardly (42.7/16) <**Awkwardly**, this tax encourages the rich colleges to minimise their cash incomes.> 1989 July 8 *Economist* 54/2.

exceptionally (86.7/37) <It was, **exceptionally**, a state restaurant, which taught us not to make assumptions.> 1989 Aug. 28 *Daily Telegraph* 17/7–8.

famously (45.6/33.7) <The Prince of Wales is **famously** a welly-booted and Barbour-suited champion of the countryside who farms organically in muddy Gloucestershire.> 1999 Mar. 20 *Times* Weekend 12/1.

funnily (18.5/0.2) <[Clive Bradley:] **Funnily** enough, a Brit like me found himself relatively shy turning up for the case method of teaching [at Yale Law School].> 1990 Critchfield 257.

importantly, more (69.3/47.6) <I had momentarily forgotten that she probably didn't know who George was, nor, **more importantly**, who his daughter was.> 1987 Bawden 60.

interestingly (64.3/33.6) <**Interestingly**, he [John Major] says of her [Margaret Thatcher], "Apart from admiring her, I *like* her. She is a jolly nice woman."> 1990 Critchfield xxiv.

irony, by an (0.2/0) Ironically <**By an irony**, it was Grade's peremptory departure from the Beeb the previous year that had cleared the way for him.> 1988 Apr. *Illustrated London News* 58/1.

more like More likely <Called by cockerels **more like**.> 1987 Feb. 2 *Evening Standard* 23/2.

regrettably (17.8/9.5) <And, **regrettably**, many colleges only teach their students to type at the bare minimum words per minute; what's needed is over 60wpm, and an *accurate* 60wpm, plus.> 1988 Sept. 15 *Times* 41/1–2.

remarkably (148.4/94.9) <**Remarkably**, this was upheld in 1983 in the High Court.> 1988 Sept. 14 *Times* 18/2.

sadly (241/58.6) <. . . the *Queen Elizabeth* and the *Queen Mary*. **Sadly**, they are no more.> 1988 Dec. *In Britain* 35/4.

seriously (570.8/494.7) Really <My God, . . . you haven't **seriously** locked the door?> 1976 Raphael 132.

surprisingly (265.2/177.3) <In March he **surprisingly** accepted the job of managing director of BBC Television.> 1988 Apr. *Illustrated London News* 58/1.

unexpectedly (78.1/64.3) <More **unexpectedly**, she shares an allotment on the south side of the river with a retired postman called Prime.> 1987 Bawden 17.

uniquely (47.9/30.5) <[World Cup rugby:] Of course, extra time is added (in Australia, **uniquely**, by timekeepers who record it from the referee's signals and sound a hooter at the end).> 1987 June 18 *Times* 40/8.

unusually (103.7/98.4) <I noticed that Tim, **unusually**, asked for a double Scotch.> 1991 Barnard 76.

usefully (34.5/5.5) <More **usefully**, perhaps, the guide clearly shows students wishing to study, say, dentistry which 16 institutions offer it, what A-level subjects they need to have passed and how stiff the competition is.> 1987 June 20 *Times* 24/2.

worryingly (12.1/0) <**Worryingly**, he then tries convincing me that my arm's lost feeling.> 1994 Sept. 28–Oct. 5 *Time Out* 8/4.

6.3 Comparison

Only a few differences in the comparison of adverbs have been noted.

far/further/furthest Far/farther/farthest: CIC shows a British/American preference for *further* (2756.7/1402.9) over *farther* (90.6/169.8), with the British preference being stronger, and a British preference for *furthest* (27) over *farthest* (10.5), with a slight American preference for *farthest* (13.9) over *furthest* (10.7). <Lewis drove half a mile or so **further**.> 1992 Dexter 101. <Career worries were **furthest** from the former marine's mind.> 1987 Feb. 27 *Evening Standard* 13/1.

The choice between inflectional or periphrastic comparison is variable in common-core English, but some choices are more characteristic of one variety than the other.

badly, more Worse: Although the normal comparative of *badly* is *worse*, *CGEL* (7.83) reports that periphrastic comparison is required in British after *need* and *want*: *I really need that job* ***more badly*** *than you*. CIC has 1.2 iptmw of *more badly* in British texts and 0.4 in American.

oftener More often: CIC has 5.7 iptmw of *oftener* in British texts, and 0.7 in American. <You ought to do this **oftener**.> 1940 Shute 145.

Also the choice between positive, comparative, and superlative forms is sometimes characteristic of national varieties.

best Better <Well, I'd **best** hop along to class.> 1989 Oct. 5, undergraduate English major at University College London.

best pleased Well pleased: CIC has 3.6 iptmw of *best pleased* and 10.1 of *well pleased* in British texts; it has none of *best pleased* and 2.4 of *well pleased* in American texts. <His editor had not been **best pleased**.> 1991 Critchley 151.

6.4 Adverb order

Different adverbs have different typical positions in a clause (*CGEL* 8.14–23, 150–2). Although there is often considerable latitude in positioning an adverb, certain positions may be more preferable for a given adverb than others. The positions of adverbs can be identified with the following symbols (*CGEL* 8.14), in which *I* or *i* is initial, *M* or *m* is medial, and *E* or *e* is end:

> *I* They *iM* must *M* have *mM* been *eM* watching *iE* us *E*.

The order of adverbs of probability (such as *certainly* and *probably*) before or after an operator (such as *has*) differs between British and American (Swan 1995, 26; Johansson 1979, 200). Those adverbs have the following order distributions in CIC texts (the numbers are iptmw):

	British	American
has certainly	22.7	13.4
certainly has	11.7	22.2
has probably	21.2	14.5
probably has	8.8	18.6

These figures do not take account of whether or not the operator was emphasized (which Swan reports as an influencing factor), but they support the generalization that American prefers the iM position rather than the M (or later) position for these adverbs and British has the opposite preference.

Adverbs of frequency (*generally, never, usually*), like those of probability, tend to occur in medial position, after the first auxiliary, if there is one. However, with these also American has a higher tolerance for placement before the first auxiliary than does British: *She* ***usually*** *is at work from nine to five* versus *She is* ***usually*** *at work from nine to five* (Johansson 1979, 200). In the next example, the adverb of frequency would be expected in the medial position, after the first auxiliary verb (*Previously he had* ***always*** *been . . .*); here it occurs instead before the main verb.

always <He had previously been **always** negotiating with Islamic Jihad.> 1987 Jan. 27 BBC1 morning news.

An adverb of time-when typically occurs initially or at the end of its clause. The initial position is favored except in relative clauses, where the initial position of the relative has priority. However, in the following examples, adverbs of time occur in one of the medial positions (like *previously* in the immediately preceding example). These examples are from journalistic (or in one case advertising) prose, which may explain the shift of the time adverb, since journalistic writing prefers the subject in first position.

during the week <He . . . lives **during the week** in a grace-and-favour residence in Admiralty House . . .> 2003 June 25 *Guardian* international ed. 9/2.

earlier in the week <We did **earlier in the week** publish a complete costing of our manifesto.> 1987 May 18 BBC1 morning news (Alliance spokesman).

last night/year <A girl aged four was **last night** waiting for a life-saving liver transplant in a London hospital.> 1987 Apr. 23 *Times* 2/6. <Priscilla . . . is a Brit living in America, where she **last year** earned £30,000.> 1987 May 11 *Evening Standard* 27/4–5.

now <Eric can **now** hold a saucepan.> ca. 1987 tube train poster ad for arthritis treatment.

this afternoon <The Home Office was **this afternoon** going to the High Court to try to overturn the judge's ruling.> 1987 Feb. 18 *Evening Standard* 2/3–4.

today <The conference is **today** to give its assent to the joint strike.> 1987 Apr. 20 *Times* 1/3. <The Government will **today** announce an innovative structure for the £1 billion-plus flotation of BAA.> 1987 June 22 *Times* 1/7.

yesterday <Retailers were **yesterday** ordered not to stock a so-called "Viagra pop" due to go [on] sale in Britain next week, which claims to use herbs to boost sexual performance.> 2003 June 26 *Guardian* international ed. 8/6. <Culture Secretary Tessa Jowell **yesterday** announced plans to bring some democracy into the lottery.> 2003 July 4 *Daily Express* 12/2.

In the following example with two adverbs of time, an alternative is to put the larger time unit first, followed by the smaller one (*last year in February*) or to subordinate the larger time unit to the smaller one (*in February of last year*). <. . . the vice-chancellors . . . argue that the 1988 pay round was covered by a settlement negotiated **in February last year**.> 1988 Oct. 16 *Sunday Telegraph* 2/6.

When an adverb of time or duration cooccurs with an adverb of place, the expected order is place + time/duration. The reverse order is exemplified by the following citations.

late home *Late home* occurs in CIC British texts a little more than one-third as often as *home late* but not at all in American texts. <His missus would go on a vinegar trip if he was **late home** again.> 1989 Bainbridge 150.

longer here Here longer <What a pity you can't stay **longer here**!> 1986 Benson 53.

As a modifier of the subordinating conjunction *since, ever* usually precedes: *ever since*. The reverse order, however, is exemplified in the following citation.

since ever <He has a cottage near the church, and **since ever** anybody can remember he's been saying he has lived in it for eighty-seven years.> 1983 Innes 109.

Other matters of order are illustrated by the following citations.

anyway The usual positions for *anyway* are clause initial or final. But medial position is also attested, albeit exceptionally. <But the measure . . . would subsidise many of those who would **anyway** go private.> 2003 June 12 *Times* 20/2.

better had Had better (Swan 1995, 226). The same order of *better* first is possible in American, though the CIC has no American examples and 9 in British texts. Two are from fiction: <Somewhere along the line, Rosemary supposed, there might have been a question raised about whether the wife had been informed, and a bit of perhaps we **better had**.> and <I'm sure you're astute enough to work it out, and for all your sakes you **better had**.>. The others are from spoken texts, such as <Yes you **better had**>.

defiantly <Marjorie looked **defiantly** at him.> (an American clerk in copying the quotation typed: "at him defiantly") 1988 Lodge 234.

just <Have **just** a think on your own, OK? [i.e., "We'll give you a moment to think about it."]> 1989 Jan. 28 ch. 9 San Francisco *Mystery: Inspector Morse*.

marginally <"Anyway, I'm too old and fat to model a fur coat," she said. [¶] "Of course not," said Hugo, gallantly, while thinking that in fact she, **marginally**, was.> 1980 Drabble 7.

matter not, to Not to matter: There are no tokens of *to matter not* in CIC for either British or American texts. <It seemed **to matter not** to Ball that it was the filthy elements that reduced Portsmouth's attendance from the hoped-for biggest of the season to one of under five figures.> 1986 Oct. 25 *Times* 41/4.

6.5 Adverbial particles

Although British and American share a common inventory of adverbial particles, with only a few differences of form (e.g., *on and off* vs. *off and on*), they differ significantly in their use of those particles. The following list is of a few adverbial particles. For many others that complement particular verbs, see § 11.1.6.

about Around (Andersen 1972, 861; Swan 1995, 53–4) <They don't like being shunted **about**. You start moving men **about** from one job to another, and they start complaining.> 1988 Lodge 124. <. . . apart from occasionally being knocked **about** a bit it has not been physically or psychologically menacing.> 1988 May *In Britain* 39/4. Cf. § 6.1 ABOUT.

down Away from an important place (cf. UP) <In more hierarchical days, . . . London was generally accepted as the most important centre in the United Kingdom, and all journeys . . . away from London were *down*, even if they went north. In 1846 Lord Chancellor Campbell wrote: 'At Christmas I went *down* (from London) into Scotland and, crossing the Cheviots, was nearly lost in a snowstorm.' Miss La Creevey, miniature painter and London landlady in *Nicholas Nickleby*: 'You don't mean to say that you are really going all the way *down* into Yorkshire this cold winter's weather, Mr Nickleby?' British trawlermen used to speak of making a trip *down* north, even when they were heading to the Kara Sea or somewhere else within a few degrees of latitude of the North Pole, very rightly regarding Grimsby or Aberdeen as the centre of the world, and all voyages from there as by definition *down*. . . . To go *up* to Oxford means to take up residence at the beginning of term, until you come *down* at the end of term, unless you have had the bad luck to be sent *down* (expelled) earlier. But if your parents come to visit you, they will come *down* to Oxford from London, and you will take a trip *up* to London for the day. This is merely an extension of the hierarchical system of *up* and *down*. As a member of the university, you go *up* to the centre of your universe. As an ordinary citizen, you go *up* to London from Oxford or Cambridge.> 1990 Howard 107–8.

in **1.** Inside <They've got real cream-horns and brandy snaps with cream **in**.> 1986 Clark 202–3. **2.** "*Brit.* (of a fire) alight: *do you keep the fire* **in** *all night?*" (*CED* s.v. *in*). **3.** In the middle of a quarrel <Well, as I said, we quarrelled,

Hereward and I, as we always did. We were well **in**, when Dersingham barged in.> 1991 Greenwood 200.

on and off Off and on; intermittently: Although *on and off* is the favored order in both national varieties, American is relatively more favorable to *off and on*, particularly in the sense "intermittently." *MW* so defines *off and on*, with only a cross reference to that form from *on and off*. The *OED* documents *off and on* from 1535, but *on and off* only from the nineteenth century. CIC has 4.5 times as many tokens of *on and off* as of *off and on* in British texts, and only twice as many in American texts. <He lived for forty five years in Italy **on and off** but never learnt to speak Italian.> SEU w1-1.106.

***number* out** *Number* off <As it turned out, she was correct on the first two counts, but on the last she was **one out**.> 1994 Oct. 1 *Times* Magazine 54/5.

over to *someone* Up to *someone* <They are happy to have done their bit in rescuing a historic building that was well on its way to oblivion. But now it is **over to** someone else to complete the task.> 1991 Feb. 9 *Daily Telegraph* Weekend 20/5.

up Toward an important place (cf. DOWN) <Saves a special journey **up** to town.> 1985 Bingham 47.

6.5.1 Omission of a particle

home from home Home away from home: CIC has 5.0 iptmw of *home from home* in British texts and 0.1 in American texts. It has 0.4 iptmw of *home away from home* in British texts and 4.2 in American texts. <**Home from home** was what people wanted then and they achieved that by taking their holidays in English ghettos eating chips.> 1991 Feb. 18 *Girl about Town* 10/1.

7 Qualifiers

Qualifiers (also called degree adverbs) are expressions that modify adjectival or adverbial constructions. They seem to be more frequently used in British than in American, a generalization that is statistically supported for *quite* and *very* according to the LOB and Brown corpora. On the other hand, some qualifiers are characteristic of American, such as *kind of* in *The argument was **kind of** compelling*, *mighty* in *It's **mighty** hot today*, *plenty* in *The nights were **plenty** cold* (a *MW* usage note points out that, despite advice against the use, it is more precise in some contexts than the alternatives, although it is informal), and *some* in *He's feeling **some** better today*. Other qualifiers identified as primarily American are *pretty, real, really, so*, and *totally* (*LGSWE* 564–7).

7.1 Modifying adjectives or adverbs

(a) **bit** A little; rather: CIC has 1833.7 iptmw in British texts and 670.7 in American texts. <After the judge had said he hoped that the women would "be able to arrive at some sort of truce", Lady Archer, 58, remarked to her solicitor: "That's **a bit** rich."> 2003 July 4 *Times* 7/1.

absolutely <How **absolutely** super!> 1985 Mortimer 229. Cf. *LGSWE* 564.

as near as makes no difference/matter/odds Very nearly: CIC has no American tokens but a number of British ones. <There are new options. These are mostly based upon the realisation, which has come upon the Irish like a cloudburst at a race meeting, that the country is **as near as makes no odds** bankrupt.> 1987 Feb. 9 *Evening Standard* 7/2.

at all Very *in a negative context* <He didn't feel he knew either **at all** well.> 1983 Innes 55.

awfully, most Very <"Well . . ." The man paused diffidently ". . . it's **most awfully** kind of you – "> 1975 Price 28.

barking Completely, before *mad*; *barking* is also used alone as an adjective in the sense "mad." CIC has 3 iptmw of *barking mad* in British texts and none in American texts. <The man's **barking mad,** thinks Faro.> 2001 Drabble 252.

best, not (before *pleased*) Very little; not at all: CIC has 3.6 iptmw in British texts and none in American texts. <They were**n't best pleased** about that; what with her being new and them being so busy just now.> 2000 Aird 76.

blasted Damned <Well, don't look so **blasted** boot-faced about it, then! That's the trouble with you, you've no bloody sense of humour.> 1968 Porter 13.

bleeding *euphemism for* bloody <Just **bleedin'** bored and nosey.> 1985 Ebdon 86.

bloody Very: CIC has 709.7 iptmw of *bloody* in all uses in British texts and 150.5 in American texts. <I'd forgotten about that **bloody** awful one-way system.> 1993 Smith 167. <The show is **bloody** good.> 1998 Jan. 7 *Evening Standard* 53/2. Cf. §§ 5.1.1 MINDED, 5.2, 6.1, 10 BLOODY; *LGSWE* 564.

bloody sight Much <**Bloody sight** too interesting, if you ask me.> 1940 Shute 111–2.

blooming *euphemism for* bloody <Our geraniums are fantastic this year . . . and so are our roses / In fact the whole garden is **blooming** lovely!> (*here a pun*) 1997 July 10 "Fred Basset" (British comic strip) *Chicago Tribune* 5 12.

crashingly <Bernard Shaw had seized on the **crashingly** obvious point that no Englishman can open his mouth without being despised by some other Englishman.> 1984 Smith 13.

cringingly <To compensate for their lack of thought, he accuses [TV] writers of "fobbing us off with **cringingly** appalling anecdotes about bottoms and urinals, with a lot of arm-waving and screaming."> 1987 May 29 *Evening Standard* 31/2.

dead Extremely <Paul and Fatima who run it [a café] are **dead** friendly and nice.> 1994 Sept. 14–21 *Time Out* 33/4.

deuced <He painted my grandfather – **deuced** well.> 1937 Innes, *Hamlet* 233.

devilish Very <We know **devilish** little about that sort of thing, after all.> 1983 Innes 69.

effing CIC has 2.6 iptmw in British texts and none in American texts. <Oh yes, I'm good with people. I'm **effing** brilliant.> 1994 Sept. 24 *Guardian Weekend* 84/1. Cf. § 5.2.

ever *post-head qualifier of superlative adjectives* Although originally an Americanism as a qualifier in connection with superlatives, *ever* is now common-core English. The *OED* reports this use (s.v. *ever* adv. 7.f) with early American examples, such as <1906 'O. Henry' *Four Million* (1916) 71 Anna and Maggie worked side by side in the factory, and were the greatest chums **ever**>, in which *ever* is at the end of a noun phrase containing a superlative adjective. However, later British citations place *ever* immediately after a superlative adjective within a noun phrase. The use of *ever* as a post-head modifier of the adjective is 2.3 times more frequent in CIC British texts than in American. <Neil Kinnock had one of his best **ever** results with 22,947 majority in Islwyn, David Owen had his biggest **ever** win in Plymouth Devonport by 6,470.> 1987 July *Illustrated London News* 21/1.

ever so CIC has 56.5 iptmw in British texts and 14.6 in American texts. <You're **ever so** close to a "Touch of Pine" store.> 1995 May 26 radio commercial.

fair <By the time they arrive north of the border, . . . they have worked themselves up into a **fair** old lather.> 1999 Mar. 6 *Economist* 37/1.

flipping <I had caught a **flipping** awful cold.> 1960 Feb. *Lilliput* 61/2.

frightfully CIC has 10.3 iptmw in British texts and 2 in American texts. <. . . it really was **frightfully** good.> 1989 Mar. *In Britain* 37/4.

full Very: *Full well* is about 1.5 times more frequent in British CIC texts than in American. <The letter centre is that way, as I'm sure you know **full well**.> 1987 Apr. 20 ITV *Crossroads*.

full on On full; fully on: In the sense "all the way on" (of lights, sound, heat, water, etc.), *on full* is the norm in common-core English, as opposed to *full on* "precisely on" as in *full on the lips* or "directly, straight ahead" as in *hit the car full on*. But *full on* is more than 3 times as frequent in CIC British texts as in American. <Although it was a warm day the radiators were **full on**.> 1987 Graham 97.

hellish <These things are always **hellish** difficult to decide.> 1976 Bradbury 29.

hugely CIC has 73.3 iptmw in British texts and 28.8 in American texts. <Graduates are **hugely** important to us.> 1994 Sept. 25 *Sunday Times* 3 2/6.

incredibly <It's . . . **incredibly** lyrical.> 1986 Dec. 4 *Midweek* 21/1–2.

jolly CIC has 76 iptmw in British texts and 11.7 in American texts. <That was **jolly** clever of you!> 1990 Rowlands 57. <'Tis the season to be **jolly** . . . pleased that everything you're looking for is in one place.> (syntactic pun) 2002 Nov. 17 underground train car poster for John Lewis store. Cf. § 6.1. – **jolly good** CIC has 21.1 iptmw of *jolly good* in British texts and 1.1 in American texts. <So you found Ryan, Mrs. Clutton. **Jolly good**.> 2003 James 242. – **jolly well** CIC has 4.8 iptmw of *jolly well* in British texts and none in American texts. <If he's the one who did it in the first place, you should **jolly well** make him do it in his own time.> 1990 Rowlands 22.

near Nearly <. . . it has sadly made it **near** impossible to watch the film with an open mind.> 1988 Sept. 13 *Metropolitan* 10/1–2. – **near enough** CIC has 18.3 iptmw in British texts and 6 in American texts. <At night, provided the alarm system was switched on, Cort Place was **near enough** impregnable.> 1987 Hart 85.

nothing like Not nearly <None of them would have ever been asked to . . . Holland House, **nothing like** clever enough.> 1979 Snow 226.

over the top <. . . she's always been a bit **over the top** vitriolic about Hermione Orwell.> 1987 Bawden 57.

proper(ly) Really, very <**Proper** upset, he was.> 1968 Aird 122.

quite The word *quite* is significantly more frequent in British than in American English. LOB has 484 occurrences, compared with Brown's 281 (Hofland and Johansson 1982, 522; also *LGSWE* 566). CIC has 4523.6 iptmw in British texts and 1541.4 in American texts. <**Quite** Another of those English words that has been not only changing but is now even reversing its meaning. Thus, while it originally meant 'totally' ('I was **quite** alone'), it also meant 'actually' ('she was **quite** ill'); and out of this second sense has grown the use of quite to mean 'fairly' or 'somewhat'. So, when we say 'his work is **quite** satisfactory' do we mean it 'somewhat' or 'totally' satisfies? Americans still, and not only in this instance, tend to prefer the old sense; in England the original meaning now sounds distinctly affected – and not just **quite** affected.> 1984 Smith 198. **1**. *with simple adjectives* <. . . they have been known to get **quite** nasty.> 1989 Mar. 19 *Manchester Guardian Weekly* 24/5. **2**. *with superlatives* Certainly, decidedly, much <Greenbaum's book provides **quite** the best discussion of the problem that I have read.> 1989 Apr. *English Today* (5.2) 48/1. **3**. *with numbers* Fully <Sergeant Forsyte struggled with them for **quite** ten minutes.> 1977 Barnard 80. **4**. *with adjectival nouns* Really <It might be **quite** fun.> 1959 Innes 5. **5**. *with adverbs* Very < . . . it can drip away **quite** happily.> 1987 Oliver 81.

rather CIC has 3880.3 iptmw in British texts and 1943.8 in American texts. <I'm afraid they were **rather** good, weren't they?> 1988 Stoppard 20.

right **1**. *with adjectives* Very; real <At the photo-shoot, the band suggested a **right** royal knees-up round the old Joanna.> 1994 Sept. 28–Oct. 5 *Time Out* 6/3. – **right little** CIC has 1.5 iptmw in British texts and none in American texts. <In fact, those banks could be **right little** hotbeds of alien intelligence.> 1985 Clark 61. – **right old** CIC has 3.3 iptmw in British texts and none in American texts. <She was a **right old** so-and-so, his mum.> 1992 Charles 128. **2**. *with adverbials* Completely; altogether; all <"We've scared them away." [¶] "**Right** away?"> 1987 Nov. *Illustrated London News* 82/4–84/2. – **right the way** <We costume you in frock coats **right the way** through.> 1987 Bradbury 24.

ruddy "*Informal, chiefly Brit. . . .* bloody" (*CED*). <**Ruddy** great engine in front of you to keep the bullets off.> 1940 Shute 112.

seriously Very: CIC has 1.4 times as many of this use in British texts as in American. <. . . if the Labour Party ever gets back into power, she will be a **seriously** important adviser to Downing Street.> 1988 June *Illustrated London News* 36/3.

sincerely Very <Stay put while I phone my editor. Don't budge if you want to be **sincerely** rich.> 1991 Critchley 175.

spanking In common-core English, this qualifier collocates mainly with *clean* and *new*. CIC has 3.8 iptmw of *spanking new* in British texts and 1.5 in American texts. It has no tokens of American *spanking fine* or *spanking good*. <*The Sun* in Scotland had a **spanking** good exclusive story about the President of the Scottish Conservative Association and an Edinburgh prostitute.> 1989 Sept. 14 *Times* 17/4.

stone-bonker <Tomorrow we all try to make **stone-bonker** sure that Hopcraft was shanghaied from here.> 1985 Clark 124.

streets "*chiefly Br* FAR AND AWAY < ~ *ahead of the other girls*>" (*LDEL*). CIC has 3.6 iptmw of *streets ahead* in British texts and none in American texts. <London Rents **Streets** Ahead.> 2004 Jan. 2 *Times* Business 27/2–3.

that So; very "*dial Br* to such an extreme degree" (*LDEL*). <I'll be **that** grateful.> 1995 Sept. 11 BBC1 "The Chamber." <I'm **that** excited.> 2003 July 4 *Times* T2 2/2.

that bit A bit; somewhat <. . . she was wrongly dressed: her powder-blue suit and hat were **that bit** too formal and old-fashioned for the fête.> 1985 Barnard 54.

thumping CIC has 0.5 iptmw of *thumping great/good* in British texts and none in American texts. <. . . we insist on a **thumping** great order or a high price.> 1988 Lodge 76.

thundering "*Br informal* VERY 1 – chiefly in ***thundering** good* and ***thundering** great*" (*LDEL*). <A prolonged round of applause from the ground distracted Charters. 'Someone out, by the sound of it.' [¶] 'Or a **thundering** good six,' said Caldicott.> 1985 Bingham 179.

too . . . by half Much too <Mavis didn't seem the type to kill herself. **Too** self-satisfied **by half**.> 1991 Charles 199.

very Although *very* is common-core English, it is more often used in British than in American; LOB has 1229 tokens, and Brown 796 (Hofland and Johansson 1982, 540). CIC has 12,966.6 iptmw in British texts and 9442.5 in American texts.

well + alone Well enough + alone, after *leave* or *let*: CIC has 7.7 iptmw of *well alone* in British texts and 0.2 in American texts. CIC has 4 iptmw of *well enough alone* in British texts and 18 in American texts. **1**. *with intransitive verb* <Good God, Pam, leave **well** alone.> 2000 Granger 43. **2**. *with transitive verb* <It would be possible, and much more comfortable, to backtrack now, this minute, out of the whole conversation and leave things **well** alone.> 1998 Joss 242.

well + in with "*Brit. informal.* on good terms (with): *the foreman was **well** in with the management*" (*CED*). <I am **well** in with the police.> 1986 Dec. 4 *Midweek* 7/2.

well *posthead modifier of emphasizing adverbs* bleeding, bloody, ruddy, *etc.*, see §6.1.

whacking + great "*Informal, chiefly Brit.*" (*CED*). <We'd still need a **whacking** great bank loan.> 1988 Lodge 372.

7.2 Modifying prepositional phrases

a bit A little; rather <. . . it looks **a bit** like brown-nosed sucking-up to shower your boss with frequent individual presents.> 2003 June 28 *Times* Weekend 2/5.

anything As much as: CIC has 10.5 iptmw of *anything up to* in British texts and 1.2 in American. <Express mail which normally took three days to arrive

was now taking **anything** up to eight weeks.> 1987 May 28 *Evening Standard* 10/5.

bang Exactly; completely <. . . brings the story **bang** up to date.> 1999 Mar. 13 BBC1 News.

hard Close; right <If you're running a pub **hard** against a 2,000-acre privately owned estate, it would ill-behove you to slag off the owners.> 1998 Jan. 3 *Times* Weekend 3/4.

quite <Nothing **quite** like the Commonwealth has ever been created or evolved before.> 1990 Mar. 12 a printed program for "An Observance for Commonwealth Day."

right <She's in two parts, sir – **right** in two separate pieces.> 1940 Shute 232.

spot + on Exactly at <Mrs Denny, the medium, came in **spot** on two o'clock.> 1989 Sept. 1 *Times* 12/6.

too Too much <Embarrassed, feeling **too** like a Peeping Tom for comfort, he scrambled to the floor.> 1988 Lodge 108–9.

very Very much <Both men, safely on the other side of the door, felt **very** like naughty schoolboys who had avoided a wigging but had been given a talking down which was almost worse.> 1977 Barnard 142.

7.3 Modifying comparative structures

7.3.1 Equivalences

nothing like *modifying "as/so . . . as" constructions*: Although *not nearly* is the norm in common-core English, CIC British texts have 4.8 iptmw of *nothing like* and American 0.1. <The food is **nothing like** as imaginative in content or in preparation as it is in neighbouring Spain.> 1992 newspaper CIC.

nowhere near CIC British texts have 9.2 iptmw and American 3.9. <They [New York unions] are **nowhere near** as Luddite as British unions were at their worst.> 1994 Sept. *Tatler* 92/2.

quite Just <He took a taxi across to Waterloo, although the tube would have been **quite** as quick.> 1959 Innes 21.

7.3.2 Superlatives

much the most The very most; by far the most: CIC has 3.8 iptmw in British texts and 0.2 in American. <**Much the most** difficult bit was hiding them in the cupboard.> 1998 Rowling 160 (*US ed.* By far the hardest part).

8 Prepositions

Dieter Mindt and Christel Weber (1989) concluded from a comparative study of prepositions in the Brown and LOB corpora that 99.9 percent of all prepositional tokens are of forms used in both British and American and that the six most common prepositions (*of, in, to, for, with, on*) have the same rank order in both varieties and account for nearly three quarters of the occurrences of prepositions in the two corpora. It is clear that prepositional differences are not mainly of form. There are, however, a good many differences in collocation and frequency.

8.1 Choice of preposition

The most significant prepositional differences are in the choice of one preposition over another in particular contexts, that is, the meaning of the preposition in context or its idiomatic use or collocational probabilities, especially in regard to the preposition's object. Cf. also §§ 11.1.1.2, 11.1.6.1, 11.1.6.2.1, 11.2.1, and 11.4.1.

Prepositions that are primarily American include *(in) back of* (Burchfield 1996, 85; Peters 2004, 60–1). CIC has 0.5 iptmw of *in back of* in British texts (four-fifths of them oral and the other fifth from popular journalism) and 7.3 in American texts (in all text categories except oral talk about lexicography, which is the smallest of all text categories and therefore unrepresentative).

about 1. Around; in the vicinity of <I am aware that all **about** me people are watching, assessing, storing up tit-bits of information to pass on.> 1977 December 7 *Punch* 1120/2. 2. Around; on every side or in every part of <"The trouble with your hair," he sniffed as he faffed his fingers **about** in it, "is that it's not saying anything."> 2005 Jan. 15 *Daily Telegraph* 27/5. 3. With; on; on the person of: The idiom *keep/have one's wits about one* is more frequent in CIC British texts (5.7 iptmw) than American (0.7). <Was glad Ross had his wits **about** him sufficiently to watch out for traffic when visibility was so dodgy.> 1983 Radley 144. In the sense of physical possession, the use is clearly

British. <*I haven't any money* ***about*** *me.*> *CED*. <*have you a match* ~ *you?*> *LDEL*. Cf. § 11.1.6.1 GO ABOUT WITH.

across On the other side of <A large Asda superstore stands **across** the road.> 1995 June 8 *London Review of Books* 8/3. – **across to** Across from; opposite <The tea party was in rooms overlooking the main court, **across to** the chapel.> 1985 Byatt 129.

against **1.** For; in anticipation of <He sent some of his books and papers for Mr Caldicott to keep in storage **against** his return.> 1985 Bingham 16. **2.** In accordance with <Mr Rhodes also says that your department insists on ordering all pens . . . centrally, and then distributing them **against** departmental requisitions.> 1982 Lynn and Jay 170. **3.** In compensation for <Charters glared at him. 'Official Mourner? What's that?' [¶] 'Appointed by the Home Office, Unpaid, of course, though one receives a small honorarium **against** expenses – black tie allowance and so on.'> 1985 Bingham 58. **4.** Because of; to protect from <He . . . put on his tweed coat **against** a blustery autumnal morning.> 1986 James 18. **5.** Next to <On your answer sheet, indicate the letter A, B, C or D **against** the number of each item 26 to 40 for the answer you choose.> 1987 May directions on a sample Cambridge Syndicate examination. – **hard against** Very near; right next to <If you're running a pub **hard against** a 2,000-acre privately owned estate, it would ill-behove [*Amer*. "behoove"] you to slag off the owners – particularly when several of the estate staff were in the bar.> 1998 Jan. 3 *Times* Weekend 3/4. – **claim** ***something*** **against tax** Claim *something* as an exemption; claim *something* on one's taxes <. . . actors will be taxed at source and will not be able to **claim** a whole range of vital expenses **against tax**.> 1993 Feb. 7 *Sunday Times* 8 18/3.

along (a road or passageway) Down (from one location to another on a road, etc.); on (a road, etc.) <Straight into the school, through the swing doors. Right, and all the way **along** the passage.> 1991 Dickinson 41. – **along at** At <Perhaps this afternoon, **along at** the cottage hospital.> 1987 Hart 18. – **along to** To <Simply visit a local bank or building society or go **along to** your post office.> SEU w7-16.78.

amidst Amid; in the middle of (Peters 2004, 35): In CIC, British *amidst* is less than one-third as frequent as *amid*; but American *amid* is approximately 23 times more frequent than *amidst*. <Even **amidst** the solemnity and dead seriousness of this stake-out, there was something very funny about the man from the *Star*.> 1995 June 8 *London Review of Books* 8/4.

amongst Among (Peters 2004, 35): The BNC has 4447 instances (17 percent) of *amongst* versus 22,441 instances (83 percent) of *among*. The Michigan Corpus of Academic Spoken English (MICASE) has 19 instances (12 percent) of *amongst* versus 146 instances (88 percent) of *among*. LOB has 45 instances (13 percent) of *amongst* versus 313 instances (87 percent) of *among*; Brown has 4 instances (1 percent) of *amongst* versus 370 instances (99 percent) of *among*. Similarly, CIC has 13 percent of *amongst* versus 87 percent of *among* in British texts, but 1 percent of *amongst* versus 99 percent of *among* in American texts, the same percentages as in LOB and Brown. <A dozen or so newspapers . . . lay in a staggered pile on a table just inside the breakfast room – *The Sunday Times* not **amongst** them.> 1992 Dexter 82.

apart from Aside from; except for; in addition to; other than: The BNC has 6411 instances of *apart from*, and only 298 of *aside from*, and the text of the *OED* has 606 instances of *apart from*, and only 113 of *aside from*. (A majority of the *OED*'s citations are British, as is all of its editorial language, in which *apart from* features prominently.) CIC has 563.7 iptmw of *apart from* in British texts and 109.3 in American texts. It has 46.8 of *aside from* in British texts and 89.1 in American texts. <**Apart from** anything else, it is not fair on the little people to make them sit quietly while great-uncle Tony and his friends rabbit on about Iraq and the European constitution.> 2003 July 9 *Times* 2/3–4. Cf. § 6.1 APART.

as from As of: CIC has 40 iptmw of *as from* in British texts and 27.1 in American. Conversely it has 74.1 iptmw of *as of* (in all uses) in British texts and 234.7 in American texts. <**As from** the beginning of this term, Professor Sidney Greenbaum has taken early retirement as Quain Professor of English Language and Literature.> 1991 Mar. *UCL NEWS* (University College London magazine) 19/1.

at The *at* of British English often corresponds to different prepositions in American. In some cases, the entire prepositional phrase introduced by *at* is expressed otherwise in American.

at *an* attempt On *an* attempt <She . . . got caught (and prosecuted) **at** her first **attempt**.> 1990 Aug. 24–30 *Good Times* 5/7.

at the back (of) In back (of): CIC has 257.4 iptmw of *at the back* in British texts and 39 in American. Conversely it has 6.1 iptmw of *in back* in British texts and 35.9 in American texts. <Their council flat, in a high-rise block, had garages for the tenants **at the back**.> 1989 Williams 179.

at *a* bungalow In <He knew that she lived **at** a **bungalow** outside Taunton, Somerset.> 1994 Oct. 4 *Daily Telegraph* 3/1.

at college In: CIC has 27.9 iptmw of *at college* in British texts and 15.9 in American texts. Conversely it has 9.9 iptmw of *in college* in British texts and 147.9 in American texts. <My biggest thieving phase was when I was **at college** in a small town.> 1990 Aug. 24–30 *Good Times* 5/7.

at dead of night In the dead of night: CIC has equal British and American frequency for *in the dead of night*, but 0.8 iptmw for *at dead of night* in British texts and none in American. <. . . there is just no evidence that the Bank of England is dumping French francs and Danish kroner, **at dead of night**, on the Tokyo market.> 1993 Feb. 13 *Spectator* 14/2.

at the double On the double: The idiom, with either preposition, is more frequent in British than in American, but whereas *on the double* occurs only sporadically in either variety, CIC has 2.8 iptmw of *at the double* in British texts and none in American. <The Government is moving **at the double** to

increase the maximum penalty for insider trading from two to seven years.> 1987 Jan. 20 *Guardian* 12/3.

at *some* election (campaign) In some election: An American clerk, transcribing a British citation with *at*, mistyped *in*. <**At** this **election** people will have a clear choice. . . . What I'm concerned about is that people understand the nature of the choice that people have **at** the **election**.> 2005 Jan. 16 BBC1 *Breakfast with Frost*.

at *an examination*, grades Grades on *an examination* <The diploma will be awarded to students at four levels of ability. . . . foundation level would be the same as the lower **grades at** GCSE.> 2003 July 16 *Times* 1/3.

at half-cock Halfcocked: In CIC, *half-cocked* occurs with approximately equal frequency in British and American, but *at half-cock* (used with about the same frequency as *half-cocked* in British) is not used at all in American.

at hand On hand, available: In CIC, *at hand* is used with approximately equal frequency in British and American; but *on hand* is almost twice as frequent in American as in British. <. . . about two dozen hospitals already have GPs **at hand** in casualty departments.> 1999 Mar. 13 *Times* 1/6. Cf. TO HAND below.

at Home Office In: According to random samples of CIC citations, British favors *at* over *in* with *home office* by more than 2 to 1; American favors *in* over *at* by 4 to 3. <But we have a liaison officer **at** the **Home Office**.> 1986 Clark 30.

at interview In/during an interview: Two factors are involved in this construction: the choice of preposition and the presence or absence of an article before the noun. CIC has no instance of *at interview* in American texts and 1.8 iptmw in British texts; it has 0.5 iptmw of *in interview* in American texts and 1.3 in British texts. When one word (generally a determiner) falls between the preposition and the noun, CIC has 11 iptmw of *at a/the/etc. interview* in British texts and 2.6 in American texts, but 51.8 of *in a/the/etc. interview* in British texts and 300.0 in American texts. <Many graduates are made to feel ashamed of a 2.2 **at interview**.> 1993 Feb. 13 *Spectator* 21/3.

at the moment Right now: CIC has 655.3 iptmw of *at the moment* in British texts and 146.9 in American texts. By contrast, it has 138.7 iptmw of *right now* in British texts and 1035.8 in American texts. <**At the moment** companies can make their claims and it is up to the Trading Standards officers to dispute them.> 2003 June 28 *Times* Magazine 57/2–3. Cf. FOR THE MOMENT below.

at a pinch In a pinch: CIC has 4.3 iptmw of *at a pinch* in British texts and none in American. It has 0.3 iptmw of *in a pinch* in British texts and 3.7 in American.

at *place name* British uses *at* with place names more than American does (*OED* s.v. *at* 2; *CGEL* 9.17 for the contrast of *area in which* versus *point at which*). CIC has 1.5 iptmw of *at the Isle* in British texts and 0.1 in American. <I was actually on board with regular commuters – the staff of the *Daily Telegraph*, which is now based **at** the Isle of Dogs.> 1988 Dec. *In Britain* 19/1.

at risk In danger: Although *at risk* was popularized in America as part of a 1983 report about education and is used in medical contexts, it is used in wider contexts in Britain and may have originated there. The oldest citation for it in the *OED* is <1965 *New Statesman* 10 Dec. 951/2 (Advt.), The appointment should be of interest to those who are prepared to assist in training child care officers and actively supervising casework of '**at risk**' families.> *OED* risk *n*. 1.d. All four of the *OED*'s citations of the form without an adjective are from British sources; its first American citation is *at high risk* from a 1973 issue of *Scientific American* magazine. The expression appears to be a Briticism that extended to American use through professional fields like education and medicine. CIC, however, has more citations in American texts (161.6 iptmw) than in British (130 iptmw). <The caretaker of the block said that Gemma was "only alone for about a day. She wasn't really **at risk**".> 1993 Feb. 13 *Daily Telegraph* 1/6.

at school In school; (while) enrolled in a school: In British *Sid is at school* is likely to mean he is enrolled in a school, rather than being physically located there instead of at home; the equivalent American expression for enrollment is *Sid is in school* (*CGEL* 9.17). CIC has 244.9 iptmw of *at school* in British texts and 83.9 in American texts. It has 56.9 iptmw of *in school* in British texts and 189.5 in American texts. <A single certificate . . . would radically reduce the number of exams students take and encourage more 16-year-olds to stay **at school**.> 2003 June 29 *Times* 26/1.

at second reading On/during a second reading <It is possible that an amendment is tabled **at second reading** but would almost certainly be defeated.> 1999 Mar. 12 *Times* 14/4.

at source (Of tax) on gross wages < . . . actors will be taxed **at source** and will not be able to claim a whole range of vital expenses against tax.> 1993 Feb. 7 *Sunday Times* 8 18/3.

at speed At high speed; fast; quickly: CIC has 15.2 iptmw of *at speed* in British texts and 0.2 in American texts. It has 11.9 iptmw of *at high speed* in British texts and 5.8 in American texts. The use of the prepositional phrase, rather than an adverb such as *quickly* or *fast*, is British, but when the prepositional phrase is used in American it usually takes the adjective. <Francesca . . . was excusing herself and leaving **at speed** with the girl.> 1993 Neel 130.

at stall In the next stall <*En route* from the crush bar Joshua paused at the palatial Gents. His neighbor **at stall** was Charles Harvey.> 1992 Critchley 59.

at table, serve/wait Wait (on) tables: CIC has 2.1 iptmw of *serve/wait at table(s)* in British texts and none in American texts. It has 0.8 iptmw of *wait (on) table(s)* in British texts and 4.2 in American texts. <The outside caterers, who wore teeshirts with the word GNOSH on them as they served **at table**, were as noted for their *nouvelle cuisine* as they were for their *nouveau Beaujolais*.> 1987 Bradbury 18.

at (the) weekend(s) Over/on/during (the) weekend(s): Cf. *CGEL* 9.34, 40. CIC has 66 iptmw of *at weekends* and 77 of *at the weekend* in British texts, and 0.8 and 12 respectively in American texts. It has, on the other hand, 35.2 iptmw of *over (the) weekend(s)* in British texts and 110.8 in American texts,

26.8 of *on (the) weekend(s)* in British texts and 92.6 in American texts, and 3.8 of *during (the) weekend(s)* in British texts and 12.9 in American texts. Thus, *at* is the favored British preposition in this construction, but *over, on*, and *during* are favored in American. <Shall I buy a new pair of jeans? Yes, it will give me more chance of pulling ["sexually attracting women"] **at the weekend**.> 2004 Dec. 15 *Daily Telegraph* 13/6.

at past *cardinal* o'clock After *cardinal* o'clock: There are no instances in CIC. <**At past** three **o'clock** on a Sunday, the public dining-room was empty.> 1969 Amis 229.

bar Except; except for, leaving out of consideration; unless there are: The preposition *bar* is recorded from the early eighteenth century, but is more frequent in British (4 iptmw) than in American (0.1 iptmw), except for restricted contexts, such as the collocation *bar none*, which is slightly more frequent in American use according to CIC texts. <When all was over, **bar** the disappointment, the only enthusiast I could find was Michael.> 1996 July 24 *Times* 15/2–3.

before time Ahead of time: CIC has 6 iptmw of *before time* in British texts, including 3.7 of *not before time*. It has only 1 iptmw of *before time* in American texts, and none of *not before time*. <1961 M. Spark *Prime of Miss Jean Brodie* iii. 71 She had been retired **before time**.> *OED* s.v. *retire* v. 11a. – **not before time** None too soon <Swavesey provides – **not before time** – the encouragement I need to continue this quest for evidence that the meridian means anything to the people who live along it.> 1999 Mar. 20 *Times* Weekend 3/8.

beneath The CIC has 423.9 iptmw in British texts and 270.4 in American. **1**. Underneath <From a cupboard **beneath** the stairs were exhumed a silver multi-tier cake stand . . . and a leather ledger.> 1996 Aug. 9 *Daily Telegraph* 16/2. **2**. Beside but lower than <They came to South Harting presently, a village close **beneath** the down.> 1940 Shute 143.

but Except: British and American prepositional use of *but* is similar, except in certain contexts, for example expressions like *last but one*, for which CIC has 2.5 iptmw in British texts, but only 0.1 in American texts. <. . . for several moments they sat silently together, the last pair **but** one in the dining room.> 1992 Dexter 17. Cf. FROM LAST below, § 8.2.2 SECOND LAST, § 11.3.1 LAST BUT.

by British *by* has various American alternatives in a few expressions.

by auction At auction: The word *auction*, in all of its inflected forms as noun and verb, is used more frequently in American texts of CIC (225.9 iptmw) than in British texts (182.6 iptmw). However, *by auction* is 7.5 times more frequent in British (1.5 iptmw) than in American (0.2 iptmw). <Millend was advertised for sale **by auction** on several occasions.> 1989 nonfiction CIC.

by *oneself* With; near: *By* meaning "near" with a pronoun object coreferential with the subject, as in *She wants to have a book by her* with stressed *by*, is characteristically British, and is distinct from the same sentence with unstressed *by* and stressed, non-coreferential *her*, meaning "written by some other woman," which is common-core English (*CGEL* 9.9). <I'll keep it **by** me – you never know, I may need to force a lock.> 1986 Oct. 27 *Times* 15/5.

by reference to With reference to: Pam Peters (2004, 464) reports that *by reference to* "is used across a range of writing styles in the UK, whereas in the US it's mostly found in academic writing." In CIC texts, *by reference to* is about 6.5 times more frequent in British use than in American. *With reference to* is also more frequent in British than in American, but only about 3.3 times more so. <For obvious reasons, it is desirable that the termination of a trust should NOT be **by reference to** the death of the settlor.> 1960 Feb. 12 *Evening Standard* 3/6.

by the sea On; next to: *By the sea* is not usual in present-day American English; compare the following definitions of *coaster*: "One who dwells **by the sea** coast" (*OED*); "a resident of a seacoast" (*MW*). CIC has 22.4 iptmw of *by the sea* in British texts and 3.4 in American texts.

by way of In CIC texts, *by way of* is about twice as frequent in British use as in American. **1.** Into; given to <"Do you know that as a young man he went in for extravagant hoaxes?" [¶] "I . . . shouldn't suppose him to be much **by way of** that sort of thing now."> 1959 Innes 158. **2.** In the way of (gear/equipment) <. . . most had arrived with only sleeping bags and little else **by way of** kit to keep out the cold of an English winter.> 1991 Feb. 2 *Times* 4/6.

cum This loanword, which was a preposition in Latin, is so identified in many English dictionaries. For that reason, it is treated here among the prepositions. *MW*, however, more appropriately calls it a conjunction. It sometimes functions like the preposition *with* (cf. *bedsitter-cum-bathroom-cum-kitchen* below). It more often functions like the conjunction *and* (cf. *friend-cum-housekeeper* below). But it most often functions like a lexical formative making dvandva compounds (cf. *study-cum-den* below); a dvandva compound denotes coequal aspects, such as *prince-consort* or *secretary-treasurer. Cum* is very popular in British, but much less so in American. The following examples are arranged alphabetically. <. . . a woman was seated alone in an upstairs flat, **bedsitter-cum-bathroom-cum-kitchen**.> 1983 Dexter 29. <Mairead, the family's **friend-cum-housekeeper**, lives with them now.> 1989 Sept. 11 *Daily Express* 15/1. <And off the sitting room . . . is the writer's **study-cum-den**.> 1988 Feb. *Illustrated London News* 46/1.

down American has an archaic or regional use of *down cellar* "in/into the cellar" and a contemporary regional use of *down-home* "back home; of one's home area" (usually attributive) that have something in common with the British locational uses. Common-core English uses *down* as a preposition when its object is a path (as contrasted with a goal), as in the following: <I strolled back **down** the lane.> 2001 Lodge 232. Cf. UP below. **1.** At; down at <When he sells it [condemned meat] **down** the Jockey, the entire estate gets food poisoning.> 2004 Dec. 17 *Independent* Arts & Books Review 2/2. **2.** To; down to: "*Br nonstandard*" (*LDEL*). <'We'd better go **down** the chippie then.' . . . They all . . . trail off dispiritedly down the hill to the chip shop.> 1991

Glaister 8. **3. down the (tele)phone** On/over the (tele)phone: CIC has 8.7 iptmw of *down the (telephone)* in British texts; it has only a few examples in American texts (one from a novel set in England, and another of data coming down the phone line). <. . . the negligent printer . . . could have been called on at any time within reason or even castigated **down the telephone** without much loss of effect.> 1988 Amis 256. **4. down the years** Through the years: CIC has 7 iptmw of *down the years* in British texts and 0.7 in American texts. On the other hand it has 8.5 of *through the years* in British texts and 24.7 in American texts. <Sassoon . . . gave voice to an anguish that has screamed **down the years**.> 2003 Nov. 11 *Times* T2 3/4.

down to, be (all) **1.** Be attributable to (cf. *put something down to a cause*, which is common-core English) <But now I can see the menu as clearly as I can my fellow diners and the waiter hovering in the distance. And it's **all down to** my Varilux spectacle lenses.> 1999 Mar. 20 *Times Magazine* 28. **2.** Be up to; be the responsibility of <Whitehall would have a part to play in promoting good health, but it would also **be down to** the public.> 1991 Apr. 25 *Evening Standard* 2/4.

for British *for* has American variants in a few expressions, and a few distinctive combinations.

for *cost* a time At *cost* each: CIC has a few examples in British texts but none in American texts. <Mr Christian [descendant of Fletcher Christian] registered Pitcairn as a domain on the Internet and planned to sell the "PN" electronic addresses **for £100 a time**.> 1998 Jan. 3 *Times* 3/1.

for *hour* (o'clock) By *hour* (o'clock): This construction is common-core English in other senses, for example, one can set an alarm, book a table, order a cab, or schedule a meeting *for* a particular hour. But only in British English will a train get one in **for** three o'clock, or will one have been in bed **for** eight o'clock last night. CIC has approximately 7.2 iptmw of the construction with *for* in this distinctive sense in British texts and none in American texts. <I've got to be back up at the castle **for one o'clock**.> 2000 Rowling 284 (*US ed.* by).

for it In for it: "*chiefly Br informal* likely to get into trouble <*you'll be* for it *when teacher catches you*>" (*LDEL*). "*Brit. informal.* liable for punishment or blame: *you'll be for it if she catches you.*" (*CED*). This construction, with or without *in*, is rare; queries of CIC produced just one instance of *be for it* and one of *be in for it* in British texts and none in American texts. *MW* has a run-on entry under *in* adv.: "**in for**: certain to experience <*in for* a rude awakening>," which underlies *be in for it*. <"I've made you some real coffee." She filled two mugs. [¶] "You'll **be for it**. We're a caffeine-free zone here."> 1993 Graham 190.

for long enough For a long while: CIC has 11.4 iptmw in British texts and 2 in American texts. <My missus has been trying to get hold of one of those **for long enough**.> 1986 Clark 121.

for the moment Right now: CIC has 101.2 iptmw of *for the moment* in British texts and 57.5 in American. By contrast, it has 138.7 of *right now* in British texts and 1035.8 in American. <Confined though he is **for the moment** by shadow cabinet elections every autumn, he will have more latitude in office.> 1994 Sept. *Tatler* 96/3. Cf. AT THE MOMENT above.

for ***a period of time*** In *a period of time* (*CamGEL* 707) <He's an extremely pleasant dog, the first I've had **for** 20 years.> date n/a newpaper CIC.

for ***one's*** **view** In *one's* view: No examples with *for* were found in CIC; the construction with *in* is common-core English. <'Do you gents want something to drink?' though said in a perfectly friendly manner, was not, **for** my **view**, the right way for a wine waiter to address First Class passengers.> 1967 Frost and Jay 65.

hour **for** ***hour*** Specifying the earliest hour for arrival at an event (such as a meal) and the hour at which the event is to begin <I'm going to be late. It's **seven for seven-thirty**.> 1985 Mortimer 102.

number **for** ***number*** A pattern for specifying cricket scores, specifically "With the result of (so many runs), at the cost of (so many wickets) . . . (Cricket) The score stood at 150 for 6 wickets" (*OED* s.v. *for* prep. 15). <. . . the score rose to 63 **for** 3.> 1985 Ebdon 138.

from ***a date*** From *a date* onward; after *a date* <Euros will be issued in both coin and note form **from** 1st January 2002.> 1998 Barclays Bank leaflet *Economic and Monetary Union: What It Will Mean to You* 4. <. . . the television series Dad's Army . . . ran for nine years **from** 1968.> 2004 Jan. 4 *Sunday Times* Money 6 8/1.

from ***a month*** **to/until/till** ***a time*** From *a month* through *a time*: The preposition *through* makes it clear that the end point in *from May through July* is the last of that month. The other prepositions leave the end point ambiguous (*CamGEL* 708). CIC shows that *until* and *till* are minor options for this construction in common-core English, although both of those prepositions are more frequent in British than in American. The major options are *to* and *through*. CIC has 45.5 iptmw of *from [a month] to [a time]* in British texts, and 21.2 in American texts. It has 0.9 of *from [a month] through [a time]* in British texts, and 14.6 in American texts. Thus *to* is the most often used preposition in both national varieties, but *through* is a strong second option in American but a weak one in British Cf. TO *A DATE* below.

from last, second Next/second to last: CIC has 0.3 iptmw of *second from last* in British texts and none in American texts. It has 0.4 of *next to last* and 0.9 of *second to last* in British texts, and 7.6 of *next to last* and 2.6 of *second to last* in American texts. <Their **second from last** exam . . . > 1999 Rowling 234 (*US ed.* to). Cf. BUT above, § 8.2.2 SECOND LAST, § 11.3.1 LAST BUT.

gone 1. ***an hour of the day*** After/past *an hour of the day* <Loretta looked at her watch. "Just **gone** six."> 1993 Smith 140. 2. ***an age*** Over *an age* "I'd never have thought he was **gone** 60 – he looks amazingly young for his age" (*CIDE*).

in British *in* often corresponds to different prepositions in American. In some cases, the entire British prepositional phrase introduced by *in* is expressed otherwise in American.

in *so many* acres On *so many* acres: CIC has 12.3 iptmw with *in* and 2.6 with *on* in British texts. It has 0.6 with *in* and 19.6 with *on* in American texts. <Spikemead Farm, a 16th-century listed detached cottage **in** two **acres**, priced at £195,000.> 1995 Aug. 30 *Daily Telegraph* 36/3.

in arrivals In CIC, with *arrivals* or *arrival(s) hall/lounge, in* outnumbers *at* by 6 to 1 in British texts. The American evidence is sparse, other expressions, such as *at the gate*, being favored. <People are likely to say goodbye to friends *at* passport control, but would they not wait for friends ***in*** International **Arrivals**?> 2001 Apr. *English Today* 29/1.

in Cambridge At: When *Cambridge* refers to the town, the preposition *in* is common-core English. When it refers to the university, however, *at* is usual in common-core English, but *in* occurs in a number of CIC citations, some of which are ambiguous in reference to town or university. <When he goes for his interview **in Cambridge** and they ask him why he thinks he should be accepted as an undergraduate, he will reply, with his usual charm: "Because I am a ghastly little oik, Sir."> 1991 Feb. 5 *Daily Telegraph* 16/6.

in *a* card On <Of course, you might write "Best Wishes" ***in*** the **card** (if it is big enough or folded).> 2001 Apr. *English Today* 30/2.

in care Under supervision by the child welfare system: This expression is about 4 times more frequent in British than in American, in all its uses. <Despite their earnings, many were homeless and almost half who had started begging had been **in care**.> 1994 Sept. 14 *Times* 3/1.

in chambers At a lawyer's office: The expression is frequent in British English, but not used in American. <Miss Aldridge could be **in Chambers** in about twenty minutes.> 1997 James 133.

in college At the college: In American use, *in college* typically means "enrolled in a college" not "physically present at a college." <Dr. Alan Hardinge decided that Monday evening to stay **in college**.> 1992 Dexter 202.

in construction Under construction. The preposition *under* is more frequent for this expression in both British and American, but especially in the latter. <. . . the new Ackroyden Estate [is] part complete, part **in construction**.> 1954 Aug. 8 *Observer* 6/3.

in *a* date At; on: This use is rare and may result from blending with *in which year*. <The show was founded in 1863 and revived in 1952, **in** which **date** many events seem to have become stuck.> 1995 Aug. 28 *Daily Telegraph* 17/3.

in the decline On the decline: In CIC British texts, *on the decline* is more than twice as frequent as *in the decline*; in American texts, it is 4 times as frequent. <However, do not infer from this that vegetarianism is **in** the **decline**.> 1987 May 29 *Evening Standard* 26/4.

in discussion with Talking with: *In discussion with* is slightly more frequent in CIC British texts than in American; but *talking with* is more than 4 times more frequent in American texts than in British. <We are listening to the arguments and are **in discussion with** English Heritage and the Corporation of London.> 1991 Mar. 17 *Sunday Times* Magazine 3/3.

in dock (Of cars) in a repair shop; (of people) in a hospital: CIC has 1.9 iptmw of *in dock* (in various uses) in British texts and none in American texts. <Morse's old Jaguar was **in dock** again ("Too mean to buy a new one!" his colleagues claimed).> 1993 Dexter 46.

in drink Drunk: CIC has 2.3 iptmw in British texts and none in American texts. <Anyway, a man **in drink** might babble any old nonsense.> 2000 Granger 403.

in education In school: In American use, the sense of this expression is often "in the field of education," not the sense illustrated here. <There are a million young people not **in education**, not in work.> 2005 Jan. 16 BBC1 *Breakfast with Frost*.

in employment Employed: The expression is about twice as frequent in British use as in American, and has no American use in the sense illustrated here. <He had four children, not all of whom were **in** gainful **employment**.> 1991 Critchley 5.

in *a* farm At/on *a* farm: In both British and American CIC texts, *on a farm* is usual in constructions like the following; however, British texts have 0.5 iptmw of *in*, and American texts have none. <We always stayed **in** the Peter Aragons' **farm**.> 1983 Mann 82.

in the force On the force: CIC has 6.1 iptmw of *in the force* in British texts and 2.3 in American texts. It has almost exactly the opposite distribution of *on the force*, namely 2.4 in British texts and 6.1 in American texts. Also, American use of *in the force* is primarily military rather than police. <How long have you been in the [police] Force?> 1981 Dexter 83.

in gate CIC has no instances of this sequence; it is, as the text comment suggests, probably a syntactic blend. <Wait ***in*** **Gate 5** / – announcement at UK departures at London's Heathrow Airport. / [text comment:] This announcement seems to have overlapped with "please wait in the departure lounge".> 2001 Apr. *English Today* 29/1.

in goal, play Play goal: CIC has 1.8 iptmw of *play in goal* in British texts and only a single example in American texts. It has none of *play goal* in British texts and 0.5 in American texts. <None of this changes the fact that I [former soccer player] have only one eye . . . that I'll never be able to **play in goal** again.> 1991 Bishop 38.

in (the) grounds On (the) grounds: CIC has 40.2 iptmw of *in [some] grounds* in British texts and 1.4 in American texts. Of the latter, only 6 instances are in the use illustrated by the following British citations, and 5 of those are in reference to locations in Britain. **1**. The area surrounding and belonging to a house <There's an old potting shed **in** the **grounds**.> 2000 Granger

270. **2**. An area used for sporting events <In spite of policing measures taken **in grounds**, . . . the Government says there are still too many incidents of violent hooliganism **in grounds**, in town centres, and on trains involving rival spectators.> 1989 Mar. 5 *Manchester Guardian Weekly* 31/1.

in hand, task Task at hand: CIC has 5.9 iptmw of *task in hand* in British texts and 0.1 in American texts. It has 1.1 of *task at hand* in British texts and 5.8 in American texts. <. . . the **task in hand** seemed possible.> 1985 Byatt 163. – **time in hand** Free time: CIC has 0.2 iptmw of *time in hand* in British texts and none in American texts. <But having a bit of **time in hand** I thought I'd pull in here for a few minutes.> 2001 Lodge 149.

in the hearth On the hearth: CIC has 1.6 iptmw of *in the hearth* in British texts and 0.6 in American texts. *On the hearth* is 3.5 times more frequent than *in the hearth* in British texts; the two prepositional phrases are about equal in use in American texts. Britons talk about hearths nearly 5 times more often than Americans do. *Hearth* may refer either to the fireplace (hence *in the hearth*) or to the floor of the fireplace or the area in front of a fireplace (hence *on the hearth*).

in the holidays During/over the holidays: The preposition most frequently collocating with *holidays* in British texts is *in*; and in American texts, *during*. CIC has the following British/American iptmw: *in* 5.1/0.3, *during* 3.6/8.0, *over* 1.5/3.2. <We gave balls for her and she had friends to stay **in the holidays**.> 1990 Aug. 26 *Sunday Times* Magazine 9/1.

in (a) job(s), be Working: CIC has about 2 iptmw of this use in British texts and none in American texts. <But many people might choose periods of their lives when they **are** not **in jobs**.> 1991 Feb. 11 *Girl about Town* 4/3.

in loss In the red; losing money: The expression is rare in both varieties. <. . . 1990 will see Lloyd's **in loss** for the first time since 1966.> 1990 Aug. 2 *Evening Standard* 18/2.

in *the* lunch hour On/during *the* lunch hour: CIC has the following British/American iptmw: *in* 2.2/0.1, *on* 0.0/2.0, *during* 0.7/1.5. <Once, **in** the **lunch hour**, he invited her to accompany Bunny and himself to church.> 1989 Bainbridge 84.

in mistake *By mistake* is more frequent in both varieties, but CIC has 1.2 iptmw of *in mistake* in British texts and none in American texts. <It could even explain why that wretched Helen Appleyard was murdered **in mistake** for poor Jenny.> 1985 Bingham 53.

in *a month* 1. *In* is used with months (*in January*) in common-core English, but if the name of the month is modified, for example, *in the January before last* (*CGEL* 9.40), American tends to omit the preposition altogether or to use some other. <. . . the child is registered **in the January** of the year when it will be three.> 1987 Mar. 16 *Times* 11/7. **2**. ***ordinal weekday* in the month** *Ordinal weekday* of the month: CIC has 1.1 iptmw of *in a month* in British texts and none in American texts. It has 3.4 *of a month* in British texts and 1.1 in American texts. <. . . the School holds regular introductory meetings on the first and fourth Thursday and the third Sunday **in the month.**> 1999 Mar. 10 sign on a London tube train.

in the newsagent('s) At the newsstand: CIC has 1.5 iptmw of *in the newsagent('s)* in British texts and no instances of *newsagent* in American texts. It has no instances of *at the newsstand* in British texts and 0.5 iptmw in American texts. <Anyway **in the newsagent**, I happened to glance at some of those, er . . . you know, those things they have in there.> 1986 Brett 69.

in the night, get up CIC has 1.5 iptmw of *get up in the night* in British texts and 0.4 in American texts. <. . . he **gets up in the night** for William.> 1993 Neel 70.

in ***particular category of person*** **occupation** Occupied by a *particular category of persons*: CIC has 0.3 iptmw of this use in British texts and none in American texts. <Even to owners determined to keep their houses **in** family **occupation** – and open to the public – the temptation to sell land and/or contents to keep the show on the road is overwhelming.> 2003 June 28 *Times* Weekend 2/1.

in one go At once; at the same time: CIC has 18.6 iptmw of *in one go* in British texts and 0.7 in American texts. <. . . when it comes to furniture, . . . they want to rush out one Saturday afternoon and get it all **in one go.**> 1987 Apr. 1 *Evening Standard* 26/1.

in the order of On the order of: CIC has 11.4 iptmw of *in the order of* (in several senses) in British texts and 4.9 in American texts. It has 2.4 of *on the order of* (also in several senses) in British texts and 12.9 in American texts. <In early February London hotels would expect to be quiet. But quiet means something **in the order of** 60 per cent occupancy.> 1991 Jan. 28 *Times* 1/2.

in/of patter, line Line: CIC has 0.3 iptmw each of *line in patter* and *line of patter* in British texts. It has no instance of either form in American texts. American use is more likely to be simply *line* "a glib often persuasive way of talking" (*MW*). <Dark strangers and unexpected fortunes – I ask you. But you've got a nice **line in patter**, we can work on that: it's worth its weight in gold.> 1988 Taylor 32.

in the porch On the porch: CIC has 6.8 iptmw of *in the porch* and 3.5 of *on the porch* in British texts, and 0.1 of *in the porch* and 18.3 of *on the porch* in American texts. <. . . in my rush left the boots **in the** guest-house **porch.**> 1987 Apr. 9 *Times* 14/6.

in post On the job: CIC has 2.6 iptmw of *in post* in a relevant sense in British texts and 0.3 in American texts (when the contexts are telegraphic in style). CIC has 23.2 iptmw of *on the job* in British texts and 107.8 in American texts. <You're hoping that . . . there might be someone still **in post** who knew her and would remember incidents of twelve years ago.> 2001 James 319.

in the pound Per dollar: CIC has 11.7 iptmw of *in the pound* in uses comparable to the following citation in British texts and 0.1 of *in the dollar* in American texts. It has 2.6 comparable British uses of *per pound* and 5.2 American uses of *per dollar*. <The party also wants to slap national insurance on all earnings,

taking an extra 10p **in the pound** on earnings.> 1994 Sept. 25 *Sunday Times* 3 6/3.

in practice Practicing <The girls duly don their ear muffs while I am **in practice** [playing the saxophone].> 1991 Mar. 10 *Sunday Times* Magazine 58/3.

in the premises *On the premises* is the dominant form in both varieties, but more so in American. In CIC texts, the American ratio of *on* to *in* with *premises* is 20:1, whereas in British it is 8:1. The word *premises* is 4.5 times more frequent in British than in American. <. . . we had every reason to believe he was **in the premises**.> 1991 Feb. 20 *Times* 4/7.

in(to) profit In the black; profitable; into profitability <The Royal Mail has announced that it is back **in profit**. . . . "We hope we can stay **in profit** . . . move **into profit** . . . make itself **in profit**."> 2003 Nov. 13 BBC News.

in the Riviera *On the Riviera* is usual in both varieties. <The weather caught the south of France by surprise, with snow up to 8in deep **in the Riviera**.> 1991 Feb. 9 *Daily Telegraph* 1/2.

in the sale(s) On sale; at the/a sale: In the sense of "at a reduced price," British uses *in* with *sale*; American does not. <I would have bought it even if it hadn't been **in the sale**.> 2003 July 8 *Times* T2 13/1.

in *some* shelf On *some* shelf: Both varieties customarily use *on* in this construction, but CIC has sporadic British instances of *in*, but no American ones. <I'm just putting a book back **in** my **shelves**.> 1994 Sept. 24 *Spectator* 63/2. Cf. INTO *SOME* SHELF below.

in *a ship* *On* is usual in both varieties. <Uncle Ernest, **in** the ***Iron Duke*** – he's coming to see us tomorrow night, and I said I'd be home early. His ship came in yesterday.> 1940 Shute 40.

in *a* side On *a* team: With reference to sports teams, *on* is usual in American English. <Fraser is now the best bowler **in** the England **side**.> 1990 Aug. 24 *Times* 38/1.

in street/avenue/drive/lane/road/roadway (and proper names of streets) On: For specifying the position of something relative to a street, British generally uses *in*, and American *on*. When the street in question is noted as a shopping location, British uses *on* or *in*. Thus, CIC has approximately equal numbers of British *in the High Street* and *on the High Street*, but no instances of American *in Main Street*, only *on Main Street*. <Houses **in Fentiman Road** are relatively inexpensive and very spacious. . . . Having a gastropub **in** the **street** is handy, too.> 2004 Dec. 12 *Sunday Times* Bricks and Mortar 16/2–5. <I'm not desperate, and neither are any of the others who live **in** the **street**.> 2005 Jan. 9 BBC1 *Frost on Sunday*.

in the street, man Man on the street: CIC has *in* for this idiom 13 times more frequently than *on* in British texts, and *on* 3 times more frequently than *in* with American texts. <For all her much-vaunted support of the small businessman, the Prime Minister has done bog all for the **man in the street**.> 1989 July 29 *Times* 28/1.

in *some* table At *some* table: Although in combination with *in*, *table* often has the sense of "tabulation" rather than an article of furniture, it is notable that in CIC, the frequency of *at* + *table* is similar in British and American, but *in* + *table* is 4.5 times more frequent in British than in American. <Some non-University guests sitting **in** high **table** for the first time took their verbal battles seriously.> 1987 Archer 181.

in *some* team On *some* team: CIC data indicate that British *in* + *team* is 3 times more frequent than *on* + *team*, but American *on* + *team* is 4 times more frequent than *in* + *team*. <Students would also get credit for extra curricular activities. . . . Mr Tomlinson said last week that even playing "**in** the local village cricket **team**" should be recognised.> 2003 July 16 *Times* 1/3. Cf. OUT OF TEAM below.

in *one's* own terms CIC data suggest that *on one's own terms* is the most frequent version of this expression and is equally common in British and American, but that *in one's own terms* is three time more frequent in British than in American. <Here are some 'on's that are current, and sound wrong, or rather novel, to me: . . . children's learning ought to be evaluated *on* its **own terms**. . . . I should have used . . . **in**.> 1990 Howard 104–5.

in *some* test, mark Mark on *some* test: This is not a frequent construction, but CIC has 0.2 iptmw of *marks/results in* + *test* in British texts and 0.8 of *marks/results on* + *test* in American texts. <[question from the Singapore Primary School Leaving Examination:] The highest **mark** _____ the Mathematics **test** was 76 out of 100. . . . The correct answer . . . is . . . ***in***, but the norms for prepositions in Standard American English would dictate . . . *on*.> 2001 Peter L. Lowenberg in Thumboo, *Three Circles of English* 391–2.

in their *large numbers* By/in the *large numbers*: In CIC, 79 percent of the British instances of such constructions have *in (their)*; the American instances are nearly evenly divided with 51 percent *by (the)* and 49 percent *in (the)*. <Merely within the last 90 years, Sikhs have suffered and died **in their** hundreds of thousands.> 1999 Mar. 24 *Independent* Wed. Review sec 5/3. Cf. § 2.3.1.

in *some* timetable On *some* timetable: In CIC British texts, *in* and *on* occur about equally with *timetable*, but American texts have 5 times as many instances of *on* as of *in*. <There's been a cock-up **in** the first-year **timetable**.> 1987 Smith 79.

in trade On the Trade Commission; in business <'What was he doing in Hong Kong?' [¶] 'He was **in Trade**.' [¶] 'Shopkeeper?' [¶] 'The British Trade Commission,' said Charters severely.> 1985 Bingham 15.

in two minds Of two minds; unsure: CIC has 5.8 iptmw of *in two minds* in British texts and 0.1 in American; it has 1.5 iptmw for *of two minds* in American texts and none in British. <David Swan was **in two minds**: should he return . . . or should he hang around . . . ?> 1992 Critchley 173.

in the university At the university: *In the university* is of approximately equal frequency in CIC British (10.1 iptmw) and American (11.6) texts, but *at the* *university* is more than twice as frequent in American (41.9 iptmw) as in British (18.1). <I occasionally go to films or lectures **in the university**.> 1990 Aug. 26 *Sunday Times* Magazine 54/3.

in the uptake *On the uptake* is the usual version of this expression in both varieties with approximately equal frequency; *in the uptake* occurs sporadically in British, but not in American CIC texts. <. . . the illusion that the Westcountry is inhabited by . . . straw-sucking yokels . . . slightly slow **in the uptake**, is still perpetuated and cherished.> 1985 Ebdon 170.

in vacations On/during vacations: *In vacations* occurs occasionally in British CIC texts, but not in American; *on vacations* occurs at a frequency of 2.2 iptmw in American CIC texts, but not at all in British. *During vacations* occurs in both varieties. <And he talked about his holidays in expensive and remote places that other students wouldn't be able to travel to, at least not **in vacations**.> 2001 James 7.

in the week During the week: Although both expressions are common-core English, in constructions like the following, *in the week* seems improbable in American use. <Kate Garely . . . runs a free aerobics class here **in the week** as well.> 1989 Williams 37.

in work This expression is 3.3 times more frequent in CIC British texts than in American. It is not used in either of the following senses in American. **1**. With a job; employed <There are a million young people not in education, not **in work**.> 2005 Jan. 16 BBC1 *Breakfast with Frost*. **2**. At work <I broke down **in work** today because I heard the news on the radio and my son's in the 7th Armoured Brigade.> 1991 Feb. 26 *Times* 5/2.

in aid of For; in support of; for the purpose of: CIC has 20.1 iptmw of *in aid of* in British texts and 1.2 in American texts. Moreover, the American uses tend to be more literal references to aid and cannot be adequately paraphrased by *for*. <It's **in aid of** Survival International (which supports tribal peoples).> 1994 Sept. 28–Oct. 5 *Time Out* 7/2.

in case of This complex preposition can be used in either of two senses: to indicate a possible later event, as in *The house has a smoke detector in case of a fire* (smoke detector first, fire possible later), or to indicate a prior condition, as in *In case of a fire, use the stairs not the elevator* (fire first, consequent action later). British favors the first sense; American uses both (Peters 2004, 271–2). Cf. § 9.2 IN CASE.

in front of *apparently financial jargon* Before (in time) <Apart from a slight dip **in front of** the New York opening futures were well supported. Dealers felt there was some buying **in front of** today's Uruguay tender.> SEU w2-2. 227-8.

in reference to See WITH REFERENCE TO below.

in respect of With respect to: CIC British texts have 96.6 iptmw of *in respect of* and 66.0 of *with respect to*; American texts have, respectively, 1.2 and 102.9. <£3,592 was paid. It was only some months after this main settlement that you received a further £350 **in respect of** the pearl necklace.> 2005 Jan. 15 *Daily Telegraph* B8/2.

into "*Into* is commonly confused with the combination *in to*, where *in* is an adverb. *In to* is correctly used in <*we went in to breakfast*> <*they came in to see me*> <*reports should be sent in to the chief executive*>" (*LDEL*). The confusion is common to British and American (Gilman 1994), but here are British examples of it in both directions: **in to** for *into* <I pulled **in to** the next lay-by.> 1996 Aug. 9 *Daily Telegraph* 15/2 and **into** for *in to* <. . . a petition . . . will be handed **into** the House of Commons next Wednesday.> 1986 Oct. 30 *Times* 22.

into the bargain In the bargain: CIC has 11.8 iptmw of *into the bargain* in British texts and 0.5 in American texts. *In the bargain* occurs in both varieties in similar frequencies (British 4.8, American 4.1). <1962 *Guardian* 7 Aug. 5/1 A child can have ten days skiing for under £25 and be kitted out by Moss Brothers **into the bargain.**> *OED* s.v. *kit* v. 2.

into *some* shelf Onto/on *some* shelf: Both varieties customarily use *onto* (or *on*) in this construction, but there are sporadic instances of *into*, CIC American examples involving a closet or beneath a bar. <He slotted the book back **into** its **shelf.**> 1977 Dexter 61. Cf. IN *SOME* SHELF above.

into work Find work: The expression *into work* is about 1.7 times more frequent in British than American CIC texts; the general British sense is rare in American, which generally uses the expression in reference to a particular job as in *I'm going into work* ["to my job"] *today*. <However, we deplore the muddled thinking which suggests that helping a minority **into work** requires further reductions in incapacity benefits.> 1998 Jan. 3 *Times* 23/3.

next Next to: The sequences *next me/him/her* occur in CIC British texts at the rate of 1.3 iptmw, and not at all in American texts. <The Irishman wedged in **next** him.> 1994 Freeling 1.

of British *of* has a few characteristic uses, notably with times of the day. On the other hand, American uses *of* as the second element in compound prepositions: *off of*, *out of*, and *inside of* and *outside of* in locative senses (*CamGEL* 639). British uses these combinations also, but not as frequently as American does; notably *out of* is 4 times more frequent in American than in British in CIC.

of an evening In the evening: *Of an evening* is almost 4 times more frequent in CIC British texts than in American. <To quell these moments of panic she hardened her resolve . . . by joining Annie and Rosie in the boot-room **of an evening** to watch television.> 1980 Sharpe 202.

of a lunch time At lunch time <In my town council days we used to get four or five of us bright lads in there **of a lunch time.**> 1953 Mortimer 11.

of *a month* In *a month* <Sunday was fine, a windy sunny day **of** late **February**.> 1940 Shute 141.

of a morning In the morning: *Of a morning* is 4 times more frequent in CIC British texts than in American, very few of whose instances were in this sense. <He has four children. "It's a fight **of a morning** to see who gets certain tracksuits and shirts."> 1991 Feb. 15 *Evening Standard* 51/1.

of nights At night: *Of nights* in this sense is extremely rare in American texts; *at night* is frequent. <What d'you say I come and sleep here **of nights**? No meals, just sleeping night watchman.> 1949 Tey 121.

of a *weekday* (afternoon/evening) On *weekdays* / [no preposition] *weekday* (afternoons/evenings) <George always went for a drink about nine o'clock **of a weekday**.> 1974 Price 67. <But while we were tolerated in the bar of the George and Pilgrims **of a** Saturday **afternoon**, the travellers ["Gypsies"] were barred.> 1993 Feb. 10 *Evening Standard* 23/1.

Other nontemporal differences:

of *some* education With *some* education <I always doubt whether someone **of** a public school **education** gains much from Borstal training.> 1983 Brooke-Taylor 90.

of that order, something Something on that order: CIC British texts have only *of* in this expression, and American have only *on*. <Two or three hundred doctors to each rep, I believe. **Something of that order**, anyway.> 1986 Clark 51.

off This preposition has some characteristic British uses, including "not inclined towards: *I'm off work; I've gone off you*" (*CED*). A characteristic American colloquial compound is *off of* "off."

off *one's* head Out of *one's* mind: *Off one's head* in this sense is frequent in British and rare in American. <Peach had stated frankly that the prospective sitter was **off** his **head**.> 1974 Innes 20.

off plan From a plan; on the basis of a house plan before construction <Gone are the days when a contractor could build a row of identical box-like houses, fill them with identical fixtures and fittings and expect them to sell **off plan**.> 1993 Feb. 17 *Times* 18/2.

off the ration Unrationed; without ration coupons: This expression is dated in British, but non-occurring in American. <. . . a poor quality coal, obtainable **off the ration**.> 1959 Opie and Opie 163.

off retirement From retirement <No job for . . . someone ten years **off retirement**.> 1998 Joss 40.

off school Out of / off from school: In CIC texts, *off school* is 5.3 times more frequent in British than in American; *out of school* is 2.5 times more frequent in American than in British; *off from school* is the rarest combination of the three in both varieties, but is 12 times more frequent in American than in British, where it is very rare. <You'll just get some days **off school**.> 1994 Symons 140.

off *a source* From *a source* <I get ties and shirts anywhere – some of my best are **off** the airport at Milan, and my handkerchiefs are **off** Paddington station.> 1989 Aug. 13 *Sunday Times* Magazine 66/1. <Took us three weeks to get a new door **off** the council.> 1990 Sept. *Evening Standard* magazine 37/2.

off the train, meet ***someone*** Meet *someone* at the train: This expression is rare in British, but non-occurring in American. <Luke and Marie **met** me **off the train.**> 1997 James 245.

off work This expression is more than twice as frequent in British as in American CIC texts. 1. Away from work; off *adv.* <Mrs Routley had been **off work** for a week with a back problem.> 1994 Oct. 1 *Times* 3/2. **2.** Out of work; not working <When I was first **off work** I was in a bad state and I knew something had gone wrong in my head.> 1999 Mar. 15 *Daily Telegraph* 7/3.

on This preposition is one that has many differences in use between British and American English, most of which are lexically linked, either to its following object or to a preceding word that it complements (cf. § 11 passim).

on "compared with another person or thing: *This essay is a definite improvement on your last one.* | *Sales are 10% up* **on** *last year*" (*LDOCE* 18). **1.** (*of a decrease in percentage*) From; below <Experts estimate that prices are down 5 per cent **on** last year.> 1989 Aug. 11 *Times* 29/7. **2.** (*of an increase in percentage*) Over; above <However, graduate salaries were rising fastest in Northern Ireland, up 9.1 per cent **on** last year.> 2003 July 16 *Times* 9/2.

on ***some*** **account** In *some* account <An imbalance **on** the tuition **account** was a familiar problem.> 1993 Neel 46.

on any view(s) In any view: CIC has 0.5 iptmw of *on any view* in British texts and none in American texts. <**On any views**, it would have been discourteous to Mr Barker, who was Lord Archer's friend.> 2003 June 21 *Times* 1/3.

on addresses At addresses: CIC has 0.3 iptmw of *raids on addresses* in British texts and no instances of *on addresses* in American texts. <British Transport Police said last night that they were found in dawn raids **on addresses** in Acton, west London, on Tuesday.> 1989 Sept. 14 *Times* 5/1–2.

on behalf of In behalf of: *On behalf of* is the overwhelming choice in common-core English; however, the minority option, *in behalf of*, is 12 times more frequent in American than in British CIC texts. "In current British use, *on behalf* (*of*) has replaced *in behalf* (*of*); both are still used in American English" (*MW* usage note). Pam Peters (2004, 67–8) reports also a British variant without an initial prepositional element: *to speak* ***behalf of*** *individual students.* No American instances of the short form are known.

on ***some*** **benefit(s)** With/receiving *some* government financial help: CIC has 24.2 iptmw of this sequence in British texts and 13.5 in American texts (many of which have a different sense). The usual American analog would be *on welfare*, which is 10 times more frequent in American use than in British. <. . . she needed money to feed and clothe Jessica, especially now she was no longer **on benefits.**> 2002 Smith 173.

on the bins With the garbage department: CIC has only sporadic British instances of this expression and no American ones. <. . . their own children, who have double firsts in Latin, can't get a job **on the bins.**> 2005 Jan. 9 *Sunday Times* 4 4/7.

on the cards In the cards: In CIC *on the cards* is 15 times more frequent in British than in American; *in the cards* is nearly 7 times more frequent in American than in British. <Dr Dabbe says the disease is always **on the cards** if you don't take the proper precautions when handling the contents of a mummy case.> 2000 Aird 198.

on *some* car park In *some* parking lot: The salient national difference for this expression is in the noun: British *car park* versus American *parking lot*. With either of those terms, the most frequent preposition in both varieties is *in*. However, British uses the minority preposition *on* more often than American does. <You theorized they would take ["abduct"] him **on** the **car-park**.> 1985 Clark 146–7.

on *some* catalogue In *some* catalog: The overwhelmingly dominant British spelling of the noun is *catalogue*; American uses *catalog* about 3 times more frequently than the longer form. The most frequent preposition in both varieties is *in*. British uses the minority preposition *on* about twice as often as American does; however, since British also uses *catalog(ue)* about twice as often, the prepositional difference may be incidental. <. . . you should find virtually everything except the collection of ritual material, which is not yet available **on** the **catalogue**.> 2003 Dec. *Square* 40/1–2.

on the cheap Cheaply: Now a part of common-core English, *on the cheap* seems originally to have been British. It is still somewhat more frequent in British texts (British 8.8 to American 6.9 iptmw). <Alan Beith, home affairs spokesman, criticised the "privatisation of police work" as a botched attempt to do everything **on the cheap**.> 1994 Sept. 21 *Times* 11/3–4.

on closing time At closing time: This combination is rare, having no instances in CIC. <. . . we shall have to decide on the best time to go in. . . . Just **on closing time** in the afternoon?> 1985 Clark 174.

on *some* computer In *some* computer: Both *on* and *in* are used with *computer* in common-core English, and *on* predominates. British uses *on* about 64 percent of the time; American 56 percent. <His name went down **on** the Eurotunnel **computer** as someone whose support should not be overlooked.> 1994 Sept. 30 *Daily Telegraph* 15/3.

on *some* concourse In *some* concourse: Both *on* and *in* are used with *concourse* in both varieties; *on* is somewhat more frequent in British (1.6 iptmw of *on* to 1.1 of *in*), and *in* is only slightly more frequent in American (0.7 iptmw of *in* to 0.5 of *on*). <Le Cafe de Piaf . . . transformed into a French restaurant and one of the first private caterers allowed **on** the station **concourse**.> 1987 July 1 *Daily Telegraph* 5/4.

on *some* count By *some* count: *On* is more frequent than *by* with *count* in both varieties, but in British it is nearly 4 times more frequent, and in American less than twice. <Even **on** the most conservative **count** . . . there were 7,780 racially motivated attacks last year.> 1992 Dec. 5 *Economist* 59/1.

on *some* course In *some* course (an educational program): *On* + *course* (in all senses) is some 2.3 times more frequent in CIC British texts than American ones. In the use exemplified below, the difference would be even greater. <Plus there are assorted spouses . . . enrolled **on** the chateau's cookery **course**.> 2005 Jan. 9 *Sunday Times* 5 1/3–4. Cf. § 11.1.7 GO ON A COURSE.

on *some* **crossing** At *some* crossing: British talks more about crossings (level or railway or grade, pedestrian, pelican, zebra) than American does, probably because they are more prominent in Britain than in America. The British choice of preposition to use with such crossings is 2.5 times *on* versus *at*; the American choice is 3 times *at* versus *on*. <They crossed **on** the pelican **crossing**.> 1993 Stallwood 170–1.

on (the) ***day*** *Day*; that day; the day *of a particular event*: An analysis of British news reports (*LGSWE* 800) concludes that prepositions are generally used with names of the days of the week to form adverbial phrases, whereas American news reports tend to use the days of the week without a preceding preposition: Br. *on Monday* versus Am. *Monday* (cf. also Swan 1995, 451). <. . . having sampled so many turkeys, we'd all rather have goose **on the day**.> 1997 Dec. 13 *Times* Weekend 10/4. Cf. also ON THE NIGHT below and §§ 2.1.4, 11.2.1 WEEK ON *DAY OF THE WEEK*.

on ***day of the week, a period of time (e.g., a week on Friday)*** *A period of time* from *a day of the week*: This method of specifying dates in the future is 4 or 5 times more frequent in British than in American. And when British uses it, the preposition *on* is about 26 times more frequent than *from*, whereas when American uses it, *from* is 27 times more frequent than *on*. <. . . school resumes after half-term a week **on** Monday.> 1993 Feb. 13 *Daily Telegraph* 3/2.

on *some* **desk(s)** At *some* desk(s): The use of *on* rather than *at* with *desk* is rare in British, but even more so in American. <Slowly the voters shuffled forward to give their names to the lady clerks sitting primly **on** their **desks**.> 1991 Critchley 97.

on *some* **door** At *some* door <Tickets Booked in Advance: £2.50 . . . Tickets **on** the **Door**: £3.00> 1987 London flier advertising a play.

on *some* **drill** In *some* drill <He hadn't been **on** a fire **drill** since he was at school.> 1977 Dexter 34.

on *some* **estimate** 1. At/for *some* estimated amount <. . . lot 232 in Christie's sale of garden statuary . . . sold, not **on** its **estimate** of £3,000–£4,000, but for £715,000.> 1989 Sept. 14 *Daily Telegraph* 1/8. **2.** By *some* estimate <**On** a generous **estimate**, there are at most ten possible future Cabinet ministers among middle-ranking and junior ministers.> 2003 June 19 *Times* 20/1.

on *some* **figures** According to *some* figures <**On** the Government's **figures**, the cost will be twice as high as rates, although experts predict the true cost to be substantially higher.> 1987 Oct. *Illustrated London News* 14/4.

on *some* **file(s)** In *some* file(s) <Of course we always knew in the Exchange that nothing **on** the **files** was dead certain – intelligence work isn't like that.> 1994 Dickinson 90.

on (the) film(s) 1. In the movies <Love [a character] . . . was played **on film** by David Niven.> 1989 July 22 *Times* 41/5–6. 2. For camera film <Boots Film Processing Same Day Monday to Friday **on films** handed in before 9.30 am ready for collection after 5 pm.> 1990 May 31, sign outside Boots, Charing Cross Road.

on Foodworth At/of Foodworth <Magistrates have also made an emergency closure **on Foodworth**, a large supermarket at 244 Kilburn High Road NW6.> 1987 Mar. *Camden Magazine* no. 46 7/3.

on (*some*) form 1. In (top) form/shape <'I 'ope I find you well?' [¶] '**On** excellent **form**, I thank you.'> 2000 Rowling 215 (*US ed.* in). <Baroness Blackstone is **on** top **form** this evening.> 2003 June 29 *Sunday Times* News Review 7/1. 2. Judging by / according to past experience <**On form**, it would have ended round about nine-thirty or ten.> 1986 Barnard, *Political* 177.

on full scale At/in full scale <Looking at the remarkable set for the first time **on full scale**, I was able to recognise an old favourite prop from *Merry Widow*.> 1986 Sept. 25 *Hampstead Advertiser* 21/3.

on *some* grade(s) At/in *some* (pay) grade(s) <You start moving men about from one job to another, and they start complaining, or demanding to be put **on** a higher **grade**.> 1988 Lodge 124.

on Greenland In Greenland: Both British and American use *in Greenland*, treating the place as a land; British has *on Greenland*, treating it as an island, only rarely. <A thousand years ago the Vikings established a settlement **on Greenland**. Financial Times 13 Jul 99.> 2001 Apr. *English Today* 66 30/1.

on the halls In vaudeville (houses) <Father was an acrobat and is in the Middle East now. Name of Valoroso. It's an old name **on the halls**.> 1942 Thirkell 25.

on heat In heat; sexually excited: Except for a few sporadic instances of *in heat* in British texts, *on heat* is British and *in heat* American. <Kingsland may have been a kitten **on heat**, but he was a shameless seducer.> 2003 July 13 *Times* Culture 45/2.

on *income(s)* With / [start] at *income(s)*: For the phrase *on/with (x) income(s)*, CIC British texts favor *on* by nearly 3 times; American texts have approximately equal numbers of the two prepositions, with a slight preference for *with*. <Graduates from 1996, who started **on** an average of £14,774, were now earning an average of £17,000. Recruits from 1994, who started **on** £13,500, were now **on** £21,000.> 1998 Jan. 6 *Times* 8/3. <All too often people **on** very low **incomes** with debts face a barrage of threats designed to bully and intimidate.> 2003 July 16 *Daily Express* 31/1. Cf. also ON SOME SALARY below.

on insurance 1. For insurance <She has two monthly standing orders: £30 for her pension, £15 **on** house **insurance**.> 1991 Feb. *Evening Standard* magazine 20/3. 2. With/through insurance <Father Leo treats religious addicts in clinics across America and charges them £5000 a month. "Most of them get it **on** medical **insurance**."> 1989 Sept. 4 *Evening Standard* 26/1–2.

on *a* junction At *a* junction: *At* in this construction is common-core English. CIC has 2.7 iptmw of *on* in British texts and none in American texts. <In Maida Vale, **on** the **junction** of Castellain and Lauderdale Roads, there are three Redwood Trees.> 1994 Sept. 14–21 *Time Out* 39/2.

on the lorries Driving trucks: CIC has a few examples in British texts; there is no direct analog in American. <How the rich live. . . . I must want my head tested sorting mail all day when I could be picking up wads of it **on the lorries**.> 1969 Rendell 10.

on *certain* lunches At *certain* lunches <**On** monthly Saturday **lunches** (in March, April and June) Mr Tucker and Sir Ronald sat down with the Mr and Mrs Thatcher to discuss the lastest poll findings.> 1987 June 13 *Times* 28/4.

on *some* market At/in *some* market <There are other secrets at Smithfield, suggestions that "famous gangsters" have worked **on** the **market**, but no one names names.> 1988 June *Illustrated London News* 70/2.

on marriage After marriage <**On marriage**, I could buy food at the same time as washing powder.> 1986 Oct. 1 *Times* 11/7.

on *a* meter At *a* meter; in *a* metered parking place: British uses both *on* and *at* in this rare construction; American uses only *at*. <. . . where's the best place to park in Cambridge? I'm **on** a **meter** at the moment.> 1995 Wilson 99.

on National Service In the army: This expression is rare in British use. <After leaving school each of them spent eighteen months **on National Service**.> 1979 Dexter 94.

on the night American English would be inclined to omit the preposition but would require a modification of *night* to identify it: either a phrase like the one in square brackets or a determiner like *that* rather than *the*. <. . . viewers will be encouraged to pledge money **on the night** [of a BBC1 charity program].> 1988 Feb. *Illustrated London News* 24/4. Cf. also ON (THE) DAY above and § 2.1.4.

on the North-East In the northeast: In CIC, the expression is rare in British texts and does not occur in American. <Jobclubs, pioneered **on the North-East** five years ago, are open to anyone unemployed for more than six months and looking for a job.> 1989 Aug. 7 (Durham) *Evening Chronicle* 8/4.

on oath Under oath: In CIC, both prepositions are used in British texts, with a slight preference for *under*; American texts have only *under oath*, which occurs 18.5 times more frequently than the same expression in British texts.

on *cardinal number* o'clock At *cardinal number* o'clock: The preposition *at* is usual in both British and American. CIC has 1.0 iptmw of *on* in British texts; the only such instances in American texts are 0.3 in the idiom *going on*, i.e., "nearing," which does not occur in the British texts. <Mrs Denny, the medium, came in spot **on** two o'clock.> 1989 Sept. 1 *Times* 12/6. <Pick it up *on* nine o'clock on a Wednesday.> 1996 spoken text in a tearoom CIC.

on offer Available; being offered: In CIC, *on offer* occurs 42 times more frequently in British texts than in American. <. . . you'll buy whatever's **on offer**.> 2005 Jan. 15 *Daily Telegraph* Books 5/3.

on *some* park In/at *some* park: *In* is the most frequent locative preposition with *park* in common-core English. CIC has some 5.1 iptmw of *on* with *park* in British texts, but only 0.1 in American texts. <Dribbles [a giraffe] is 104 in human terms, the oldest animal **on** the [zoological] **park**.> 1993 Feb. 13 *Daily Telegraph* 12/4–6.

on a party At/in a party: CIC has a few instances in British texts, but none in American texts. <Don't catechize people **on a** swimming **party**.> 1985 Byatt 83.

on *certain* patterns With/by/according to *certain* patterns: CIC has very few instances in British texts, and none in American texts. <**On** present smoking **patterns**, the future is going to be considerably worse than the past.> 1994 Sept. 20 *Times* 6/3.

on *some* photograph In *some* photograph: CIC has a few examples in British texts, but none in American. <"Are *you* **on** this **photograph**, Mrs Prokosch?" "Do I look as if I'm **on** it?"> 1976 Bradbury 78.

on *a place* See ON FOODWORTH, TYNESIDE, THAMES.

on *some* plans According to *some* plans: CIC has a few instances of *on current plans* in British texts, none in American, and at least one instance of *according to current plans* in American texts, none in British. <Nonetheless, it [a new bank building] has thirty-eight storeys **on** current **plans**.> 1982 Lynn and Jay 139.

on the pools The whole expression is British; a somewhat parallel American expression, *on/in the lottery*, uses either preposition, but *on the pools* is the regular British form rather than **in the pools*. <. . . my dad, Selwyn, won a couple of thousand pounds **on the pools**.> 2004 Dec. 12 *Sunday Times* Bricks and Mortar 3/1.

on prescription By prescription: With *prescription*, CIC British texts have *on* nearly 9 times more often than *by*; in American texts, the two prepositions are approximately equal in frequency. <It's not **on prescription**, so you can buy it across the counter.> 1990 Hardwick 145.

on *a* rehearsal At/in *a* rehearsal: *At* and *in* are more frequent with *rehearsal* in both varieties, but *on* occurs only in British in CIC texts. <OK, everybody, what can we do, **on** one **rehearsal**?> 1993 Neel 191–2.

on release **1. go on release** Be released; premiere: This idiom is found in British with the adjectives *controlled, general, limited*, and *national*; it is not usual in American. <The leaflets, which will be handed out at cinemas all over Scotland when the film **goes on** general **release** on Friday, have a picture of Gibson as Wallace.> 1995 Sept. 4 *Daily Telegraph* 2/4. **2. be on release** Be playing: This idiom is applied to films in British but is not used in American CIC texts. <And that afternoon I had to queue to see *Four Weddings and a Funeral*, a British movie that is still packing them in, despite having **been on release** for months.> 1994 Sept. *Tatler* 92/3.

on *some* salary At *some* salary: In CIC, *on* is used with *salary* about equally in British and American texts, but *at* is used about twice as often in American texts as in British. <She [Connie Chung] recently jumped ship at NBC News to became [sic] an anchor at CBS **on** a starting **salary** of $1.3m a year.> 1989 Sept. 10–16 *Sunday Telegraph* magazine 17/2. Cf. also ON *INCOME(S)*.

on sale For sale: In American English, *on sale* has two senses, the common-core "for sale" and "for sale at a reduced price." <. . . a three-bedroom period semi . . . is **on sale** for £99,000.> 1995 Aug. 30 *Daily Telegraph* 36/2.

on *some score* With/at *some score*: This use, which occurs in CIC British texts, appears to be rare in American. <Tied in first place, **on** eighty-five points each. . . . In second place, **on** eighty points. . . .> 2000 Rowling 439 (*US ed.* with).

on the scrounge Scrounging; on the prowl: Although not common in CIC British texts (0.4 iptmw), this idiom does not occur in CIC American texts. American texts have a somewhat higher incidence of *scrounging* and *on the prowl* than do British texts. <Always **on the scrounge** for money, always in trouble with the law.> 1994 Fyfield 66.

on *some periodical* section In *some periodical* section: This construction is rare. <If we have space, some opinions may appear **on** the Letters **section.**> 2002 Sept. *Square* 27.

on show Being shown/displayed: CIC has 54 iptmw of *on show* in British texts and 2.2 in American texts. <. . . hardly any of the work **on show** is of the twig-woven variety.> 1995 Sept. 6–13 *Time Out* 56/2.

on *some* skip In *some* Dumpster: *On* (versus *in*) is rare with *skip* in British texts, a 1:13 ratio, but only *in* occurs with the American analog *Dumpster*. <Dumping your aubergine bidet **on** someone else's **skip** is fly-tipping, a criminal offence.> 1997 Mar. 19 *Evening Standard* Homes & Property 17/2–3.

on *some* stall In *some* stall: CIC has 5.6 iptmw of *on* + *stall* in British texts and none in American texts. It has 1.6 iptmw of *in* + *stall* in British texts and 6.2 in American texts. <But the question remains, since you were rarely **on** the **stall**, where were you?> 1985 Barnard 148.

on *some (train)* station In/at *some (train)* station: CIC has no instances of *on* for this construction in American texts. <He was last seen getting off a train **on** Waterloo **station.**> 1992 Walters 71.

on *some* suburb(s) In *some* suburb(s): This use of *on* is clearly exceptional; the *OED* text and CIC have many instances of *in* with *suburb(s)*, but no relevant example of *on*. The exceptional use is perhaps a blend with *live on the* [Hampstead] *Heath*. <Residents of Hampstead Garden Suburb say that they live ***on*** the **Suburb**, perhaps to distinguish themselves from lesser breeds who live commonly in the suburbs.> 1990 Howard 105.

on income support With income support: In CIC British texts, *on* is 27 times more frequent than *with* in this construction. The construction does not occur in CIC American texts. <A single mother **on income support** describes how she goes scrimping at markets and jumble sales.> 1994 Oct. 3 *Times* 47/3.

on ***some system*****, fault/leak** Fault/leak in *some system*: In CIC British texts, *in* is more frequent than *on* with this construction. CIC American texts have no instances of the construction with *on* and only 1 with *in*. <An electrician who allegedly failed to spot a **fault on** a central heating **system** faced a manslaughter charge.> 1989 Aug. 31 *Times* 1/2.

on ***some*** **table** At *some* table <I dined **on** High **Table**.> 2000 Caudwell 322.

on tank maintenance In tank maintenance: The construction is rare. <Mary and Terry have been putting on a brave front; they've a son **on tank maintenance** somewhere in the Saudi desert.> 1991 Feb. 23 *Telegraph Weekend Magazine* 8/1.

on taxis In taxis: The construction is rare. <Here are some 'on's that are current, and sound wrong, or rather novel, to me: . . . he rode **on taxis** (rather than buses). I should have used . . . in [taxis]>. 1990 Howard 104–5.

on + ***telephone*** **1. on** ***a telephone number*** At a number; by calling: This use is frequent in British and lacking in American. <I suggest you ring the dean **on** 4673140.> 1993 Greenwood 53. **2. be on the telephone** Have a telephone: Judging from CIC, this sense is now rare in British, with only a few instances in the negative (*not on the telephone*). The sense "be using the telephone" is, however, common-core English. <Of course that is not including those who **are** not **on the telephone**.> 1977 Dec. 7 *Punch* 1144/1.

on ***some*** **temperature** At *some* temperature <If you pop a quilted bedspread in the freezer overnight, this will kill the dust mites and means you can wash it **on** a cooler **temperature**.> 2004 Jan. 4 *Sunday Times* Home 7 24/1.

on-Thames, Henley- This naming pattern is characteristically British. <**Henley-on-Thames**. . . . Prepositions and place-names are two of the most erratic elements in the English vocabulary.> 1990 Howard 106.

on a roasting tin In a roasting pan: CIC has about equal numbers of British *in a roasting tin* and American *in a roasting pan*, and no instances of *on* for this construction in either variety. <Arrange the potatoes and lamb **on a roasting tin**.> 1994 Oct. 3 *Evening Standard* 60/3.

on the top of ***some*** **scale** At the top of *some* scale: CIC has no instances of *on* for this construction in either variety. <. . . senior registrars **on the top of** their salary **scale** will get an extra £400 taking their salaries to £27,210.> 1993 Feb. 13 *Daily Telegraph* 6/4.

on tow In tow: CIC has similar numbers of *in tow* from British and American texts. It is the overwhelmingly dominant form, used chiefly of people, but also of land and water vehicles and other objects. *Under tow* is rare in both varieties, used mainly, though not exclusively, of ships. *On tow* does not occur in CIC texts of either variety. <The Aberdeen coastguard said that the rig was **on tow** in rough seas.> 1990 Aug. 21 *Times* 16/7.

on Youth Training In Youth Training: CIC has twice as many instances of *on* as of *in* with *Youth Training scheme* in British texts. *Youth Training* does not occur in CIC American texts, but those texts have more than twice as many instances of *in* + *training* as of *on*. <Just 4 per cent of girls **on Youth Training**

were in jobs such as construction, engineering and computing.> 1994 Sept. 12 *Independent* 6/2.

on *one's* travels In *one's* travels: CIC has about 7 times as many instances of *on* as of *in* with *travels* in British texts. It has about twice as many instances of *in* as of *on* with *travels* in American texts <She . . . wrote . . . a slim guide to the unusual water closets she had encountered **on** her **travels**.> 1985 Richardson 101.

on present trends This is a set phrase in British English; there are no instances of it in CIC American texts, which use instead *if/should present trends continue/persist*. <**On present trends**, the jobless total will top 3m in a year.> 1991 Mar. 17 *Sunday Times* 1 14/6.

on Tyneside CIC British texts have more than 12 times as many instances of *on Tyneside* as of *in Tyneside*, and 3 times as many of the latter as of *at Tyneside*. By contrast, CIC American texts have twice as many instances of *in Riverside* (a comparable place name) as of *at Riverside*, and none of *on Riverside*. <A startled horse trampled a bus driver . . . **on Tyneside** today.> 1989 Aug. 8 (Durham) *Evening Chronicle* 1/3.

on *the* Underground In *the* subway: CIC British texts have twice as many instances of *on* as of *in* with *Underground*; its American texts have 1.5 times as many instances of *in* as of *on* with *subway*. <Customers are reminded that smoking is not permitted (*on* any part of the **Underground** /–Tube announcement, Surbiton Station, Greater London, 14.6.00).> 2001 Apr. *English Today* 29/1.

on *some* ward In *some* ward: CIC British texts have about equal numbers of *on* and *in* with *ward*; its American texts have about 4 times as many instances of *in* as of *on*. <Nor did the deceptively cheerful lemon-coloured decor and ample supply of toys **on** the children's **ward** raise his spirits one little bit.> 2002 Aird 94.

on last year, up/down Up/down from/over last year: In *up/down ____ last year*, the dominant form in CIC British texts is *on*, with *from* a distant second, and no instances of *over*. In CIC American texts, the dominant form is *from*, with *over* a very distant second, and no instances of *on*. <. . . 50 of its London staff would get a Christmas bonus of £1 million each, substantially **up on last year**.> 2000 Dec. 18 *Times* 1/2. <[income is] well **down on last year**.> 2002 Feb. 25 BBC1 evening news.

on to, onto The spelling *on to* is the older one, dating from the sixteenth century, but *onto* has been used since the eighteenth century. A distinction is now made between the two forms comparable to that of *in to* and *into*, that is, an adverbial particle followed by the preposition *to* and a compound preposition (Gilman 1994). In CIC's British texts, the spaced spelling *on to* outnumbers the solid *onto* by 2.25 to 1; in its American texts, the ratio is more nearly even: 1.15 to 1. The spaced spelling sometimes gives rise to a confusion by which the adverb plus preposition is spelled solidly: <She was a precocious child, . . . the first of her family to go **onto** grammar school.> 1993 Feb. 15 *Daily Mail* 26/2.

<. . . they . . . had moved with their glasses [from inside the riverside pub] out **on to** the almost deserted decking.> 2003 James 128.

onto "*chiefly Br* in or into contact with <(*been* ~ *him about the drains*" (*LDEL*). "*especially Br E* to get in contact with someone: *Get* **onto** *the hospital and see if they can spare extra nurses*" (*LDOCE* 1995).

onto *a* degree course Into *a* degree program <. . . if I were applying for a university place today I could get **onto** a **degree course** in engineering or even physics.> 1994 Sept. 21 *Times* 16/2.

onto *a* flat Into *an* apartment <The apartment has the benefit of a lift giving private access directly **onto** the **flat**.> 1988 Nov. *Illustrated London News* 71/3.

opposite (to) *Opposite* has been used alone as a preposition since the eighteenth century and is common-core English; however, it is more frequent in British than in American (Peters 2004, 396). A random sample of 250 British and 250 American instances of the form *opposite* in CIC found 50 in prepositional use in British texts and 25 in American texts (many of which involved statements about one actor playing opposite another, or one structure being opposite another on a street or river). CIC has 19.1 iptmw of *opposite to* in British texts and 2.6 in American texts. American seems to prefer other wordings for the concept: *across from, different from, facing, on the other side of the street from*, etc. <Lorton sat down **opposite** Dougal.> 1988 Taylor 97. <The woman . . . was so **opposite to** David's expectation that he almost cried out in protest.> 1991 Charles 72.

out / out of The preposition *out* is used chiefly with *door* and *window*, but also in American with other objects occasionally and as "not quite part of the mainstream" (Gilman 1994). A study (Estling 1999) based on parts of four corpora reports that in collocation with *door* and *window*, the norm in British is *out of* and in American, *out*. Specifically, British uses *out of* twice as often as *out* (67 to 33 percent) whereas American uses *out* between 6 and 7 times as often as *out of* (87 to 13 percent). However, the dominant British form in spoken texts is *out* (72 percent), and in written texts *out of* (80 percent), indicating a striking divergence between written and spoken usage. In that study, *out* is favored in American English and in British speech; *out of*, in British written material. An examination of the frequency of the two prepositions with *door* and *window* as objects in CIC texts agreed with Estling's general conclusions, but differed in the percentages. In CIC texts, both British and American prefer *out* over *out of* with *door* and *window*, but American more strikingly so: British by 68 to 32 percent (roughly 2 to 1) and American by 91 to 9 percent (roughly 10 to 1). There is also a notable difference with the two objects. In American, *out* is preferred with both *door* and *window* by fairly similar percentages (93 and 89 percent respectively); in British, the preference for *out* with *door* is less (70 percent), but with *window*, British preference is actually for *out of* (57 percent), thus making the object apparently a significant factor. With regard to writing versus speech, CIC data also agrees in general conclusions with the earlier study: American texts, both written and spoken, have a preference for *out* by 90 and 94 percent, respectively; British spoken texts also prefer *out* by 91 percent, but British written texts prefer *out of* by 58 percent. – **out** Out of: "*Br E* used in a way which some people think is incorrect, to say that someone or something is removed from inside something, leaves somewhere etc: *Get out the car and push with the rest of us!*" (*LDOCE* 1995). In CIC British texts, *out the car* accounts for 8 percent and *out of the car* for 92 percent of the total uses; American texts have no instances of *out the car*. < . . . **out** the way, Fang . . . ***out*** *the way*, yeh dozy dog.> 2003 Rowling 372. – **out of** Some British uses of *out of* also seem less likely in American: **1**. From: CIC British texts have about equal numbers of *out of* and *from* with *King's Cross*; American texts have no instances of either preposition with *Grand Central*. <Consider this report in an English newspaper: "Princess Margaret travelled last night to Balmoral as an ordinary first class passenger in the Aberdonian night train **out of** King's Cross."> 1967 Frost and Jay 31. **2**. After (hours): In CIC British texts, *out of hours* accounts for 21 percent and *after hours* for 79 percent of the total uses; American texts have no instances of *out of hours*. <The new council will reward further-education colleges for . . . keeping libraries open **out of** hours.> 1992 Dec. 5 *Economist* 61/3. **3**. Out of (a team): In CIC British texts, *out of the team* accounts for more than 96 percent and *off the team* for less than 4 percent of the total uses; American texts have no instances of *out of the team*. <He missed two practice sessions and now he's **out of** the team.> 1995 *CIDE*. Cf. IN *SOME* TEAM above. **4**. Beyond: In CIC British texts, *out of all recognition* accounts for 28 percent and *beyond all recognition* for 72 percent of the total uses; American texts have no instances of *out of all recognition*. <If the situation did not improve **out of all recognition**, it did, nevertheless, at last improve – but very, very slowly.> 1993 Mason 165.

outside Outside of: These two related forms have been the subject of usage controversy (Gilman 1994, 702–3); *outside* has been said to be "overwhelmingly the normal use in BrE" (Burchfield 1996, 562); yet *outside of* has also been said to be "established in British English, and used across a range of prose styles for the general reader" (Peters 2004, 401). In random samples from CIC, British texts had approximately equal numbers of *outside* and *outside of* (49 and 51 percent, respectively); American texts had slightly more than a third as many instances of *outside* as of *outside of* (26 and 74 percent, respectively). <. . . a service station **outside** Hull.> 2003 June 14 *Times* 26/1.

over **1**. Across; on the other side of <Most of us probably look at the house **over** the road more often than our own.> 2003 June 21 *Times* Weekend 12/1. **2**. Over/across to <"Are you in this evening, Mr. Daley?" asked Morse. [¶] "Wha' – I usually go **over** the pub for a jar or two at the weekends but – "> 1992 Dexter 119. **3**. Above; more than <He admired John O'Hara **over** all writers.> 1986 Oct. 30 *Times* 18/5. – **over the odds** Above (the) average: In CIC, *above average* is the more common expression in both varieties and of approximately equal frequency in both, but British has almost half as many instances of *over the odds*, and American has none. <Health-conscious consumers are paying **over the odds** for "inferior" imported cooking oil.> 1993 Feb. 13 *Daily Telegraph* 5/1.

over *so many* floors On *so many* floors: CIC British texts include 5 times as many examples as American texts do, and the latter all refer to spreading or scattering something, not to area measurement. <Boasting 13,957 square foot, **over** five **floors**, the store will house the famous footwear alongside accessories and men's and women's clothing.> 1994 Sept. 21 *Times* 17/3.

over that score, lose no sleep Lose no sleep on that score <They knew their standards were almost anachronistic, probably "pi", but they **lost no sleep over that score**.> 1963 Ashford 44.

over *a season* During *a season*: In CIC texts, *during* is more common with seasons in both varieties; but British has 6 times as many instances of *over* as American does. <We get housewives with kids who . . . need six weeks off **over** summer.> 1994 Sept. 24 *Guardian Careers* 3/2.

over the top Exaggeratedly, unreasonably: In CIC, this expression is 2.75 times more frequent in British texts than in American. <The widow of one of the most famous alcoholics of the 20th century behaving a touch **over the top** as her husband's coffin made its way six foot down seems to me pretty small beer in the great scheme of unacceptable behaviour.> 1994 Sept. 17 *Times Magazine* 3/4.

over to *someone* Up to *someone*: As an expression meaning "the responsibility of," *up to* is common-core English; CIC British, but not American, texts also have *over to* as an occasional variant (approximately 0.9 iptmw). <But now it is **over to** someone else to complete the ***task***.> 1991 Feb. 9 *Daily Telegraph* Weekend 20/5.

past *an hour* After *an hour*: In CIC, with hours (including *noon* and *midnight*), British texts have *past* in 31 percent of the instances and *after* in 69 percent; American texts have *past* in 16 percent of the instances and *after* in 84 percent. "In American English *after* is often used instead of *past* (e.g. *ten **after** six*)" (Swan 1995, 582).

qua Disregarding *sine qua non*, which has about equal use in the two varieties, *qua* is twice as frequent in CIC British texts as in American. <Anita Roddick, supremo of the eco-friendly Body Shop, has written her memoirs, *Body and Soul*, due out in September. However, there is precious little in the book about Roddick ***qua*** woman.> 1991 Feb. 17 *Sunday Times* Books 7/5.

round Around: In combined prepositional and adverbial uses, *round* outnumbers *around* 7:6 in the British LOB corpus; in the American Brown corpus, *around* outnumbers *round* 40:1 (Peters 2004, 48). CIC classifies 954.6 iptmw of *round* in British texts as prepositional and 59.3 in American texts (compared with 2561.1 iptmw of prepositional *around* in British texts and 2883.3 in American texts). British notably uses *round* for circular movement or position (*walk round the car, sit round the table*) and for everywhere (*look round the house*), but uses *around* for indefinite movement or position in the sense "here and there in" (*wander/stand around the place*) (Swan 1995, 53): <And so he [comedian Steve Coogan] turned down the naff jobs and concentrated on a new, character-based routine and took it **around** arts centres.> 1994 Sept. 14–21 *Time Out* 21/3. American uses *around* more widely. Although the number of senses listed for a word in dictionaries may represent the style of the lexicographer as much as the semantics of the language being described, it is noteworthy that *MW* has 7 senses or subsenses for the preposition *around* but only 2 for the preposition *round*, whereas *NODE* has 5 for *around* and 8 for *round*. **1.** Around <The boyfriend greased **round** her by giving back all her things – and the money he'd nicked. . . . So she decided not to do him for assault.> 1996 Neel 45. **2.** Around to <My father . . . has gone **round** Pandora's house to borrow a bottle of spirits.> 1985 Townsend 151. **3.** On <The Thurso Boy . . . cheeked two bobbies in a cafe and one of them gave him . . . a cuff **round** the back of the head.> 1989 Sept. 6 *Evening Standard* 7/2. **– round the twist** Eccentric <And she is a bit **round the twist**.> 1991 Neel 121. Cf. §§ 5.1.4 ALL-ROUND and 6.1 ALL ROUND and ROUND.

save (for) Except (for) <However, the party agents, middle-aged men with hairy tweeds and bad teeth, who read nothing **save for** the *Daily Mail*, always insisted on holding public meetings.> 1991 Critchley 54.

saving Except <He had done the round so often that he didn't need a clock to know that, **saving** Christmas and a General Election, he would finish his . . . delivery at a quarter to eight in the furthest farmhouse.> 1968 Aird 6.

since (when) Since (which time): The sequence *since when* is about 5 times more frequent in British than American according to CIC. Two of its uses are as an interrogative and as a relative. In British texts, the relative is 2.5 times more frequent than the interrogative; in American texts, the interrogative is about 5.5 times more frequent than the relative. (Cf. also *CGEL* 15.29n, 57.) <. . . he gained his BA in Fine Art from 1963 to 1989, **since when** he has devoted himself to his painting.> 1993 *Artist's and Illustrator's Magazine* (BNC).

till Until; to: In CIC, British and American texts have roughly the same number of instances of *until*, but British has about 5 times more instances of the preposition *till* than does American. <She's in the casino **till** nearly dawn most nights.> 1992 Walters 141. Cf. § 9.2 TILL.

to *To* is the fourth most frequent word in the LOB corpus (after *the*, *of*, and *and*) and the second most frequent preposition. Its British-American differences involve cooccurrence with objects.

to budget Within budget: CIC has 0.4 iptmw of this use of the phrase in British texts and none in American. <Thus, thirdly, any given National production is under that much greater pressure to keep **to budget**; which Lear has duly done.> 1991 Feb. *Evening Standard* magazine 53/3.

to camera On camera: CIC has 4.3 iptmw of this use of *to camera* in British texts and none in American. It has 8.1 iptmw of *on camera* in British texts and 23.1 in American. <The resulting work is strange and disturbing: a sequence of

oddballs wearing wigs and masks confess their innermost secrets **to camera**.> 1998 Jan. 3–9 *Times* Metro 22/2.

to commission On commission: CIC has 0.3 iptmw of *to commission* in British texts and none in American. It has 0.2 of *work on commission* in British texts and 1.1 in American. <You have to remember that they were professional painters, they worked **to commission**.> 1993 Smith 91.

to contract, out Up for bid: CIC has 0.5 iptmw of *out to contract* in British texts and none in American. It has no instances of *for bid* in British texts and 3.3 iptmw in American, often in the combination *up for bid*. <London Regional Transport . . . has put many of its other routes out **to contract**.> 1989 Autumn *Illustrated London News* 26/2.

to *a date* Through *a date*: For indicating inclusive time periods, British and American differ notably in five ways. British characteristically uses the following four constructions (the figures are iptmw in CIC British texts, followed by those in American texts after a virgule): *from [a month] to [a later period of time]* 45.9 / 22.3; *from [a period of time] to the end of [another period of time]* 3.5 / 0.5; *from [a period of time] through to [another period of time]* 3.1 / 0.6; *from [a period of time] to [another period of time] inclusive* 0.6 / 0.0. The characteristic American construction is *from [a period of time] through [another period of time]*: American 53.7 iptmw, British 1.3. <But even the news that annual wage rises **to August** had reached 9.25 per cent did little to disturb the equanimity of the party faithful.> 1988 Oct. 16 *Sunday Telegraph* 23/5. Cf. FROM *A MONTH* above.

to *a* design In/from *a* design <Three generations have worn the same style [of ring] **to** an old family **design**.> 1994 Sept. 25 *Sunday Times* Magazine 48/4.

to *some* direction At/by/following/according to *some* direction <But they were all easy-mannered, answering Sarah's questions readily as they placed files in piles **to her direction**.> 1993 Neel 66.

to form According to form <. . . it was Lewis's job that day to ferry the chief inspector around; doubtless, too (if things went **to form**) to treat him to the odd pint or two.> 1993 Dexter 46.

to hand 1. On/at hand; available: In CIC texts, *to hand* is about 1.5 times more frequent in British texts than in American; *on hand* is about twice as frequent in American texts as in British; *at hand* is about equally frequent in both varieties. <Having your national insurance number **to hand** will speed up the process.> 2003 June 21 *Times* Money 6/8. **2**. In hand <By ten past nine the entrance and drive-way of the Grand Hotel had filled up with eager Tories, . . . conferences agendas **to hand**.> 1992 Critchley 76. Cf. AT HAND above.

to *hour* Of: In expressions like *a quarter to/of nine*, British CIC texts have *to* more than 7 times as often as American texts do. American texts have *of* 15 times as often as British texts do; however, British uses *of* rarely (0.1 iptmw), so *of* in the American construction is minor (1.5 iptmw). Moreover, other prepositions (*before, till*) in this construction are also of minor or negligible importance in British and are unrecorded in CIC American texts. Thus it appears that American prefers other constructions for telling time, such as 8:45, which constructions are about 1.4 times more frequent in American than in British CIC texts. <[traveler on platform:] Train to King's Cross? . . . Leaves when? [traveler on train:] Quarter **to**.> 1990 Jan. 29 conversation at the Cambridge station.

to interview For an interview; to be interviewed <Local Tory worthies often harbour ambitions to be selected as their association's candidate; parish pump courtesies dictate that many of these are called **to interview**, but few are, in fact, ever chosen.> 1991 Feb. 9 *Daily Telegraph* 10/1.

to *a meal* At/for *a meal*: Common-core English collocations are *invite to dinner, sit down to dinner*, etc. Others exist in British English; e.g., *entertain to dinner*, for which American is more likely to have *entertain at dinner* or a completely different construction, such as *invite for dinner*. <They had been a large party **to dinner**.> 1956 Robinson 27. Cf. § 11.1.1.2 ENTERTAIN *SOMEONE* TO A *MEAL*.

to *some* meeting For *some* meeting; to go to *some* meeting <Mr Clarke, Education Secretary, was leaving his office **to** the Cabinet **meeting** when the attack happened.> 1991 Feb. 8 *Daily Telegraph* 2/6.

to *one's* peak At *one's* peak <They believe a person needs the right environment to perform **to** his **peak**.> 1989 July 19 *Daily Mail* 7/5–6.

to someplace Someplace: CIC has 0.4 iptmw of *go someplace* (without *to*) in British texts, and 7.1 in American texts (cf. also Swan 1995, 452).

to plan As planned: CIC has 5.2 iptmw of *go to plan* in British texts, and none in American texts. It has 1 iptmw of *go as planned* in British texts, and 6.9 in American texts. <Everything was working **to plan**.> 1989 Quinton 261.

to ransom For ransom: CIC has 2.5 iptmw of *hold to ransom* in British texts and 0.2 in American texts. It has 0.5 iptmw of *for ransom* in British texts and 3.9 in American texts. <The gazunderer is making a conscious decision to hold somebody **to ransom**.> 1989 July 30 *Sunday Times* A-9/4.

to schedule On schedule: The ratio between the prepositional phrases *to schedule* and *on schedule* in CIC British texts is 1:10, and in American texts, 1:18; moreover, in the American texts, nearly two-thirds of the instances of *to schedule* are *according to schedule*, which represents less than one-third of the British instances. <. . . sailings . . . had operated **to schedule**.> 1986 Aug. 30 *Times* 2/3.

to the highest/higher standard(s) This expression is almost 6 times more frequent in CIC British texts than in American. <The work of the carpenter . . . has been . . . all **to the highest standard**.> 1990 Sept. 1 *Times* (Saturday) Review 31/3–4.

to a timetable, work This construction is rare in British, but has no instances in CIC American texts. <During the long vacation both **worked to a** gruelling **timetable**.> 1987 Archer 167–8.

to wife As a wife: This phrase echoes Leviticus 21.14: "he shall take a virgin of his own people to wife"; the construction, which comes from Old English, is used archaically in British English; there are no instances in CIC American texts. <Be glad you've got Jean and not Lee Garfield **to wife**.> 1989 Quinton 239.

towards Toward: *Towards* in LOB outnumbers *towards* in Brown by 318 to 64; *toward* in Brown outnumbers *toward* in LOB by 386 to 14 (Hofland and Johansson 1982, 537). Christian Mair (1997, 144) reports the following ratios for *towards:toward* in limited portions of the 1961 LOB and Brown corpora: 45:3 and 6:67; and in the 1991 or 1992 FLOB and Frown updates: 32:0 and 2:41. Their ratios in CIC are British 14:1 and American 1:4.4. These figures indicate that *towards* is predominantly British and *toward* American on a continuing basis. <'Over here,' says Helen, taking her arm and guiding her **towards** the downstairs cloakroom.> 2001 Lodge 136.

under A few collocational differences distinguish British and American use.

under *one's* face *Under one's nose* is common-core English. CIC has 0.3 iptmw of *under one's face* in British texts and none in American texts. <Should your partner fail to maintain the level of devotion you consider essential, these yellowing fragments of newsprint should be . . . thrust **under his face**.> 1991 Feb. 11 *Ms London* 4/2.

under offer CIC has 0.3 iptmw of *under offer* in British texts and 0.2 of sense 2 below (none of sense 1) in American texts. **1**. Contract pending; with an offer received, but awaiting the signing of a contract <Its "For Sale" board is a hopeless bit of cardboard. . . . On it he has written, "**Under Offer**: £172,000".> 1990 Aug. 18 *Daily Telegraph* Weekend 14/2. **2**. Available for sale <Superb offices **under offer**> 1999 March sign at a Hampstead estate agency.

under *place name* <Newcastle-***under***-Lyme. Prepositions and place-names are two of the most erratic elements in the English vocabulary: if you try to find logic in them when they are combined, you will surely go mad.> 1990 Howard 106.

under preparation In preparation: CIC has 0.2 iptmw of *under preparation* in British texts and none in American texts. <Malise Ruthven is the author of *Islam in the World* . . . a new edition of which is now **under preparation**.> 1996 Aug. 1 *London Review of Books* 2/4.

underneath the down Next to a low hill: Neither the preposition nor the noun is used in these senses in American English. <Three hours later they dropped down a muddy lane into Cocking, another hamlet **underneath the down**.> 1940 Shute 143.

up This prepositional use corresponds to an optional adverbial *up* followed by various prepositions of location. **1**. (Up) at <He wanted nothing to do with his father's brick semi **up** the Liverpool bypass.> 1993 Greenwood 20. **2**. (Up) to "*Br nonstandard* (up) to *<going ~ the West End>*" (*LDEL*). <He's going **up** the post office to cash his giro.> 1991 Glaister 21. **3**. (Up) on <The dog . . . jumped **up** the policeman's tunic with its muddy paws.> 1985 Townsend 15. – **up the spout** Pregnant: This phrase has several other senses in British English: "pawned"; "useless or ruined"; "lost"; "dead"; (of a bullet) "in a gun barrel ready for shooting." CIC has 1.98 iptmw of the phrase (in various senses) in British texts and one instance in an American text, in which it is glossed "vanished." <Harriet described her boyfriend . . . and the fright they'd had in May when Harriet had thought she was **up the spout**.> 2001 Drabble 235. Cf. DOWN above.

upon Christian Mair (1997, 145) reports that, in limited portions of the 1961 LOB and Brown corpora and of their 1991–1992 FLOB and Frown updates, *upon* was more common in American than in British use at the earlier time but has declined in frequency in both varieties, and so much more in American that now the two varieties show no significant difference in its use. CIC, however, shows a difference: whereas British and American have similar frequencies of the preposition *on*, British has almost twice as many instances of *upon* as American (2105.8 versus 1112.6 iptmw); because *on* is so much more frequent (more than 62,000 iptmw in each variety), American *upon/on* occur at the respective percentages of 2/98, and British *upon/on* at 3/97.

upon *some* bottom On *some* bottom: *Upon* here is rare and may be obsolete. <. . . the discovery of a terribly battered car **upon** the concrete **bottom** of an empty dry dock, with two dead naval officers in it.> 1940 Shute 60.

upon *place names* This pattern of place names is characteristically British. <Burton-***upon***-Trent and Kingston-***upon***-Thames, . . . Newcastle ***upon*** Tyne.> 1990 Howard 106.

upon *some* side On *some* side: CIC British texts have about 5 times as many instances of *upon (some) side* as American texts do. <A middle-aged lady . . . sat opposite to her **upon** the far **side** of the fireplace.> 1940 Shute 213.

upon the telephone On; by telephone: *Upon* here is rare and may be obsolete. <I'll get in touch with you **upon the telephone** after I've been to Emsworth.> 1940 Shute 162.

upsides Beside: CIC has 0.4 iptmw of *upsides* in British texts and none in American texts. <I could tell tales of being **upsides** Terry Biddlecombe on Fearless Fred at Warwick [racecourse].> 1999 Mar. 16 *Independent* Review 4/6.

with Several collocations with this preposition involve British-American differences.

with *some* bank, deposit *something* Deposit something in a bank: CIC has 0.5 iptmw in British texts and 0.1 in American texts. For the construction using *in* instead of *with*, it has 0.3 iptmw in British texts and 0.8 in American texts. <I'll deposit it **with** your bank.> 1985 Bingham 116.

with next/last *time period*, start Start next/last *time period*: CIC has 0.5 iptmw of the construction using *with* in British texts and none in American texts. For the construction lacking *with*, it has 19.9 iptmw in British texts and 32.1 in American texts. <Interviews should have started **with last April**.> 1989 Sept. 10 *Sunday Telegraph* 7/8.

with effect from In effect from: CIC has 4.4 iptmw using the preposition *with* in British texts and 0.1 in American texts. For the construction using *in* instead of *with*, it has no instances in British texts and 0.6 iptmw in American texts.

<The following members of staff have been promoted to chairs, **with effect from** October 1.> 1990 Aug. 22 *Times* 12/7.

with it As well; in addition: The construction in this sense is listed in *NODE*, but not in *MW*. <She's a pretty lady and fast **with it**.> 1991 Critchley 201.

with reference to CIC British texts have 2.3 times as many instances of *with reference to* as of *in reference to*; American texts have 1.4 times as many of *in reference to* as of *with reference to* (the latter primarily in academic texts). A sampling of British texts collected by Algeo and Read for lexical purposes has *with reference to* outnumbering *in reference to* by 3:1. <It first appeared **with reference to** the Iraq dossier.> 2003 July 9 *Daily Express* 27/1.

with/in regard(s) to CIC texts show a British preference for *with* versus *in* of about 4.5 to 1, but an American preference of little more than 2 to 1. British preference for singular *regard* is about 19.4 to 1, and American preference is also for the singular, but only about 4.3 to 1. Therefore, although both varieties have more instances of *with regard to* than of the other three options combined, it accounts for 82 percent of all the British forms, but only 68 percent of the American forms.

within the hour In less than an hour: CIC has 4.4 iptmw of *within the hour* in British texts and 2.0 in American texts. It has 1.9 iptmw of *in less than an hour* in British texts and 2.8 in American texts. <He hobbled and hopped across to the telephone and rang Lewis, and **within the** half **hour** he was sitting disconsolately in the accident room of the Radcliffe Infirmary.> 1975 Dexter 79.

without "Outside of, beyond (in various senses): opp. to *within* prep. Now only literary or arch." (*OED*). <**Without** the house and within there was much mellow opulence on view.> 1973 Innes 113.

8.2 Omission of any preposition

8.2.1 In collocation with a following object

The omission of a preposition in the following citations leaves what would have been its object as a noun phrase functioning adverbially.

bottom At the bottom <. . . opinion polls regularly place them **bottom** of the royal league.> 1989 July 25 *Evening Standard* 22/3.

care of In care of "In the address of a letter or package *'care of—'*. *in care of* (US): = *care of*" (*OED* s.v. *care* n. 4.a).

century With a shorter period of time (*year, month, week*), omitting any preposition is common-core English, but with *century* it is more typically British. In CIC, British texts have approximately 2.8 times as many instances of both *last century* and *this century* used adverbially as do American texts. – **last century** In/during/of the last century <Nash got involved in the canal scheme early **last century** when he became entranced by the idea of boats sailing through

his newly-designed Regent's Park.> 1986 Aug. 28 *Hampstead Advertiser* 8/1. – **this century** In/during/of this century <Our report concluded that up to 200,000 houses a year were likely to be built **this century** in England and Wales.> 1990 Aug. 24 *Times* 11/5.

corner, fight *one's* Defend *one's* interest: This idiom is British; CIC has 2.8 iptmw of it in British texts and 0.1 in American texts (specifically in a Cable News Network report, where British influence is likely). If an American version existed, one would expect *fight for one's corner*. <If he hadn't seen him with his back against the wall **fighting** his **corner**, . . . he might well have got the impression that the DCI was a touch soft-headed.> 1996 Graham 220.

end, this At/on this end: A sampling of CIC American texts produced no instances of adverbial *this end*; a sampling of British texts did. <. . . it wasn't Beevers I should have been worried about – it was who Beevers was dealing with **this end**.> 1985 Bingham 142.

fashion, a valedictory In a valedictory fashion <. . . he actually shook hands with me **a valedictory fashion**.> 1983 Innes 70.

front In front <It was looks that first led her **front** of screen when she was a researcher on *Wogan*.> 1991 Mar. 9 *Telegraph Weekend Magazine* 18/1.

late, too Until too late <No one could talk to them about things like that. If I could have done, I might have been able to get an abortion. I left it **too late**.> 1987 Bawden 82.

latest At the latest <Only if he doesn't fit me in at half-past one sharp, he can't fit me in at all. So that means leaving ten past one **latest**.> 1985 Bingham 19–20.

period, this In/during this period <The vendor is asked to undertake not to accept any other bids **this period**.> 1987 Apr. 20 *Times* 18/8. Cf. CENTURY above.

side, *some* On some side: In random samples of 100 instances of *either side* from both British and American CIC texts, the British instances included 19 in which *either side* functioned adverbially without a preposition, and the American instances included 2. <Kingsley Shacklebolt and a tough-looking wizard . . . were positioned **either side** of the door like guards.> 2003 Rowling 538 (*US ed.* on either side).

time, a At a time <In any event, concentration was limited to ten seconds **a time**.> 1994 Fyfield 9.

weather, this In this weather <"The other two were in a little rubber boat." [¶] "Too bloody cold for that **this weather**."> 1940 Shute 33. – **all weathers** In all (kinds/sorts of) weather <He sits out there **all weathers** now.> 1985 Mortimer 317.

8.2.2 In collocation with a preceding word

born *year* Born in *year* <Beatrix, **born 1866**, was a plain and sickly child, starved of companionship.> 1986 Oct. 30 *Times* 15/1.

buttered A proverbial expression with three grammatical variations is *(on) which side one's bread is/was buttered (on)*. The variations are in the presence and location of the preposition *on*. **1**. Without the preposition *on*: <1863 Kingsley *Water Bab*. 289 He . . . understood so well **which side his bread was buttered**, and which way the cat jumped.> *OED* s.v. *cat* n. 13.e. **2**. With *on* at the end of the clause: <Brenda Maddox has a funny story about the American publisher of her biography of James Joyce's wife, *Nora:* [block quote] Not only were they trying to copy edit me, they were trying to edit Joyce. He's got this line: "Earth knows **which side her bread is buttered**." And this editor came back with a query, "Surely he meant '**buttered on**'?"> 1990 Critchfield 251. **3**. With *on* before the relative: <1834 Macaulay in Trevelyan *Life* I. 373, I quite enjoy the thought of appearing in the light of an old hunks who knows **on which side his bread is buttered**.> *OED* s.v. *light* n. 9. The BNC has 7 instances of the expression and CIC British texts 5 instances, which are, respectively: 4 and 2 of *which side one's bread is buttered*; 2 and 2 of *which side one's bread is buttered on*; 1 and 1 of *on which side one's bread is buttered*. CIC American texts have only 1 instance, of *on which side one's bread is buttered*; despite that evidence, the most usual American form is doubtless with the terminal preposition, *which side one's bread is buttered on*, as indicated by the reaction of the American editor under 2. above.

fortnight ***day*** Two weeks from *day* <President Mitterrand's daughter-in-law Elizabeth Mitterrand is standing in the French senate elections a **fortnight today**.> 1989 Sept. 10 *Sunday Telegraph* 8/7.

half ***hour*** Half an hour after *hour*; half past *hour*; e.g., half eleven = 11:30: A search of CIC produced some 441 instances in British texts and none in American texts. <Make him bring you home by **half eleven** – anyhow, by midnight.> 1940 Shute 136. <I went in just before **half twelve**.> 1996 Graham 209.

month ***day*** Month from *day* <First rehearsal call – **one month today**.> 1987 Apr. 16 *Hampstead Advertiser* 14/3.

second last Second to/from last (cf. common-core *second best*): A search of CIC produced 27 instances in British texts and 2 in American texts. <Even further behind was the fancied second favourite, Shadeed, . . . which bumbled home **second last** in a field of 14.> 1985 June 6 *Times* 1/3. Cf. § 8.1 BUT and FROM LAST, § 11.3.1 LAST BUT.

sides, both Both sides of <I say, have you considered acquiring all the rights to Noel Coward? . . . I should nobble him, if nobbleable, on **both sides** the Atlantic: if I were a publisher.> 1938 Lawrence 696.

week day Week from *day*: CIC has 6.0 iptmw in British texts and none in American (cf. *CamGEL* 1562). <I've got cakes to bake – the fête is a **week today**, you know!> 1991 Charles 76. Cf. § 17.4 DAY WEEK.

year last ***time period*** Year ago/before last *time period*: CIC has 0.3 iptmw in British texts and none in American texts. <We presented him with one [a gold watch] a **year last December** for general good work.> 1986 Clark 41.

year next *time period* Year from *time period*: CIC has no instances in either British or American texts. <If I want to search Wytham Woods I'll bloody well search 'em till a **year next Friday**.> 1992 Dexter 93–4.

8.3 Omission of the prepositional object

The use of prepositions without an expressed object, when the implicit object is expressed earlier in the clause, has been reported with such examples as *My socks have got holes in (them)*, *I'd like a piece of toast with butter on (it)*, *All the trees have got blossom on (them)*, and *He was carrying a box with cups in (it)* (Swan 1995, 174, 433). CIC has sporadic instances of this construction in its British spoken corpus: <. . . the speech therapist suggested . . . that she made flashcards **with** letters **on**.> 1998 CIC spoken corpus. No American instances have been located.

8.4 Prepositional phrase versus noun adjunct

captain of games Team captain: CIC has 0.1 iptmw of *captain of games* in British texts and none in American texts. It has 6.3 iptmw of *team captain* in British texts and 5.6 in American texts. <He became **Captain of Games** in my house [at Eton] and used the position to pick on me unjustly, more than once.> 1994 Dickinson 15.

hall of residence Residence hall: CIC has 3.0 iptmw of *hall of residence* in British texts and none in American texts. It has no instances of *residence hall* in British texts and 2.7 iptmw in American texts. <They . . . went off . . . towards the **hall of residence**.> 1993 Neel 123.

8.5 Order of numbers with *by*

In specifying a two-dimensional size, British tends to put the larger size first, and American the small size. For the three pairs of dimensions *4 by 2* versus *2 by 4*, *5 by 3* versus *3 by 5*, and *6 by 4* versus *4 by 6*, CIC British texts have 2.0 iptmw of the larger size first and 0.3 of the smaller size first; American texts have 0.1 of the larger size first and 2.7 of the smaller size first.

<The most common size is **28 × 18** cm (**11 × 7** in), but it is also useful to have a slightly larger size, **33 × 23** cm (**13 × 9** in).> 1986 Pettigrew 19. <We're still working in the conventional manner with **six by four** cards.> 1988 Edmund Weiner, co-editor Oxford English Dictionary, at MLA in New Orleans Lexicography Discussion Group. <I . . . send a written-up entry on a 3” × 5” flimsy (we say **5” by 3”**!) back to her for eventual keying in to her machine.> 1989 July 25 private letter from British lexicographer Paul Beale.

9 Conjunctions

9.1 Coordinating conjunctions

and 1. When numbers such as *310* are written out or spoken, they may be either *three hundred and ten* or *three hundred ten* (Swan 1995, 385). In random samples of 1000 tokens of the word *hundred* from British texts, CIC's ratio of *hundred **and*** followed by another number to *hundred* followed directly by another number was 329:10; from American texts, the ratio was 149:42. In both national varieties, the norm is *hundred **and***, but in American there is a greater tendency to omit *and*. **2.** Before the introduction of decimal currency, the expression *X (shillings) and X (pence)*, with optional omission of *shilling(s)* or of both currency terms, was common. The pattern is now historical only. <Diva scuttled away to the other table without even waiting to be paid the sum of **one and threepence** which she had won from Elizabeth.> 1931 Benson 216. <Did you know, in 1958 you could get bed and breakfast in a one-star hotel in Morecambe for **seven-and-six** a night?> 1988 Lodge 174.

Certain paired-word collocations with *and* have different preferred orders for the paired words in British and American.

board and lodging The American analog is *room and board*. In CIC texts, each national variety has only sporadic tokens of the term regularly used in the other variety, often with reference to life in the other country. <workhouse . . . a public institution in which the destitute of a parish received **board and lodging** in return for work.> *NODE*, s.v. *workhouse*.

egg(s) and bacon; e&b *Bacon and eggs* is the norm in common-core English; but *egg(s) and bacon* accounts for 31 percent of the tokens in CIC British texts and only 23 percent in American. <I myself only rarely tuck into **e&b** [eggs and bacon] by choice.> 1988 June *Illustrated London News* 80/4. <By two in the morning Annabelle was eating **egg and bacon** in a huge kitchen.> 1996 Neel 10.

on and off Off and on: *On and off* is the norm in common-core English, but accounts for 90 percent of the occurrences in CIC British texts and for only

69 percent in American. <[They] have been phoning me **on and off** all day with questions about the house.> 2001 Lodge 86.

out and in *In and out (of)* is the norm in common-core English, but *out and in* has sporadic representation in CIC British texts and none in American. <[Glaswegian Jimmy Boyle:] . . .we kids were **out and in** each other's houses as if they were our own.> 1990 Critchfield 174.

there and then Then and there: *There and then* is the choice by more than 2:1 in CIC British texts; *then and there* is the choice by more than 4:1 in American texts. <Bernard made a telephone call **there and then** to the Chaplain's office at St Joseph's, and arranged it.> 1991 Lodge 305.

British prefers asyndetic compounds in some cases.

macaroni cheese Macaroni and cheese: CIC British texts prefer the conjunction-less form by nearly 3:1; it is unknown in American texts. <. . .such larder standbys as . . . **macaroni cheese**.> 2003 June 12 *Times* 9/1.

Double coordinating conjunctions *and nor* and *but nor* are characteristic of British, corresponding to common-core English *and neither* and *but neither*. CIC has 9.8 iptmw of *and nor* versus 3.4 of *but nor* in British texts, and 0.6 versus 0.4 of the two forms respectively in American texts. Those figures accord with the Algeo corpus, in which *and nor* outnumbers *but nor* by 2 to 1. Cf. also NOR MORE, OR NOR below.

and nor And neither <You haven't had supper **and nor** have I.> 2003 James 144.

but nor But neither <Mrs Pargeter didn't know much about computers, **but nor** apparently did the reception staff at Brotherton Hall.> 1992 Brett 47.

neither When it serves as a conjunction between sentences, *neither* is typically followed by inverted operator-subject order: A: *They don't gamble*. B: *Neither do I*. However, it may exceptionally occur in British English with subject-operator order. CIC had no examples of this exceptional order in a random sample of 100 tokens of sentence-connector *neither* in all texts, nor in a random sample of 85 tokens in spoken texts. <**Neither he will**, my dear, if he knows it.> 1935 Firth 310. Cf. NO MORE 2, NOR 3 below.

no more Neither; nor **1**. Used to introduce a sentence with operator-subject order that responds to a preceding negative sentence (*CGEL* 10.58n). In a randomly selected sample of 1000 examples of sentence-initial *No more*, CIC had 12 tokens of this construction. <He . . . doesn't see much of her. **No more** do her father and mother for that matter.> 1994 Symons 28. **2**. Used similarly, but with subject-operator order (*CGEL* 10.58n). In a randomly selected sample of 1000 examples of sentence-initial *No more*, CIC had 6 tokens of this construction, 5 of them from nineteenth-century fiction. <**No more** it was.> 1981 Innes 16. Cf. NEITHER, NOR 3.

nor As a clause coordinator, *nor* is slightly more characteristic of British than of American. CIC has 278.2 iptmw of clause initial *Nor* in British texts and

200.7 in American texts. **1.** Neither (contrasting the subjects of two clauses) <"And she won't like the fact that Tolby's involved." [¶] "**Nor** do I," Lorton snarled.> 1988 Taylor 66. **2.** And . . . not (either) (emphatically contrasting the predications of two clauses) <'In referring to Jock Beevers' cricket accomplishments, you said his school batting average had never been surpassed.' [¶] '**Nor** has it.'> 1985 Bingham 10–1. **3.** *followed by noninverted subject-operator order* <. . . that blasted baby feels his parents do not understand him as she does. **Nor** we do, I'm afraid.> 1993 Neel 78. Cf. NEITHER, NO MORE 2.

nor more And . . . not either/anymore: This is a rare construction; neither the BNC nor CIC has any examples of it. <She says you're not yourself. **Nor more** you are.> 1988 Lodge 316.

only As a conjunction, *only* is common-core English in the sense "but, however, except," as in *We intended to be there. Only it rained.* However, in the following example, its use was sufficiently odd to cause the American publisher to omit the word altogether: <Madam Hooch? Is it OK if Harry has the Firebolt back? **Only** we need to practise.> 1999 Rowling 188 (*US ed.* [deleted]).

or nor Or not: CIC has 0.4 iptmw of the form. <Believe it **or nor**, they even buy in bottles of midges.> 1999 magazine CIC.

For the pseudo coordination in *They've **been and (gone and)***, cf. § 1.4.2.

9.2 Subordinating conjunctions

Like is used as a subordinating conjunction in both British and American English as an alternative to *as* in sentences such as *You talk **like** my mother (does)* and to *as if/though* in sentences such as *You look **like** you need a drink*. Though sometimes castigated, the use is standard. It has been reported as somewhat more widespread and less exclusively informal in American use than in British (*CamGEL* 1158).

The conjunctive use of *other than* in the sense "except" is entered without comment by *MW* and dated to 1605, but it is sometimes criticized (Kahn and Ilson 1985, 414–5; Gilman 1994, 699–700) or is said to sound awkward to British ears (Peters 2004, 399). Nevertheless it occurs in British use: <The Yard does not break down the cost of individual murders **other than** by overtime.> 1993 Feb. 3 *Times* 3/3.

Some subordinating conjunctions with characteristic British uses are listed below.

as **1.** That <If he's there, [come] back into the office and tell Trixie **as** I sent you.> 1991 Dickinson 41. **2.** As it <Well, sir, that's **as** may be.> 1983 Innes 93. **3. as was** As *he/she* was <I got a call from Elsie Prosser. Elsie Inglefield **as was.**> 2001 Mortimer 80.

cos Because: The American spelling is *'cause*. CIC has 2077.4 iptmw of *cos* in British texts and 0.3 in American texts. <I am sure he won't mind me letting you know, **'cos** it's what he always says.> 2002 Sept. *Square* 26.

directly As soon as (*CGEL* 14.12, 15.25; Kjellmer 1997) <I cycled back home here **directly** work was finished.> 2000 Granger 17.

for all (that) Despite the fact that <You look at two respectable women in their eighties, but on the posh side **for all** they're skint.> 2000 Granger 308.

immediately As soon as (*CGEL* 14.12, 15.25; Kjellmer 1997) <The two youths sauntering along Oxford Street became targets **immediately** they started shopping for knives in a tobacconist's store.> 1997 Dec. 12 *Evening Standard* 5/1.

in case If; lest: *In case* has two uses, depending on the priority in time of the main and subordinate clauses. In *Have an extinguisher in your house* ***in case*** *a fire breaks out*, the main clause has temporal priority and the subordinate clause is a future contingency; and *in case* = "lest" or "as an anticipation of the possible event that." In *Use the fire extinguisher in case a fire breaks out*, the main clause is a result following upon the prior condition of the subordinate clause; and *in case* = "if." The Michigan Corpus of Academic Spoken English has more than twice as many tokens of the "if" sense of *in case* as of the "lest" sense. Among 50 examples in the BNC, none had the "if" sense. The "lest" sense is the norm in British; American has both senses. <It's typical of Ron Gladstone to keep it to himself **in case** we were upset.> 2000 Granger 188. Cf. § 8.1 IN CASE OF.

lest In the mid twentieth century, *lest* was apparently 5 times more frequent in American English than in British, the ratio in the Brown and LOB corpora being 17:3. CIC, however, now shows *lest* to be actually more frequent in British use than in American. It has 53.7 iptmw in British texts, mainly fiction, and 32.6 in American texts, mainly academic.

no matter Even though: The common-core use of *no matter* as a subordinating conjunction is in the sense "without regard to; irrespective of" (*MW*), followed by a relative or conjunction (*how, what, when, where, whether, which, why*, or more rarely *if, that*, or *though*), as in *We will come*, ***no matter*** *what the weather is* or *We will come* ***no matter*** *if it rains* (or as a preposition followed by a noun phrase, as in *We will come*, ***no matter*** *the hour*). The following use is apparently a reduction of the rare common-core conjunctive use with *if, that*, or *though*, having the sense "even though": <Frederick Clinton was too important to waste his time merely putting the boot into the CIA, **no matter** it was a recognised international sport.> 1975 Price 166. CIC has 1 such token out of a randomly selected 1000 British examples with *no matter*: <**No matter** they had, or aspired to, Bentleys and Rolls and MGs and Rovers . . . it was somehow too vulgar.> 1989. A comparable American sample contained no tokens of the construction.

not but what Granted that: The *OED* says it "often occurs . . . and is still dial. and colloq." *MW* lists it without comment in a different sense ("that . . . not"), as in *I don't know* ***but what*** *I will go*. <'Tain't so difficult to make a ship the way he done it. . . . **Not but what** he made a good job of it.> 1940 Shute 137.

now Now that: The simple form *now* has such use also in American, but generally only in highly colloquial contexts in which phonological reduction and elision are also found, so the forms are not stylistic equivalents. <**Now** Potter and Weasely have been kind enough to act their age, . . . I have something to say to you all.> 2000 Rowling 336 (*US ed.* Now that). <**Now** the venerable briefcase has been consigned to the status of endangered accessory, why should metrosexuals be forced to endure the hardship of lopsidedly bulging pockets?> 2003 July 8 *Times* T2 13/4.

seeing as Since; in as much as: In comparable random samples, CIC has 7.5 times more British than American tokens of this use (152 to 20). <The agent gave his consent, **seeing as** it was doing nothing. I did hear, mind, that Sir Marcus was none too pleased.> 1989 Burden 86.

since In its temporal sense, *since* is often modified by *ever*. In common-core English, *ever* comes first: *ever since*, but CIC British texts have a few (0.3 iptmw) examples of *since ever*, whereas American texts have none. <He has a cottage near the church, and **since ever** anybody can remember he's been saying he has lived in it for eighty-seven years.> 1983 Innes 109.

so (that) The *OED*'s first citation of *so* [*swa*] used in this way without *that* is from *Beowulf*, but the editors add (sense 23), "*so that* (also *so* alone), denoting result or logical consequence; also sometimes = 'in order that'. In the revived use of *so* alone, orig. U.S." The *OED*'s modern citations of *so*, rather than *so that*, are evenly divided between British and American. Ward Gilman (1994, 856–7) finds no difference in formality between *so* and *so that*. Robert Burchfield (1996, 721–2) comments on the history of the two forms: "Constructions using *so* alone are recorded from medieval times, but are no more than sporadic. First in America in the 19c., and gradually elsewhere, *so* alone has gradually established itself in standard use, esp. in spoken English." John Kahn and Robert Ilson (1985, 570) distinguish the forms semantically in British use: "There is a slight preference in British English for *so that* to indicate purpose [*He filled the tank so that he could drive all the way without stopping*], and *so* to indicate result [*The tank was full, so he drove all the way without stopping*]; it is possible to use them the other way round."

straight after Immediately after; as soon as: Although the two national varieties use *immediately after* with similar frequency, CIC has 10.2 iptmw of *straight after* in British texts and 2.6 in American texts. <**Straight after** he'd finished he spirited off his Rent-A-Tottie for a naughty weekend at his country cottage.> 1984 Brett 90.

suppose/supposing (that) What if; "if by way of hypothesis : on the assumption that" (*MW* s.v. *supposing*, conj.). As signals of a hypothesis, an assumption, or a suggestion, these terms differ in frequency of use between British and American, with the *suppose* forms more frequent in British use, and the *what if* form in American. – **suppose** CIC has 64.8 iptmw of clause-initial *Suppose* in British texts and 32.2 in American texts. This use of the verb in expressions like *Suppose it rains* and *Suppose we stay home* is common-core English, although more frequent in British. However, in the following British example, it appears to be a subordinating conjunction with the sense "even if," introducing an initial concessive clause: <**Suppose** you've got official business with God Almighty, you can't leave your car here.> 1984 Gilbert 29. – **supposing** The LOB corpus has 14 tokens of *supposing* to Brown's 2. Of 50 randomly selected tokens of the form *supposing* out of 504 total in the BNC, 7 or 8 are interpretable as suggestions (although the context is often ambiguous). The Michigan Corpus (MICASE) is much smaller, but of its 6 tokens of *supposing*, none appears to be a suggestion. CIC has 14.8 iptmw of clause-initial *Supposing* in British texts and 1.3 in American texts. It also has 41.9 iptmw of noninitial *suppose* in any use in British texts and 6.3 in American texts, thus confirming the LOB/Brown statistics that the verb *suppose* is more frequent in British than in American. – **suppose that** CIC has 6.2 iptmw of clause-initial *Suppose that* in British texts and 2.6 in American texts. <**Suppose that** the strontium rate in grass . . . goes bumping up sharply just after the Russians have done a series of experiments.> 1959 Innes 7. – **supposing that** CIC has 1.1 iptmw of clause-initial *Supposing that* in British texts and none in American texts. – **what if** On the other hand, CIC has 109.3 iptmw of *what if* in British texts and 170.6 in American texts.

that *in noninitial clause position* Though; as: Common-core English has constructions like *Fool that he was, he managed to evade his pursuers* = "Even though he was a fool . . . ," with a noun subject complement front shifted (minus its article), followed by the conjunction *that*. British in addition can front shift an adjective followed by *that* rather than *as*: *Poor that they were, they gave money to charity* = "Even though they were poor . . . " (*CGEL* 15.39).

till Until: CIC has 3727.2 iptmw of *until* in British texts and 3688.3 in American texts, making that form approximately equal in the two varieties. However, CIC has nearly 5 times more tokens of *till* in British texts than in American (369.7 to 74.5). <. . . the porter wouldn't let them into Dr. Bennett's room **till** he'd spoken to the warden.> 1993 Smith 256. Cf. § 8.1 TILL.

whether or nor Whether or not: This construction is rare, occurring not at all in the text of the *OED* and only once in the BNC (in *The Alton Herald* of Farnham, Surrey). CIC has <**whether** they're satisfied **or nor**> in a quotation from Dickens. The following citation also attests it. <. . . computer-assisted sperm analysis (Casa) . . . predicts . . . **whether or nor** it is able to fertilise the egg.> 1993 Feb. 27 *Times* (Saturday) Review 6/1–2. Cf. § 9.1 OR NOR.

whilever While; as long as: This parallel to *wherever* is rare. The *OED* has 2 tokens of *while ever*, 1 of *while-ever*, and 1 of *whilever*; the BNC has 3 tokens of *while ever* in this use and none of *while-ever* or *whilever*. Similarly, CIC has 3 tokens of British *while ever* and none of the other two spellings, as well as no American forms. <Nor do *I* believe in fairies. . . . But **whilever** he's

firmly fixed to the top of the Christmas tree, what else?> 1989 Wainwright 43.

whilst While: *Whilst* is a popular form in British English although secondary to *while*, with 1388 versus 11,180 tokens of the two forms in the *OED*, 5775 versus 54,778 in the BNC, and 379.8 versus 5890.1 iptmw in CIC British texts, compared with 8.8 versus 6674.2 in American texts. The Michigan Corpus (MICASE) has no tokens of *whilst* versus 458 of *while*. In LOB the number of tokens are 66 versus 590; in Brown, 0 versus 680. In American English *whilst* is rare. <. . . **whilst** I see you as a dear and valued friend, I don't see myself as your wife.> 2000 Granger 296. <Ron was . . . at a loss for anything to say, **whilst** Hermione looked on the verge of tears.> 2003 Rowling 64 (*US ed.* while).

9.2.1 Omission of a subordinating conjunction

Subordinating conjunctions are sometimes omitted before clauses with various functions in their sentences. This is a common-core possibility, but seems to be more prevalent in British than in American.

DIRECT OBJECT

appreciate [that] <The "tankies" **appreciate** they are going to war and so treat the vehicles better.> 1991 Feb. 16 *Daily Telegraph* 4/5.

check [that/if] <**Check** no one's watching.> 1998 Rowling 56 (*US ed.* Check that no one's). <He likes to . . . **check** I'm happy.> 1999 Rowling 317 (*US ed.* check if I'm happy).

complain [that] <Of those who received substituted items, more than 40% **complained** they were often of a poorer quality to those ordered.> 2004 Dec. 12 *Sunday Times* 1 1/5.

confirm [that] <The Office of Fair Trading (OFT), the government's consumer watchdog, **confirmed** this weekend it had launched an inquiry into the online services of Tesco and Sainsbury's.> 2004 Dec. 12 *Sunday Times* 1 1/1.

ensure [that] <He repeated that the Government wanted to **ensure** vulnerable groups would take proper steps to keep warm.> 1991 Feb. 13 *Daily Mail* 3/1.

SUBJECT COMPLEMENT

be [that/if] <[Baroness Warnock:] . . . one of the things that would motivate me [to die] **is** I couldn't bear hanging on and being such a burden on people.> 2004 Dec. 12 *Sunday Times* 1 1/2.

APPOSITIVE

fact [that] <[a sometime head of Mrs. Thatcher's policy unit:] She used the **fact** she was a woman very powerfully to get her way.> 1990 Critchfield 437.

EXTRAPOSED SUBJECT

it . . . [that] <**It**'s Malfoy's problem he wasn't listening.> 1999 Rowling 92 (*US ed.* problem that he).

COMPLEMENT OF AN ADJECTIVE

frightened [that] <And they're **frightened** other people have got a tool [weapon].> 1987 Nov. *Illustrated London News* 76/3.

sure [that] <Harry felt **sure** there ought to be a security person there.> 2003 Rowling 678 (*US ed.* sure that there).

ADVERBIAL

operator subject If *SUBJECT OPERATOR* <. . . she would take her drink in with her to dinner **should dinner** be ready.> 1984 Drabble 24. <**Had they gone** to the pub, William and Darryl would doubtless have discussed music over a pint of Strongbow.> 2003 June 20 *Times* 11/3. <The running costs of any new Centre would need to be assessed and form part of a business plan **were the purchase of a new Centre** to be seriously considered.> 2004 Jan. minutes from a financial meeting, London.

10 Interjections

Interjections, whether single-word or multiword forms, are numerous and are particularly apt to vary between national varieties. The class of interjections is close to open-ended. The following list is therefore of examples only. Some of the items occur also in American use, and some are old-fashioned in use but nevertheless seem characteristic of British English.

Characteristically American interjections include *uh huh* (CIC 3478.4 iptmw in American texts versus 30.9 in British texts) and *wow* (CIC 282.8 iptmw American versus 78.9 British). For *huh*, see EH below. For *hi* and *howdy*, see HELLO below. The form *OK* or *okay*, which has been called America's most successful export to the world, has approximately equal use in British and American English; CIC has 2720 iptmw in British texts versus 2710.1 in American texts.

aargh, aaargh CIC has 25.3 iptmw in British texts versus 0.2 in American texts. <'I think we're doing the drawing room tomo – **AARGH!**' [¶] With two loud cracks, Fred and George . . . had materialized out of thin air in the middle of the room.> 2003 Rowling 66.

ah This interjection has been reported as nearly 4 times more frequent in British conversation than in American (*LGSWE* 1097). CIC has 1247 iptmw in British texts versus 262.8 in American texts.

aha This interjection has been reported as more than 4 times as frequent in British conversation as in American (*LGSWE* 1097). CIC has 247.3 iptmw in British texts versus 6.8 in American texts. Cf. also HA and OOH below.

aye Used as a response in discourse, *aye* is a distinctively British form seldom used in American (*LGSWE* 1098). CIC has 606.9 iptmw in British texts versus 21.4 in American texts, many of them parliamentary language.

blast (it) CIC has 8.4 iptmw of the exclamatory collocation *blast it* in British texts and none in American.

blimey CIC has 36.7 iptmw in British texts, often in the collocations *cor blimey* or *oh blimey*, and no American tokens. <**Blimey**. . . . That sounds even more dangerous.> 2005 Jan. 15 *Daily Telegraph* Weekend 18/1.

bloody hell CIC has 52.1 iptmw in British texts, often in the collocation *oh bloody hell* and occasionally *cor bloody hell*, and 1.3 in American texts. <He

recalls his poetry classes by the Christian Brothers of St Illtyd as characterised by 'Daffodils, Skylarks, Cuckoos, Jug-jug, pu-we, to-witta-woo! **Bloody hell**, it was, I thought, cissy stuff.'> 1988 Apr. *In Britain* 43/3. Cf. §§ 5.1.1 MINDED, 5.2, 6.1, 7.1 BLOODY.

Bob's your uncle Everything works out as expected or desired: CIC has 1.8 iptmw in British texts (as well as a few examples of *Bob's your auntie*) and no American tokens. The expression is often used as a concluding comment but also as an interjection. <I was getting out of the car when – **Bob's yer uncle** – there was Peter Finch paying off his taxi.> 1994 Oct. 3 *Times* 19/7.

brilliant This word, in all of its uses, is more frequent in British English than in American. CIC has 535.4 iptmw in British texts and 184.8 in American texts. There is also a British popular clipping to *brill*, as in <Youths: "**Brill**", "Excellent!"> 1991 CIC. <"Daddy has gone to live with Elaine," I burst out. [¶] "**Brilliant**. Now I can stay up and watch Red Dwarf."> 1994 Sept. 24 *Guardian Weekend* 84/3.

bugger me "a general excl. of surprise, annoyance, alarm" (Green 1998). CIC has 2.4 iptmw in British texts and no American tokens.

cheerio "When leaving people: . . . *Cheerio*" (Swan 1995, 543). An American comparable expression is *take care* (*LGSWE* 1097). CIC has 20.4 iptmw in British texts, including the collocation *Cheerio now*, and 0.4 in American texts. Cf. also CHEERS and TATA below.

cheers CIC has 62.5 British tokens of *Cheers*, most being interjections in one of the following senses, and 20.3 American tokens, most being references to a popular TV program. **1**. Goodby "**Cheers**, see you" (*CIDE*). **2**. Used as a toast when drinking alcohol; skoal, here's to you (Swan 1995, 545). **3**. Thanks <'**Cheers**,' said George, taking the slip of parchment Bagman handed him and tucking it away into the front of his robes.> 2000 Rowling 82.

come on (then) An exclamation used to introduce an utterance (*LGSWE* 1118). CIC has 247.7 iptmw of *Come on* in British texts, including 31.7 of the collocation *Come on then*, and 110 in American texts, including 0.4 of *Come on then*. Cf. also RIGHT below.

cor Gosh! *from* God, *euphemistic expression of surprise*: CIC has 79.6 iptmw in British texts and no American tokens. <"**Cor**," I thought to myself, "look who's talking!"> 1976 Mar. 17 *Punch* 461/1.

crikey Golly! *from* Christ, *dated euphemistic expression of surprise*: CIC has 14.1 iptmw in British texts, including the frequent collocation *oh crikey*, and no American tokens. <**Crikey**, he is Barclays' . . . worst nightmare.> 2005 Jan. 15 *Daily Telegraph* 34/2.

eh /ei/ "*exclamation infml* used to express surprise or confusion, to ask someone to repeat what they have said, or as a way of getting someone to give some type of reaction to a statement that you have made • *'Janet is leaving her husband.' 'Eh?'* • *'Did you hear what I said?' 'Eh? Say it again – I wasn't listening.'* • *Going overseas again, eh? – it's a nice life for some!*" (*CIDE*). It is relatively rare in American although common in Canadian. An American analog is *huh*, which is rare in British (*LGSWE* 1097). CIC has 380.4 iptmw of *eh* in British texts and 87.1 in American texts. For *huh*, on the other hand, CIC has 169.8 iptmw in British texts and 391.8 in American texts. <Jonathan Gathorne-Hardy claims that there was never any strain between the upper-class 'What', the lower-middle 'Pardon' or the working-class '**Eh**'.> 1979 Cooper 80.

er; erm These British spellings represent, respectively, an oral and nasal vocalic sound that marks a hesitation in discourse. The typical American equivalents are spelled *uh* and *um*, which represent exactly the same sounds respectively as the British spellings (*LGSWE* 1053, 1096). Americans unfamiliar with *r*-less British pronunciation sometimes pronounce the British spelling *er* with rhotic quality when they encounter or adopt it, a pronunciation consequently recorded in *MW*. **1. er** Uh: CIC has 13,822.5 iptmw of *er* in British texts and 59 in American texts, which however include tokens of the suffix *-er* and *'er* (for *her*). On the other hand, CIC has 85.3 iptmw of *uh* in British texts and 5410.3 in American texts. <I'm from Rummidge University. I'm, **er**, taking part in, that is to say . . . I'm on a kind of educational visit.> 1988 Lodge 102. <Well, **er**, no.> 2005 Jan. 9 *Sunday Times* 4 31. **2. erm** Um: CIC has 9912.6 iptmw of *erm* in British texts and 3.5 in American texts. On the other hand, it has 134.6 iptmw of *um, umm*, and *ummm* in British texts and 2942.2 in American texts. <Well . . . **erm** . . . well, you know why you're here.> 2003 Rowling 303. Cf. also MM below.

God As an expletive, *God* has been reported to be used twice as often in British conversation as in American (*LGSWE* 1098).

good-oh CIC has 1.3 iptmw in British texts and no clear American tokens. <**Good-oh**. Which is it to be? Lord's or the Oval?> 1985 Bingham 78.

ha As an interjection, *ha* is four times as frequent in British conversation as in American (*LGSWE* 1097). CIC has 409.3 iptmw in British texts, some of which are in a sequence representing laughter, and 146.3 in American texts. Cf. also AHA above.

hear, hear CIC has 5.3 iptmw in British texts and no American tokens. <The raucous give-and-take of parliamentary debate, with frenzied shouts and jeers of "Question! Question!" "Reading!" "**Hear, hear**!" as the Speaker furiously cries, "Order! Order!" is something totally out of the American experience.> 1990 Critchfield 114.

hello The most usual British greeting, *hello* has been reported as half again as frequent in British conversation as in American (*LGSWE* 1097). CIC has 533.7 iptmw in British texts and 202.1 in American texts. A predominantly American greeting is *hi*, which is eight times as frequent in American conversation as in British according to *LGSWE* (1097); CIC has a smaller spread, with 183.3 iptmw in British texts and 315 in American texts. A less frequent American form is *howdy*, for which CIC has 0.3 iptmw in British texts and 11.8 in American texts. Cf. also HIYA below.

hey presto CIC has 6 iptmw in British texts and no American tokens. <. . . all you need is the shell of an old local authority college of further education and,

hey presto, you can syndicate university degrees around the world.> 1995 Sept. 2 *Spectator* 16/3.

hiya This is a less frequent British greeting (*LGSWE* 1097). CIC has 24 iptmw in British texts and 1.3 in American texts. Cf. also HELLO above.

I say <Oh **I say**, ta most awfully.> 1987 Feb. 23 ITV *Rumpole of the Bailey*. <[Bernard Levin:] It is of course the best way to make your opponents spit blood, to say not "How dare you!" but "**I say**, what fun!"> 1990 Critchfield 320.

lawks Lordy! "*dial. or archaic Br* – used to express surprise" (*LDEL*). CIC has no British or American tokens. <Oh, **lawks**! . . . *There*, look. Just to the left of my fringe, a nasty little breeding colony of silvery grey hairs.> 1998 Jan. 3 *Times* Weekend 6/3–4.

lor CIC has 1.3 iptmw in British texts and no American tokens. <**Lor**, how they go on.> 1978 Jan. 18 *Punch* 98/3.

mate A particular kind of interjection is the vocative use of nouns, either proper names or common nouns, chiefly for persons. *Mate* is the most characteristic British common noun so used. American analogs are *bro*, *bud*, *buddy*, *dude*, *folks*, *guys*, *man*, and *pal*.

mhm CIC has 1380.4 iptmw of this response signal in British texts and 373.4 in American texts. See also MM below.

mind (you) According to CIC data, *Mind you* is about seven times more frequent in British than in American. Two-thirds of the British uses are clause initial, but only about a quarter of the American ones. <**Mind you**, I don't say I mightn't have chatted her up a bit even if I hadn't had to – she was looking quite fanciable.> 1984 Caudwell 80. <"I gather you also do a Good Samaritan act with stranded caravans." [¶] "About twice a year when idiots cut the corner. It's good for business, **mind**. They usually feel obliged to come in and eat something."> 1992 Walters 94–5. <**Mind you**, people do get raped on the Inner Circle [tube], these days. Even men.> 1995 Lodge 16. <He still loves his son, **mind**. He just feels he should have been hanged [for two murders and 26 assaults].> 2003 July 3 *Times* T2 28/2.

mm, mmm, mmmm Used as a response in discourse, the prolonged nasal *mm* is the major distinctively British form and is 4 times more frequent in British conversation than in American (*LGSWE* 1096). In a wider spread of texts, CIC finds the form much more distinctively British, with 8325.8 iptmw in British texts and 131.6 in American (including abbreviations for *millimeter*). Cf. also AYE, MHM above.

never mind CIC has 128.5 iptmw in British texts and 63.7 in American texts. <Archer, short, wiry, athletic, came striding out, telling me I was too early, **never mind**, ordering coffee and shouting to his secretary.> 1990 Critchfield 287.

not a bit of it CIC has 6.0 iptmw in British texts and 0.2 in American texts. <Recalling the intellectual snobbery which has, once or twice, crept into this

column, you may have thought that I disapprove of Pugin jewellery and Pugin headscarves. **Not a bit of it**.> 1994 Sept. 12 *Guardian* 21/2–3.

not at all A reply to an expression of thanks. CIC has 53.4 iptmw of *Not at all* in British texts and 26.4 in American. "British people, especially, do not usually answer when they are thanked for small things. If a reply is necessary, we can say *Not at all* (rather formal), *You're welcome, Don't mention it, That's (quite) all right* or *That's OK* (informal British)" (Swan 1995, 439). Most of the alternatives seem to be common-core English. A relatively recent alternative among the younger generation is *No problem*.

now Used to indicate a transition in the discourse, *now* is more than twice as frequent in British conversation as in American (*LGSWE* 1097). Cf. also YOU SEE below.

ooh, oooh, ooooh As an interjection, this form is three and a half times as frequent in British conversation as in American according to *LGSWE* (1097). CIC has 627.7 iptmw in British texts and 83.9 in American texts. Cf. also AHA above.

oy, oi A characteristically British, although rare, interjection to gain attention. CIC has 64.3 iptmw in British texts and no clear American tokens, although the quite different Yiddish expression of surprise or concern *oy vey* is not unusual in American. <**Oy**, where do you think you're going?> 1985 Bingham 90. An American equivalent is *hey*, which is six times as frequent in American conversation as in British (*LGSWE* 1097), and for which CIC has 249.4 iptmw in British texts and 472.5 in American texts.

pardon An apology seldom used in American according to *LGSWE* (1098), although CIC shows the extended form *Pardon me* to be somewhat more frequent in American than in British, by 12.4 to 10.5 iptmw. Cf. also SORRY below.

please As an interjection, *please* is twice as frequent in British conversation as in American (*LGSWE* 1098).

quite (so) Right: a response of agreement in the sense "I quite agree" or "It is quite so" (in which *quite* is an adverb or a qualifier) (*CGEL* 8.120n, 130n). CIC has 4.4 iptmw of *Quite so* in British texts and no American tokens. <"So sad. . . . An entire home going under the hammer." [¶] "**Quite so**."> 1988 Taylor 3. <"I hope the news from the infirmary will be . . ." [¶] "**Quite, quite**."> 1990 Aug. 25 BBC1 *Miss Marple: Nemesis*.

quite right Some speakers of British English think *right* used as a response signal of agreement to be an Americanism. But in the modified form **quite right**, it is British. CIC has 8.1 iptmw of *Quite right* in British texts and only 0.4 in American texts. <"It doesn't bother me." [¶] "**Quite right**."> 1987 Oliver 53–4.

rather "often used interjectionally, esp by British speakers, to express enthusiastic affirmation <"*will you come?*" "**Rather**!">" (*LDEL*). <'That *is* what you meant, isn't it, Cantrip?' 'Oh **rather**,' said Cantrip.> 1984 Caudwell 43.

right An exclamation used to introduce an utterance. Characteristically American analogs, in their order of frequency are *well, okay*, and *yeah* (*LGSWE* 1118). <'**Right**,' I said, 'into my office and we'll get this sorted out.'> 1986 Simpson 77. Cf. also COME ON above.

righto, right oh; righty ho/oh; right you are; too right CIC has 7.5 iptmw of *righto* and *right oh* in British texts and 0.6 in American texts. It has 0.5 iptmw of *righty ho/oh* in British texts and no American tokens. It has 4.9 iptmw of *Right you are* in British texts and 0.8 in American texts. It has 5.5 iptmw of *too right* in British texts and no American tokens. An American analog is *all righty*, of which CIC has no British tokens and 5.6 iptmw in American texts. <'Come to Larking Post Office and then fork left and she's about a quarter of a mile down the road on the bad bend.' [¶] '**Right you are**. You get back to her then.'> 1968 Aird 7. <'**Right-oh**,' roared the chaps as time was called, 'but do up your flies – it's cold outside!'> 1985 Ebdon 131. <"That's not usual, is it?" [¶] "**Too right** it isn't."> 1985 Taylor 76–7.

sod it Expletive: CIC has 5.9 iptmw in British texts and 0.2 in American texts. <Barnaby grabbed the paper just before it knocked over a coffee cup. There was a lengthy pause, then Christopher said, "**Sod it**."> 1993 Graham 232.

some hope(s) <He wanted Swan to settle down, raise a family and do a bit of good for himself. **Some hopes**!> 1972 Rendell 92.

sorry An apology used four times as often in British conversation as in American (*LGSWE* 1098). It is also used as a polite request for repetition or clarification of a remark. <'We're going out,' he said. [¶] '**Sorry**?' [¶] 'We – that is to say, your aunt, Dudley and I – are going out.'> 2003 Rowling 45. Cf. also PARDON above.

ta A less common expression for *thank you* or *thanks*. The latter expressions are twice as frequent in American conversation as in British according to *LGSWE* (1098); however, in a wider range of texts, CIC shows them to be similar, with British incidents slightly more numerous. <It is always "Please, Mrs Spilling" and "**Ta**, Mrs Spilling" whenever he's offered a cup of tea.> 1994 Sept. 25 *Sunday Times* Magazine 32/1. Cf. also NOT AT ALL above.

ta ta, tata, tara Goodbye. CIC has 11.9 iptmw of these forms in British texts and no American tokens. <**Ta ta** for now, Liz.> 1982 Symons 135. <Time for zizz! **Ta-ra**! Nighty-night!> 1991 Feb. 2 *Times* (*Saturday*) *Review* 6/4. Cf. also CHEERIO above.

tchah "An exclamation of impatience or contempt" (*OED*). CIC has no tokens. <'There are directories too,' Butler snapped. [¶] 'But not walking ones.' [¶] '**Tchah**!'> 1974 Price 54.

urgh Ugh (cf. ER, ERM above), a spelling representing "the sound of a cough or grunt or to express disgust or horror" (*MW*). CIC has 45.5 iptmw in British texts and no American tokens. It also has 47 iptmw of *ugh* in British texts and 10.4 in American texts. The use of either spelling is more characteristic of British than American, but the *r*-spelling is exclusively so. <'**Urgh**!' . . . A jumble of assorted rags and smelly old blankets were piled on the floor.> 2003 Rowling 445.

well done CIC has 46.4 iptmw of *Well done* in British texts and 2.6 in American texts. <**Well done**! Did you get rid of them?> 1990 Critchfield 287.

you see Used to indicate a transition in the discourse, *you see* is eight times more frequent in British conversation than in American (*LGSWE* 1097). The most characteristic American term in this function is *you know*, which is more than twice as frequent in American as in British (*LGSWE* 1096). Cf. also NOW above and § 6.1 YOU + *VERB OF PERCEPTION*.

II

Syntactic Constructions

11 Complementation

Complementation concerns the forms or constructions required by other forms or constructions. For example, the verb *postpone* normally requires a noun phrase as its direct object complement (*They postponed a decision*, **They postponed*); the approximately synonymous verb *delay* does not (*They delayed a decision, They delayed*). Complementation is thus a particular type of collocation.

11.1 Complementation of verbs

11.1.1 Noun phrase complement

11.1.1.1 As direct object

A verb may have a direct object in British English that would not collocate with it in American. An instance is *pull a cracker*; crackers containing hats and small gifts are not part of American Christmas celebrations. The American holiday association of crackers is with the Fourth of July, and they are firecrackers, which are not pulled, but set off.

pull a cracker <[At Christmas] They sat now, with the food eaten and the **crackers pulled**, round the table.> 1985 Mortimer 263.

shit *oneself* An example of a verb that is more often reflexive in British than in American is *shit*. In CIC, the reflexive use – as in <I remember when Rufus bit me I was **shitting** myself.> 1994 CIC spoken corpus – occurs once in approximately every 3 tokens of the verb in British texts versus once in every 27 tokens of the verb in American texts.

11.1.1.1.1 Versus prepositional complement

A number of verbs in contemporary British take a nominal complement, whereas in American (and older British) use, they would normally have a prepositional complement instead. One of the most frequent is *agree*. The transitive use of *agree* is recent, and its acceptability is still debated. *LDOCE* 1978 labeled *agree a plan* nonstandard in the sense "accept after unwillingness or argument." Kahn and Ilson 1985 say that British usage "allows – just –" the omission of the prepositions *on, upon*, or *about*, but that omission of *to* is informal and unacceptable to careful users of English. Gilman 1994 finds British transitive *agree* corresponding to either *agree on* or *agree to*. *LDOCE* 1995 calls *agree a plan* more formal than *agree on a plan*. Burchfield 1996 finds transitive *agree* to be "common but somewhat controversial". Despite divided opinions about the acceptability of the construction, it is widespread in standard use. The inferable prepositions are usually *on* and its synonyms, but sometimes also *to*, as in the 1986 Oct. 9 citation below, for which American and older British would typically have *agree to a draw*.

A random sample of 100 instances each of CIC British and American texts produced the following numbers of complementations (intr. = intransitive use; inf. = infinitive complement; nom. = noun or pronoun complement). A larger sample would certainly refine the comparative figures, but noun or pronoun complements of *agree* are primarily British:

	with	intr.	*that*	*to*	inf.	*on*	nom.	*upon*	*about*
British	37	20	14	8	8	5	4	2	2
American	39	17	24	3	4	13	0	0	0

The unusual 1986 Oct. 10 construction below is based on a complex transitive use of *agree*. The corresponding active, pruned of irrelevancies, would be *They agreed the game drawn*. Although consultants judge the construction in the citation to be odd and constructing plausible transformational analogs for it is difficult, its occurrence is certainly due to the vogue for transitive *agree*.

agree ***something*** Agree on/upon/about/to *something* <Kasparov . . . refused to **agree** the draw.> 1986 Oct. 9 *Times* 2/7. <The twenty-fourth and final game of the World Chess Championship was **agreed** drawn yesterday.> 1986 Oct. 10 *Times* 2/8. <European Union foreign ministers . . . **agreed** the outline of a deal.> 1994 Sept. 12 *Guardian* 22/1. The vogue for transitive *agree* extends also to its use as a participial modifier of nouns: <. . . at some **agreed** date in the future.> 1986 Aug. 23 *Times* 23/1. – **sales agreed** Sale pending; sold <**Sales Agreed**> 1994 Sept. sign on a lot, London.

A number of other verbs can also be used with a noun phrase direct object in British. In American too there has been a recent tendency to omit prepositions: *vote* (*for the*) *Democratic* (*Party*), *shop* (*at*) *Macys, fly* (*by*) *United, joke* (*with*) *someone*, which individually may seem odd or marginal to some Americans. The innovative pattern is shared by the two national varieties, but the specific realizations of the pattern often differ. One of the following constructions, *graduate college*, is also in American use, though uncommon in edited prose (Gilman 1994); some such overlap is to be expected, as is variation within a national variety.

ask ***something*** Ask for *something*: In 750 comparable samples each from CIC British and American texts, British was nearly 3 times more likely to use this construction than American and to have a larger number of different complements after *ask* (in order of frequency): *advice, permission, pardon, help, directions, forgiveness, leave, opinions, things*, and *views* versus American *permission, directions*, and *information*. <. . . she had to **ask** the day off school in order to play.> 1985 July 2 *Times* 25/3.

bitch ***something*** Bitch about *something* <For the next hour or so, he **bitched** everything in sight.> 1986 Oct. 5 *Sunday Times* 54/4.

disapprove ***something*** Disapprove of *something* <Actually, this is a tactic I don't strongly **disapprove** and it worked a treat on this occasion.> 1994 Sept. *Tatler* 57/2.

dispose ***something*** Dispose of *something*; discard *something* (*somewhere*) <Please don't **dispose nappies** in toilets.> 2003 Nov. 13 sign in lavatory at Heathrow airport.

excuse ***something*** Excuse from *something* "*Br* to free from (a duty) <*the class was* excused *homework*>" (*LDEL*). <As usual, the grammar of cricket is tricky. (American readers are **excused** this paragraph.)> 1990 Howard 106.

flunk university Flunk out of college: The construction is rare. <I **flunked university** at Newcastle, but then I took a degree at the Army College of Science at Shrivenham and got a First.> 1991 Feb. 16 *Daily Telegraph* 4/1–2.

fuss ***someone*** Fuss at/with *someone* <The way she was **fussing** him, I wouldn't bet on that.> 1975 Price 223.

graduate ***an educational institution*** Graduate from *an educational institution* <. . . it was assumed that once Charles had **graduated** Oxford, he would succeed his father at Hampton's Bank.> 1984 Archer 8.

operate ***a tradition*** Operate in/by/according to *a tradition*; follow *a tradition* <MP's are continuing to **operate** the tradition whereby one MP does not handle the affairs of a constituent of another MP.> 1986 Aug. 21 *Guardian* 12/6.

run ***fuel*** Run on *fuel* <. . . cars which **run** leaded fuel account only for fewer than four in 100 sales.> 1989 July 28 *Times* 31/7.

slum ***a place*** Slum in/along *a place* <I'd **slummed** that same route long before, mostly hitch-hiking and sleeping semi-rough.> 1985 Price 134.

squat ***a place*** Live in *a place* as a squatter <A black theatre group faces eviction today from a Camden Town church hall they **have squatted** for more than a year.> 1987 Apr. 2 *Hampstead Advertiser* 1/4.

In the following instances, an implicit goal is left unspecified in the British examples.

hand ***something*** Hand *something* to *someone* / *somewhere*: The construction is rare. <They sat down together to dinner, served by a maid with fat red hands, who breathed heavily as she **handed** the vegetables.> 1940 Shute 166.

relegate ***someone*** Relegate *someone* to *somewhere*; consign to an unimportant position: Of 50 random CIC tokens of *relegate*, British texts had 12 without a *to* complement; American texts had none. <A few token extremists have been expelled, those many more who remain are to be **relegated.**> 1986 Oct. 1 *Times* 13/1.

11.1.1.1.2 Versus a different verb

In some cases, the British construction of a particular verb would be unusual in American, which would have a different verb and sometimes different complementation as well.

attend hospital Go to the hospital: *Attend* "to be present at" is general English when the verb collocates with objects like *church, college, meetings, school*, but the collocation with *hospital* is rare. <She . . . received a telephone call to **attend hospital**.> 1991 Feb. 20 *Times* 4/5.

buy shopping Do shopping: Rare in CIC British texts and lacking in American. <I tend to **buy** the weekly **shopping** with a debit card.> 2004 Jan. 4 *Sunday Times* Money 6 8/2.

drink soup Eat soup: *Eat soup* is the norm in common-core English, but *drink soup* is about twice as frequent in British as in American. <You'll have to **drink** the **soup** yourself.> 1985 Benedictus 164.

hire ***something*** Rent *something*: British uses *hire* of things, either as "hire from" or "hire out to" for shorter periods of time but *rent* and *let* (*out to*) of dwellings for longer periods (*LDOCE* s.v. *hire* usage note). American may use *hire* similarly as "hire from" (not "hire to") but generally prefers *rent* of things and *hire* for beginning to employ a person. In a sample of 100 tokens each of *hire* from CIC British and American texts, British used *hire* of things in 64 percent of the tokens and of persons 36 percent; American used it of things in 2 percent and of persons 98 percent. < . . . the only car to be seen was their family-sized four-door saloon **hired** from Pisa airport.> 1988 Mortimer 51.

hop it Leave quickly: Rare in CIC British texts and lacking in American. <My girlfriend **hopped it**.> 1992 Walters 207.

pull a face *Pull a face* is slightly more frequent than *make a face* in CIC British texts; but *make* is 3 times more frequent than *pull* in American. <Daphne **pulled a face**.> 1991 Charles 131–2.

sit ***an exam*** *Take* with *exams* is about 1.5 times more frequent than *sit* in CIC British texts, but is practically the only option in American. < . . . it was the easiest exam any of them had ever **sat**.> 1999 Rowling 233 (*US ed.* taken).

take fright Become/be frightened: The construction is almost 12 times more frequent in CIC British texts than in American. <President Saddam Hussein has **taken fright**.> 1991 Feb. 16 *Daily Telegraph* 2/1.

want ***something*** Need *something*: Want is from Old Norse *vanta* "to lack, be lacking," which was the word's earliest sense in English. What one lacks, one needs; and what one needs, one desires. And so those two later senses developed, and all three senses are still attested in common-core English, as in, respectively, *He wants [lacks] common sense*; *They want [need] a little more experience*; *She wanted [desired] a better life*. Although all three senses still exist, the last (and most recent, dating only from the eighteenth century) is now the usual sense, the others being less common, especially in American use. British seems to preserve especially the "need" sense more actively, as in the following. <What you **want**, Rumpole, . . . is a complete makeover.> 2001 Mortimer 69.

11.1.1.1.3 Versus other complement

draw ***someone*** Draw *someone* out <The smooth and urbane Rose is not foolish enough to be **drawn** on whether he thinks that the profit warning marks the bottom for M&S.> 2005 Jan. 9 *Sunday Times* 3 5/1.

obsess ***someone*** *Obsess* is generally transitive, usually in passive constructions (in more than 90 percent of its uses in the BNC, Peters 2004, 387). CIC British texts have only a few tokens of *obsess* followed by a noun phrase beginning with *the*; American texts have none. In both British and American texts, *obsessed with* is the norm; *obsessed by* is 3 times more frequent in British than in American. An intransitive use, as in *You are just obsessing*, is labeled chiefly North American by *NODE*. <M Duhamel spends 275 pages . . . exorcising the demons **obsessing** the populace.> 1993 Feb. 3 *Times* 16/7. <. . . men **are obsessed** by the size of women's breasts.> 1993 Feb. 12 *Sun* 28/1.

11.1.1.2 As direct object with prepositional phrase

commit ***someone*** **against** ***something*** Commit *someone* to oppose *something*: The construction is rare. <. . . the SLD voted overwhelmingly against attempts to **commit** them **against** the use of nuclear weapons in any circumstances.> 1989 Sept. 13 *Times* 1/5.

compare ***one thing*** **with** ***another*** Compare *one thing* to *another*: The BNC has 5502 citations of *compared with* and 2176 of *compared to*. The Merriam-Webster files "show that *with* and *to* are used about equally after the past participle" (Gilman 1994). CIC has 342.2 iptmw of *compared with* in British texts and 211.9 of *compared to*; it has 413.9 of *compared with* in American texts and 283.7 of *compared to. Compared with* is favored in common-core English, but slightly more strongly in British. <And **compared with** the way they used to live, the Gersons' simple-lifery is just a sham.> 1985 Mann 84 (an American typed "compared to" in copying the citation). Cf. § 11.3.1 COMPARABLE.

direct ***someone*** **at** ***a place*** Direct *someone* to *a place*: The construction is rare. < . . . people who needed advice . . . were simply **directed at** the casualty department.> 1986 Sept. 30 *Guardian* 2/7.

drive ***a vehicle*** **on headlights** Drive *a vehicle* with headlights on: The construction is rare. <'Was it being **driven on headlights**?' . . . 'My client . . . did have his headlights on in the dipped position.'> 1978 Underwood 20.

entertain ***someone*** **to** ***a meal*** Invite/have *someone* for *a meal*: CIC British texts have *entertain to tea/lunch(eon)/dinner/coffee*; American texts have none of those. <He would **entertain** his local Party members **to** lunch on Thursday.> 1992 Critchley 14. Cf. § 8.1 TO *A MEAL*.

give ***an answer*** **to** Give *an answer* for: Of 16 Americans consulted informally, 8 preferred *for* and 8 preferred *to*, several expressing doubt about the choice; of 4 Britons resident in the UK, all preferred *to* without hesitation, and one commented "*to* . . . would be the English/English. I don't know which the American/English would be." The sample is too small to be reliable, but it is suggestive. <**Give** one answer only **to** each question.> 1987 May directions to a sample Cambridge Syndicate examination.

hire ***a car*** **from** ***a place*** See 11.1.1.1.2 HIRE *SOMETHING*.

hold ***someone*** **to ransom** CIC British texts have 11 times as many tokens of *hold to ransom* as of *hold for ransom*; American texts have 5 times as many *hold for ransom* as of *hold to ransom*. <The gazunderer is making a conscious decision to **hold** somebody **to ransom**.> 1989 July 30 *Sunday Times* 9/4.

invest ***a sum*** **on** ***a company/product/etc***. *Invest in* is the norm for this construction in common-core English. CIC British texts have a few tokens of *invest on*; American texts have none. <My advice to every cricket team captain is to **invest** £3.95 **on** "Howzat" [a book] . . . , then leave it lying around the changing room.> 1987 May 10 (Scotland) *Sunday Post* 15/4.

kick ***someone*** **up the backside** *Up the backside* is not used in American, where the usual expression is *in the ass*, whose variant *in the arse* is used also in British. <Fox-Strangways . . . **kicked** Bevan **up the backside**.> 1987 Feb. 10 *Evening Standard* 6/2.

laid to lawn Planted with grass: Rare in CIC British texts and lacking in American. <The garden . . . was **laid to lawn**.> 1993 Smith 7.

leave ***somewhere*** **to** Leave *somewhere* for: CIC texts have approximately the same frequency of *leave for* in British and American texts, but 1.6 times as many tokens of *leave to* in British texts as in American. <Mr Clarke, Education Secretary, was **leaving** his office **to** the Cabinet meeting when the attack happened.> 1991 Feb. 8 *Daily Telegraph* 2/6.

make ***something*** **to** ***a recipe*** Make *something* from /according to *a recipe*: Rare in CIC British texts and lacking in American.<. . . it really can't claim its toffee is "**made to** a traditional recipe".> 1994 Sept. 22 *Times* 19/5.

market ***something*** **at** Rare with *at* in CIC British texts but lacking in American.
1. ***a purpose*** Market *something* for *a purpose* <. . . it [Dairylea cheese] has been ruthlessly **marketed at** children's packed lunches.> 2003 July 2 *Times* 3/4.
2. ***a consumer*** Market *something* to *a consumer* <The sort of cars **marketed at** women.> 2003 June 25 *Guardian* international ed. G2 5/1.

name ***someone/thing*** **after** ***someone/thing*** Name *someone/thing* for *someone/thing* (Peters 2004, 364): CIC British texts have 6.5 times as many iptmw of *named after* as of *named for*; American texts have 1.3 times as many of *named for* as of *named after*.

persuade ***someone*** **of** ***something*** **to be** ***done*** Persuade *someone* to *do something*; persuade *someone* that *something* needs to be *done* <Mr Gorbachev has **persuaded** Mr Reagan **of** a long agenda of business **to be** done.> 1988 June 12 *Manchester Guardian* 1/2.

place ***an amount*** **to** ***an account*** Place *an amount* in *an account*; credit *an amount* to *an account* < . . . at least £75,000 a year should have been **placed to** buildings reserve.> 1993 Neel 45.

plant ***an area*** **with** ***vegetation*** CIC British texts overwhelmingly favor *planted with*, the alternative *planted in* occurring in less than 3 percent of the tokens. American texts also favor *planted with*, but less strongly, *planted in* occurring in 29 percent of the tokens and *planted to* in 7 percent. <. . . the garden carefully **planted with** aubretia and spiky little tulips.> 1985 Levi 94.

put ***someone*** **off** ***doing something*** Discourage *someone* from *doing something* <A Labour council has been accused of trying to **put** tenants **off** buying their homes.> 1987 Feb. 27 *Evening Standard* 13/2.

put ***one's*** **hand to** ***something*** Put *one's* hand on *something*; come up with *something* < . . . he had first to invest money in it, more money than he could **put** his **hand to**. > 1989 Quinton 265.

save ***something*** **off** ***doing something*** Save *something* by *doing something* <I promised to give her that bit of sugar I **saved off** not having it in my coffee since the war.> 1942 Thirkell 7.

spare ***someone*** **to** ***something*** Spare *someone* for *something* <. . . a mathematician who was no longer producing creative work . . . could also be best **spared to** the task.> 1993 Neel 14.

strike ***someone*** **blows to** Strike blows on *someone's (head)* <He . . . was **struck** several **blows to** the top of the head.> 1987 July 1 *Daily Telegraph* 3/5.

take ***a child*** **into care** *Take into care* is not used in American texts. <A boy has been **taken into care**.> 2004 Dec. 13 *Times* 22/6.

take it in turns (*to do something*) Take turns (*doing something*): In CIC British texts, 54 percent of the tokens are *take turns* and 46 percent, *take it in turns*; in American texts, 99.4 percent are *take turns*, and 0.6 percent are *take it in turns*. <Each day she and her husband **take it in turns** to deliver James to his secondary school.> 2005 Jan. 14 *Daily Telegraph* 8/4.

take it out of "exact satisfaction from" (*OED* s.v. *take* v. 88f). *Take it out of one's hide* is common-core English. The common-core *take it out on* "vent one's anger, frustration, etc., on an object other than the cause of it" (*OED* s.v. *take* v. 89) seems to be the sense in the following two citations from the same source: <He wouldn't allow for mistakes, he used to **take it out of** himself, his equipment –; and, of course, the nearest guy at hand.> <I had to take his sand-iron off him because he was threatening the guy with it. He really **took it out of** this photographer, and I can tell you he's lucky to be alive today.> 1990 nonfiction CIC.

take ***something*** **off** ***someone*** Take *something* from *someone* <Lib Dems – they **took** the seat **off** the Tories at the last election.> 2001 Lodge 129.

The following are instances with an exchange of roles between the direct object and the object of the preposition.

circulate ***somebody*** **with** ***something*** Circulate *something* among/to *somebody* <Sir Jeffrey **has circulated** his staff **with** some critical remarks about . . . the Zeebrugge disaster.> 1989 July 21 *Private Eye* 5/2.

exchange ***X*** **for** ***Y*** Exchange *Y* for *X*; change into *X* from *Y*: An earlier thing is usually exchanged for a later thing; the reverse order is, however, exemplified in the *OED* (s.v. *exchange* 1c) and in the following: <Amy came in and stared at me until I had noticed the dirty sweater and holed jeans she had **exchanged for** her earlier get-up.> 1969 Amis 52.

issue ***someone*** **with** ***something*** Issue *something* to *someone* (frequently passive: *someone* is issued with *something*): Although uncommon in the LOB Corpus (with only 1 example), the construction is highly acceptable in British use. In a completion test by Christian Mair, 24 respondents added *with* to "They issued all visitors —— identity badges," and 1 added *their*. This response confirms the judgment of one consultant that the straight ditransitive use (*issue someone something*) is marginal in frequency. <. . . the Serbs were **issued with** a fresh ultimatum to accept Nato peacekeepers.> 1999 Mar. 19 *Times* 16/4.

notify ***something*** **to** ***someone*** Notify *someone* of *something* <He must **notify** details of his earnings **to** the Official Receiver during the period of his bankruptcy.> 1996 Aug. 7 *Daily Telegraph* 3/3.

recommend ***a patient/client*** **to** ***a specialist*** Recommend *a specialist* to *a patient/client* <And they in turn **recommended** me **to** Eric Gustavson, a long-established consultant plastic surgeon.> 1991 Feb. 3 *Sunday Times* 3 4/5.

substitute ***X*** **with** ***Y*** Substitute *Y* for *X*; replace *X* with *Y* <We recently printed a letter in *The Times* that advised '**substituting** junk food **with** fresh fruit'.> 1990 Howard 173.

11.1.1.3 As predicate noun

A group of copular verbs (*feel, look, seem, sound*, etc.) have predominantly adjectival complements in common-core English, but also have nominal subject complements in British more frequently than in American.

appear Appear to be / like <As he did so, what had **appeared** an outside chance of Britain winning its first track gold of the Games moved closer to evens.> 1996 Aug. 3 *Times* 45/1.

come top Be at the top; be first; hold the highest place: *Come top* is a collocation, frequently used of academic standing, but also of any ranking, as in *Diana came top*. In various uses, it is represented by 59 citations in the BNC. <Hermione, of course, **came top of** the year.> 1997 Rowling 204 (*US ed.* had the best grades of the first years).

feel Feel like <I **felt** a fool, my breasts wedged up like a buxom serving wench.> 1994 Sept. *Tatler* last page.

get Get to be; become <People tend to invent all sorts of nouns and verbs and make words that shouldn't be. I think we have to be a bit careful; otherwise the whole thing can **get** rather a mess.> 1995 Mar. 25 *New York Times* 24/5–6 (quoting Prince Charles).

look Look like <Names ["Lloyd's insurance underwriters"] . . . **look** a dying breed.> 1994 Oct. 5 *Times* 16/6. – **look a treat** Look very good <Their five acres of garden **looked a treat**.> 1991 Feb. 2 *Times Saturday Review* 35/3.

prove Prove to be <But the lone wildebeast **proves** a better proposition [for a hunting lion to catch].> 1989 July 22 ch. 4 "Kingdom of the Sun."

seem Seem to be / like <Mr. Shapiro's unfortunate encounters . . . **seem** an astonishing excuse.> 1960 Nov. 6 *Newcastle Sunday Sun* 8/6. – **seem certainties** The construction is rare. <Essex **seemed certainties** to win when Northants left them needing only 147.> 1986 Aug. 20 *Daily Mirror* 28/4.

sound Sound like <It **sounds** a good idea but research evidence shows that these programmes do not work.> 1993 Feb. *Woman's Journal* 40/2.

turn Turn into; become <. . . the hole in the wall **turns** fruit machine and churns out bank notes.> 1991 Feb. 7 *Times* 11/1.

11.1.1.4 As adverbial

drop *someone* home Drop *someone* (off) at home <She was **dropped home** about 10.30 p.m.> 1993 Neel 38.

go walkies Go for a walk (with a dog) <Hilda and Stanley [dogs] . . . are on 24-hours notice to **go walkies** with any guest who fancies a turn around Green Park.> 1994 Oct. 3 *Evening Standard* 15/2.

11.1.2 Double noun phrase complement

11.1.2.1 As indirect and direct objects

do *someone food* Do/fix *food* for *someone* <Course I can **do** you bangers and mash!> 2000 Granger 284.

recommend *someone something* Recommend *something* to/for *someone*: Ditransitive use of *recommend* is not often attested. There is only one example in the *OED*, taken from an 1826 novel by Disraeli: "Let me recommend you a little of this pike!" Historically it is perhaps a syntactic backformation from the prepositional construction *recommend something to/for someone*. <Can you **recommend** me a nice hotel?> 1985 Apr. 8 *Times* 10/1.

write Ditransitive use of *write* (*I wrote them a letter*) is common-core English. But some ditransitive verbs can also be used with either object alone: *I told* *them a story. I told a story. I told them.* In American English, *write* belongs to that category: *I wrote a letter. I wrote them.* In British English, however, if *write* has a single object, it is normally the ditransitive direct object, and when the ditransitive indirect object occurs instead, it is the object of a preposition: *I wrote to them.* Also in British, if the direct object function is filled by direct or indirect discourse, the same prohibition against the ditransitive indirect object exists: *I wrote to them, "I'll come on Sunday,"* not ?*I wrote them, "I'll come on Sunday." I wrote to them that I would come on Sunday*, not ?*I wrote them that I would come on Sunday* (*CGEL* 16.59; *LGSWE* 662; Swan 1995, 614; Peters 2004, 583).

11.1.2.2 As direct object and object complement

appoint ***someone something*** Appoint *someone* as *something* <Mr. T. Thirkill, Labour M. P. for Leicester East, has been **appointed** an additional Financial Secretary to the Treasury.> 1979 Snow 201.

describe ***something something*** Describe *something* as *something* <The man accused of melting down bullion from Britain's biggest robbery in his back garden can now return to . . . the timeshare scheme he has **described** a "little goldmine".> 1987 Apr. 2 *London Daily News* 5/2–4.

promote ***someone a rank*** Promote *someone* to *a rank* "British English sometimes omits prepositions where American English retains them, whereas the reverse is rare: for instance, . . . (almost universal) British 'he was **promoted** colonel' for American 'he was promoted to colonel'" (Partridge and Clark 1951, 317).

reckon ***someone something*** Reckon *someone* to be *something* <In LA he [André Previn] is **reckoned** a champion of British music.> 1987 June 19 *Times* 20/4.

think ***something something*** Think *something* to be *something*; think that *something* is/was *something* <Despite the inventor's assurances of the safety of this new tomato I do not **think** it a very good idea.> 1989 July 22 *Spectator* 18/1.

11.1.3 Noun phrase and adjectival complement

11.1.3.1 As direct object and object complement

expect ***a business in profit*** Expect *a business* to be *profitable* <Arnault has announced he is prepared to sink £22 million into Lacroix before he **expects** it in profit.> 1989 July 24 *Times* 3/6.

order ***someone*** **off work** Order *someone* to stay away from work <A psychiatrist **ordered** him **off work** for nine months.> 2003 July 14 *Times* 5/2.

think ***something adjectival*** Think (that) *something is adjective* <[of skinny-dipping:] My children **thought** it weird that they should be in the water with bare bums and bits.> 1989 Sept. 13 BBC1 *Points of View*.

11.1.3.2 As direct object and subject complement

strike ***someone adjective*** Strike *someone* as *adjective*; seem *adjective* to *someone* <[of the temperature in a flat:] Does it **strike** you warm? . . . I'm glad it **struck** you warm.> 1989 Oct. 29 English woman in conversation.

11.1.4 Noun phrase and verbal complement

11.1.4.1 Passive participle

know ***someone/something done*** Know *someone/something* to be *done* <I've **known** as many as two hundred and fifty deck-chairs occupied along there.> 1985 Clark 131.

need ***something done*** Need to have *something done* <I suggest to Heald that he **needs** his head examined, getting involved in this sort of stunt.> 1989 July 23 *Sunday Telegraph* 43/1.

want ***something done*** Need to have *something done* < . . . whoever she is, she **wants** her head seen to.> 2000 Granger 143.

11.1.4.2 Present participle

get ***someone/thing doing something*** Get *someone/thing* to *doing something* / to (be able to) *do something* <Freezing August has **got** even Russia's famous Bolshoi Ballet shivering.> 1986 Aug. 27 *Daily Mirror* 4/3.

need ***something doing*** Need (to have) *something done*: *Need* can be followed by a noun phrase and a present participle, with the latter having the semantic effect of a passive participle. *LDOCE* labels this use as North of England English, but it seems to be widely acceptable. It is recorded without limitation by Kahn and Ilson. <High Trees [a house] . . . **needed** a lot doing to it.> 2003 James 35.

want ***something doing*** Want *something* (to be) *done*: *Want*, like the verb *need*, can be followed by a noun phrase and a present participle. Kahn and Ilson (1985) cite letters from the popular press defending the usefulness and propriety of constructions like *I want the car parking = to be parked*, but call the use regional. <Where do you **want** it putting, miss? By the coffin?> 2000 Aird 47.

want ***something doing*** Need to have *something done* <Vic . . . said I **wanted** my eyes testing.> 1986 Hardwick 213.

11.1.4.3 Infinitive

A significant difference between British and American is whether the infinitive is marked by *to* or is a bare infinitive.

ask ***someone do something*** Ask *someone* to *do something*: This construction is rare. <On St Valentine's Day, she **asked** me marry her.> 1993 Feb. 12 *Sun* 22/1.

have *someone* **to** *do something* Have *someone do something* <We're **having** this man **to** come and . . . **to** do some things to the kitchen.> SEU s.7.1a.41. – **have** *someone* **to stay** Have *someone* stay: The parallel construction with the *to*-less infinitive is common-core English, and American consultants disagree about the acceptability of the construction with *to*. One British consultant suggested a semantic difference: *She had her to stay* implies an invitation, whereas *She had her stay* suggests an unwilling imposition. <We gave balls for her and she **had** friends **to stay** in the holidays.> 1990 Aug. 26 *Sunday Times* Magazine 9/1.

help *someone* **to** *do something* Help *someone do something*: After *help*, both options are possible in common-core English: *Sarah helped us (to) edit the script*. However, preferences for the two variations are almost exactly opposite in the two national varieties (*CGEL* 16.52). British (in LOB) uses the *to* infinitive 73 percent of the time (out of 44 tokens); American (in Brown) uses the *to-less* infinitive 75 percent of the time (out of 75 tokens). <I **helped** collect the soiled plates and glasses from various rooms on the ground floor, and **to** stack them in the kitchen.> (note that both options are used) 2001 Lodge 143.

know *someone do something* Know *someone* to *do something*: After *know*, British can use a *to-less* infinitive, which is less likely in American. There are 5 examples of the construction in LOB and none in the Brown Corpus. <I've **known** you eat a cheeseburger yourself, sir.> 1994 Symons 31.

tip *someone* **to** *be/get something* **/ as** *something*; **tipped to** *be something* Suggest that *someone* is going to *be/get something*; rumored as *being/getting something*: *Tip* in the sense "regard as a likely choice" is a British lexical item with grammatical consequences (*CGEL* 16.50). It has a direct object followed by an infinitive (or possibly *as*): *They tipped him to be the next president*. Unlike similar verbs (*report, rumor*), however, it cannot have a *that*-clause as complement: **They tipped that he would be the next president*. Moreover, the verb is used more often and more naturally in the passive: *He was tipped to get the appointment*.

11.1.5 Adjectival complement

One of the senses of *go* in common-core English is "become" or "turn," restricted to certain complements; the principles of the restriction are unclear. In many cases the complement has a negative value or is a departure from a norm. One can *go crazy*, but not **go sane*. One can *go sound asleep*, but not **go wide awake* (though it is possible to *come wide awake*). However, one can also *go straight*, but not **go crooked*. And one can either *go limp* or *go rigid* (*with fear*), but neither **go happy* nor **go sad*.

In British, the choice of possible complements after *go* "become" is somewhat different from that in American. A currently fashionable collocation, which has also been the subject of popular comment and is now appearing in American (Safire 2004), is *go missing*. But other adjectival complements are also used after *go* "become, turn" in British that are less probable in American.

After each of the following lemmas, British/American iptmw figures are given in parentheses. If only one figure is given, it is British, and American texts had no tokens. If no figures are given, there were no CIC tokens or the construction could not be conveniently identified.

go absent (0.7) <. . . a confused elderly gentleman who had **gone absent** from an old people's home in Kinnisport.> 2000 Aird 22.

go bonkers (1.4/0.9) Go crazy <. . . the kids can get up and spend all day **going bonkers** in the sea, without the mothers having to move off their fat arses.> 2005 Jan. 9 *Sunday Times* 5 22/1–2.

go clean (0.7) <[boy who has fallen into the water:] Gar, I've **gone** all **clean**.> 1985 Apr. 5 TV cartoon.

go cold (8.1/3.7) <. . . his hands had broken out in sweat and his feet had **gone cold**.> 1953 Mortimer 102.

go *color* (4.7/0.4) Turn *color* (Cf. Swan 1995, 112) <Two weeks later I started radiotherapy. I **went** red, but otherwise it didn't bother me either.> 1995 Sept. *Marie Claire* 275/1–2.

go dead (1.4 other than of lines, phones, etc.) <. . . the blasted chap has **gone dead** on us.> 1983 Innes 145.

go fat <I knew I looked sinister, like an unfrocked parson or a spy **gone fat** in a neutral country.> 1953 Mortimer 18.

go fuzzy <Prussian ideas on orderly change **go fuzzy** when it comes to describing a point at which East Germans will be happy with an extra ration of freedom, without asking for more.> 1989 Oct. 7–13 *Economist* 14/2.

go green (1.2/0.7) Become sensitive to environmental issues <Ministers share their concern that, with more people "**going green**", there is a danger of some firms exploiting the trend by using misleading claims that their goods are environment friendly.> 1989 Aug. 3 *Evening Standard* 3/4.

go into profit (0.3) Become profitable <The party was ambitiously conceived and the guests' sartorial aspirations were high. . . . Costume hire shops **went into profit** overnight.> 1994 Sept. *Tatler* 140.

go mad Get mad "angry" <Mum **went mad** at them . . . . she's furious at them.> 2000 Rowling 52.

go missing (31.7/6.1) <Mr Wren said he is attempting to locate the money which **went missing**.> 1990 Aug. 18 *Daily Telegraph* 19/2.

go nap on *something* Commit oneself wholly to *something*; go all out for *something*; bet everything on *something* (From *nap* "a bid to win all the tricks in a card game"; though etymologically a noun, *nap* here seems adjectival) <Again, a road-building policy designed for closer links with Europe might not be expected to **go nap on** the Conway estuary.> 1989 Sept. 2 *Spectator* 21/2.

go off Go bad; spoil <There are only two reasons for irradiating food. One is to clean up dirty food. . . . The other is to stop it **going off** in storage.> 1999 Mar. 21 *Sunday Times* 11/7–8.

go operational <Europe's biggest vertical axis wind turbine . . . **goes operational** this week.> 1990 Aug. 20 *Times* 6/3–6.

go pale (1.0) <Seamus . . . was **going pale.**> 2003 Rowling 197 (*US ed.* turning).

go quiet (9.1/1.8) <The matter **went quiet** until 1973.> 1996 Aug. 4 *Sunday Times* 8/7.

go rogue <. . . cancer is caused by a cell in the body **going rogue.**> 1985 Clark 88.

go rural <. . . they tended to offer such jobs to . . . single girls with no particular ties, who were willing to **go rural** for the sake of a few extra pounds a week.> 1985 Clark 51.

go rusty (0.5) Become rusty; rust <. . . they [hedge-clippers left out in the rain] have **gone** all **rusty.**> 1985 Townsend 26.

go shapeless <Somewhere there is an outfit that we have had for five years, which never seems to **go shapeless** or tatty.> 1993 Feb. *Woman's Journal* 28/1.

go sick (1.0) **1.** Become/get sick <. . . all of a sudden Rolley had **gone sick** inside, dreading the pain from a fractured rib or collar bone.> 1953 Mortimer 102. **2.** Take time off work on sick leave <Each time her bosses . . . send her a warning letter she puts in a brief appearance at work – before **going sick** again.> 1993 Feb. 5 *Daily Express* 3/3.

go spare (1.6) Become angry or distraught <Hermione was **going spare**, she kept saying you'd do something stupid if you were stuck all on your own without news.> 2003 Rowling 61.

go woolly/wrinkly <Try to ripen them and, overnight, they suddenly become geriatric – the flesh **goes woolly**, the skin **goes wrinkly** – and you might as well eat a prune.> 1996 Aug. 3 *Times* Weekend 3/1.

go wrong (177.6/101.6) Go bad <However, the marriage **went wrong**. She claimed that Mr Dale was becoming more violent.> 1989 July 20 *Times* 3/2.

Other verbs also have adjectival complements.

come expensive/valuable Are expensive/valuable <And mind that Ali Baba vase as you go. . . . They can **come valuable**, too.> 2000 Aird 9.

come good (6.3/0.3) Turn out well <I risked everything for the company and it's **come good.**> 2005 Jan. 15 *Daily Telegraph* 34/2.

leave well alone Leave (*someone/thing*) (well (enough)) alone: The BNC has 54 tokens of *leave (X) well alone* (where X is a single word) and 4 of *leave (X) well enough alone*. CIC has 6.7 iptmw of *leave (X) well alone* in British texts and 0.3 of *leave (X) well enough alone*. It has 0.1 iptmw of *leave (X) well alone* in American texts and 1.7 of *leave (X) well enough alone*. <If I were you I'd **leave well alone.**> 1992 Green 22.

look ***adjective*** Look like / as though *pronoun is adjective*: CIC British texts have 1.4 times as many tokens as American texts do. <Tom Hanks **looks** set to get another Oscar.> 1994 Sept. 25 *Sunday Times* Style 42/4.

look ***done*** Look like / as if *pronoun is done* <The fiction **looks** put in to embellish the ideas.> 1987 Nov. 8 *Manchester Guardian Weekly* 24/5.

look ***prep phrase*** Look like / as though *pronoun is prep phrase* <He [Salman Rushdie] comes over as a bespectacled chappie in a double-breasted blazer who **looks** in need of a tennis partner.> 1990 Aug. 20 *Evening Standard* 7/3.

look likely (19.6/2.2) Seem likely <. . . interest rates **look likely** to remain high because of consumer spending.> 1989 Feb. 12 *Manchester Guardian Weekly* 6/1.

look set (43.6/3.2) Look as if *pronoun is* set <[The bill] was stalled in the Commons . . . and now **looks set** to fail.> 2003 June 25 *Guardian* international ed. G2–7/1.

need ***doing*** Need to be *done*: *Need* can be complemented directly by a present participle in a construction for which American would have a passive infinitive. <The [TV] licence fee . . . **needed** raising.> 1995 Aug. 28 *Independent* 4/4.

need ***done*** Need to be *done*: According to Kahn and Ilson, the past participle directly after *need* is limited to regional dialect. <She and her husband Lloyd . . . have just bought their house and there's lots **needing done**.> 1987 May 10 (Scotland) *Sunday Post* 12/3.

say sorry (9.5/0.6) Say *one is* sorry <Harry **Says Sorry** For Dressing Up As Nazi> 2005 Jan. 13 *Daily Telegraph* 1/5–6.

seem set for (1.6/0.5) Seem to be set for <Harry **seems set for** success.> 1991 Feb. 17 *Sunday Times* Magazine 19/1.

strike lucky (2.9) Become lucky <. . . the 54-year-old nuclear scientist still had to . . . **strike lucky** when his name was drawn from more than 20,000 entries.> 2003 June 21 *Times* Travel 4/2.

want rid of (1.3) Want to be/get rid of <He just **wanted rid of** them.> 1998 Joss 244.

want shot of (0.2) Want to be rid/shut/shet/shed of <I just **wanted shot of** her.> 1986 Simpson 212. The construction with the infinitive expressed also occurs. <Mr Lawson . . . clearly **wants to be shot of** his other house.> 1991 Jan. 29 *Daily Telegraph* 8/5–6.

11.1.6 Adverbial particle complement

be off Be out; be off work <We've two chief inspectors and two DIs **off** with flu.> 1993 Neel 25.

begin off Begin; start off <I once wrote up for an autograph . . . Well I **began off** 'Am heartily ashamed to write up but – '> 1971 Mortimer 76.

break down (of a marriage) Break up <So you don't think he was too upset about his marriage **breaking down**?> 1986 Simpson 60.

brew up "Brit . . . . to make tea" (*CED*). <Afternoon tea is one of those quintessentially English rituals that time seems to have forgotten. Thankfully, at some London venues **brewing up** is still an event.> 1988 May *Illustrated London News* 96/1.

budge up Move over <**Budge up**, yeh great lump.> 1997 Rowling 39.

clock on Arrive at work, esp. by registering the time on a sheet or clock; clock in; punch a time clock <The head waiter had said that Wayne was due to **clock on** at five.> 1991 Critchley 233.

come through Come in <Shall I tell her to **come through**?> 1996 Dexter 215.

come with Come along <Sorry about tonight. Tina insisted on **coming with**.> 1985 Mortimer 319.

cut along "*Brit. informal.* to hurry off" *CED*. Cf. American *cut out*. < 1949 'M. Innes' *Journeying Boy* ii. 25 'And now you'd better **cut along**.' Captain Cox was a great believer in the moral effects of abrupt dismissals on the young.> *OED* s.v. *cut* v. 19.b.

fall about Fall down <It's nice to think of those [cigarette-smoking] foreigners coughing themselves silly and **falling about** all over the place.> 1977 Dec. 7 *Punch* 1095/1. Cf. § 11.1.6.4.1 FALL ABOUT LAUGHING.

follow on Follow (after) <You go ahead. . . . I'll **follow on** in the van.> 1989 Daniel 4.

get on Get along; make out <How did you **get on**?> 1992 Granger 181.

give in Give up: *Give in* and *give up* are both common-core English, but they are used in different contexts in the national varieties. In the following contexts, American is likely to have *give up*: <You'll never guess the answer – do you **give in**?> *CIDE*. <1805 *Sporting Mag*. XXVI. 56 According to the boxing phrase, [he] shewed the white feather and **gave in**.> *OED* s.v. *give* 59.a.

give over Give up; stop it <Oh, **give over**, will you?> 1972 Rendell 112.

pack in Be packed in; crowd in <Normally more than 100 customers would **pack in** to watch the game.> 1998 Jan. 3 *Times* 19/2.

pay out Pay up <My 21-year-old son's E-reg Vauxhall Astra was stolen but his insurer is refusing to **pay out** on the grounds that the company was not told he had fitted his car with alloy wheels.> 1999 Mar. 14 *Sunday Times* 415/2.

phone through Phone <1932 T. S. Eliot *Sweeney Agonistes* 13 She says will you ring up on Monday. . . . All right, Monday you'll **phone through**.> *OED* s.v. *phone* v. b.

potter about Putter around <We all know some people who . . . **potter about** and do not know what to do.> 1925 Leadbeater 223.

pull in Pull over <She was trying to wave down cars and my first thought was that she was in danger of being run over. I **pulled in**, wound down the window and asked what on earth she was doing.> 1993 Smith 222.

ring through Call <Just before twelve the hospital **rang through** to say that Carpenter was now fit for a brief interview.> 1986 Simpson 140. Cf. § 11.1.6.1 RING THROUGH TO.

rub up Jack off; masturbate <1963 C. Mackenzie *My Life & Times* II. 115 Just as I was going down the steps into our area B— asked me if I ever **rubbed up**. . . . In bed that night I tried the experiment recommended by B—.> *OED* s.v. *rub* v. 14.d.

sell up Sell (out/off) <We also discussed . . . how we'd **sell up** – offer each other first refusal and use the average of three estate agents' quotes or put it on the open market.> 2000 Jan. 16 *Sunday Times* Money 9/5. Cf. § 11.1.6.2 SELL *SOMETHING* UP.

sign on Sign up (for unemployment compensation) "(*Br infml*) To **sign on** is to report to a government unemployment office that you are unemployed and wish to receive unemployment benefit" (*CIDE*).

stay off Stay out (of schoool) <OK, you'd better **stay off** today.> 1991 Glaister 127.

strip off Strip down <Of the three doctors . . . Paul Mari . . . is so timid that when he introduces himself he is mistaken for a patient and told to **strip off**.> 1987 Mar. 25 *Punch* 59/3. Cf. § 11.1.6.2 STRIP *SOMEONE* OFF.

turn in Turn up; come in <In the old days when we got paid weekly on a Thursday we used to go out for some beer at night and not bother to **turn in** Friday.> 1999 Mar. 21 *Sunday Times* 10/7.

wash up In British this combination refers to washing dishes after a meal; in American, to washing one's hands (and face). <After supper . . . Charlotte said she would **wash up**.> 1991 Trollope 131.

write up Write off/away <I once **wrote up** for an autograph . . . 'Am heartily ashamed to **write up** but – '> 1971 Mortimer 76.

11.1.6.1 Adverbial particle and preposition

be on about *something* Be going on about *something* <Good Lord, girl, I wondered what you **were on about**!> 1992 Granger 12.

call out at *someone* Call out to *someone* <. . . men . . . would **call out at** him, asking him questions about his uneventful sex life, which he pretended not to hear.> 1985 Mortimer 82.

carry on with *something* Go on or continue with *something* <. . . they wanted me to **carry on with** my brace. You know, they're dentists.> 2000 Rowling 353.

drop back to *someplace* Drop back by/in/at *someplace*; come back to *someplace* <. . . **drop back to** the vicarage for a sherry.> 1985 Bingham 118–19.

get on for *an age/time* Get on to *an age/time*: CIC British texts have 7.1 iptmw of *get on for*; American have 0.3. <He must be **getting on for** fourteen now. Doesn't look much like a teenager, does he?> 1999 Apr. 5 "Fred Basset" (British comic strip) *Chicago Tribune* 5 6.

get on with *something* Do *something*; go ahead with *something*: CIC British texts have 184.8 iptmw; American have 48.1. <They are not trying to convince us

to let them wed; we need to tell them [Charles and Camilla] that they should **get on with** it.> 2004 Dec. 15 *Daily Telegraph* 18/7.

get up to ***a baby*** Get up with *a baby* <The New Man . . . **gets up** at night **to** the crying baby.> 1987 Apr. 6 *Guardian* 10/1.

give on to ***someplace*** Open onto *someplace* "*Brit*. (of a window, door, corridor, etc.) overlook or lead into: *a plate glass window* ***gave on to*** *the roof*" (*NODE*).

go about with ***someone*** Go around/out with *someone* <Anthea has been allowed to **go about with** young men ever since she was fifteen or sixteen.> 1985 Pym 83.

going on with, be Get started with <It'll do to **be going on with**. . . . It gives us enough to get him to the police station for questioning.> 1993 Cleeves 194.

pop down to ***someplace*** Stop by or drop in at *someplace* <Just **popping down to** the tavern for a quick drink.> 1997 June 20 "Fred Basset" (British comic strip) *Chicago Tribune* 5 6.

ring through to ***someone*** Call/phone *someone* <Sergeant Robinson **rang through to** Walsh.> 1992 Walters 253. Cf. § 11.1.6 RING THROUGH.

rub up on ***something*** "*Chiefly Brit* . . . . to refresh one's memory (of)" (*CED*).

sign up to ***something*** Sign on for *something* <Mr Leighton believes that he is not getting the reforms that he needs – even if union leaders **sign up to** them.> 2003 July 9 *Times* 1/3.

turn up to ***an event/place*** Turn up at/for *an event/place* <Hamnet **turned up to** No 10 wearing an outsize T-shirt.> 2003 June 28 *Times* Weekend 9/1.

11.1.6.2 Adverbial particle and noun phrase

answer ***someone*** **back** Talk back to *someone* <There were Fenians, Suffragettes, daughters **answering back** their parents.> 1987 June 8 *Evening Standard* 24/3.

bring ***someone*** **on** Bring *someone* in <Mrs Margaret Thatcher's changes aimed at . . . **bringing on** new blood.> 1989 July 24 *Times* 1/1.

buy ***something*** **in** **1**. Buy *something* (from a subcontractor) <If your company **buys in** mailing lists, you may sometimes wonder why they cost so much.> 1998 Jan. 7 *Times* 35/1. **2**. Stock up on *something* <I can't afford to start **buying** things **in**.> 1990 Hardwick 120.

catch ***someone*** **out** The expression occurs also in American use but is more than 5 times as frequent in British CIC texts. **1**. Take *someone* by surprise <'The other road?' countered the man on the telephone, who had been **caught out** by bad directions before.> 1968 Aird 7. **2**. Catch *someone* <Blunkett's real gaffe was to be **caught out**> 2004 Dec. 15 *Daily Telegraph* 18/1.

catch ***someone*** **up** Catch up to/with *someone* <An investigation by two London University experts has revealed that the [GCSE] exam fails to help boys **catch up** girls.> 1991 Feb. 15 *Evening Standard* 5/3.

chase ***someone/thing*** **up** Track *someone/thing* down <Obstinately he'd worked on the matter over the weekend, **chasing up** every lead.> 1992 Granger 14.

cover ***something*** **over** Cover *something* (up) <In the outer office . . . two other girls were **covering over** their typewriters.> 1968 Aird 50.

cut ***a driver*** **up** Cut *a driver* off <The most common grievance is motorists saying they have been **cut up**, followed by complaints of tail-gating.> 1996 Aug. 3 *Times* Car 96 9/1–2.

do ***someone*** **down** Do *someone* in; take advantage of *someone* <You couldn't make out that I was to blame. Trying to **do** you **down**.> 1990 Hardwick 100.

do ***something*** **up** Do *something* over; redecorate *something* <. . . property values have risen, and it is not so easy now to find a cheap house to **do up**.> 1989 Mar. *In Britain* 15/1.

dosh out ***food/drugs*** Dish up *food*; give out *drugs* (*Dosh out* is not recorded in dictionaries.) <'How much did you hear?' [¶] 'Not a lot. I was busy **doshing out** Lonnie's seconds.'> 1985 Mortimer 345. <He'd sooner get to the root cause of it . . . and he'll treat that rather than just **dosh out** the Valium.> 1993 spoken citation CIC.

draft ***someone*** **in** Draft *someone* <Then last November, . . . Jones was **drafted in** [for a round-the-world balloon trip].> 1999 Mar. 21 *Sunday Times* 14/5.

dust ***someone/thing*** **down** Dust/brush *someone/thing* off <So bring them out, **dust** them **down**, and give them a new lease of life.> 2005 Jan. 15 *Daily Telegraph* Weekend 3/6.

eye ***something*** **up** Eye *something*; look intently at *something* <Yesterday, Kensie [a terrier] was **eyeing up** the big swans grazing by the Round Pond.> 1999 Mar. 17 *Evening Standard* 31/1.

fill ***a form*** **in** Fill *a form* out <"And . . . and you've had the forms, you say?" [¶] Morse nodded. [¶] "And . . . and you've actually **filled** 'em ***in***?"> 1994 Dexter 16.

fill ***someone*** **in** "*Brit. slang*. to attack and injure severely" (*CED*). <1959 *Times* 3 Mar. 3/4 A naval rating accused of murdering . . . an antique dealer . . . was alleged to have said: 'I **filled in** a chap and took his money.'> *OED* s.v. *fill* v. 15.f.

fit ***someone*** **up** Incriminate *someone* <If Mr Daniloff was **fitted up**, Mr Zakharov was set up, just a week earlier.> 1986 Sept. 12 *Daily Mirror* 6/4.

give ***prizes*** **away** Give *prizes* out <. . . Sir Ralph's kind suggestion that he might one day **give away** the prizes at the school's speech day.> 1991 Critchley 144.

give ***something*** **in** Turn *something* in "*Brit.* hand in a completed document to an official or a piece of work to a supervisor" (*NODE*).

give ***a player*** **out** (*of an umpire in cricket*) To declare a man at bat to be out in response to an appeal by the other side <The Majarajah of Kashmir . . . tampered with the laws of cricket with the effect that he could only be **given out** lbw [leg before wicket, grounds for giving out].> 1983 Brooke-Taylor 74.

glance ***something*** **over** Glance over [*prep.*] *something*; look *something* over <He picked up the sheets of buff typewritten paper, and **glanced** them **over** rapidly.> 1940 Shute 62.

hatch ***something*** **out** Hatch *something*: *Hatch out* is nearly 3.5 times as frequent in CIC British texts as in American. <. . . **hatching** Aragog **out** in a cupboard wasn't his idea of being innocent.> 1998 Rowling 208 (*US ed.* hatching).

have ***a day*** **off** Take *a day* off <Yes, he was **having** a day **off** to take the twins to Mum and Dad's.> 1991 Charles 37.

have ***someone*** **round** Have *someone* come around; ask *someone* in <**Have** some people **round** in the evening.> 1985 Barnard 28.

hide ***something*** **up** Hide *something* away <There's a dozen places and more where you could easily **hide up** any amount of drugs.> 2000 Aird 165.

hire ***someone*** **in** Hire *someone* <With three of the remaining Bad Seeds, he decamped to Paris . . . to start writing for the album, and there struck on the idea of **hiring in** gospel singers to enhance the songs.> 2004 Dec. 16 *Daily Telegraph* 15/4.

invite ***someone*** **along** Invite *someone*; ask *someone* to come along <Charles Richards should be **invited along** to talk about the small publishing business.> 1981 Dexter 215.

knit ***something*** **up** Knit *something* <He had been especially enamored of a multicolored Fair Isle beret, and an aunt had **knitted** it **up** for him.> 1991 Graham 92.

lay ***something*** **on** "*chiefly Brit.* provide a service or amenity" (*NODE*). <. . . he can **lay on** some Falkland veterans for you to be photographed talking to.> 1989 Dickinson 81.

lay up ***tables*** Set *tables* <Wayne was due to . . . begin **laying up** the tables in the Members' and Strangers' dining rooms.> 1991 Critchley 233.

look ***something*** **out** Look for and find *something* <I'm fine to . . . **look out** the spanner they need for tinkering.> 1991 Grant-Adamson 15.

measure ***something*** **up** Measure *something* <The [bowling] lanes were apparently **measured up** by laser.> 1989 Sept. 5 *Evening Standard* 31/2.

mess ***someone*** **around** 1. Mess around with *someone*; play games with *someone*; give *someone* problems <I'm supposed to be getting a flight to Moscow but those wankers at the embassy are **messing** me **around** about a visa.> 1993 Smith 266. 2. Mess around with *someone*; i.e., engage in casual sexual activity with someone < – If you're **messing** her **around** . . . – I'm *not* **messing** her **around**.> 1999 Mar. 22 BBC1 *EastEnders*. 3. Mess *someone* up; confuse *someone* <I do think you can **mess** children **around** by having theories about them.> 1991 Dickinson 78.

miss out ***someone/thing*** Miss/omit/overlook *someone/thing*; leave *someone/thing* out <The islands are rightly popular, but **miss out** Dubrovnik and you miss a rare gem of a tourist town.> 2003 June 21 *Times* Travel 1/1.

pack (it/*something*) in Stop (it/working/doing *something*) <Well, . . . they don't like it, so **pack it in**.> 1991 Graham 132. <Your pancreas has **packed in** completely.> 1996 Dexter 234.

pack ***a place*** **out** Pack *a place*; fill *a place* up <They **packed** the restaurant **out**, moved the chairs, rearranged the tables.> 1953 Mortimer 19.

pass ***something*** **through** Pass *something* on <I would like to think they [the savings] would be **passed through** to the consumer.> 1999 Mar. 12 *Times* 13/7.

pay ***someone/thing*** **out** Pay *someone/thing* back; get even with *someone* or for *something* <Killed is just what he was. But I'll **pay** them **out**.> 1983 Mann 50.

phone ***someone*** **up** Phone *someone*; call *someone* (up) <I've got this jeweller friend who's going to **phone** you **up**.> 1987 Feb. 23 *Mirror* Week 4/5.

post ***something*** **on** Mail *something*; send *something* on <You dropped it on the station, did you, and some kind soul's **posted it on**?> 1990 Hardwick 151.

pull ***doors*** **to** Close *doors*: Infrequent; CIC British texts have 0.4 iptmw; American have 0.1. <. . . he . . . **pulled** the doors **to**.> 1998 Rowling 42 (*US ed.* closed).

put ***something*** **by** Put *something* away, save *something*: <. . . you still **put by** a bit each week to ensure you could pay for a decent funeral.> 2003 James 12.

put ***an amendment*** **down** Put forward *or* propose/move *an amendment* <The bill is short, just three clauses, but already the antis have **put down** hundreds of amendments.> 1992 Nov. 7 *Economist* 63/2.

put the (tele)phone down CIC has 23.7 iptmw of this expression in British texts and 1.8 in American texts. The American option is likely to be *hang the (tele)phone up*, which also occurs in British use, though only about one-fifth as frequently. <I **put the phone down**.> 1987 June 8 *Evening Standard* 13/1.

put ***washing*** **on** Put *a load of wash* in; do *a load of wash* <Is there any washing you'd like me to do? I'm going to **put** one **on** this morning.> 1993 Smith 118.

rained off, be (Of an event) be rained out <If you have paid for admission to a baseball game and the game is **rained off**, your ticket will become valid as a 'rain check'.> 1982 Trudgill 115.

read ***something*** **up** Read up on *something* <I've spent ages **reading up** stuff for him.> 1999 Rowling 232 (*US ed.* reading up on).

rub up ***something*** **1.** Bone up on *something*; review *something* <1885 *Pall Mall G.* 9 June 1/2 Now is the time for all fiddle lovers to go and **rub up** their fiddle lore.> *OED* s.v. *fiddle* n. 7.b. **2.** "*Chiefly Brit.* . . . (*tr.*) to smooth or polish" (*CED*). <1924 M. A. Burbridge *Road to Beauty* 115 Finish by using a bit more of the tinted polish and **rub up** with the buffer.> *OED* s.v. *polish* n. 3.b.

rub ***someone*** **up the wrong way** Rub *someone* the wrong way <In his determination to be a modern prince, he [Prince Charles] **rubs** many modern commentators **up the wrong way**.> 2003 Nov. 10 *Times* 18/2.

run ***a machine*** **in** Break *a machine* in: *MW* labels the sense "chiefly British." "*Brit.* prepare the engine of a new car for normal use by driving slowly, usually for a particular period of time" (*NODE*).

run ***typeset matter*** **on** Run *typeset matter* in: Hence also the derived noun and adjective denoting such matter in dictionaries are British *run-on* and American *run-in*. Both variations are used in both varieties, but the preferences seem to be as stated. *MW* has a cross-reference from *run on* to *run in*, but not vice versa; *NODE* defines *run on* in the relevant sense, but not *run in*.

run *someone* over Run over *someone*; run *someone* down <I could arrange to **run** you **over** in University Avenue. Make it look like an accident.> 2001 Lodge 283.

sell *something* on Resell *something* <Classic cars can be **sold on** fairly easily.> 2000 Aird 105.

sell *something* out Sell out of *something* <It had been said of Essex that 'even the newsagents were white'. But the fact would not prevent them from **selling out** the *Essex Bugle* were it ever to carry the story.> 1991 Critchley 26–7.

sell *something* up Sell *something* (off) <I told one Indian shopkeeper in Crawley recently that all he could do if he wanted to make money was to **sell up** his shop and get out.> 1994 Oct. 1 *Times* Weekend 13/3. Cf. § 11.1.6 SELL UP.

send *someone* down Send *someone* to prison <. . . the press fantasising the while about the pretty blonde policewoman and what a story it would all make when Mr Stagg was **sent down**.> 1994 Sept. 24 *Spectator* 8/3.

share *something* out Share *something*; pass *something* out; divide *something* up <Could it be . . . that Lizzie has all the emotional, sensual and reproductive instincts that should by rights have been **shared out** between us?> 1993 Trollope 63.

spend *money* out Spend *money* (foolishly) <You're always **spending out** your money on the boy.> 1985 Mortimer 102.

stock *something* up Stock up on *something* <. . . shoppers, fearing even worse weather to come, **stocked up** food.> 1991 Feb. 9 *Daily Telegraph* 1/4.

strip *someone* off Strip *someone* down <He smelt rotten so we **stripped** him **off** and put him in the bath.> 1985 Townsend 356–7. Cf. § 11.1.6 STRIP OFF.

take *a phone* out Take *a phone* off the hook: Rare. <Oh, we were in. We were in all right. I'd of **taken** the phone **out**.> 1991 Dickinson 244.

take *time* out Take *time* off: CIC British texts have approximately the same frequency of *take a year out* and *take a year off* (respectively 2.8 and 2.6 iptmw); American texts have almost only *take a year off* (4.1 iptmw), with very few *take a year out* (0.1 iptmw). <He has been **taking** a year **out** from Edinburgh, but returns this autumn to complete his degree in psychology.> 1989 July 19 *Daily Mail* 17/2.

take *someone* through Take *someone* in; admit/escort *someone* <That's the last patient gone . . . . Come along, Inspector. I'll **take** you **through**.> 1996 Graham 113.

take up *premises* Occupy/rent *premises* <Whether Tobacco Dock will live up to its claim to be the new Covent Garden remains to be seen, but virtually all the shop and restaurant space has been **taken up**.> 1988 May *Illustrated London News* 67/3.

throw in *a job* The particle *up* is usual in common-core English; CIC has no examples of *throw in a job*. <He was unusual to the degree that, aged 51, he **threw in** his job on a farm in Kent, left a note for his wife and five children

saying that he wasn't coming back and became a rough-sleeping tramp.> 1993 Feb. 15 *Daily Mail* 39/2.

throw up the sponge The norm in common-core English is *throw in the towel*, with *sponge* as a minor variant. The particle *up* instead of *in* is not represented in CIC. <It would be absolutely unlike Elizabeth . . . to **throw up the sponge** like that.> 1931 Benson 220.

tidy *something* away Put *something* away/up "The children were expected to **tidy away** their toys / to **tidy** their toys **away** (= put them in the correct place)" (*CIDE*).

tidy *drawers* out Straighten *drawers* up "(*Br*) Next week I'm going to **tidy out** my drawers / **tidy** my drawers **out** (= tidy them up by removing unwanted things)" (*CIDE*).

trigger *something* off Trigger *something*; set *something* off: CIC British texts have 8.1 iptmw of *trigger off*; American texts have none. <1983 *Daily Telegraph* 23 Apr. 21/4 The arrival of the new pound coin has **triggered off** something.> *OED* s.v. *pound* n. 4.b. *pound coin*.

try it/*something* on Try *something* <I'm not just threatening you, Daley – I'll bloody *kill* you if you **try it on** again.> 1992 Dexter 235.

tuck *someone* up (in bed) Tuck **someone** in(to bed) <And **tucked up** in bed.> 1991 Critchley 217.

turn *someone* off "*Brit. informal.* to dismiss from employment" (*CED*). <1892 *Temple Bar Mag.* Mar. 321 A packer had been **turned off** for carelessness.> *OED* s.v. *turn* v. 74.b.

turn *heat* out Turn *heat* off <**Turn** the heat **out** [under a pan of rice].> 1995 Sept. 6 BBC2 *Delia Smith's Summer Collection:* "The Summer Kitchen Garden."

turn *a place* over Rob *a place* <The room must already have been **turned over**.> 1993 Apr. 22 GPTV ch. 8 *Mystery: Inspector Morse*.

turn *someone* up Cause *someone* to vomit (*CED*); cf. *turn off* "disgust" <If there was one thing that **turned** him **up**, it was white women dressing like blacks.> 1993 Graham 212.

turn *something* up Turn down / pass up *something* <Alan Clark, a former Tory minister, asserted that Churchill was a warmonger who had **turned up** opportunities to get "first reasonable, then excellent, terms from Germany".> 1993 Jan. 9 *Economist* 82/2.

wind *someone* up "*Brit. informal* tease or irritate someone" (*NODE*); put *someone* on <He looked at her, saw the amused lift of her lips and laughed. " . . . You're **winding** me **up**."> 1992 Walters 248.

In the preceding citations, the nominal functions as direct object. In the following, however, it functions adverbially.

go down a storm Be enthusiastically received; go over like gangbusters: CIC has 1.8 iptmw in British texts and none in American. < . . . the Screen Two film 'Priest' . . . is currently **going down a storm** at festivals.> 1994 Sept. 28–Oct. 5 *Time Out* 16/2.

go down a treat Go over well: CIC has 1.5 iptmw in British texts and none in American. <It **went down a treat** with the studio audience too, apparently.> 1995 Lodge 320. Cf. § 6.1 A TREAT.

In the following, the object is a subject-headed gerund:

find out *someone doing something* Find/discover *someone doing something* <There is a mood of uncomfortable deafening silence. It's as if your granny has been **found out** shagging the butler.> 2004 Dec. 8–15 *Time Out* 8/1.

11.1.6.2.1 With preposition

bring *someone* **out in a rash** Cause a rash (on *someone*): CIC British texts have 0.4 iptmw; American texts have none. <These plants **bring** you **out in an** unpleasant, spreading **rash.**> 1982 Trudgill 19.

do *something* **out in** *a style* Decorate *something* in *a style*: CIC British texts have 1.3 iptmw of *done out in*; American texts have none. <There was the same dull reception foyer **done out in** light oak veneer and worn-looking splay-legged furniture.> 1988 Lodge 194.

learn/know *something* **off by heart** Learn/know *something* by heart <. . . trying to . . . **learn** charms and spells **off by heart.**> 1997 Rowling 179 (*US ed.* learn spells by heart). <. . . we **know** it **off by heart.**> 1999 Rowling 142 (*US ed.* know by heart).

put *something* **out to contract** Put *something* out on/for bid <London Regional Transport, the body set up . . . to run London's public transport, has **put** many of its other routes **out to contract.**> 1989 Autumn *Illustrated London News* 26/2.

11.1.6.3 Adverbial particle and adjective

come over all *adjective* Begin to feel *adjective* <Annie, 68, **comes over all** funny.> 1994 Sept. 14–21 *Time Out* 8/4.

cut up rough "*Brit. informal.* to become angry or bad-tempered" (*CED*). <Did Mlle Bardot **Cut Up Rough**? / Brigitte Bardot, the film star turned animal rights defender, has been accused of castrating a neighbour's pet donkey, Charly, to end a romance with her own donkey Mimosa.> 1989 July 23 *Sunday Telegraph* 3/1–3.

11.1.6.4 Adverbial particle and verbal

11.1.6.4.1 Present participle

carry on *doing something* Continue *doing something* / to *do something*: In CIC British texts this construction is about 10 times more frequent than in

American texts. <Waiting lists [for NHS services] **carried on** growing.> 1993 Feb. 17 *Times* 14/6.

fall about laughing Fall down laughing <They **fell about laughing** when we told them what we were doing.> 1989 June *In Britain* 8/2. Cf. §11.1.6 FALL ABOUT.

11.1.6.4.2 Infinitive

come on to *do something* Start/begin to *do something* <She would look much more sensible in her comfortable blue felt [hat] if it **came on to** rain.> 1985 Pym 108.

tell *someone* off to *do something* Tell/order *someone* to *do something* <You know that David has been **told off to** help me?> 1985 Price 148.

11.1.7 Prepositional complement

admit to *doing something* Admit *doing something*: The construction with *to* is about 10 times more frequent in CIC British texts than in American. <I certainly wasn't going to **admit to** touching the bowl in the kitchen.> 1992 Green 43.

affiliate to In CIC British texts, *affiliate to* is 4.5 times more frequent than *affiliate with*; in American texts, *affiliate with* is 27.5 times more frequent than *affiliate to*. <Unions . . . ask to join [the Trades Union Congress], to be **'affiliated' to** it.> 1988 Brookes and Fraenkel 91.

aim for Aim at: In CIC British texts, *aim for* is about twice as frequent as in American texts. <Suggest that he **aims for** a compromise.> 1989 Dickinson 115.

allow of Allow <By this definition, then, a word has the kind of stability which does not **allow of** further reduction in form.> 1987 Carter 5.

answer to *interrogation* Answer *some questions* <In the old days I could have said, would you **answer to** some interrogation?> 1994 Freeling 6.

appeal against According to one count (Hundt 91), of 100 randomly selected tokens of *appeal* in the British *Guardian*, 99 were followed by *against*, and only 1 by a nominal; in contrast, the American *Miami Herald* contained no tokens of *appeal against* in an entire year's issues.

average at *a sum* Average *a sum* <. . . *prêt-à-porter* evening dresses **average at** £1,200.> 1987 Oct. *Illustrated London News* 64/2.

be on income Have income <. . . women and older pensioners . . . are more likely to **be on** a low **income**.> 2003 July 16 *Daily Express* 35/1.

be on the phone Have a telephone <This week he's gone to visit his sister in Scarborough. . . . And she's not **on the phone**.> 1995 Jones 302.

breathe on *some* air Breathe in *some* air <Morse **breathed** deeply **on** the early-morning air – cigarettes were going to be *out* that day.> 1992 Dexter 20.

bucket with rain Pour down rain <God, it was a foul night – **bucketing with rain.**> 1995 Wilson 110. Cf. POUR WITH RAIN below.

call into Visit; drop by <**Call into** your local Barclays branch or ring 0 800 000 929> 1999 Mar. 13 poster for Barclays Bank in a London underground station.

cater for ***someone/thing*** Cater to *someone/thing*: In CIC, *cater for* is more than 100 times as frequent in British texts as in American; *cater to* is 3 times as frequent in American texts as in British. In the sense "provide food (at a party)" British prefers *cater for* or possibly *cater at;* American also uses the verb transitively: *cater a party*. <Abbey National, another of the biggest high street lenders, does **cater for** people who buy abroad.> 2005 Jan. 23 *Sunday Telegraph* http://www.telegraph.co.uk/.

chat to ***someone*** Chat with *someone*: CIC British texts have comparable numbers of *to* and *with* after *chat* (with slightly more tokens of *to*); American texts have 26 times as many tokens of *with* as of *to*. <[Prince] William **chatted to** the residents on subjects ranging from garage music to trendy hairdos.> 2003 June 20 *Times* 11/1.

claim for Claim; file a claim for <Anyone over 16 can **claim for** low-income benefits.> 1986 July *Family Income Supplement*, *FIS.1* (leaflet issued by the Department of Health and Social Security), back page.

claim on insurance Claim insurance; file a claim on insurance <He'll just **claim on** his **insurance**.> 1993 Stallwood 71.

comprise of The complementation of *comprise* is one of the shibboleths of prescriptive usage guides. The range of options in standard use (Gilman 1994) are these (using "whole" and "parts" in a wide sense): (a) the whole comprises its parts = "consists of"; (b) the parts comprise their whole = "make up, constitute," or the whole is comprised of its parts = "is made up of, is constituted by"; (c) a thing or things comprise(s) or is/are comprised of another thing or things = "is/are." The citation below illustrates yet another alternative to (c): *comprise of* ("consist of"). CIC British texts have 0.2 iptmw of *comprise of*; American texts have none. <These [gifts] **comprise** mostly **of** tee shirts.> 1989 Aug. 31 *Midweek* 13/2.

consist in Consist of (Peters 2004, 124): In CIC British texts, *consist* has *of* 15 times more often than *in*; in American texts, 22 times. < . . . a quaintly-named duty which **consisted in** parading with the guard in steel helmets and peeling potatoes for two hours.> 1962 Lodge 59.

could do with ***doing something*** Would like to *do something / have something done*: This construction is fairly common in British, accounting for about 10 percent of the tokens of *could do with* in a sample from CIC. It is very rare in American. <I **could do with** paying for these two days.> 1992 Green 30.

dabble on ***the stockmarket*** Perhaps a blend of *dabble in* and *on the stockmarket*. <. . . he had broken the resolution of a lifetime not to **dabble on** the stockmarket.> 1980 Sharpe 131.

dine off ***food*** Dine on *food*: This construction is rare in British, but has no CIC American tokens. "<***dined*** **~** *oysters*>" (*LDEL*).

do for ***someone*** Do *someone* in <No, whatever they tell us today, it wasn't really Nannygate that **did for** Blunkett. . . . [¶] So what was it, then, that **did for** Blunkett?> 2004 Dec. 16 *Daily Telegraph* 22/6–7.

do with, to Having to do with; about <. . . there was some strange footage **to do with** a man who had once tended Adolf's boiler and sitting-room fires.> 1989 Sept. 8 *Evening Standard* 30/6. Cf. § 11.1.8.2.2 BE TO DO WITH.

doing with, not be Not put up / be bothered with <I **can't be doing with** spending an enormous amount of money on clothes.> 1994 Sept. *Tatler* 24/1.

engaged on In common-core English, *engaged in* is the norm, but *engaged on* is 4 times more frequent in CIC British texts than in American. < . . . someone here . . . can cook when not **engaged on** overcomplicating the food.> 1995 Sept. 9 *Times* Magazine 77/5.

enrol on ***a course*** In CIC British texts, *enrol* is followed by *in* 2.5 times as often as it is by *on*. But American texts have no tokens of *enroll on*. <Annette **enrolled on** an intensive course to become a childminder.> 2004 Jan. 4 *Sunday Times* News Review 5 5/5–6.

enter ***tickets*** **to** ***a draw*** Enter *tickets* in *a draw*: Rare construction. <Thousands of tickets [were] never **entered to** the prize draw.> 1993 Feb. 22 *Evening Standard* 17/2.

get up ***a place*** Get (up) to *a place* <[Of a ripple in a swimming pool:] It's prob'ly doing 20 miles an hour, time it **gets up** the deep end.> 1991 Feb. 26 *Times* 14/3.

go off ***someone/something*** Begin to dislike *someone/something* <**Gone off** me a bit, hasn't she?> 2000 Rowling 532.

go on a course Start/take a course <I've **gone on a** relentless self-improvement **course** in losing weight.> 1989 Sept. 7 *Midweek* 19/3. See also § 8.1 ON *SOME* COURSE.

go to it Go at it < . . . he had been **going to it** for a decade or so: experience does count for something.> 1991 Feb. 2 *Times* 11/4–5.

increase on Increase over <Calls have been **increased** by 77 **on** last year.> 2005 Jan. 13 BBC News24.

lay about Lay into; criticize <Howard has **laid about** the prime minister in the Commons.> 2004 Jan. 4 *Sunday Times* 13/4.

look like ***doing something*** CIC British texts have 12.5 iptmw of *look like being*; American texts have 0.1. <Middleton's merger . . . **looks like** causing a boardroom crisis.> 1995 Aug. 28 *Daily Telegraph* 22/1.

natter to Chat with <Sir Andrew said he had just been **nattering to** his brother.> 1994 Sept. 22 *Times* 18/3.

operate to ***something*** Operate according to / by *something*: CIC British texts have 3.5 times as many tokens of *operate to* as of *operate according to*; American texts have nearly 3 times as many tokens of *operate according to* as of *operate to*. <. . . she **operates to** a formula that invariably incorporates certain ingredients.> 1991 Feb. 10 *Independent* Sunday Review 4/3.

play to the rules In common-core English, *play by the rules* is the norm. <. . . the inability to **play to** the rules . . . amounted to a sort of conspiracy.> 1987 Mar. 25 *Punch* 60/4.

play at Although CIC American texts have a marginally higher number of tokens of the verb *play*, British texts have 1.3 times more tokens of *play at*. <He . . . recalled **playing at** cowboys.> 1992 Granger 14.

point at *Point to* is the norm in common-core English; but in CIC British texts it exceeds *point at* by 3.3 times, whereas in American texts it does so by 5.3 times. <Eight of the [clock] hands were currently **pointing at** the 'home' position, but Mr Weasley's, which was the longest, was still **pointing at** 'work'.> 2000 Rowling 135 (*US ed.* pointing to).

pour with rain In CIC British texts *pour with rain* has 3.0 iptmw, and in American texts none. <. . . it was **pouring with rain**.> 2003 Nov. 7 *Daily Express* 3/5. Cf. BUCKET WITH RAIN above.

presume upon ***something*** In CIC British texts *presume upon* has 0.6 iptmw, and in American texts none. <Mrs. Thatcher replied: "What happens to Mr Kinnock is a matter for the British people. I would not **presume upon** their choice."> 1986 Dec. 10 *Times* 1/5.

protest against/at/about/over Protest: According to one count (Hundt 90), the British *Guardian* typically complements *protest* by a preposition: *against* 45.5 percent, *at* 26.5 percent, *about* 20 percent, *over* 6 percent, and with a nominal only 2 percent of the time; American, on the other hand, complements with a nominal 97 percent of the time, and with the preposition *against* by only 3 percent. <They were **protesting about** my proposed new legislation.> 1981 Lynn and Jay 122. <More than 200 French removal vans choked the centre of Paris yesterday . . . to **protest against** new public allowance cuts for families moving house.> 1986 Oct. 30 *Times* 7/3–6. <Those who . . . **protested over** its waste . . . can say a simple hurrah.> 1999 Mar. 17 *Times* 20/3. <. . . a consultant gynaecologist was **protesting at** a reduction in the number of beds for women patients.> 2005 Jan. 14 *Daily Telegraph* 27/2.

reckon to/on CIC American texts have no tokens. "have a specified view or opinion of: *What do you **reckon on** this place?*" (*NODE*). <What do you **reckon to** the old boy? Think he was genuine?> 2000 Granger 280.

sit on a working party CIC British texts have 31.9 iptmw of *working party* and 0.3 of *on* before it; American texts have 0.2 of the noun but none with a preceding preposition. <. . . members would normally expect to **sit** . . . ***on* a** . . . **working party**.> 2001 Apr. *English Today* 30/1.

speak to *Speak to* is the norm in both varieties, but it is 7 times more frequent than *speak with* in CIC British texts and only 2 times more frequent in American. In the BNC also, *speak to* is between 7 and 8 times more frequent than *speak with*. Cf. Swan 1995, 553.

stay to ***a meal*** Stay for *a meal* <They **stay to** tea and supper.> 1988 Brookes and Fraenkel 4.

subscribe for Subscribe to: CIC British texts have 3.5 iptmw of *subscribe for* and 35.6 of *subscribe to*; American texts have 0.2 and 68.1 respectively. <The thrust of the privatisation campaigns has been to persuade individuals to **subscribe for** shares.> 1991 journal CIC.

train to success Train for success <**Train to** Success / Diploma Courses in Commercial Typing / Word Processing> 1989 Sept. 4 *Girl about Town* 28/1.

whip round Make an informal collection of funds from <She . . . **whipped round** the family, parents, uncles and aunts, bullied a bank manager, and produced enough to buy and furnish a boarding house.> 1987 Bawden 8.

work at ***something*** *Work at* is a characteristic British option to *work on* (*CGEL* 9.46n): "She is working at her new play." For Americans *work at* may imply resistance, difficulties, obstacles to be overcome: "It's a problem, but I'm working at it!" <. . . a **fourth-class degree** . . . was something of a class-conscious badge of not having **worked at** studies, or having been a swot.> 1976 Grotta-Kurska 35.

work to 1. ***a schedule/plan*** Work by/on/according to <Primary teachers have to **work to** rigid targets set by the Department for Education and Skills.> 2005 Jan. 23 *Independent* (Web edition). 2. ***a person*** Work for/under <Mr Duncan Smith has built a strong team at the top . . . . chosen by and **working to** him.> 2003 July 14 *Times* 16/5.

11.1.8 Verbal complement

11.1.8.1 Gerund

11.1.8.1.1 Catenative gerund

become accepting of Accept <Daniel is gradually **becoming** more **accepting of** his handicap.> 1991 Mar. 10 *Sunday Times* Magazine 49/1–3.

face being arrested Face arrest <Thousands of motorists . . . **face being arrested** this week . . . to collect unpaid parking fines.> 1988 Oct. 16 *Sunday Telegraph* 2/7.

intend ***doing something*** Intend to *do something* <Having got this far I do not **intend** giving up.> 1991 Feb. 2 *Spectator* 16/2.

like ***doing something*** Like to *do something*: Michael Swan (1995, 285) suggests that in British *like doing* implies enjoyment, whereas *like to do* implies habitual choice, as in *I like climbing mountains* and *I like to put the milk in first when I pour tea*. Stig Johansson (1979, 212) concludes that there is a weak tendency for Britons to choose a gerund complement and Americans an infinitive. <Beckham is a nice lad who **likes** being with kids.> 1999 Mar. 17 *Evening Standard* 83/3.

need ***doing*** Need *to be done*: In both acceptability judgments and choice of alternatives, British tends to favor the gerund complement and American the infinitive (Johansson 1979, 212). <P. **needs** editing out.> 1992 Walters 249.

show willing Show oneself willing (to do something) <He asked me to make a private retreat. . . . To **show willing**, I went to a Carmelite monastery.> 1991 Lodge 211.

want ***doing*** **1.** Want to be *done* <We just **want** leaving in peace. Goodbye.> 1990 Byatt 303. **2.** Need to be *done* <You homicidal maniac. You **want** bloody locking up.> 1991 Graham 252. **3.** Want/need to be *done*: In some cases, it is impossible, without larger context, to distinguish between the "desire" and "need" senses of *want*. In some cases, the senses may be indistinguishable; see the discussion of their history above (§ 11.1.1.1.2 WANT *SOMETHING*). <A proper chartered accountant, who is going to **want** paying properly.> 1993 Neel 64.

11.1.8.1.2 Gerund with subject

benefit ***someone doing something*** Benefit *someone* in *doing something* <. . . can Mr Tebbit say whether the agreement on exhaust emissions will **benefit** this country selling cars?> 1985 July 4 *Times* 4/6.

excuse ***someone doing something*** Excuse *someone* for *doing something* <You will **excuse** me speaking, won't you? . . . I wouldn't have done as a rule, of course.> 1977 Barnard 9.

prevent ***someone/something doing something*** Prevent *someone/something* from *doing something*: The option without the preposition *from* is a relatively recent British innovation, not used in American (Mair 1998, 150). <. . . traffic humps are not only damaging ambulances and fire engines but are also slowing them down so much as to **prevent** them doing their work.> 2004 Jan. 4 *Sunday Times* 13/6. Cf. STOP *SOMEONE / SOMETHING DOING SOMETHING* below.

recommend ***someone doing something*** Recommend that *someone do something* <But I would not **recommend** women walking alone at night.> 1987 Feb. 23 *Mirror Weekend* 7/3.

stop ***someone/something doing something*** Stop *someone/something* from *doing something*: British prefers the construction with *from* by a ratio of 3 to 2 (according to 10 examples in the LOB Corpus), but there are no similar *from*-less examples in the Brown Corpus. <. . . he had to blink to **stop** his eyes watering.> 2003 Rowling 117 (*US ed.* stop his eyes from). Cf. PREVENT *SOMEONE/SOMETHING DOING SOMETHING* above.

11.1.8.2 Infinitive

In common-core English, the verbs *dare* and *help* can be complemented by an infinitive with or without a preceding *to*: *They dared/helped (to) solve the puzzle.*

The infinitive may also have a separate subject or not: *They dared/helped (their friends) to solve the puzzle. Helped* may also be complemented by a *to*-less infinitive with a subject: *They helped their friends solve the puzzle. Dare* is less likely to be so complemented: ?*They dared their friends solve the puzzle.*

However, these options are not used equally by the two varieties. According to a corpus-based study (*LGSWE* 735), both varieties prefer the bare infinitive over the *to*-infinitive, but American does so more strongly. After *help*, American preference for the bare infinitive is greater than 9:1 in conversation, and 14.5:1 in news sources. By contrast, British preference is 4:1 and 3:1, respectively. Moreover, the preference for bare infinitives over *to*-infinitives grew over the three decades of 1961–91 in both British and American English (Mair 1998, 148–9).

11.1.8.2.1 Catenative infinitive

In common-core English, when a verb is complemented by a subjectless infinitive, the infinitive is usually preceded by *to*. The following, however, seem characteristic of British.

accept to *do something* Accept an offer to *do something*; agree to *do something* <Olivier . . . had **accepted to** do [the film] *Term of Trial* because he had been offered nothing better.> 1994 Oct. 1 *Times* Weekend 1/4.

afford to install *something* Afford *something*; afford the installation *of something* <. . . she **had afforded to install** a proper open fire.> 1991 Dickinson 5.

be to do with See § 11.1.8.2.2.

begin to *do something* Begin *doing something*: Although the infinitive complement is the majority choice in both British and American, American has a higher percentage of gerund complements, and that percentage has been increasing, especially in the press (Mair 1998, 151). Cf. START TO below.

come to think Come to think of it: The long form is the norm in common-core English, and the short form rare. <And perhaps there'd been a streak of puritanism in Eamonn's Irishness, because **come to think**, he couldn't remember Eamonn ever making that sort of joke.> 1994 Freeling 17.

could do to *do something* Would like to *do something*: This construction is rare. <Please – yeah, please try to make it, will you? I really **could do to** see you.> 1989 Daniel 74.

enjoy to *do something* Enjoy *doing something* <We thought you would **enjoy to** have Ianthe Hoskins herself come and talk to us.> 1987 chair introducing a London lecture.

feel to *have* Feel that *one has* <Each of us **feels** in our ordinary being **to** have a unitary consciousness.> 1986 Oct. London lecture.

invest to save Invest in order to save <The trouble is that the Treasury and the MoD never learnt to **invest to save.**> 1991 Feb. 16 *Daily Telegraph* 4/6.

know to *do something* Know enough to *do something*: The construction with *enough* is more than twice as frequent in CIC American texts as in British. <Dunkirk showed the Brits . . . as game-players who **know to** give luck a chance.> 1984 Smith 83.

look to *be/do something* Seem to *be/do something* <It **looked to** have got it all right.> 1989 July 23 *Sunday Telegraph* 28/7.

look to *do something* Hope/expect/work to *do something*: In 1990 Philip Howard (*Word in Time* 44) called this use a recent innovation from sports jargon. <Brighton is now **looking to** achieve city status, after merging with its neighbouring local authority.> 1996 July 24 *Times* 20/4.

omit to *do something* Omit *doing something*; fail/neglect to *do something*: This construction occurs 5 times in the LOB Corpus but only once in Brown. CIC has only 0.1 iptmw in British texts, but none in American. The Algeo corpus has some 15 examples from popular fiction and periodicals. <. . . she **omitted to** tell the police it was there.> 1992 Walters 51.

ordered to be *done*, **be** Be ordered *done* This doubly passive verb construction, as in *The incinerator was ordered to be closed immediately*, is more usual in British than in American; CIC British texts have 6.9 iptmw of it, and American texts 1.2. An American analog, as in *The incinerator was ordered closed immediately*, has no tokens in some 400 CIC British citations of *ordered*, but a comparable number of American citations include 4.3 iptmw.

reckon to *do something* Think/intend to *do something*: *Reckon* is more frequent in British use than in American; CIC British texts have 522.3 iptmw, and American texts have 16.7. Use of the verb in the sense "believe, suppose" is dialectal in American English, chiefly Southern and South Midland (*DARE*). CIC has 2.5 iptmw of *reckon to* in British texts and none in American texts. < . . . so she's **reckoning to** spend most of her time sailing.> 1984 Caudwell 83.

require to *do something* Need to *do something*: *Require* in the sense "need" with an infinitive complement is a construction with no examples in the Brown Corpus, but 9 in LOB. CIC has 10.2 iptmw of *require(s) to* in British texts and 2.7 in American. <He [Lord Chief Justice Taylor] said: "Judges do **require to** have decent vacations."> 1993 Feb. 7 *Sunday Times* 22/5.

seen to, be Appear to: CIC has 124.5 iptmw in British texts and 24.4 in American. <. . . it's a line [of merchandise] that we cannot **be seen to** be undercut on.> 1994 Oct. 5 *Times* 21/1.

settle to *do something* Settle on *doing something* <Lucia had **settled to** leave Riseholme without the least thought of what injury she inflicted on him.> 1931 Benson 159.

sound to *be something* Sound like / as though *clause* <. . . you **sound to** have been very moderate with him.> 1990 Hardwick 39.

start to *do something* Start *doing something*: British uses both complementations, about equally; American prefers the gerund and that preference has been growing, especially in press reports (Mair 1998, 152). <Any minute now

the telephones would **start to** ring with complaints from car owners.> 1993 Mason 97. Cf. BEGIN TO above.

think to *do something* Intend to *do something*; think about *doing something*: The construction is about 50 percent more frequent in British than in American CIC texts. <The boys took it back to their home in Clapton, where they wiped it down, and **thought to** keep it.> 1995 June 8 *London Review of Books* 8/3.

want to *do something* Need to *do something*: <You don't **want to** worry about that.> 1991 Cleeves 195.

11.1.8.2.2 Infinitive with subject

The verb *want* is complemented by an infinitive with a subject in common-core English: *They want us to meet only twice a year.* In some American dialects, *want* may be complemented by a *that*-clause: *They want that we should meet only twice a year* (*CamGEL* 1422).

be (anything/more/nothing/something) to do with Have (anything/more/nothing) to do with: In this construction, the norm in common-core English is the verb *have*. Use of the verb *be* is a recent Briticism, appearing in less than 20 percent of the tokens in the BNC (Peters 2004, 380). A random check of the *OED* text found 100 tokens of *have* and none of *be* for this construction. In the more recent texts of CIC, however, the *be* construction is gaining ground, accounting for more than 33 percent of the tokens in British texts. In CIC American texts, the *be* construction accounts for only 6 percent of the whole, and *have* for 94 percent. <Tough luck. **It's nothing to do with** us.> 2005 Jan. 11 BBC News24. <It **is to do with** common sense.> 2005 Jan. 16 BBC1 *Breakfast with Frost*.

know *someone do something* Know *someone* to *do something*: Complementation of *know* by a *to*-less infinitive occurs in British English in the perfect aspect. <I'd never **known** him lose his temper before.> *CamGEL* 1244.

permit *someone* be *affected* Permit *someone* to be *affected* <. . . a flimsily clad female "spirit" would . . . glide between members of the audience, **permitting** herself **be** groped in the process.> 1991 Feb. 7 *Midweek* 17/1.

recommend *someone* to *do something* Recommend (that) *someone do something*: This British construction corresponds to an American mandative subjunctive; its oldest date in the *OED* is 1856. The construction is entered without comment in *LDOCE*. <Mrs Barefoot . . . would certainly **recommend** younger women **to** look ahead.> 1993 Feb. 1 *Times* 12/4.

11.1.8.3 Participle

need done Need to be done <She and her husband . . . have just bought their house and there's lots **needing done**.> 1987 May 10 (Scotland) *Sunday Post* 12/3.

11.1.8.4 Verbless nonfinite clause

allow *someone* **back to** Allow *someone* to go back to/*someone* back in(to): This verbless clause structure is rare in British English, but has no tokens in CIC American texts. <My father . . . told him that if he didn't **allow** me **back to** school in whatever colour socks I liked he would protest to his MP.> 1985 Townsend 83.

11.1.9 Clausal complement

Some verbs can be complemented either by a noun phrase or by a *that*-clause. For the following verbs as a group, CIC British texts have clause complementation 3.6 times more frequently than American texts do. The subordinating conjunction *that* is optional.

absorb that *something is the case* <Girls, on the other hand, **absorb** early on **that** in the most profound sense they must rely on themselves as there is no-one to take care of them emotionally.> 1986 Oct. 7 *Today* 15/4.

accept that *something is the case* <Michael Howard and Mr Letwin **accept that** moves have to be made.> 2005 Jan. 14 *Daily Telegraph* 1/3.

appreciate that *something is the case* <The "tankies" **appreciate** they are going to war and so treat the vehicles better.> 1991 Feb. 16 *Daily Telegraph* 4/5.

denounce that *something is the case* <This is a country where humbug is a great virtue. You **denounce** something is being done and rush to read about it.> 1990 Critchfield 424.

reinforce that *something is the case* <John Broome . . . has **reinforced that** the Battersea scheme will remain dominated by the leisure park concept.> 1989 Sept. 12 *Evening Standard* 17/1.

Similarly, *depend* can be complemented by a preposition (*on, upon*) or by an indirect interrogative clause. In CIC British texts, the clause is 4 times more frequent than it is in American texts.

depend *what happens* <I think it **depends** what they're offered.> 2003 Rowling 81.

11.1.10 No complement

Occasionally, verbs that would normally have some complementation are used without any. The lack of complementation is of several different sorts. The complement may be understood: *She's been (here/there)*. Or there may be a change in role relationship, so that a verb's subject is what, in other uses, would be its object: *She closed the door / The door closed*. The latter sort, sometimes called "ergative," may be more frequent in British than in American (McMillion 1998).

been Been here; come <Later maybe, after Audrey's **been**.> 1993 Smith 97.

deliver Be delivered <The delivery of first-class mail within 24 hours is a hit and miss affair and it is not unusual for properly addressed and pre-stamped mail to take three days **to deliver**.> 1988 Sept. 25 *Manchester Guardian Weekly* 2/5.

feature Be featured <Ancient craft restored to at least river-worthiness will be back in their element. . . . Modern craft, too, **will feature**.> 1986 Oct. 30 *Times* 16/2.

go Go off; make a sound <Your alarm's **gone**.> 1991 Dickinson 165.

make Be made <Ransome has always had a key to the gates and although we knew that fresh keys were **making** we didn't think they would be forthcoming so soon.> 1937 Innes, *Seven* 180.

notice Be noticed <They've got half a dozen already so one more won't **notice**.> 1987 Graham 44.

prepare Be prepared <Even now, strange events are **preparing**.> 1937 Innes, *Hamlet* 12.

settle Settle down/in <He was a good worker and he steadied down as he got older. He seems to have **settled** well, to have fitted in.> 1993 Cleeves 147.

tidy Tidy (*something*) up: In a random sample of 143 tokens of the verb *tidy* (and its inflected forms), the BNC has 89 tokens of *tidy (something) up*, 37 of simple *tidy something* (*tidy a house/room/drawer/etc.*), 9 of *tidy away*, and 8 of *tidy* as intransitive. <Give lavender bushes a light trim now to **tidy**, but leave their main cut until the spring.> 1994 Oct. 1 *Times* Weekend 11/4.

11.2 Complementation of nouns

11.2.1 Prepositional complement

advantage from/in/of *doing something* Advantage to *doing something*: CIC texts have comparable proportions of the four prepositions *from, in, of*, and *to* after *advantage* in British and American texts, with not more than one percentage point difference between the two varieties (respective percentages of British/American: 1.2/0.3, 9.9/9.0, 81.4/82.2, and 7.5/8.5). However, when the object of the preposition is a gerund, *to* is notably more frequent in American texts, and the other three prepositions are somewhat more frequent in British texts (percentages as before: 1.4/0.5, 41.0/35.5, 49.0/40.0, and 8.6/24.0). <For Mr Kinnock there are **advantages from** being brought back into the fold.> 1991 Feb. 9 *Daily Telegraph* 5/2. <There are additional **advantages in** setting up a timeshare.> 1989 nonfiction CIC. <. . . students see significant **advantages of** entering the workforce after two instead of three years.> 1989 Aug. 5 *Times* 10/7.

appointment to *the sovereign*, by This use does not occur in American English. <By **Appointment** To Her Majesty Queen Elizabeth II / Soft

Drink Manufacturers / Schweppes International Limited / London> 1989 Sept. 17 notice on a can.

appreciation of Appreciation for: In CIC British texts, *of* occurs in 94 percent and *for* in 6 percent of the tokens; in American texts, in 55 and 45 percent, respectively. <Then he sits nervously twining his long fingers until I walk in and express **appreciation of** his efforts.> 1989 Daniel 2.

audience of Audience with <The Right Hon Margaret Thatcher, MP (Prime Minister and First Lord of the Treasury) had an **audience of** The Queen this evening.> 1985 May 1 *Times* 18/1.

bruising to Bruises on: In CIC British texts, *bruising to* is nearly twice as frequent as *bruising on* (2.0 to 1.1 iptmw); *bruising* does not occur with either preposition in American texts. *Bruises on* is preferred over *bruises to* in both varieties, somewhat more in American (British 3.6 iptmw to 0.4, American 4.6 to 0.4). <. . . she came home with bad **bruising to** her handicapped leg.> 1994 Sept. 30 *Daily Telegraph* 2/4.

burns to Burns on: In CIC texts, national preferences for the two prepositions after *burns* is opposite (British *to* 3.4 iptmw and *on* 1.5, American 1.7 and 3.9, respectively). <He was taken to hospital with **burns to** his hands and knees.> 1995 Aug. 28 *Independent* 2/8.

chat to Chat with: CIC British texts have more than 2.0 iptmw of *to* after the noun *chat*, but American texts have none. <I had a brief **chat to** him to say that I hoped they turned up and that the kids returned safely home.> 2003 Nov. 7 *Daily Express* 6/5.

change to Change in < . . . the editor . . . is famous for her last-minute **changes to** the mix.> 1991 Feb. 10 *Independent* Sunday Review 5/1.

claim to *something* Claim for *something* <These figures will have to be specific to items such as . . . **claims to** reliefs.> 1994 Oct. 1 *Times* 29/3.

closure on *a business*, make an emergency Close *a business* as an emergency measure: The construction is rare. <Magistrates have also **made an emergency closure on** Foodworth, a large supermarket.> 1987 Mar. *Camden Magazine* (local London borough), no. 46, 7/3.

contribution to Contribution for: CIC has a slightly larger percentage of *for* versus *to* after *contribution* in American texts (4.4 versus 95.6) than in British (2.3 versus 97.6). < . . . his efforts to raise **contributions** from other countries **to** the British effort in the Gulf.> 1991 Feb. 8 *Daily Telegraph* 2/1.

decision over Decision on/about <Without having a **decision over** it, we had to abide by the university regulation.> SEU s3-4.966-8.

defence to Defense against <. . . merely being depressed did not amount to a **defence to** that charge.> 1991 Feb. 13 *Daily Mail* 2/3.

delight to Delight in <So skilfully was I able to blend [the dog] Addo into the plot, though, that even Nicol eventually began to enjoy the audience's **delight to** him.> 1994 Oct. 5 *Times* 14/2.

difference of Difference in <I greatly doubt whether anyone but an expert can tell the **difference of** flavour between a pasteurized cheese and the unpasteurized varieties.> 1987 July *Illustrated London News* 73/1.

difference to, make ***a*** Make a difference in: In CIC British texts, *to* is 7.4 times more frequent than *in* for this construction; in American texts, *in* is 2.2 times more frequent than *to*. <That [being an Arabic speaker] **makes a** distinct **difference to** his reporting.> 2005 Jan. 16 BBC1 *Breakfast with Frost*.

divorce to *Divorce to*, rather than *from*, is rare in British use, the only examples being journalistic. <They popped into a supermarket but the petite star [Felicity Kendall] was saying nothing about her **divorce to** Michael Rudman.> 1991 Mar. 2 *Daily Express* 15/3.

doubt at/of *Doubt about* is the norm in common-core English. But CIC British texts have 3 times as many tokens of *doubt at* as American texts do, and 4.4 times as many of *doubt of*. <Hilary Steinberg saw the film in the making and has no **doubt at** its brilliance.> 1986 Aug. 28 *Hampstead Advertiser* 17/2–3. <Convicted defendants were left in no **doubt of** his disapproval.> 1995 newspaper CIC.

edge on ***one's voice*** Edge to *one's voice*: In this construction *to* is the norm in common-core English. CIC British texts have only 0.1 iptmw of *on*; American texts have none. <The sudden sharp **edge on** Morse's voice made Walters look up anxiously.> 1981 Dexter 83.

end on it, an An end to it: In this construction *to* is the norm in common-core English. CIC British texts have only 0.1 iptmw of *on*; American texts have none. <I'll not do it and there's **an end on it**.> 1989 Daniel 71.

example to Example for: CIC British texts have 61 percent with *to* and 39 percent with *for*; American texts have 27 percent with *to* and 73 percent with *for*. <Club officials should set an **example to** their players!> 1987 Jan. 29 *Deptford & Peckham Mercury* 10/1.

experience of Experience with: CIC British texts favor *of* by 2.8 times, and American texts favor *with* by 2.3 times. <I now have some **experience of** the subject.> 1999 Mar. 8 *Guardian* 16/2.

files of Files on: This construction is rare. <West End vice squad officers closed their **files** yesterday **of** "Operation Circus".> 1987 Feb. 18 *Daily Telegraph* 3/3.

fuss of, make a Make a fuss over: The construction with either preposition is rarer in CIC American texts (0.9 iptmw) than in British (6.4); British texts prefer *of* by 7 to 1, and American texts prefer *over* by 2 to 1. <Get off home as early as you can, and **make a** proper **fuss of** him.> 1993 Mason 147.

grip of Grip on: In this construction *on* is the norm in common-core English. CIC British texts have 3.0 iptmw with *of*; American texts have 0.4. <After just a few seconds, I got a **grip of** myself.> 1997 Sept. 3 CNN British speaker.

guide on Guide to: In this construction *to* is the norm in common-core English. CIC British texts have 1.9 iptmw of *on*; American texts have none. <. . . a complete **guide on** where to find what is particularly timely.> 1997 Apr. *Businesslife* (British Airways) 6.

increase of ***an amount*** **on** ***a time*** Increase of *an amount* over *a time*: In CIC British texts, 71 percent have *on* in this construction and 29 percent have *over*; in American texts all have *over* and none have *on*. <Average starting salaries

have risen . . . to £20,300, an **increase of** 4.1 per cent **on** 2002.> 2003 July 16 *Times* 9/1.

key of *a place* Key to *a place*: In common-core English, *to* is the norm in this construction. CIC British texts have *of* in 2.6 iptmw, and American texts in 0.4. < . . . you must have a **key of** the house.> SEU s1-10.1031.

kick up the backside/arse/bum Kick in the ass; a reproof, esp. one serving as motivation to act: The British and American idioms differ in both the preposition and its object. CIC British texts have *up* in 4.3 iptmw; American in only 0.1. Other objects of *up* in British use include *behind, fundamentals, pants, rear*, and *rump*, of which *pants* and *rear* also occur in American texts after *in*, along with *butt* and *tail*. <Snivelling little oik needs a **kick up the backside**.> 1995 Aug. 29 *Evening Standard* 11/2.

lease of Lease on: CIC British texts have *of* after *lease* 3.2 times more often than *on*; American texts have *on* 2.3 times more often than *of*. <He had . . . the **lease of** the flat.> SEU w16-7.36. **– new lease of life** New lease on life: The phrase is 3 times more popular in British use than in American. In CIC British texts, the ratio between *of* and *on* is 43:1; in American, nearly 1:10. <So bring them out, dust them down, and give them a **new lease of life**.> 2005 Jan. 15 *Daily Telegraph* Weekend 3/6.

legalization on Legalization of: The phrase with *on* is rare. <[Baroness] Warnock, 80, a Lords' cross-bencher . . . helped frame Britain's **legalization on** embryo research.> 2004 Dec. 12 *Sunday Times* 1 1/3–4.

luck on *someone*, bad Bad luck for *someone*: This construction is infrequent in CIC British texts, but there are no tokens of it in American texts. <I think she identified the school with the Union Jack, which was rather **bad luck on** the school.> 1994 Sept. 25 *Sunday Times* Magazine 10/1–2.

member for Representative from: Both noun and preposition differ between the two varieties. <. . . that instinct for survival . . . had kept the **Member for** Arden in Parliament for so long.> 1992 Critchley 27–8. Cf. also MP FOR.

membership of Membership in: CIC British texts have *of* in this construction 7 times as often as *in*; American texts have *in* 33 times as often as *of*. <. . . my **membership of** the London Library eventually determined the direction of my interest.> 2005 Jan. 15 *Daily Telegraph* Books 2/5.

Minister for CIC British texts have *Minister of* (as also in the American analog *Secretary of*) twice as often as *Minister for*, which occurs in 30.0 iptmw. <Cornelius Fudge, **Minister for Magic** . . .> 2003 Rowling 537 (*US ed.* of).

misconception on Misconception about: The construction is rare. <There is one very common **misconception on** this.> 1987 Aug. *Illustrated London News* 47/2–4.

MP for CIC British texts have this construction in 91.1 iptmw. The American analog is *Representative from*. <David Harris, the Tory **MP for** St Ives, could bear it no longer.> 1993 Feb. 7 *Sunday Times* 2 3/2. Cf. also MEMBER FOR.

name to *a book* Name on *a book*: The construction with *to* is rare. <Rather jolly to have one's **name to** a book.> 1973 Innes 21.

one thing for it, only The norm in common-core English is *only one thing to do*; CIC has 0.5 iptmw of *only one thing for it* in British texts and none in American. <**Only one thing for it**. He hobbled and hopped across to the telephone and rang Lewis.> 1975 Dexter 79.

pass at *a particular grade* The construction, which is normal in British, does not occur in CIC American texts; if it did one might expect *with* rather than *at*. <The intermediate diploma would be roughly equal to five GCSE **passes at** grade C or better.> 2003 July 16 *Times* 1/3.

pattern to Pattern for: The construction is rare. <. . . activism . . . set a **pattern to** their future lives together.> 1994 Sept. 25 *Sunday Times* Magazine 25/1–2.

preference for, in CIC British texts have 0.9 iptmw; American texts have 0.1. *X in preference for Y* means "not X, but Y, by preference" as in <. . . they avoid salaries **in preference for** commission payments or fees directly related to their performance.> 1994 nonfiction CIC.

processing on Processing of/for: The construction is rare. <Boots Film **Processing** Same Day . . . **on** films handed in before 9.30 am> 1990 May 31 sign outside Boots, Charing Cross Road.

recommendation to CIC British texts have only a few examples with *to* in the sense "for" or "in favor of." *Recommendation for* is the norm. <They dispersed . . . to get a **recommendation to** a security firm.> 1993 Neel 145.

report into The norm in common-core English is *report on* or *investigation into*. CIC British texts have 12.1 iptmw of *report into*; American texts have 0.7. <Ministers are currently completing a green paper on children at risk, in response to the Laming **report into** the death of Victoria Climbié.> 2003 June 25 *Guardian* international ed. 17/1.

respect of, in CIC British texts have 96.6 iptmw of *in respect of* and 66.0 of *with respect to*; American texts have, respectively, 1.2 and 102.9. < . . . the position taken by local government **in respect of** community care.> 1989 Aug. 9 *Times* 15/3.

return of *investment* This construction with *of* is rare; the norm is *on*. < . . . donations which can yield a threefold **return of** investment.> 1987 Jan. 20 *Guardian* 1/6.

return of post This construction is exclusively British (2.0 iptmw), which also uses *return post* and *return mail* (0.2 each), the latter being the American choice at 0.5 iptmw. <. . . write to me by **return of post**.> SEU w7-9.38.

revulsion of CIC British texts have only 0.1 iptmw of this combination, and American texts none. The norm is *revulsion against*. <. . . environmental leaders have begun to reassess their **revulsion of** nuclear power.> 1989 Aug. 25 *International Herald Tribune* 1/1.

room for manoeuvre CIC British texts have 7.0 iptmw with *for* and 1.5 with *to*. American texts have 1.5 of *room for maneuver* and 5.0 with *to*. <Mr Brown may seem to have plenty of **room for manoeuvre**.> 1999 Mar. 6 *Economist* 36/1.

Secretary for *cabinet office* The norm in common-core English is *Secretary of*, which is notably more frequent in CIC American than British texts (362.9 versus 150.9 iptmw). Thus although the frequency of *Secretary for* is not very different in the two varieties (American 5.4, British 6.7), *Secretary for* accounts for only 1.5 percent of the two options in American texts but for 4.2 percent of them in British texts. <**Secretary for** Employment.> 1987 Feb. 4 *Evening Standard* 13/4–5. Cf. MINISTER FOR above.

substitution of *X* **by/with** *Y* This construction appears 2.5 times more often in British than in American CIC texts, and with four variations in British versus two in American. The norm in common-core English is *the* ***substitution of*** *X* ***for*** *Y*, with a minor variation, *the* ***substitution of*** *X* ***in place of*** *Y*, in both of which X replaces Y. They are the only such constructions in CIC American texts. CIC British texts have two other constructions: *the* ***substitution of*** *X* ***by*** *Y* and *the* ***substitution of*** *X* ***with*** *Y*, in both of which X is replaced by Y, the reverse of the usual relationship. <. . . the **substitution of** Jeffers **by** Moore was greeted with boos.> 2000 newspaper CIC. <Most changes . . . are the **substitution of** old-fashioned words **with** others regarded as new.> 1987 June 7 *Sunday Telegraph* 20.

trawl of CIC British texts have 6.6 iptmw of the noun *trawl*, most metaphorical; American texts have 1.2, all references to fishing, and none for *trawl of*. <. . . they will run software checks – such as a **trawl of** the electoral register.> 2004 Dec. 14 *Daily Telegraph* 31/3.

value for money Value; one's money's worth: CIC British texts have 76.4 iptmw of *value for money*; American texts have 0.5. <. . . we're not giving **value for money**.> 2003 James 38.

week on *day of the week* Week from *day of the week*: CIC British texts have 10.9 iptmw with *on*; American texts have none. <. . . school resumes after half-term a **week on** Monday.> 1993 Feb. 13 *Daily Telegraph* 3/2.

win on Win in: This construction is rare, but the few tokens in CIC British texts have *on*, and the few in American texts have *in*. <'But I'll tell you what would have helped her. . . .' [¶] 'A **win on** the National Lottery?'> 1996 Dexter 67.

word on *something* The construction with *on* is rare; in CIC British texts it is usually *word about something*; American texts have no tokens of either form. <May we have a **word on** this?> SEU s3-4.583.

11.2.1.1 With verbal object

opportunity of *doing something* Opportunity to *do something*: *Opportunity to do* is the norm, but *opportunity of doing* is a secondary British alternative (Peters 2004, 396), of which CIC British texts have 53.2 iptmw and American texts 6.9. <One must never let slip an **opportunity of** teasing the next man about his geographical origins. Geordie, Scouse, Taff, Paddy, Jock.> 1962 Lodge 65.

preparation for *doing something* Preparation to *do something*: CIC British texts have 4.7 iptmw of the construction; American texts have 2.6. <. . . an IRA man who worked as a police informer was being interrogated in **preparation for** being shot.> 1991 Feb. 20 *Times* 8/6.

11.2.2 Verbal complement

omission to ***do something*** Not *doing something*: This relatively rare construction is 3 times more frequent in CIC British texts than American (0.6 to 0.2 iptmw). <The **omission to** ask Stephen was another instance of Mrs Annick's tact.> 1970 Johnson 148.

something **to be going on with** *Something* to work/deal with: *Enough* and *plenty* are frequent as heads in this construction. CIC has 0.6 iptmw in British texts and none in American. <With both a dead body and a missing person on his plate, he had more than enough **to be going on with**.> 1996 Graham 106.

11.2.3 Clausal complement

time (that) ***someone did something*** Time (that) *someone does / (should) do something*: In a small sample (28 tokens) of CIC British texts with this construction, the ratio of preterit to nonpreterit verbs was 8:1; in a smaller sample (13 tokens) of American texts, the ratio was 1:2. <It is high **time** the local education authorities got their act together on these issues and agreed some guidelines.> 1986 Oct. 6 *Times* 12/7.

11.3 Complementation of adjectives

11.3.1 Prepositional complement

In common-core English, *enough* and *sufficient* may be followed by a prepositional phrase with *for*, as in *They have enough/sufficient money for a taxi* or by an infinitive complement, as in *They have enough/sufficient money to take a taxi*. American English has, as a minority option, a *that*-clause as complement (*CamGEL* 396; Peters 2004, 183): *They have enough/sufficient money that they can take a taxi*. This option is also available for *enough* as a pronoun and *enough* and *sufficiently* as qualifiers (*CamGEL* 969).

bored of *Bored with* is the usual collocation in common-core English, but *bored of* is an option (Peters 2004, 76), of which CIC British texts have 3.1 iptmw and American texts 0.7. <Gary . . . got **bored of** having so little to do.> 2004 Dec. 17 *Independent* 10/3.

comparable with Although *compared with* and *compared to* have similar relative frequencies in British and American, and *with* is preferred in both, *comparable with/to* is different, *to* being preferred in both varieties, but much more strongly in American. In CIC British texts, *to* is more frequent than *with* by

1.8 times, but in American texts, by 11.7 times. <They [civil service jobs] should be for fixed-term contracts, with pay **comparable with** the private sector.> 1991 Jan. 31 *Times* 13/2. Cf. § 11.1.1.2 COMPARE.

concerned at/for Concerned about: CIC has the following British/American iptmw for *about* 133.3/375.3, *at* 17.1/3.5, *for* 14.5/9.5. <The Prince . . . has become **concerned at** some of the opinions of his unpaid adviser.> 1987 Mar. 13 *Evening Standard* 6/1–2. <Thompson is now secretly **concerned for** his health.> 1993 Feb. 7 *Sunday Times* 5 2/3.

cover in Cover with: American generally prefers *with* and British *in*. < . . . the far end of Alice's office with the walls **covered in** bookshelves and her desk piled with proofs.> 1990 James 126.

different to Different than: Both British and American also use the prescribed *different from* (cf. *CGEL* 16.69n). According to one count (Hundt 1998, 87), the percentage of tokens in which *different* is followed by various prepositions in the British *Guardian* and the American *Miami Herald* is as follows: *from*, British 89 percent, American 65 percent; *than*, British 3 percent, American 35 percent; *to*, British 8 percent, American none. A study based on a corpus of American English spoken by professional people (Iyeiri, Yaguchi, and Okabe 2004) found 98 tokens of *different from* and 91 tokens of *different than* (followed by a nominal). CIC British texts have the following iptmw of *from, to*, and *than* after *different*: respectively, 242.7, 44.3, and 5.0; American texts have 234.2, 1.0, and 91.1. <. . . the sort of detailed information that patients need . . . will be **different to** the kind of information the NHS thinks patients *ought* to want.> 2003 July 16 *Times* 16/7. Cf. § 11.4 DIFFERENTLY TO.

down to Up to; be the responsibility of <The ethics of sex selection [of babies] should not be **down to** the public.> 2003 Nov. 12 *Times* 22/6.

due to Due: British is said to favor the prepositional complement in *$750 is now due to you* and American the nominal complement in *$750 is now due you* (*CamGEL* 546).

earlier to Earlier than <. . . the arching braces . . . are of an **earlier** type **to** those in the kitchen block.> 1990 Aug. 15 *Daily Telegraph* 26/5.

exempt *something* Exempt from *something* <More than 40 soldiers . . . applied to be **exempt** service.> 1991 Feb. 5 *Daily Telegraph* 1/1.

fair on Fair to: CIC has 8.2 iptmw with *on* in British texts and 0.4 in American. <. . . it is not **fair on** the little people to make them sit quietly while great-uncle Tony and his friends rabbit on about Iraq and the European constitution.> 2003 July 9 *Times* 2/3–4.

fed up of Fed up with: CIC has 6.2 iptmw with *of* in British texts and 0.5 in American. <It's a different form of exercise, good for the horses who are **fed up of** their daily runs.> 1988 Apr. *In Britain* 51/1.

furious at Furious with: CIC British texts have 11.4 iptmw of *at* and 9.7 of *with*; American texts have respectively 4.8 and 5.1. <. . . she's **furious at** them.> 2000 Rowling 52.

good on Good for: CIC British texts have a few tokens with *on*; American texts have none. <Nick said they'd stolen the name from a manor house in Somerset. . . . If so, **good on** them.> 2001 Drabble 146.

good to *one's* word As good as *one's* word <He vowed he would return with a vengeance. He has been **good to** his **word**.> 1991 Jan. 29 *Daily Telegraph* 34/5.

identical with *Identical to* is the norm in common-core English, but *identical with* is an option, especially in British (Peters 2004). CIC British texts have half as many tokens of *identical with* as of *identical to*; American texts have only a third.

last but *cardinal number* CIC British texts have 2.5 iptmw of *last but one* and 0.4 of *next to last*; American texts have respectively 0.1 and 7.6. <The **last** week **but** one in May.> 1969 Rendell 69. Cf. NEXT BUT, SECOND (TO) LAST below, § 8.1 BUT, FROM LAST, § 8.2.2 SECOND LAST.

lined in The preposition *with* is the norm for this construction in both British and American, but CIC British texts have 2.1 iptmw of *lined in* and American texts 0.8.

nervous of Nervous about: CIC British texts have more than 2 times as many tokens with *about* as with *of*; American texts have more than 55 times as many. <We are **nervous of** financial advice –> 2005 Jan. 15 *Daily Telegraph* B 10/6.

next but *number* CIC British texts have 3.3 iptmw; American texts have 0.3. <I happen to live **next** door **but** one to a bicycle shop.> 1987 Aug. *Illustrated London News* 14/1–2. Cf. LAST BUT above, SECOND (TO) LAST below, § 8.1 BUT, FROM LAST, § 8.2.2 SECOND LAST.

nuts on *Nuts about* is the norm in common-core English, but CIC British texts have a few tokens of *nuts on*; American texts have none. <I got my Eton Schol on a Greek epigram I translated right when all the others made a mess of it, because the Captain was **nuts on** the *Anthology*.> 1983 Dickinson 60–1.

oblivious of Oblivious to: *Oblivious of* is the older form but is being replaced by *oblivious to*, which is now the norm in common-core English, with nearly 3 times as many tokens in CIC British texts and nearly 8 times as many in American texts. <Audley was . . . **oblivious of** all nuances when it suited him.> 1986 Price 281.

opposite to *Opposite to* is more frequent than *opposite from* in both varieties, but 19 times so in CIC British texts and only 3 times so in American. <The three floors of the building are connected by a lift shaft situated at the **opposite** side of the atrium **to** the entrance.> 2001 Lodge 44.

reserved to *Reserved for* is the norm in common-core English, but *reserved to* is twice as frequent in British as in American. < . . . names usually **reserved to** the upper classes.> 1969 Rendell 54.

second (to) last Next to last: CIC British texts have nearly 9 times as many tokens of *second last* as American texts do. <We pass Dronero at the **second last** [jump].> 1989 Daniel 25. <There it was, on the **second to** back page.> 1991 Greenwood 187. Cf. LAST BUT, NEXT BUT above.

separate to *Separate from* is the norm, but CIC British texts have 0.7 iptmw of *separate to*; American texts have none. <Practicalities and ease of living also call for . . . showers **separate to** the bath where possible.> 1991 Feb. 25 *Nine to Five* 20/2. Cf. DIFFERENT TO above.

shy of 1. Shy with/around <He . . . was **shy of** women and his idea of fun was a four-week holiday with his wife at a hotel in Eastbourne.> 1989 Oct. 7–13 *Economist* 109/1–2. **2**. Shy about <She's not **shy of** discussing her sex life.> 1996 magazine CIC.

smitten with/by The prepositions are used about equally in British, but CIC American texts have twice as many tokens of *with* as of *by*.

starved of Starved for: CIC British texts have 53 times as many tokens with *of* as with *for*; American texts have 9 times as many with *for* as with *of*. <. . . the poor guy must have been **starved of** affection by his ruthless career wife.> 1995 Sept. *Marie Claire* 46/2.

suited to ***something*** Suited for *something*: In general CIC British texts use terms like *suited, suitable*, and *suitability* 2 to 4 times more often than American texts do; the exception is the combination *suited for*, which is 1.7 times more frequent in American. <Mr Harris, still in his mid-thirties, appears ideally **suited to** the job.> 2003 Nov. 13 *Times* 1/5.

supportive to Supportive of: CIC British texts have *to* in 1.0 iptmw and *of* in 12.3; American texts have no tokens with *to* and 49.2 with *of*. <I made a deliberate effort not to contact our friends, so they would be **supportive to** Sarah.> 1993 Feb. *Woman's Journal* 44/3.

tight on Tight at <He needed, he decided, to get some weight off, his jaw and neck had thickened, and his shirt was **tight on** the collar.> 1996 Neel 21.

unfair on *Unfair to* is the norm in both varieties, but CIC British texts have 3.6 iptmw with *on*; American texts have none. <It would be very **unfair on** Mark to read anything too deep into that.> 1994 Sept. 20 *Times* 3/2.

violent to ***someone*** Violent with *someone*: CIC British texts have about the same numbers of *to* and *with* in this construction; American texts have *with* 6 times as often as *to*. <Had he ever been **violent to** you before?> 2003 James 202.

worst ***thing*** **for** ***years*** Worst *thing* in *years*: CIC British texts have similar numbers with *for* and *in*; American texts have 45 times as many with *in*. <The bug recently led to Australia suffering its **worst** flu outbreak **for** five years.> 2003 Nov. 7 *Daily Express* 17/5.

11.3.1.1 With verbal object

nervous of ***doing something*** *Nervous about* is the norm in common-core English, but CIC British texts have 7.6 iptmw with *of* and American 0.6. <. . . he's **nervous of** going to see a doctor.> 1991 Feb. 4 *Nine to Five* 6/3.

terrible with ***doing something*** Terrible about / when it comes to *doing something*: CIC British texts have *with* in 1.2 iptmw; American texts have none. <[British actor:] I'm **terrible with** talking about myself.> 2004 Apr. 2 *USA Today* 2D/1–2.

11.3.2 Adverbial particle complement

packed out Packed: CIC British texts have 4.3 iptmw with *out*; American texts have none. <It's a rabbit-warren of a place and it was **packed out**.> 1992 Granger 170.

11.3.3 Verbal complement

accustomed to ***do something*** Accustomed to *doing something*: CIC British texts have similar numbers of infinitive and *to* + a gerund complement after *accustomed* (respectively 53 and 47 percent); American texts have the *to* + a gerund complement overwhelmingly (94 percent to 6 percent infinitives). <He was **accustomed to** work long hours.> 1940 Shute 165.

concerned to ***do something*** Concerned about *doing something*: CIC British texts have a ratio of 5.3:1 for complements of *concerned* by an infinitive versus *about* + a gerund; American texts have a ratio of 4:1 in favor of *about* + a gerund. <The Chancellor . . . is **concerned to** keep the lid on pay.> 1989 July 23 *Sunday Telegraph* 1/2.

far to seek Hard to find: CIC British texts have 1.7 times as many tokens of *far to seek* as American texts do; American texts have 1.7 times as many of *hard to find* as British do. <The reason is not **far to seek**.> 1984 Smith 122.

interested to ***do something*** Interested in *doing something*: CIC British texts have nearly 3 times as many tokens of an infinitive complement after *interested* as of *in* + a gerund; American texts have nearly 2.5 times as many of *in* + a gerund as of an infinitive. < . . . she was **interested to** learn all about her pupil's experience.> 2003 June 14 *Times* 29/6.

worth ***doing something*** CIC British texts have more than twice as many tokens as American texts do (cf. also Swan 1995, 631). <But it is **worth** reminding the braying brigade that the aristocrat treads a narrow path between over-refinement and coarseness.> 1993 Feb. 13 *Daily Telegraph* Weekend 36/3–4.

11.4 Complementation of adverbs

differently to Different(ly) than/from: CIC British texts have 3.5 iptmw of *differently to* and 1.1 of *differently than*; American texts have none of *differently to* and 20.0 of *differently than*. The two varieties are closer in their use of *differently from*: British 12.9 iptmw and American 11.0. <They may want to live **differently to** most people.> 1987 June 16 *Evening Standard* 5/6. Cf. § 11.3.1 DIFFERENT TO.

12 Mandative constructions

A mandative construction consists of a verb, noun, or adjective (personal or impersonal) that expresses an order, direction, requirement, necessity, preference, etc. and is complemented by a subordinate clause whose verb is – variably – modal, present subjunctive, or indicative.

She insists				should leave
Her insistence	+	that he	+	leave
She is insistent				leaves
It is imperative				

It is necessary, when the complement verb is indicative, to distinguish the mandative sense of the governing expressions from the factual sense. That is, *She insists that he leaves* may have either the mandative sense "She insists that he should/must/ought to leave" or the factual sense "She insists that it is a fact that he leaves."

British and American English differ clearly in this construction (Algeo 1992). Several elicitation experiments have substantiated those differences (Johansson 1979, Turner 1980, Nichols 1987, Algeo 1992). Those studies show that –

The modal option (*should leave*) is a frequent choice in British English; it is acceptable but little used in American.

The present subjunctive option (*leave*) is the norm in American English and is a frequent choice in British, especially in passive constructions.

The indicative option (*leaves*) is approximately as frequent a choice in British English as the modal but it is very rare in American.

That is, British English uses all three of the options; American uses primarily the subjunctive but accepts the modal. The indicative option is characteristically British.

In a completion test conducted by Christian Mair on 29 January 1987, 25 students at University College London who were native speakers of British English were asked to complete the sentence *Now that the disarmament talks have been bogged down it is absolutely essential*_______________________________.

Their responses were as follows:

that + a clearly indicative verb	7
that + a verb ambiguous in mood	8
that + a clearly subjunctive verb	3
that + *should*	2
to infinitive	5

This evidence is too restricted to project it to British English as a whole, but it is suggestive. If the verbs that are ambiguous in mood are divided according to the same proportions as those that can be identified, the result is that just over half the respondents used the innovative form of an indicative verb, a fifth used the revived subjunctive, a fifth avoided the question of modality by using the infinitive, and only about a twelfth used the traditional alternative, the *should* modal.

The mandative construction has also been the subject of corpus studies. A comparison of *should* versus subjunctive forms in mandative constructions (Hundt 1998a, 163) shows that in 1961 the Brown corpus favored the subjunctive in 88.1 percent of the cases, whereas LOB favored *should* in 87.1 percent. Some thirty years later, the Frown corpus showed a slight increase in American preference for the subjunctive to 89.5 percent, whereas FLOB showed a decline of preference for the modal to 60.4 percent (with the subjunctive accounting for the other 39.6 percent). These statistics do not include the mandative indicative. It is clear from them, however, that American use of the mandative subjunctive has spread to British, which is now using it in more general contexts than it would have formerly (171).

According to another count by Marianne Hundt (1998, 78) of 252 tokens of mandative constructions in an American newspaper, the *Miami Herald*, 88 percent used the subjunctive, 8 percent modal *should*, and 4 percent the indicative; by contrast, of 262 tokens in a British paper, the *Guardian*, 35 percent used the subjunctive, 55 percent the modal *should*, and 10 percent the indicative.

The mandative indicative is the most characteristically British form, in that it is the rarest in American use and is frequently a source of confusion for Americans, who may interpret tokens of it as either factual statements or as unacceptable. When the mandative indicative is used in British, the verb of the complement clause is usually preterit when the general context is past time or else nonpreterit when the general context is present or future time. Instances of these variants are cited below. In all of the following examples, the first American choice for the verb of the subordinate mandative clause is likely to be a present subjunctive form.

12.1 Mandative present indicative

12.1.1 After verbs

advise <Some other customers . . . may well have been . . . there to purchase replacement filters which the manufacturers **advise are** changed every three months.> 1998 June 20 *Times* Weekend 3/4–5.

argue <Nobody would **argue** that at the end of every day every stall-holder solemnly **writes** down the day's takings . . . and **forwards** the figures to his local Revenue officer.> 1976 Mar. 17 *Punch* 443/2–3.

demand <Success in the movies has **demanded** that Rachel Weisz . . . **acts** as if she is in a Japanese game show.> 1999 Mar. 22 *Times* 20/7.

insist <New York's Mayor Giuliani . . . **insists** that crime **is** fully reported. [i.e., "must be" not "in fact is"]> 1998 Jan. 8 *Times* 18/2.

propose <Heseltine is **proposing** the counters division, which runs the [post] offices, **remains** in the public sector.> 1994 Sept. 25 *Sunday Times* 1 5/2.

recommend <I'll **recommend** she **gets** the crime prevention lot over and she can go through the whole security management issue with them.> 1998 Joss 138.

suggest <Might we **suggest** he **becomes** a permanent fixture?> 2003 June 20 *Times* T2 4/1.

wish <We **wish** that each man over twelve years old **gives** the oath that he would not be a thief or a thief's accessory.> (translation of OE law II Cnut 21) 1989 Aug. 7–11 International Society of Anglo-Saxonists meeting, Durham.

12.1.2 After nouns

ambition <. . . the highest **ambition** of many mothers is that their son **becomes** a doctor or dentist.> 1986 Oct. 10 *Times* 1/5.

condition <He is currently free on bail on **condition** that he **does** not leave Arizona.> 2003 June 19 *Times* 17/8.

demand <Problems are also looming over Mr Major's **demand** that the IRA **makes** a 'significant gesture' towards decommissioning its arms.> 1995 newspaper CIC.

request <Further offences will then lead to a **request** that the official **is** transferred or withdrawn.> 1985 Apr. 24 *Times* 6/2.

requirement <It is a **requirement** in most European countries that motor vehicles **are** constructed by the manufacturers to meet certain design and construction requirements.> 1998 Jan. *Registering and Licensing Your Motor Vehicle*, Driver and Vehicle Licensing Agency, Dept of the Environment, Transport and the Regions 4/2.

understanding <Naturally, this is on the **understanding** that the church **remains** open as a church.> 1989 Williams 96.

wish <Gilbert's last **wish** is that he **lives** to see his treasures safely installed.> 1996 July 14 *Sunday Telegraph* Magazine 32/4.

12.1.3 After adjectives

Personal adjectives

concerned <. . . he is **concerned** that his girlfriends **are** protected from the media spotlight.> 2003 June 21 *Times* 7/2.

Impersonal adjectives

essential <. . . it is **essential** that more decisions **are** taken by majority vote, rather than by unanimous vote.> 1985 Mar. 31 *Sunday Times* 16.

important <It's very **important** that . . . he **shoulders** the responsibility for his behaviour and **understands** the upset that this has caused.> 2005 Jan. 15 *Daily Telegraph* 2/6.

vital <. . . it is **vital** that he **receives** daily treatment.> 1991 Feb. 13 *Daily Mail* 35/2.

12.2 Mandative past indicative

12.2.1 After verbs

demand <I remembered gasping and running forward to **demand** he **told** me what was happening.> 1991 Grant-Adamson 63.

insist <Apart from **insisting** they **kept** it clean and tidy . . . she did not interfere.> 2001 Lessing 4.

matter <This was the time when it **mattered** so desperately that he **said** and **did** [= should say and do] exactly the right things.> 1979 Dexter 184.

propose <I did what I thought was the sensible and the appropriate thing to do, which was to **propose** to my son that we **went** to the police.> 1998 Jan. 3 *Times* 1/3.

recommend <Eventually, her GP **recommended** that we **took** her to see a specialist.> 1996 July 14 *Sunday Telegraph Review* 4/3.

request <Only one laureate, Henry Pye, was hard-headed enough to **request** that his wine allowance **was translated** into cash.> 1988 Dec. *In Britain* 28/2.

suggest <Then I rang the friends we were due to meet and **suggested** that they **came** to our place.> 2003 June 30 *Times* T2 8/2.

want <All I **wanted** was that Tanner **got** my request quickly and I **got** the visiting order quickly.> 1991 Grant-Adamson 172.

12.2.2 After nouns

condition <. . . council officers offered him a home improvement loan on **condition** he **used** a particular firm of builders.> 1999 Mar. 10–17 *Time Out* 42/2.

order < . . . in **order** that the premises **were** not left vacant, they were used as an antiques shop.> 1986 Aug. 25 *Times* 11/5.

suggestion <She [a political candidate] . . . was criticised about her appearance, with **suggestions** she **wore** a mini-skirt, and "re-do her highlights" to win votes.> 2005 Jan. 15 *Daily Telegraph* 10/4. (The coordinated verb "re-do" is subjunctive.)

12.2.3 After adjectives

Personal adjectives

anxious <. . . he was **anxious** that aid to people in Africa and other third-world regions **did not dry up**.> 2005 Jan. 9 *Sunday Times* 3 1/6.

Impersonal adjectives

essential <Mr McAuslan said it was **essential** that the crew **knew** who the marshal was.> 2004 Jan. 5 *Times* 4/3.
important <. . . it was **important** she **returned** to a tidy desk.> 1995 Sept. 4 *Daily Telegraph* 13/7.
necessary <. . . a set of domestic crises rendered it **necessary** that she **went** home for an hour.> 1993 Neel 100.
vital <It was **vital** that Harvey **made** contact with Emma.> 1991 Critchley 140.

13 Expanded predicates

Hovering between grammar and lexis are constructions like *have a look*, which are approximately equivalent to a simple verb, such as *look*. The construction and its varieties have received several discussions, some primarily general (Allerton 2002, Brinton and Akimoto 1999, Claridge 1997, Wierzbicka 1982), some based on British corpora (Stein 1991, Stein and Quirk 1991), and others dealing also with British-American variation (Algeo 1995).

The verb in the expanded predicate may be relatively "light" (that is, general or nonliteral) in meaning with respect to its object (*be a challenge*, *do a dance*, *get a view*, *give a yawn*, *have an argument*, *make one's way*, *pay attention*, *put an end to*, *take trouble*), or it may be relatively "heavy" semantically, being appropriate to its object (*ask a question*, *breathe a sigh*, *effect an alteration*, *find a solution*, *grant permission*, *heave a sigh*, *offer an apology*, *reach an agreement*, *submit an application*, *tender one's apologies*, *utter a curse*).

The object noun in the construction may be "eventive," that is, correspond to a verb of similar meaning, with or without some change of form from the verb (*do a dive* = *dive*, *give an answer* = *answer*, *take a walk* = *walk*, but also *have a bath* = *bathe*, and *make a discovery* = *discover*). Or the object noun may not correspond to a verb because (a) there is no equivalent single-word verb (*do homework* but **to homework*, *have mercy* but **to mercy*, *make peace* but **to peace*) or (b) the semantically equivalent verb is not cognate with the eventive noun (*have sex* = *copulate*, *take cover* = *hide*, *do a favor for* = *help*) or (c) a cognate simple verb is not semantically equivalent with the eventive noun (*make love (to/with)* ≠ *to love*, *have a bite* "eat a little" ≠ *to bite*, *take a chance* ≠ *to chance* "happen").

Central expanded predicates are those with a "light" verb followed by an eventive noun cognate with a semantically equivalent verb (e.g., *have a look* = *look*). Constructions that depart from either of those characteristics are, for that reason, related but not central examples.

British and American have some different forms of the construction. The two national varieties often differ, however, in the frequency with which they use a common form rather than in the forms used. In the following entries, the figures in parentheses after the entry form are the iptmw in CIC British and American texts, thus (54.2/0.6) indicates that British texts have 54.2 tokens per ten million words of the construction, and American texts have 0.6. Lack of such figures indicates an absence of the construction from CIC texts.

13.1 Five "light" verbs in British and American

A comparison of expanded predicates with the "light" verbs *do*, *give*, *have*, *make*, and *take* in the Brown and LOB corpora shows that the construction is at home in both national varieties, though not equally so. The Brown Corpus has 199 tokens, representing 133 types (different verb and eventive object combinations) compared with the LOB Corpus's 245 tokens and 149 types. Brown Corpus types are used an average of 1.50 times each; LOB Corpus types are used an average of 1.64 times each. To the extent that these two corpora are representative of their national varieties, we can say that, although the expanded predicate is a shared feature, British English uses it somewhat more than American.

A more striking difference, however, is in the particular verbs used in expanded predicates. The accompanying table shows that the difference between British and American is minor for four of the verbs, but not for *have*. British uses *have* as the verb of an expanded predicate nearly twice as often as American does and in about 1.75 times as many different constructions. *Have* is the British verb of preference, in this sample accounting for 41 percent of both types and tokens of expanded predicates, whereas in American, it accounts for only 28 percent of tokens and 26 percent of types.

Expanded Predicates in the LOB and Brown Corpora

	Summary of tokens/types	
	LOB	Brown
do	0	4/4
give	40/29	40/30
have	100/61	55/35
make	67/39	59/44
take	38/20	41/20

Here follow some examples of the five "light" verbs in British expanded predicate constructions, not all of which are central examples:

do a bunk (1.2/0.1) Make a sudden departure; run away <Daley had **done a bunk**.> 1992 Granger 47.

do the car hire Rent the car <I **did the car hire**.> 1988 Mortimer 157.

do a course (8.8/0.2) Take a course: In American use, *do a course* may mean "teach a course." <Having **done a** short **course**, which costs about £800, a graduate with a qualification to teach English as a foreign language can cross the Channel for a subsistence wage.> 1993 Feb. 13 *Spectator* 21/2.

do a deal (22.8/2.8) Make a deal <. . . having **done a deal** . . . I decided this weekend to consider my various options.> 1982 Lynn and Jay 11.

do a flit (0.3/0) Run away; secretly move <I hope they get him. Only, the last I heard, he'd **done a flit**.> 1990 Hardwick 140.

do a rethink Think again (about) <His chairmanship . . . puts him in a powerful position to nudge the Tories into **doing a** policy **rethink**.> 1989 July 27 *Evening Standard* 7/5.

do *one's* **round** (1.3/0) Go on / make *one's* rounds <He would now be **doing** his **round** of locking up, before descending for the night to his bedsitter in the basement.> 1986 Brett 32.

do a runner (4.7/0.1) Run away; run off; disappear; escape <His girlfriend has **done a runner** with a work-experience boy.> 2003 Nov. 8 *Times* 29/6.

do a Virgin Imitate the practices of the Virgin enterprise <According to one senior manager in Branson's Virgin empire . . . "When I read about Forgan's letter, I thought, 'She's trying to **do a Virgin**'."> 1993 Feb. 7 *Sunday Times* 2 6/2.

do a wiggle <Then go across Wandsworth Bridge . . . and then **do a wiggle**.> SEU s1/11.872–4.

give *someone* **aggravation** (0.1/0) Aggravate *someone* <"Why on earth did you lose your temper like that?" [¶] "He **gave** me **aggravation**, didn't he?"> 2003 James 241.

give *a baby* **a feed** (2.8/0) Give *a baby* a bottle <Staff changed shifts as the babies were **given a feed**.> 1993 Feb. 27 *Times* 6/1.

give *someone/thing* **a go** (13.4/2.0) Give *someone/thing* a try or chance <Surely it's worth **giving** it **a go**.> 1994 Sept. 13 TV ch. 4 *Brookside*.

give a lead (2.5/0) Take the lead (57.2/46.9) <What we do say . . . as the opposition is this: for heaven's sake, **give a lead** and try and break down this dreadful suicidal wall where no one will yield an inch.> SEU s5.4:67.

give a look (1.2/0.2) Take a look <Barrington **giving a look** round the field.> SEU s10.1:1.

give *something* **a look-in** Try *something* < . . . and do **give** fruit and vegetables **a look-in**.> 2004 Jan. 4 *Sunday Times* 10/2.

give *something* **a look-over** <He had a mind to let his cousin . . . **give** it **a look-over**.> SEU w16.4:40.

give *something* **a miss** (6.3/0.1) Skip *something* <Chutney Mary (*the* chichi restaurant) **gave a miss** to toasted Wonderloaf and processed Cheddar.> 1993 Feb. 27 *Times* Saturday Review 31/5.

give *something* **a respray** Repaint *something* <I could **give** your car **a respray**.> 1994 Sept. 27 *Evening Standard* 56/2.

give *something* **a rest** (4.6/1.9, but: **give it a rest** 1.0/0.9) Give *something* a break; let *something* go <Can't you **give it a rest**? . . . You're always having a go at each other.> 2003 Rowling 212.

give *someone* **a ring** (34.7/1.8) Telephone *someone*; give *someone* a call <Let me **give** you **a ring** tomorrow, all right?> 1992 Dexter 80.

give *something* **a wipe** (0.7/0) <Would you like me to **give** the books **a wipe** with a duster?> 1993 Dexter 142.

have a bath (24.2/1.4) Take a bath <You can **have a bath** and a sit-down there.> 1998 Joss 15.

have a bitch (about) (0.5/0) <It's good to be able to **have** a moan and **a bitch about** things.> 1997 Dec. 15 *Times* 17/4.

have a chat (32.5/2.2) <She could **have a chat** with his doctor.> 1990 Rowlands 63.

have a feed (0.7/0.1) Get fed <They'd [babies would] **have a feed.**> 1987 Jan. 27 BBC1 morning news.

have a game of *something* (3.7/0.4) Play a *something* game / a game of *something* <. . . all the drivers will be . . . **having** a chat and **a game of** cards.> 1987 Feb. 4 *Evening Standard* 33/3.

have a giggle (1.4/0.1) <It is one thing to **have a giggle** at the office party, groaning lasciviously through a rendition of *Have Yourself a Merry Little Christmas* . . . , quite another, to think that the result is a piece of art.> 2000 Dec. 15 *Times* 2 13/2.

have a(nother) go (at) (107.2/3.7) **1.** Try **1a. have a go** Give it a try; make an attempt <Jean de Florette and the other Pagnol films did **have a go** but . . . failed.> 1993 Feb. 26 *Guardian* 2 3/3. **1b. have a go at** Make an attempt at <Who . . . suggests the tomboy might like to **have a go at** ballet?> 2003 June 25 *Guardian* international ed. G2 13/3. **2.** Behave aggressively **2a. have a go** Take violent action <'What would you commit murder for . . . Money, reputation, revenge?' [¶] 'I might **have a go** for revenge.'> 1993 Greenwood 174. **2b. have a go at** Attack *someone* physically <This year, they **had a go at** Jewish protesters and Western journalists trying to cover their demonstration.> 1987 Dec. 20 *Manchester Guardian* 10/4. **2c. have a go at** Break into; tear apart *something* <The clip-on wrecked stereo kit, complete with dangling wires and broken plastic, makes robbers think that someone else has already **had a go at** the car.> 1991 Mar. 2 *Daily Express* 40/1. **2d. have a go at** Attack *someone* verbally; criticize <It's the hunting debate. . . . It's **having a go at** the class system.> 1998 Jan. 7 *Evening Standard* 3/3–4. **2e. have a go at** Bother; annoy *someone* <'Miles hasn't been **having a go at** you, has he?' [¶] 'He was trying to scrounge a cigarette.'> 1991 Charles 90. **3. have a go (of it)** Suffer/undergo an illness <Ted says malaria isn't any worse than flu. He usually works on through when he **has a go.**> 1986 Dickinson 19. **4. have a go** Take a turn <I **had a go** on Nigel's racing bike.> 1985 Townsend 61. **5. have a go** Take a chance <I've only been to one race meeting in my life . . . but London Standard looked such a super horse we felt we had to **have a go.**> 1987 Mar. 27 *Evening Standard* 64/1. **6. have a go at** Try to get information from <They [police] might **have a go at** me about Vanessa not giving them a statement.> 1992 Green 59. **7. have a go at** Work on; tackle <Richard Compton-Miller returned with a largish file for Stephen fifteen minutes later. [¶] "**Have a go at** that."> 1976 Archer 58.

have (a) holiday(s) (11.0/0) Take a vacation (in some location) <I decided to **have a** week's **holiday** in the very selfsame place.> 1974 Potter 135.

have a laugh (21.6/3.3) <People with GSOH ["good sense of humour"] are always on the lookout for a passing joke, there is an ever-readiness to **have a laugh**.> 2003 June 21 *Times* Weekend 9/3.

have a lie-in (1.1/0) Sleep late/in <We're both dead-beat. **Have a lie-in**.> 1972 Rendell 59.

have a listen (3.4/0.1) <You could have a really tricky problem, . . . and Steve would come along, **have a listen** and say, 'Ah yes, that'll be the . . .' whatever it was.> 1986 Simpson 61.

have a look (268.4/20.5) Take a look (57.6/144.0) <I'll **have a look** first.> 1991 Green 39.

have a moan (0.8/0) <**Having a moan** can be very therapeutic.> 1998 Taylor 141.

have a moult <They seem to be permanently losing a feather or two, instead of **having a** good **moult**.> 1993 Feb. 13 *Spectator* 7/1.

have a nap (1.3/0.4) Take a nap <. . . his pregnant mother . . . was **having a** lunchtime **nap**.> 1994 Sept. 30 *Daily Telegraph* 11/5.

have a peck Peck <I can't use a bird table [feeder] . . . because we're so exposed to the westerlies. It would be blown off before the birds **had a peck**.> 1993 Feb. 13 *Daily Telegraph* Weekend 2/3.

have *a* **pee** (1.3/0) <. . . the boy **had** his **pee**.> 1996 Aug. 9 *Daily Telegraph* 15/2.

have a piss (0.7/0) Take a piss < . . . there's Terry Wogan **having a piss** in the hedge!> 1988 Oct. *Illustrated London News* 59/3.

have a place Have been admitted (to an educational institution): The sequence of words occurs more than twice as often in American: 14.7/32.0, but none of the CIC American tokens have the British educational use. <We are pleased to inform you that you **have a place** at Hogwarts School.> 1997 Rowling 42 (*US ed.* have been accepted).

have a rant and rave (*rant*: 0.4/0, *rave*: 0.2/0) <Meldrew . . . is never happier than when he is **having a** good **rant and rave**.> 1993 Feb. 12 *Sun* 11/2–3.

have a rest (10.3/0.9) Take a rest <We both **had a rest**.> SEU s11/1.717.

have a rethink (1.0/0) Give it another thought <We'll have to **have a rethink** on policy.> 1987 Mar. 15 ITV morning news.

have a root (around) (0.1/0) <I **had** a bit of **a root around**. It was all pretty well in order, clothes hung up all nice and tidy, no mess.> 1989 Nicholson 7.

have a shave (2.6/0.3) <I **had a** bath and **shave** every day.> 1993 Feb. *Woman's Journal* 39/2.

have a shower (11.5/1.2) Take a shower <I must **have a shower**.> 1998 spoken text CIC.

have a sit-down (0.6/0) Take a rest; sit down for a while <While I'm **having** a bit of **a sit-down,** I might as well tell you what this feels like.> 1994 Sept. 28–Oct. 5 *Time Out* 8/3.

have a skim (0.1/0) <The Palace will be ringing with the Guidance around ten – we'll **have a skim** through the diaries and see if there's anything we want to make a fuss about.> 1989 Dickinson 13.

have a sleep (5.6/0.5) Take a nap <Ben wants you to . . . keep her here for a few hours until he's **had a sleep**.> 1992 Green 10.

have a surf Go surfing <. . . you go and **have a surf**.> 1991 Lodge 295.

have a swim (2.1/0.1) Go for a swim; go swimming <Why don't you come down and **have a swim**?> 1988 Mortimer 54.

have a tease (0.1/0) <As we lay there perfectly still, with his noble head using my bum cheeks for cushions, I thought I'd **have a tease**.> 1994 Oct. 3 *Times* 19/1.

have a test-drive (0.1/0) Take a test drive <So I **had a test-drive**. And of course I liked the car.> 1995 Lodge 35.

have a think (7.1/0.5) Give it some thought <I'm wondering where they dumped the waste. . . . You know this area well. **Have a think** for me.> 1989 Burden 155. – **have got another think coming** (0.7/0.3) <If you think I'm washing those dishes you'**ve got another think coming**.> 1987 May 10 (Scotland) *Sunday Post* 23/3.

have a tidy up (0.1/0) <tidy up [=] tidying up (e.g. – **Having a** bit of **tidy up**.)> 1988 *How to Speak EastEnders*.

have a trawl Look around; make a search <Something is incorrectly set up . . . in your autoexec.bat or config.sys or system.ini files. . . . **Have a trawl** and see what it could be.> 1998 Jan. 7 *Times* Interface magazine 10/3.

have a try (3.2/0) Give it a try <Hoped to specialize in it once. Might still **have a try**.> 1966 Priestley 45.

have a walk (6.2/1.0) Take a walk <I thought it would be nice to . . . go up on to the Downs and **have a walk**.> 1940 Shute 132.

have a wander (round) (1.2/0.1) <I'll just **have** a bit of **a wander** here, have a look at the stalls.> 1998 Joss 28.

have a wash (3.5/0.1) <Davey was **having a wash**.> 1989 Burden 95.

have a whisper (0.1/0) <We **had a wisper** [sic] for a few minutes but you know what libraries are like.> SEU w7/32.149.

have a word (57.6/6.5) Talk (with someone about something) <By all means **have a word**.> 1999 Mar. 21 *Sunday Times* 10 46/1.

have *a* worry (1.0/0) <. . . the television industry was **having** another **Worry** about the Future.> 1994 Sept. 12 *Guardian* 13/7.

made bankrupt, be (1.6/0) Go bankrupt <. . . her father **was made bankrupt**.> 2003 Nov. 10 *Times* 15/2.

make a closure (on *a business*) Close *a business* <Magistrates have also **made an** emergency **closure on** Foodworth, a large supermarket.> 1987 Mar. *Camden Magazine* no. 46 7/3.

make a cockup (0.1/0) Make a mistake/booboo <In the article on the delights of Sardinia . . . David Wickers **made** a bit of **a cockup**.> 1993 Feb. 21 *Sunday Times* 2 7/2.

make *a* loss(es) (13.1/2.0) Take *a* loss(es) <I found it hard to sell. I can't remember how long it took but I can remember I **made a loss**.> 2004 Dec. 12 *Sunday Times* 6 12/6.

make a punt (0.1/0) Take a chance <. . . any restaurant that took such a course would be **making a** rash **punt**.> 1993 Feb. 27 *Times Saturday Review* 31/2.

make savings (1.4/0) Achieve savings <. . . defence chiefs are under pressure to **make savings** after Wednesday's announcement that four famous Army regiments will not be axed.> 1993 Feb. 5 *Daily Express* 10/2.

take *a* copy/copies/carbon (2.4/1.1) Make (carbon) copies <Suppose the copiers were *slower* than they are now? Then people . . . *would* **take carbons**, wouldn't they? Rather than hang around by the copier for ages?> 1993 Mason 176.

take *a* decision(s) (53.6/8.4) Make *a* decision(s) <The Bill enables patients suffering from illnesses such as Alzheimer's to appoint a relative or friend to **take decisions** on their behalf.> 2004 Dec. 15 *Daily Telegraph* 1/2.

take dinner (1 token/none) Have dinner <. . . the lady of the establishment interrupted her with the evening's menu, and asked if she were **taking dinner**.> 1992 Dexter 11.

take exercise (2.4/0) Get exercise <. . . squash has now spread to all classes and most countries, and is one of the most concentrated modes of **taking exercise** in huge dollops known to man.> 1984 Smith 223.

take into care (usu. **taken into care**) (7.1/0) Place in the guardianship of Social Services <He . . . has the kind of background you might expect . . . **taken into care**, placed with foster parents, ran away.> 1995 Lodge 117.

take a look up (0.1/0) <I just **took a look up** while I was writing, and she gave me a great big smile.> SEU s2/7.1296.

take the mickey (out of *someone*) (9.4/0.3) Tease, ridicule, or make fun (of *someone*) <They haven't stopped **taking the mickey out of** me since I got made a prefect.> 2003 Rowling 245.

take the piss (out of *someone/something*) (16.0/0.7) Disparage or mock; deflate *someone*, run *someone/something* down <He had started turning up at events with Sting. His natural constituency was **taking the piss out of** all that. Certainly, he was on the circuit in the '60s, too. But then he'd have The Beatles round to dinner and be **taking the piss out of** them on telly at the same time. By the end of his life, he wasn't in a position to **take the piss** – he was simply a member of the celeb club.> 2004 Dec. 8–15 *Time Out* 26/3.

take a place (at) (0.1/0) Become a student; get into <She **took a place** at Oxford.> 1992 Walters 48.

take a punt (0.7/0) Take a chance; gamble (from a gambling term in some card games, hence *to punt* "to bet, speculate") <Given the dullness of this administration, I really would **take a punt** on Lord Archer of Weston-super-Mare to do the job for a three-year stint.> 1993 Feb. 2 *Evening Standard* 13/1.

take supper (0.3/0) Have supper <"Neither he [Tony Blair] nor Cherie wants to sit around and talk about the Social Justice Commission all evening," said a friend who has **taken supper** in front of the Blairs' Aga.> 1994 Oct. 4 *Daily Telegraph* 19/4.

take up work (0.8/0.3) Go to work; get a job <Mr Lilley [Social Security Secretary] said 50,000 people were expected to **take up work** as a direct result of the change [in child-care benefits].> 1994 Oct. 4 *Daily Telegraph* 6/3.

take a wander (0.2/0) <[traffic wardens passing on information about where to find good pickings in traffic violations:] Colleagues would pass on the names and tell me to '**take a wander** up so and so street at 6.00 pm. It's brilliant up there,' all of which was gratefully received at the start of an afternoon shift.> 1990 Sept. *Evening Standard* magazine 65/2.

13.2 Modification and complementation of the expanded predicate noun

If the noun in the expanded predicate is modified, the modifier may assume various forms in the corresponding construction with a semantically heavy verb. At the simplest, an adjective in the expanded predicate may correspond to an adverb with the semantically heavy verb:

<Let's squat down and **have a closer look**.> (= look more closely) SEU s10/8.240–1.

In other cases, the modifier in the expanded predicate has a more complex adverbial correspondence. A frequent modifier, *good* serves as an intensifier and corresponds to various adverbs, according to the sense of the semantically heavy verb:

<You just sat and **had a jolly good giggle** at the things he was saying.> (= giggled a lot) SEU s1/6.773-4. <A şurgeon gets right in there and **has a good look** at it.> (= looks intensely) SEU s2/9.671. <**Have a good scan** round.> (= scan thoroughly) SEU s10/8.318. <. . . sharp minds are **having a good try**.> (= trying assiduously) SEU w11/4.104. <**I had a good think** about that one [i.e., whether to be hypnotized].> (= thought carefully) 1987 Jan. 20 *Guardian* 26/7.

Other adjectives similarly have adverbial paraphrases:

<We were going to **do a little tour** round West Cumbria.> (= tour a little) SEU s8/4.923-4. <So I took one look at it and sort of **gave a great scream**.> (= screamed loudly) SEU s1/9.935-6. <We **had an advance look-in**, too, on some of his inimitable podgy character's future quips.> (= looked in advance) SEU w8/3.88. <I **had a long talk** to her about two weeks ago.> (= talked at length) SEU s5/8.99.

When the verb of the expanded predicate is ditransitive *give*, its indirect object is the direct object of the semantically heavy verb:

<It might **give them a bit of a prod**.> (= prod them a bit) 1987 Bawden 136.

Alternatively, the semantically heavy verb may be prepositional, adverbial, or adverbial-prepositional, rather than simply transitive:

<. . . **give** them **a shout**.> (= shout to them) 1988 Apr. 10 *Sunday Telegraph* 37/4. <I think I'll **give** it **a miss** for once.> (= miss it out) 1976 Raphael 41. <. . . television . . . hardly ever **gives** industry **a look-in** except as a factor in politics.> (= looks in on industry) 1967 Frost and Jay 80.

If the noun of the expanded predicate is followed by a prepositional phrase, its object may be the direct object of the semantically heavy verb:

<Do you want to **take a note of my name**?> (= note my name) SEU s9/1.77.

13.3 Other expanded-predicate-like constructions

Many other combinations are structurally similar to expanded predicates, but differ in that their verbs are "heavy," that is, semantically more specific and appropriate to their objects or in that those objects are not eventive. Some such combinations might also be treated as matters of complementation (cf. § 11). A few of such combinations are illustrated here. Their number is large.

come a cropper (4.4/0.5) Fail utterly <Predictably, it all **came a cropper**.> 1993 Feb. 7 *Sunday Times* 6 9/1.

cop a goggle (at) <[literary satire on Orwell's *Burmese Days*:] . . . when luscious Elizabeth Lackersteen arrives in Kyauktada for the wet T-shirt and vodka-gargling marathon, her Burma's not the only thing Flory **cops a goggle at**!> 2003 June 21 *Times* 16/2.

go a bomb (on) (0.2/0) Be a great success (with); to appeal greatly (to) <Franco detested the Basques, never forgiving them for their staunch republicanism during the Civil War. They didn't **go a bomb on** him either (other than literally).> 1993 Feb. 10 *Evening Standard* 27/3.

go walkabout (2.4/0.2) Ramble around <Somewhere in the distance, . . . he could hear the high-pitched sounds of a bleeper, and bleepers didn't **go walkabout** by themselves.> 1993 Mason 105.

hitch a lift (3.8/0) Hitch a ride (2.7/5.2) <Surely she wouldn't try to **hitch a lift**.> 1993 Graham 213.

move house Move (19.3/0) <He had **moved house** without giving Christine his new phone number.> 1989 Rendell 36.

pull a face Make a face (9.8/2.4) <As she **pulled a face** at her reflection, the doorbell rang.> 1993 Stallwood 131.

put the boot in(to) Treat cruelly (6.3/0.2) <Belgians **put boot into** Wellington / A group of taxpayers are taking Belgium's Finance Minister to court in an attempt to curtail the handsome rewards still being reaped by the Duke of Wellington's descendants 185 years after his victory at the battle of Waterloo. [¶] Those bringing the action cannot accept that . . . the present Duke is still receiving nearly £100,000 a year in Belgian francs.> (a pun on *Wellington boot* "knee-high waterproof rubber boot" and *put the boot in* "kick someone when they are down") 2000 Jan. 19 *Times* 3/1–7.

put paid to (12.0/0) End, stop; put an end to <Looking fondly at Sheryl, Gazza, 25, **put paid to** press reports that they had split up.> 1993 Feb. 12 *Sun* 12/3.

sit ***an examination*** (8.7/0.2) Take *an examination* <Those **sitting finals** [at Oxford] say they are more hardworking and financially stretched than those five years before them.> 1999 Mar. 17 *Evening Standard* 11/4.

14 Concord

14.1 Verb and pronoun concord with collective nouns

A collective noun is singular in form but denotes a referent (a group, such as a business, committee, team, etc.) composed of separate members and can therefore be thought of as either singular or plural. A collective noun functioning as a subject may govern a verb that is either singular or plural. Pronouns referring to a collective noun may be either animate or inanimate (*who* or *which*) and either plural or singular (*they* or *it*) (*CGEL* 5.108; 10.48n, 50; 17.11). British collective nouns are more likely than American ones to take animate and plural concord (*CamGEL* 502; Johansson 1979, 203–5; Levin 1998, 2001; Peters 2004, 24). Practically every British collective noun sometimes takes plural concord (*LGSWE* 188).

As a rough comparison of verb concord with collective-noun subjects, CIC texts were examined for seven collective nouns immediately followed by *is, was, has* versus *are, were, have*. The results are as follows, in percentage of plural concord with each noun subject. The CIC iptmw of the sequence of noun plus verb, whether singular or plural, is given in parentheses, because the larger that number, the more significant is the percentage based on it.

Collective-noun subject	British plural concord	American plural concord
team	41% (149.0)	.35 of 1% (227.0)
military	32% (5.6)	1.7% (60.1)
press	29% (45.6)	1.9% (52.5)
council	22% (143.8)	.28 of 1% (71.3)
union	16% (70.1)	.12 of 1% (82.6)
government	9% (376.6)	.26 of 1% (573.6)
company	8% (305.6)	0.0% (473.4)

These figures suggest that plural concord with collective-noun subjects is a pronounced difference between British and American English. The semantic category of the noun is, however, a factor. The following categories are exemplified by an alphabetical list of common nouns first, followed in each category by an alphabetical list of proper nouns.

SPORTS ORGANIZATIONS:
Plural and animate concord with both common and proper nouns referring to sports teams is regular in British English (*LGSWE* 189).

club <. . . the **club are** in a Catch-22 position; **they** need money to renovate the crush-barriers, but **are** unable to draw the crowd to gain this.> 1986 Dec. 10 *Times* 38/5.

side <. . . a **side who have** won their last seven Test matches [cricket].> 2004 Dec. 14 *Daily Telegraph* 2 1/1.

team *general as well as sports use* <Kaufman's **Team Are** On The Ball> 2003 June 20 *Times* T2 19.

Australia <**Australia have** named three new caps in **their** team.> 1989 July 2 *Manchester Guardian Weekly* 31/5.

Blackheath <**Blackheath were** founded in 1858.> 1986 Sept. 26 *Times* 30/4.

City <The **City were** playing at home. . . . First match of the season.> 1991 Greenwood 74.

England <It is rare for an entire [cricket] team to under-perform, but **England were** not far off that nadir.> 2004 Dec. 14 *Daily Telegraph* 2 1/1.

Everton <Saturday afternoon traffic through the tunnel . . . is greater when **Everton are** at home.> 1988 Apr. 10 *Manchester Guardian Weekly* 5/5.

Hockey Association <. . . the **Hockey Association were** founded 100 years ago.> 1986 Oct. 17 *Times* 31/1.

Leeds <Crooks landed the goal and **Leeds were** level.> 1987 Nov. 8 *Manchester Guardian Weekly* 31/5.

Luton <**Luton, who are** considering taking out a High Court injunction against the management committee's decision, **have** barred all away fans.> 1986 Sept. 24 *Times* 1/6.

Middlesex <**Middlesex are** in good form.> 1985 Bingham 78.

Palace <**Palace are** one of four clubs Wimbledon managing-director Hamman has talked with.> 1987 Feb. 18 *Evening Standard* 52/3.

Perthshire County Cricket Club <At the moment, **Perthshire County Cricket Club pay** almost as much as Lord's, and **Kirkcaldy Rugby Club** . . . **was** charged £5,500 a year.> (concord changes from plural to singular) 1986 Oct. 19 *Sunday Times* 22/8.

Saffron Walden <**Saffron Walden were** founded in 1963.> 1986 Sept. 26 *Times* 30/4.

Sweden <**Sweden** a young side **who** also just missed out of the world championships.> 1986 Sept. 19 *Times* 34/4–5.

Viking <**Viking argue**, too, that Marnham's name gives them an additional edge.> 1987 Oct. *Illustrated London News* 46/1.

Wales <**Wales were** labelled an underdog.> 1987 June 13 ITV morning news.

Wigan <**Wigan are** regarded as currently the most progressive side in the league.> 1986 Dec. 10 *Times* 38/5.

BUSINESS ORGANIZATIONS:

In British use, common and proper nouns referring to business firms often take plural verbs, but not invariably so.

airline <The **airline say** it will be delivered within 6 hours of arrival.> 1985 Apr. *Airport* magazine 53/3.

bank <I don't think it will be long before the **bank insist** that I sell it, and when **they** do . . . it's curtains for me.> 1976 Archer 66.

company <A Canadian forestry **company are** involved, too.> 1987 May 10 (Scotland) *Sunday Post* 5/3.

firm <. . . the **firm publish** a 120,000 circulation magazine.> 1987 Sept. *Illustrated London News* 78/3.

head office <**Head Office are** expecting to hear from me.> SEU w7-9.38.

industry <. . . the British Phonographic **Industry fear** it could take hold in the pirate strongholds of Camden, Portobello and Petticoat Lane markets.> 1987 Feb. 9 *Evening Standard* 19/1–2.

management <The Theatre **Management do** not accept responsibility for any tickets bought from ticket touts.> 1990 May 31, sign in front of Palace Theatre, London.

union <. . . the **union have** to make up only three-sevenths of the weekly wage.> 1985 Apr. 8 *Times* 1/2.

Chaumet <**Chaumet were** a firm making very fine jewellery.> 2000 Dec. 17 TV *Antiques Roadshow*.

Citroen <**Citroen are** now offering the Visa five door hatchback.> 1987 Jan. 21 *Daily Mail* 4/1.

City of London <The **City of London do**n't understand it.> 1986 Oct. TV report of MP speaking in Parliament.

Cox <**Cox are** building on five sites in a 30-mile radius of Evesham. . . . [¶] Earlier this year **Cox was** absorbed by the Crest Nicholson group.> (concord changes from plural to singular) 1987 Nov. 7 *Daily Express* 24/2.

Dan-Air <**Dan-Air are** going places in the UK> 1986 Aug. poster on London tube train.

David Morris <**David Morris are** offering up to 50% Discount on selected models of . . . watches.> 1987 Feb. 12 *Evening Standard* 6/5–6.

Discovery Oil <"What price **are Discovery Oil** this morning?" [¶] "**They** have fallen to $7.40," the broker replied.> 1976 Archer 46.

Eve Construction <**Eve Construction are** helping Great Ormond Street [Hospital] Get Better> 1990 May 31, sign at London hospital.

Horizon <**Horizon are** introducing . . . safaris in Kenya and fly drive holidays in the United States.> 1989 Sept. 4 *Girl about Town* 24/1.

London Electricity Board <. . . the **London Electricity Board were** charging 3.5p per unit.> 1987 Jan. 16 *Times* 17/4.

Marconi <GEC **Marconi are** Britain's largest defence **contractors. Marconi is** engaged on major contracts.> (concord changes from plural to singular) 1987 Oct. 25 *Sunday Telegraph* 1/3.

Olympia & York plc <**Olympia & York plc are** a Canadian-based company **who have** bought out . . . Canary Wharf development.> 1987 Oct. *Illustrated London News* 92/2.

Peachey <Carnaby Street . . . was bought by **Peachey, who have** been making an honest effort to upgrade it.> 1987 Mar. 16 *Evening Standard* 34/2.

Shell <**Shell have** put great emphasis on standard of service.> 1987 Jan. 29 *Deptford & Peckham Mercury* 8/4.

Travellers Fare <**Travellers Fare operate** a wide range and a large number of modern fast food outlets at main line stations.> 1987 Feb. 12 *Evening Standard* 24/3.

If the collective noun is plural in form, it sometimes takes singular verb concord but may take either plural or animate pronoun concord:

<**Designer Homes**, of Swindon, **which was** set up in 1985 . . . won with **their** first scheme at Shipston-on-Stour.> 1986 Nov. 7 *Daily Express* 25/3.

<**Jenny Moody Properties is** based in Ingatestone, but **her** brief is to cover the whole of East Anglia. **She** is on the lookout for thatched cottages.> 1986 Nov. 7 *Daily Express* 23/1.

GOVERNMENTAL AND POLITICAL ORGANIZATIONS:

council Municipal council <The **Council have** agreed . . . to have the Postal Address of Twatt changed to Dounby.> 1977 Dec. 7 *Punch* 1144/2.

government <It's going to be very safe . . . as long as the British **government don't** get greedy and try and take control of it **themselves**.> 1976 Archer 41.

jury <The **jury have** decided that . . . you were not in control of your mind.> 1987 June 11 *Times* 3/7.

CID <**CID** [Criminal Investigation Department] **were** doing the rounds of the houses, dressed in grey suits and carrying clipboards.> 1995 June 8 *London Review of Books* 8/40.

Department of Environment <The **Department of Environment do** this sort of thing magnificently.> 1976 Aug. 11 *Punch* 221/2.

Government <**Government aim** to slash your bus services.> 1985 poster on a bus, Sheffield. But: <The British **Government has** given immediate authority to **its** mission in Cameroon to spend up to £10,000 on assistance.> 1986 Aug. 27 *Times* 1/3.

Labour <**Labour were** well acquainted with these statistics.> 1988 Sept. *Illustrated London News* 24/1.

National Front <But **were** the **National Front** not still active in the area?> 1987 Nov. *Illustrated London News* 82/4.

Scotland Yard <**Scotland Yard were** unable to obtain extradition papers for him.> 1976 Archer 52.

Security <**Security have** got in on the act and his phone's being tapped.> 1989 Dickinson 36.

United States <This has been particularly true in fields of technology and of management techniques in which the **United States have** been pre-eminent.> 1986 Mort viii.

Westminster Council <**Westminster Council have** already suggested the legalisation of brothels.> 1987 Feb. 25 *Evening Standard* 8/4–5.

Despite its plural form, *Libyan Revolutionary Cells* has singular concord here:

Libyan Revolutionary Cells <The **"Libyan Revolutionary Cells" has** never been heard of before.> 1986 Sept. 6 *Times* 1/4.

MILITARY ORGANIZATIONS:

crew See § 3.3.2.

military <The **military do** not use their airways all the time. . . . The **military controls** the majority of the airspace.> (concord changes from plural to singular) 1987 July *Illustrated London News* 33/4.

squadron < . . . the **squadron were** temporarily short of pilots.> 1940 Shute 19.

Air Force <The **Air Force have** made him pilot for these trials.> 1940 Shute 166.

Postings <I can't think what **Postings were** about.> 1940 Shute 161.

EDUCATIONAL, SCHOLARLY, ARTISTIC, ENTERTAINMENT, CULTURAL, AND RELIGIOUS ORGANIZATIONS:

chapter <'What **do chapter** think of that?' [¶] 'In general, **they're** against anything which lengthens the services.'> 1993 Greenwood 66.

choir <And the **choir themselves were** being chaired round the cricket pitch – > 1988 Trollope 217.

staff <**Staff** [at Eton] **are** divided into three scales.> 1988 Oct. 16 *Sunday Telegraph* 2/5. Cf. § 3.3.2.

By contrast, *audience* here takes inanimate and singular concord, and *films* is a plural count noun that has singular concord:

<Boyd is the author of . . . novels pitched at a sophisticated **audience which turns** to him with relief after working **its** way through more taxing reads.> 1990 Aug. 26 *Sunday Times* Magazine 40/1.

<Well, **films is** just one more verse metre, one more style.> 1976 Raphael 158.

Council <If **Council invite** you to take the chair, . . . it will be because **they** are going to make me Vice-Chancellor.> 1987 Archer 183–4.

Covent Garden <**Covent Garden are** very keen that we should like them [surtitles].> 1987 June 19 *Daily Telegraph* p. n/a.

Franz Ferdinand <**Franz Ferdinand** [a guitar band] **were** nominated for five Brit awards.> 2005 Jan. 11 *Daily Telegraph* 7/7.

Hollywood <**Hollywood are** gearing up to hand out their gongs.> 2004 Dec. 13 BBC1 *Breakfast* news.

Judas Priest <**Judas Priest are** one of the most successful heavy metal outfits in the States.> 1987 Feb. 18 *Evening Standard* 20/2.

MEDIA AND PUBLISHING ORGANIZATIONS:

press <We always get a bit upset when our **Press have** a go at the USA.> 1991 March 5, letter from an Englishwoman.

BBC <The **BBC lose** out on the royal front.> 1987 Feb. 10 *Evening Standard* 6/3–4.

Cobuild <**Cobuild have** steered a middle course between the baffling and the uselessly simple.> 1990 October *English Today* 6.4:56.

Merriam <**Merriam homograph** by etymology and part of speech; . . . **Merriam do** not homograph by morphology alone.> 1986 Hartmann 133.

Press Syndicate <. . . the **Press Syndicate have** now **agreed** to publish the series.> 1987 Nov. 3 letter from an editor.

In the following example, the name of a publisher, taken as plural, has attracted a preceding appositive into the plural form:

Collins <She has been prised away from her long-standing publisher, Century Hutchison, by **rivals Collins**.> 1987 Mar. 17 *Evening Standard* 6/1.

PUBLIC SERVICE ORGANIZATIONS:

fire brigade <The **fire brigade get** called for everything.> 1988 Oct. *Illustrated London News* 44/3.

hospital <The **hospital were** very cross about it.> 1940 Shute 215.

Road works, although plural in form, may take singular concord:

<**Road works** . . . **has** reduced both carriageways to one lane.> 1987 Feb. 24 *Evening Standard* 5/6.

London Weather Centre <The **London Weather Centre forecast** even hotter weather today.> 1996 Aug. 19 *Times* 2/6.

RSPCA <My father got the dog drunk on cherry brandy at the party last night. If the **RSPCA hear** about it he could get done.> 1985 Townsend 13.

GENERAL AND MISCELLANEOUS HUMAN GROUPS:

committee <The . . . **Committee have** recently met the Metropolitan Police.> 1987 Apr. 22 *Times* 13/4.
crowd <. . . the **crowd roar** at his delts or pecs.> 1994 Sept. 12 *Guardian* 2 3/1.
family <. . . his **family were** hard up.> 1987 Mar. 16 *Evening Standard* 13/2.
gang <The Polish **gang were** responsible for the numbers racket.> 1976 Archer 3–4.
panel <The **panel were** considering the cutbacks in education.> 1985 Benedictus 18.
party <. . . your local **Party want** you to take her place?> 1992 Critchley 118.
public <Odd how the **public** always **expect** the police to be notably more virtuous than the society from which they're recruited.> 2003 James 130.
race <"Oh to be in England, now that April's there": the island **race know** what it is to be homesick.> 1984 Smith 120.

Majority is a collective noun for which plural concord might be expected, but it also takes a singular verb:

<. . . ideas which the **majority does** not like.> 1988 Apr. 10 *Sunday Telegraph* 29/7.

14.2 Verb concord in other problematical cases

Several constructions involve other decisions in subject-verb concord. Although it is not clear what decisions predominate in British and American usage, below are examples of several such constructions.

Some subjects involve a quantifying noun followed by an *of*-prepositional phrase. In such cases, the verb may agree either with the quantifying noun, which is often singular, or with a plural object of the preposition, often the notional subject of the verb. Ward Gilman (1994, 52) observes that "experts and common sense agree that the plural verb is natural and correct, [but] actual usage still shows a few holdouts for the singular verb." Examples of such holdouts are the following:

<Only a faithful **sprinkling** of bedraggled **spectators was** standing along the west-side terrace, their umbrellas streaked with rain.> 1979 Dexter 78. <There **is** a **handful** of **verbs**.> 1986 Burton-Roberts 171. <. . . an increasing **number** of school **leavers is** turning to careers in which . . . ability . . . exists entirely in the eye of the beholder.> 1986 Aug. 19 *Times* 8/1. <When we are told that a **third of them claims** to have learned the facts of life from teachers, I suspect that **most** of that **third is** lying.> 1989 Sept. 3 *Sunday Telegraph* 16/5.

However, plural verb concord sometimes occurs in cases for which both formal and semantic concord might favor the singular, as in the following, in which what was agreed upon was the package:

<A four million pound **package** of health **cuts have** been agreed.> 1986 Nov. TV news.

Similarly, the pronouns *any, each, either, neither*, and *none* may be followed by an *of*-prepositional phrase with a plural object. In these cases, verb agreement may be either formal or notional. Formal agreement has been reported for British English in formal style, and notional agreement for American and informal British style (Swan 1995, 534); or formal agreement is presented as the norm, although "sometimes contextual considerations lead to the use of a plural verb" (Burchfield 1996, 35). The following example attests British use of a plural verb in this construction:

<**Each** of **these** [guest rooms] **have** telephone points.> 1989 May *In Britain* 43/2.

With expletive *there*, the question is whether the verb agrees with a following plural nominal serving as notional subject or with *there*, taken as a singular pronoun. Pam Peters (2004, 537) reports that agreement with the following nominal is "strictly maintained in academic writing" but that *there is* and *there's* are found before plural nominals "in narrative and everyday writing" and that *there's* is commoner than *there are* in conversation. The following are examples of *there* with singular verb concord before a plural nominal:

<. . . **there was** about five French **guys** who actually tackled him at the same time.> 1985 Feb. 2 transcription of a radio commentary of an England-France Rugby match. <**There is** a further five **bedrooms** and a second bathroom.> 1986 Aug. 21 *Hampstead Advertiser* 40/2. <**There's** not a lot of **jobs** about now, **is there**?> 1986 Nov. waitress in Lancaster. <**There has** been some terrible **incidents** because people were confused.> 1987 Feb. 4 *Evening Standard* 10/2–3 (quoting health committee chairman Vivienne Lukey of Hammersmith and Fulham). <. . . **there was families** at the pit who traced their connection with coal back to the last century.> 1989 Sept. 7 *Midweek* 32/1.

15 Propredicates

In a clause commenting on or continuing a preceding clause, the predicate may be abbreviated to an auxiliary or several auxiliaries, either echoing those of the preceding clause or newly introduced, sometimes with additional predicate items: "I thought we had been there before, and we **had (been)**" [i.e., had been there before]. "The first trip exhausted us, and the second probably **will** too" [i.e., will exhaust us]. "He was thinning out his collection [of books]: authors often **do**" (1986 Oct. 30 *Times* 18/2). These second, isolated auxiliaries serve as propredicates, implying the full predicate of the preceding clause.

In addition to such common-core instances, a more limited pattern with a present participle of an auxiliary has been reported as acceptable in some varieties of British (*CGEL* 12.22n, *CamGEL* 100, 1523): *A: Why don't you sit quietly? B: I AM* ***doing****. Kim is being investigated by the police, and I think Pat is* ***being*** *too. I've been Rex's mistress for some time now, and I shall go on* ***being****, married or not. They have all volunteered, but I think some of them regret* ***having****.* None of these seem possible in American, and the last, with *having*, is said to be acceptable to very few British speakers.

15.1 Propredicate *do*

In common-core English, intransitive *do* is used as a propredicate for verbs without any auxiliaries: *She volunteered, and he* ***did*** *too*. When there are auxiliaries in the clause with the propredicate, however, a difference arises between British and American use (*CGEL* 12.22–3, 26; *CamGEL* 1524). Then British uses intransitive propredicate *do* in ways American does not. These characteristically British uses are relatively recent, at least in widespread popular use (Butters 1983), and they are at best marginal in American English (Butters 1989, Di Paolo 1993).

15.1.1 After dynamic verbs

If the verb to which propredicate **do** refers is dynamic (*listen* rather than stative *hear*, or *watch* rather than stative *see*), British may use auxiliaries, especially modals and the perfect *have*, followed by intransitive propredicate *do*. American uses only the auxiliaries or else the auxiliaries followed by transitive *do* (with the object *so*, *it*, *that*, or the like). None of the following would be normal in American, which would have instead (in the case of the first citation): *I felt I was* or *I felt I was doing so/that/* etc. The citations are listed by the auxiliary of the propredicate.

<Did I talk too much? I felt I **was doing**.> 1990 Hardwick 111. <Of course you're very lucky, Mr Noble, living so near you can walk into work. Not many people **can do** nowadays.> 1993 Greenwood 194. <Well, Leonidas still maintains that he kept on a heading of 295 degrees, . . . but from what happened afterwards it seems that he **can't have done**.> 1984 Caudwell 142. <'Doesn't it cause breathlessness and, in an extreme attack, death?' [¶] 'It **could do**, certainly.'> 2001 Mortimer 58. <'That is what you said about Maureen, do you remember?'. . . '**I couldn't have done**.'> 2001 Lessing 161. <Jeffrey Barnett drives an FX4S and **has done** for just over nine years.> 1987 May 31 *Sunday Times* Magazine 71/2. <I cannot honestly say that I have reported this monologue with absolute accuracy. If I **had done** it would have been very much longer.> 1987 Bawden 57–8. <He might do something if inspired . . . – he **may do**.> 1987 Mar. 10 *Evening Standard* 6/3–4. <You are too young to remember some old mathematician saying that in an air raid he took refuge under the arch of probability. He **may have done**, but I confess I never could.> 1974 Snow 323. <Does it [eucharistic bread] turn into flesh, during the service? . . . It **might do**.> 1985 Mortimer 29. <But he didn't notice. He **might have done** if you hadn't rung about Tim.> 1987 Bawden 186. <'So she lives in London?' [¶] 'Oh, yes. Well, she **must do** if she's always in the Muckrakers.'> 1988 Mortimer 102. <She looked round the walls and wondered if Ruth and Joe had ever sold any paintings. She supposed they **must have done**.> 1987 Oliver 34. <If you haven't read it, Howard, then you **ought to have done**.> 1984 Price 102. <I'm on holiday, actually. Staying at the Viking Hotel. . . . The carpets come up to my ankles. . . . Mind you, they **should do**, the prices they charge.> 1995 Bowker 93. <So I lied – well I realised I **shouldn't have done**.> 1990 Aug. 26 poster at train station, Didcot Parkway. <Her pa works in the dockyard, or **used to do** before the war.> 1940 Shute 119. <– So you've forgiven Uncle Tom, have you? – Well, I suppose so. I **will do**, if I have the chance.> 1987 Jan. 28 ITV *Coronation Street*. <Laura Danby, their solicitor, had told them a court would almost certainly find against Jan and they were not to worry. She **would do**, wouldn't she?> 2000 Granger 152–3. <I was hoping you'd write or at least send a wire for Christmas. I **would have done**.> 1986 Nov. TV miniseries *Lost Empires*.

15.1.2 After stative verbs

On the contrary, if the verb to which propredicate **do** refers is stative (*hear* rather than dynamic *listen*, or *see* rather than dynamic *watch*), British may still use the same pattern as above, with intransitive propredicate *do*. However, states are something one is in, not something one does. So Americans tend to avoid propredicate *do* in this environment and use instead (in the case of the first citation): *I may have*. The distinction is not one of verb form, but of stative versus dynamic senses, and the same verb may have both senses in different uses. The citations are listed by the verb to which the propredicate refers.

believe <Oh, well, I **may have done**. . . . I dare say I did believe in it once, but I've changed my mind now.> 1985 Pym 154.

care <You don't care who my father was, do you? Any more than I do. Oh, I **might have done** once.> 1987 Bawden 158.

exist <Like Mr Average with his 2.3 children and other statistical nonsense, the absolute gentleman has never existed. He **couldn't have done**.> 1983 Brooke-Taylor 31.

feel <I don't think David feels guilty at all. I **have done** occasionally but I've argued myself out of it.> 1987 Apr. 10 *Evening Standard* 19/5.

find <And *how* had Marcus found something like that out? And if he **had done**, wouldn't he have told me?> 1985 Barnard 142.

go for "like" <I suppose it depended on whether you went for the older man, which . . . Rosie didn't and never **had done**.> 1988 Mortimer 101.

grant "believe" <If you grant that the Brontës are important as a family – and Cambridge, for instance, gives them a single entry, so it **must do** – it might just be worth mentioning that Evelyn Waugh was descended from Henry Cockburn.> 1989 Jan. 22 *Manchester Guardian Weekly* 29/3.

grasp "understand" <I couldn't grasp what had happened. And I don't think many people **could have done**.> 2003 June 20 *Times* T2 5/2.

hate <I do hate wet feet, always **have done**.> 1987 May 27 *Punch* 34/1.

have <I have someone else [as a sexual partner], **have done** for years.> 2003 James 203.

hear <[reply to a question about having heard something:] No, I haven't. . . . **Should I have done**?> 1988 Mortimer 178.

hurt <"It hurts like hell when they do my arms." [¶] . . . "It **must do**."> 1940 Shute 225.

justify <"You think the end justifies the means?" [¶] "It **must do**!"> 1992 Brett 68.

know <'Barbara Darke? I don't think I know her.' [¶] 'You **might do**.'> 1993 Stallwood 196.

like <. . . Mary Coughlan whom I like very much, and **have done** for quite a while.> 1989 Sept. 7 *Midweek* 24/2.

long <Don't you long for it, Molly Coddle? You **must do**.> 1988 Mortimer 65.

love <I even love prunes, and always **have done**.> 1987 Mar. 25 *Evening Standard* 35/6.

mean <"I always thought it meant a sort of portable ghost." [¶] It **may have done**.> 1980 Household 77.

mind <She didn't mind that (though I **would have done**).> 1988 Dec. *Illustrated London News* 58/1.

recognize <Did she recognise her? Helen thought she **must have done**.> 1985 Benedictus 175.

remember <"You remember Parker, don't you?" [¶] She frowned. "No." [¶] . . . "You **must do**."> 1989 Daniel 7.

require <'So putting the burglar alarm out of action would have required special skills?' [¶] 'It **would have done**.'> 2001 Mortimer 20.

think "understand" <"Don't you think how *she* must feel at all?" [¶] I **hadn't done**.> 1987 Bawden 108.

think of "remember" <"Never thought of it." [¶] "Then you **should have done**."> 1985 Clark 180.

trust <"Of course I trusted you. . . . " [¶] "You **ought to have done**."> 1979 Snow 252.

understand <Miss Theca Meijer . . . admits that local people understand little of Daum or Lalique. "But they **will do**," she adds.> 1989 Aug. 4 *Times* 3/3.

15.1.3 After comparative expressions

Similarly, if the propredicate *do* construction follows a comparative expression, British uses the same pattern, whereas American typically uses only the auxiliaries without propredicate *do*. In place of the following, American is likely to have instead (in the case of the first citation): *as much as I should have unassisted*.

as much as <I thus ended up spending three times as much as I **should have done** unassisted.> 1989 Aug. 4 *Times* 10/7.

as promptly as <Mr Nigel Lawson, Chancellor of the Exchequer, censured the Bank of England yesterday for failing to act as promptly as it **should have done** to avert last year's £248 million collapse of Johnson Matthey Bankers.> 1985 June 21 *Times* 1/2.

more than <Had Blader taken more champagne on board than he **should have done**?> 1982 Symons 34.

However, if the verb implied by the British *do* propredicate is a form of *have* and the propredicate is in the perfect, the American equivalent expression would typically be *has/have had*. A simple *has/have* would be misinterpretable in tense. Thus for the following, the American corresponding expression would be *than the Egyptians seem to have had* instead of *than the Egyptians seem to have*.

<Athenians of the Classical period had a much clearer picture of Minoan Crete. . . than the Egyptians seem **to have done**.> 1980 Gill xi.

15.1.4 In other comparisons

Likewise, if the propredicate *do* construction follows *as* (meaning "in the way that") or expressions like *in the way that, the number/amount that*, or *the same (as)*, British uses the same pattern, whereas American typically uses only the auxiliaries without propredicate *do*. In place of the following, American would have instead (in the case of the first citation): *as I believe most of my readers would (have)*.

as <I would have given them three years each [for assault], **as** I believe most of my readers **would have done**.> 1987 May 7 *Evening Standard* 23/1.
in (the) way(s) <. . . you go to all these different places and get to know them **in ways** that you otherwise **wouldn't do**.> 1990 Aug. 26 *Sunday Times* Magazine 12/2.
in the numbers <Women have not come to us **in the numbers** they **should have done**.> 1987 June 11 BBC1 Ken Livingston on election report.
same <Do you think your image still has the **same** impact it **used to do**?> 1986 Oct. TV interviewer.

15.1.5 After the adverb so

If the propredicate expression is preceded by the adverb *so*, propredicate *do* is possible in British, but not in American. Thus in the following, the corresponding American would be *and so I would have* or, alternatively with the pronoun *so* following, *and I would have done so*. Both initial adverb *so* and postverbal pronoun *so* would not normally occur in the same construction: ?**and so I would have done so*.

<. . . not one sonofabitch had the decency to tell me. Afraid I'd bite their fucking heads off, I suppose, and so I **would have done**.> 1975 Lodge 127.

15.1.6 In relative clauses

If propredicate *do* occurs in a relative clause whose relative pronoun (*who*, *which*, *that*, or null) functions as direct object of the propredicate *do*, American has only the auxiliary as propredicate. Thus in the following, American would have *(that) he should have*.

<If Trueman had played all the Test matches [that] he **should have done** . . . he would have taken 400 wickets, not just 307.> 1990 Aug. 24 *Times* 36/2.

15.1.7 In passive constructions

If the propredicate verb is passive, British can (somewhat rarely) still use propredicate *do*. American is more likely to have in the following citation *It has been, often*. If, however, the context had been active, American would have two options: *They can give an account of Mill's "Essay on Liberty" in a double period. They have (done so), often*.

has been done <An account of J. S. Mill's "Essay on Liberty" can be given in a double period with the sixth form. It **has been done**, often.> 1986 Oct. 27 *Times* 17/6.

15.2 Complements of propredicates

British uses *that* dialectally as a complement of a propredicate where it is not usually found in American.

be that <'Ah, officer! Is that Mr Charters' court?' [¶] 'It **is that** [i.e., is Mr Charters' court]'.> 1985 Bingham 90.

do that <Don't like the rain, do you? (*Grim chuckle.*) No. You **don't that**.> 1974 Potter 92.

have that <" 'Evening, Sister," said Loring. "Got a new accident case, I see." [¶] "We **have that**," said the Scotswoman dourly.> 1940 Shute 196.

Substitutes for *that*-clauses functioning as direct objects are *so* and *not*. The verbs often followed by *so* in common-core English are *hope, say*, and *think*, and in British *suppose* and in American *guess* (*LGSWE* 752–3). The construction as a whole is more frequent in CIC British texts than in American, notably in the forms *say so* (British 69.9 iptmw to American 31.6), *suppose so* (23.4 to 3.5), *suppose not* (5.4 to 1.5), *n't think so* (45.9 to 10.7), and *think not* (24.8 to 14.7). British is significantly outnumbered by American only in the forms *guess so* (by 1 to 5) and *guess not* (by 1 to 3.6), frequencies that are relatively somewhat greater than that of the verb *guess* in all its uses in British and American (1 to 3.4).

not <Namely, is it worth paying an extra third for the shopping experience at Harvey Nichols? The Evening Standard fair-do's hounds think **not**.> 1994 Sept. 13 *Evening Standard* 43/4.

n't so <[A:] Can you explain this in some way I'd understand it? [B:] No, I do**n't** think **so**.> 1988 Stoppard 28.

so <'And he's such a handsome chap, isn't he, Rumpole?' . . . [¶] 'I suppose **so**. . . . Although I couldn't fancy him myself.'> 2001 Mortimer 104.

16 Tag questions

16.1 Canonical form

A tag question is a subordinate interrogative clause consisting of the operator of a preceding (often main) clause, typically with reverse polarity (if the preceding-clause operator is affirmative, the tag-clause operator is negative, and vice versa), followed by a pronoun whose antecedent is the subject of the preceding clause: *Julia can help, can't she? James can't help that, can he?* When the tag is negative, the contraction *n't* is usual. The tag question normally occurs at the end of the preceding clause, as in the examples cited. It may have either the rising intonation often associated with *yes/no*-questions, or the falling intonation associated with statements. In written form, a terminal question mark does not necessarily indicate intonation, but may be only conventional. A terminal period, however, is likely to suggest falling intonation. If there is no operator in the preceding clause, the appropriate form of *do* is used in the tag question: *They came, didn't they?*

The tag question is a common-core English construction, but it has some specifically British forms and uses (Algeo 1988a).

16.2 Anomalous forms

16.2.1 Constant polarity

16.2.1.1 Affirmative polarity

Constant affirmative polarity, although not the norm, is nevertheless quite normal, in the sense of being acceptable and not infrequent. Constant affirmative-polarity tag questions ask for confirmation of a statement whose truth is assumed, especially when they have falling intonation.

are you <Anyway, you're letting them go, **are you?**> 1977 Barnard 132.
did you <You put your heart into it, **did you?**> 1985 Mann 165.
do they <They do, **do they?**> 2003 Rowling 441.

do you <You think that, **do you?**> 1985 Bingham 69–70.
is it <This is your flat, **is it**, Miss Sutton?> 1987 Hart 129.
is there <There's going to be a divorce, then, **is there?**> 1976 Raphael 136.
was it <"You remember, there was an accident." [¶] "That was the same pilot, **was it?**"> 1940 Shute 215.
would you <'Something of a squirrel, our Jock,' Caldicott whispered. [¶] 'You'd say that, **would you?**'> 1985 Bingham 48.

16.2.1.2 Negative polarity

Constant negative polarity is rarer and disputed. The construction has been reported for British English (Huddleston 1970, 221; *CamGEL* 892, 895), and examples of it have been cited: *You're not going, **aren't you?*** (O'Connor 1955, 102) and *He hasn't tried, **hasn't he?*** (F. R. Palmer 1968, 41). Constant-polarity double-negative tags have been reported for regional British dialects, such as Scots: *He wouldnae do it, **wouldn't he no?*** (Millar and Brown 1979, 30) and Tyneside Geordie: *You can't do it, **can't you not?*** (Burton-Roberts 1986, 243). A normal-sounding instance is a short mirrorlike sentence with heavily ironic meaning: *You can't catch me. – I can't, **can't I?*** (cited by Jespersen 1940, 496). Quirk et al. (*CGEL* 11.9n) conclude that the construction "has not been clearly attested in actual use." It is at best marginal; there are instances, but all are exceptional in various ways.

can't he <[speaker from Leeds:] 'He's not much cop wi t'bat, or behind timbers neither, but blurry 'ell – he can't 'arf sup ale, **can't he?**'> (nonstandard dialect use) 1985 Ebdon 139.
ent 'e <Our most downwardly mobile politician gave us his jaundiced view of the nation in *The Benn Diaries* . . . an anagram of He is'n' rabid **ent 'e?**> (a stunt rather than an actual use) 1988 Oct. 9 *Sunday Telegraph* 48/5.
isn't she <I'm afraid that Kylie, however good a fighter she is, is unlikely to be worth that much, **isn't she?**> (negative prefix *un-* rather than *not* or *no*) 1995 Jones 88.
oughtn't you <You oughtn't to say that now, **oughtn't you?**> (rare use of interrogative *oughtn't*) 1979 Snow 189.

16.2.2 Elements omitted from preceding clause

In some sentences, the subject and operator (when there is one) have been omitted from the preceding clause but can be inferred from their echo in the tag question.

With reverse polarity:

<Thought it was worth it, **didn't he?**> 1991 Graham 44.

With constant polarity:

<I hope I get the right number. Number 35, **is it?**> 1989 July 29 BBC1.

16.2.3 Variation in the operator or subject

The operator in the tag question may vary from that in the preceding clause. The most frequent such anomaly is the tag *aren't I?* The history and social acceptability of *aren't I?* – like those of *ain't* – are complex (Gilman 1994, 115–6, 60–4). It is standard in British (Burchfield 1996, 97) and was once thought by American commentators to be a Briticism, as it may well have been historically, though it is now widely used colloquially in America. Cf. § 1.2.2.2.

<I'm talking too much, **aren't I?**> 1987 Hart 139.

In the following uses of *have to, have got*, and *have got to*, British has the option of treating *have* as an operator and thus using it in the tag question or of treating it as the main verb and thus inserting *do* in the tag question instead (Swan 1995, 480). American regularly uses *do* in such constructions.

<I had to see her, **hadn't I?**> 1979 Snow 34. <I've got to do something right, **haven't I?**> 1986 Oct. 19 *Sunday Times* 25/4. <I'd still got the hots for her, **hadn't I?**> 1987 Hart 101. But also: <They have to look as though they're earning their money, **don't they?**> 1979 Snow 190.

Other operator anomalies also occur:

<What's this about . . . the American Civil War, **was it?**> (The tense has changed.) 1984 Price 23. <I shall have to ask him, **won't I?**> (The operator has changed.) 1986 Dec. 21 Masterpiece Theatre *Paradise Postponed.*

In some cases, the preceding clause that the tag question echoes is not the main clause but a subordinate one, whereas an echo of the main-clause operator and subject might be expected.

<Grand office you've got here, **haven't you?**> 1979 Snow 256. <It's Mr Lincoln's war we're curious about, **aren't we?**> 1984 Price 84. (The expected tag in both cases would be *isn't it?*)

Although a negative operator in the tag question is usually formed with the contraction *n't*, the full form *not* may be used after the subject pronoun instead.

<The new man at *Private Eye*, he is a dreadful little man, **is he not?**> 1987 Mar. 25 *Punch* 55/1.

The tag question *isn't it* may be colloquially assimilated in pronunciation and reduced to two syllables, spelled variously but usually *innit*. Similarly, other tags such as *ain't it*, *didn't it*, and *isn't he* have parallel colloquial forms. Cf. § 1.2.2.2.

innit Isn't it: CIC British texts have 35.5 iptmw of *innit*; American texts have none. <"Shopping, for me, meant a sample sale or advance ordering from designers' collections at wholesale prices." Coo, another world, **innit?**> 2003 June 20 *Times* T2 3/3. Other spellings: <That's three **in'it?** [reference to

cricket]> 1985 Ebdon 138. <Still . . . that's a perk of living in the country, **in'ert?**> 1985 Ebdon 176.

in'e Isn't he <Well, Mick, 'e's on the sick, like us, **in'e.**> 1995 Jones 132.

ennit Ain't it <"Right leg amputation, **ennit?**" "No!" I exclaimed, sitting up in alarm. "Just a minor knee operation."> 1995 Lodge 9.

dinnit Didn't it <Came in the post this morning, **dinnit?**> 1992 Dexter 235.

16.3 Frequency of use

Although comparative statistics on the use of tag questions in the two national varieties are not available, their frequency in British seems greater than in American, so Americans think of it as characteristically British. British speakers also note the prevalence of the tag question in British use, responding to it with the same annoyance that Americans have for the rhetorical use of *you know* as a filler and emphasizer. The use of the tag question is certainly an old rhetorical device, but the negative response it generates suggests that its frequency may have been increasing in recent years or that some uses may be social markers:

<'So you decided to stay silent?' [¶] 'It was my right, **wasn't it?**' [¶] Judge Chaytor turned in Tanner's direction. 'Do you think you could give your evidence without adding a question to the end of every answer?' [¶] Ian Tanner [19-year-old London school dropout, incipient criminal] gave him a blank look. [¶] 'Sorry. I don't get you.' [¶] 'You said, "it was my right, **wasn't it?**" and before that, "didn't have any choice, **did I?**" '[¶] 'Well I didn't, **did I?**' [¶] 'There, you did it again! Just try and answer the questions without asking your own.'> 1978 Underwood 122. <"Yeah, well, that's right, **isn't it, luv?** We shoulda kept it, I know. Still, as I said – well, we all do things a bit wrong sometimes, **don't we?** And we said we was sorry about everything, **didn't we, luv?**" [¶] Morse was beginning to realize that the last three words, with their appropriate variants, were a rhetorical refrain only, and were not intended to elicit any specific response.> 1992 Dexter 127.

The frequent use of tag questions is a particularly downmarket British phenomenon.

<Look, we had to work together, **didn't we?** . . . And I'd had another bird in between, **hadn't I?** No point in bearing grudges, **is there?**> 1987 Hart 101. <Well I was tempted **wasn't I** . . . not paying I mean . . . so I said I'd come a couple of stops, more like ten . . . they'd been checking **hadn't they**. Silly. £400 fine for a 50p ticket – and a day off work at court – I haven't told them at work. Tricky . . . I work in accounts – it's not exactly a reference **is it** . . .> 1988 London tube train poster on the consequences of not paying for an underground ticket.

Indications of the voguishness of the tag question are the still resounding echoes of Mandy Rice-Davies's 1963 sardonic riposte:

<Mandy Rice Davies, told in court during the Profumo scandal that Lord Astor had denied her allegations, gave a reply that has passed into the language: 'He would, *wouldn't he?*'> 1984 Smith 199. <'Seems he spent a blameless life grooming horses down on some stud farm.' [¶] 'Grooming? He told me he was a vet.' [¶] 'Well he would, **wouldn't he?**'> 2000 Granger 315. <Well, they would say that, **wouldn't they**.> 2003 Mar. 21 BBC World Service reporting the Turkish response to an avowal by the Kurds that they do not intend to form a separate Kurdish state.

The following list illustrates various tag questions:

aren't they <I've grown out of that sort of book. They're all rubbish really, **aren't they?**> 1984 Lodge 258.

can't we <We can do that, **can't we?**> 1974 Snow 7.

did he <As for his schooling, well! . . . Didn't go, **did he**.> 1991 Green 266.

have I <The girl behind the counter, a stringy and exhausted blonde, was selling a packet of cigarettes to a handsome young labourer from a nearby building site. The man had held out a ten-pound note. 'Oh Christ,' said the girl, 'haven't you got anything smaller? I'll have to go next door for some change.' 'So what?' he grinned. 'Aren't I worth it?' 'Dunno,' said the girl, without a change of expression. 'Haven't tried you yet, **have I?**'> 1982 Brookner 70.

is it <Only it's not there now, **is it?**> 2000 Granger 261–2.

need I <I needn't tell you what all this is in aid of, **need I?**> 1979 Snow 273.

shan't we <We shall see, **shan't we**, one way or the other?> 1974 Snow 37.

shouldn't you <Well, you should have thought of that before you married me, **shouldn't you**.> 1989 Sept. 10 ITV preview of a coming program.

was I <'The Super rang me, sir. You told him I was running you back home.' [¶] 'So what?' [¶] 'Well, I *wasn't*, **was I?**'> 1993 Dexter 12.

will you <'I don't know what my own speed was.' [¶] 'What car were you in?' [¶] 'My Jag.' [¶] 'Then you won't have been hanging about, **will you?**'> 1988 Ashford 25.

would I <I didn't think about taking the [car's licence] number, but I wouldn't anyway, **would I?**> 2003 James 147.

wouldn't she <Laura Danby, their solicitor, had told them a court would almost certainly find against Jan and they were not to worry. She would do, **wouldn't she?** thought Damaris grimly.> 2000 Granger 152–3.

16.4 Rhetorical uses

The tag question has several rhetorical uses in common-core English. They include (1) the informational tag question, whose purpose is genuinely to ask for information (*The Bakerloo train goes to Maida Vale*, ***doesn't it?***) and (2) the conversational tag question, whose purpose is to signal that the speaker is including the addressed person as a participant in the discourse and is inviting a confirmatory reply (*It's a lovely time of year*, ***isn't it?***). These two kinds typically have rising, questioning pitch.

British English has other rhetorical uses, which are comparatively rare in American. Increasingly characteristic of British English are the following three types, all of which are rhetorical questions: (3) The punctuational tag question is used to emphasize a preceding statement. It typically has a falling, assertive pitch. Two other uses of the tag question are even more specifically British and also more recent, or at least have recently increased in the notice taken of them and therefore presumably have increased in frequency. They are (4) the peremptory tag question, which follows a statement of obvious truth and is intended to close off further discussion of the topic; and (5) the antagonistic tag question, which follows a statement whose truth the addressee does not know and often cannot know, but which is treated as though it were a statement of obvious truth. Because these kinds of tag questions are rhetorical uses, they are distinguished, not by their own form, but by their contexts, either verbal or situational.

Any of these rhetorical uses may be difficult to identify in a given instance. In the following dialog, Jean is using the tag question in a friendly, conversational way, but her husband, who is annoyed with her for other reasons, reacts negatively to her tags as a verbal mannerism and interprets them as an argumentative signal:

<Jean: I suppose I'd better unpack. [¶] Bernard: There's no hurry. Why are you always in such a hurry? [¶] Jean: We don't want our clothes to be creased, **do we?** [¶] (*His whole posture, his whole expression, shows that he has gone far beyond mere irritability into something approaching dangerous hypertension.*) [¶] Bernard: Why are you so damned argumentative, Jean? It gets on my nerves. [¶] Jean: Argumentative? Me? [¶] Bernard: About the blasted clothes. [¶] Jean: All I said was that we don't want our clothes to be creased. [¶] Bernard: No, you didn't. You said, 'We don't want our clothes to be creased, ***do we?***' It's that bloody, never ending '**do we?**' The way you seem to make a perfectly ordinary, perfectly reasonable statement sound combative and – [¶] (*He stops, hearing the grating excess in his own tongue, feeling the tense irritability in his own limbs. She looks at him, sad.*)> 1974 Potter 142.

16.4.1 Informational tag questions

Informational tag questions, which call for an active response from the addressee, are sometimes ways of making a request, as in the first example below. Otherwise, they seek information.

<You wouldn't be a dear and collect it on the way back, **would you?**> 1975 Price 123. <You know my daughter Elizabeth, I think, **don't you?**> 1974 Snow 17.

16.4.2 Conversational tag questions

<Bit of trouble, back there on the Pentonville Road, **wasn't there?**> 1987 Bawden 174.

16.4.3 Punctuational tag questions

The punctuational tag question is sometimes recognizable by its use in a soliloquy, where no response or interaction with an addressee apart from the speaker is possible:

<My son didn't tell me – I found out about his fare fiddling through a court letter . . . No job and this won't help. So what now? I don't know, things have changed, **haven't they**.> 1989 Aug. 29 poster on London tube train.

Another sign of the punctuational tag is a medial position within its sentence, which inhibits its being taken as an invitation for a response:

<We're all terribly keen, **aren't we**, on ethnic cultures.> 1989 July 21 *Punch* 6/3.

Typically, punctuational use is merely a matter of emphasis without either encouragement or discouragement of a reply by the addressee. In some contexts, British might also use *mind you*, and American might use *you know*:

<I don't want wet and mud all over my shop, **do I** now?> 1974 Potter 94. <Because you say no to everything, **don't you?**> 1988 Mortimer 182. <You can be a prat, **can't you**.> 1989 Jan. 28 ch. 9 San Francisco *Mystery: Inspector Morse*. <Why should you? They don't tell even you everything, **do they?**> 1992 Dexter 66.

16.4.4 Peremptory tag questions

Whereas the conversational tag is used to include the addressee in the discourse, the peremptory tag question is intended to close off discussion and discourage the addressee. At its gentlest, spoken with a falling pitch, it merely puts off a questioner: *[A:] Who do you think will win the game? [B:] We'll know at the end,* ***won't we***. In its more aggressive form, sometimes spoken with a low level pitch, it is rudely abrasive: *[A:] When will the taxi arrive? [B:] We'll know when it gets here,* ***won't we***.

The peremptory tag is not recent. The following comment on British use of tag questions was written shortly after the turn of the twentieth century and illustrates both the conversational and peremptory tags:

<English people end almost every sentence with a question. Your grand lady says: "It looks like rain, **doesn't it?** We shall have a muddy ride, **sha'n't we?**" You say to the girl in the shop, "These gloves are hard to get on"; and

she replies: "But all gloves are hard to get on at first, **aren't they**? And they soon wear easier, **don't they?**"> 1901 *Harper's Monthly Magazine* 103:448.

The grand lady's comments on the weather use the polite conversational tag. The shop girl's response, on the other hand, uses what is apparently a gentle peremptory tag, designed to stifle the customer's complaint. In this instance, the peremptory tag may seem to be a working-class feature; however, it extends to all social levels. In the following example, Prince Philip's annoyance during a royal tour in China was occasioned by previous press reports of his utterance of racial slurs concerning slanted eyes:

<. . . the Duke gathered a group of ocularly-suitable girls around him at a cultural performance in Kunming, demanded that the Fleet Street photographers record the event and barked to the . . . reporters . . . "I've got to do something right, **haven't I?**"> 1986 Oct. 19 *Sunday Times* 25/4.

The Duke's tag question was clearly intended to close off, not open up, discourse. The Queen's consort and the shop girl are fellows under the skin.

Peremptory tags typically follow statements of generally acknowledged, obvious, universal, or analytical truth. The implication of the aggressive variety is that everyone knows such obvious truths, and consequently even someone as dim-witted as the addressee must also know them. As a way of informing the hearer about what everyone is expected already to know, the peremptory tag is a form of insult, a put-down:

<[A:] Will it take long, the tea? [B:] It has to boil, **doesn't it**.> 1986 Oct. Peter Barnes's adaptation of G. Feydeau's *Scenes from a Marriage*, Barbican Theatre.

The purpose of the peremptory tag, whether gentle or aggressive, is to leave no room for a response, as in the following bit of rhetoric:

<Lord Wilson [Harold Wilson, former prime minister] won't say. If the Lords debate defence, "I'll have a chance to say what I think then, **won't I**. You'll have to wait."> 1987 Mar. 11 *Evening Standard* 6/3.

A telephone query to Her Majesty's Post Office about a wrong customs charge on a package of personal stationery material that postal inspectors had treated as commercial import produced the following exchange, in which the purpose of the response was to prevent what the postal official interpreted as a complaint about improper service:

<[A:] It was my property sent to me for my use. [B:] Well we couldn't know that, **could we**.> 1986 fall telephone conversation with a Post Office official, London.

Television programs with lower-class settings also provide examples:

<Well, we don't know, **do we**. That's what we're waitin' to find out.> 1987 Feb. 2 ITV *Coronation Street*. <Well, if you look through these now, you'll get an

idea, **won't you**.> 1987 Feb. 3 BBC1 *EastEnders*. <I work here, **don't I**.> 1987 Mar. 17 BBC1 *EastEnders*. <They demolished our street, so we had to move, **didn't we**.> 1987 Mar. 23 ITV *Coronation Street*.

Other examples of peremptory tags:

<'. . . you seemed in a bit of a hurry to go away again.' [¶] 'Well, I would, **wouldn't I?**' countered Taunton sullenly. 'You're the bloody Bill [police], **aren't you?**'> 1987 Hart 99. <[mystery writer Ruth Rendell:] *I* am British. I was born here. And my mother was a Swede. . . . At the time of the Falklands War I said to my aunt – my father's sister, the *English* side – something about thinking that it was an unfortunate waste of life, time, energy, and money. And she said to me, "Oh well, you would feel like that. You're not really English, **are you?**"> 1990 Critchfield 277. <Sky Television commented. "You'd better talk to News International about it," a spokesman tells me. "It's not really a Sky issue, **is it?**"> 1990 Aug. 20 *Evening Standard* 6/3. <At least I assume she is. I can't frigging see, **can I?**> 1994 Sept. 28–Oct. 5 *Time Out* 8/2.

16.4.5 Antagonistic tag questions

Still farther removed from the politeness of conversational tags is the antagonistic tag, which resembles the peremptory tag, except that its pitch is characteristically low falling. The statement that it follows is one whose truth or falseness the addressee does not and could not know. Because the addressee is incapable of knowing the truth of the statement, which the tag nevertheless implies everyone should know, the addressee is cast in the role of someone who is willfully stupid (*CGEL* 19.63).

Millar and Brown (1979, 35) ascribe use of this tag to Edinburgh Scots and illustrate it with this example: *I've got a headache, **haven't I?*** Since addressees cannot know the internal state of the speaker, but are expected by the tag to do so, they are put into a dilemma. The effect of such a tag, Millar and Brown say, is "reprimanding, hostile and aggressive." As the following examples illustrate, the antagonistic tag is by no means a Scots monopoly, although it is characteristically British:

<'Nice-looker, sir?' ventured Lewis after a couple of miles. [¶] 'I didn't bloody see her, **did I?**' growled Morse. 'She's in Spain.'> 1981 Dexter 158. <'You know its [the word *commando*'s] origin?' [¶] It was a small innocent challenge to an ex-history teacher. 'We took that from the Boers, who fought us in South Africa, **didn't we?**'> 1985 Price 38. <I talked to him all right. There was just one problem. He wasn't bloody listening, **was he**.> (The person addressed has no knowledge of the situation.) 1986 Dec. 20 BBC1 *Bergerac*. <'You didn't see Vera Jackman? Down by the front gate, say?' [¶] 'I went the other way, **didn't I?**'> 1987 Hart 101. <Oh, you stupid woman – it's his child, **isn't it**.> (The speaker is aware that addressee does not know the fact.) 1987 Apr. 1

ITV *Coronation Street*. <'Who?' [¶] 'Well, I couldn't see that, **could I?** It was much too dark.'> 1988 Mortimer 173. <"Have you still got the postcard?" [¶] "No. Threw it away, **didn't I**."> 1994 Dexter 262. <"Why on earth did you lose your temper like that?" [¶] "He gave me aggravation, **didn't he?**"> 2003 James 241.

16.5 Other forms and uses

16.5.1 After imperatives

After affirmative imperatives, British English often has a tag question: *will you* or *won't you* (Swan 1995, 480). An American question after a positive imperative like *Help yourself* (for which British might use *will you* or *won't you*) might be *why don't you?* (*CamGEL* 942).

After a negative imperative, *will you* is also possible:

<You use the handkerchief for display purposes only. . . . Don't go and blow your nose on it, **will you?**> 1985 Mortimer 100.

After *let's*, British English uses *shall we* (Swan 1995, 306), but other modals also occur:

<Let's give her another five minutes, **should we?**> 1972 Drabble 20.

16.5.2 Invariable tag questions

Invariable tag questions are occasionally used in English. The following are two well-established ones:

eh? Although associated by Americans with Canada, the invariable tag *eh?* is also found in British, which is doubtless the source of the Canadian use. **1.** Following a statement <'You reckon he spent the night with Taunton's body dangling over his head?' [¶] 'Better than taking a chance of being seen sloping back to the house though, **eh?**'> 1987 Hart 171–2. **2.** Following a question <And to what do you attribute Waltham's excellence, **eh?**> 1985 Price 235. **3.** Reduplicated <Killing animals, killing people. . . . Who's to say he didn't kill that poor girl? I ask you. **Eh? Eh?** Snares and strangling by rope? Very little difference. **Eh? Eh?**> 1987 Hart 48.

what? "informal, dated used for emphasis or to invite agreement: *pretty poor show, what?*" (*NODE*). <[ref. to cricket] Think we contained them pretty well, **what?**> 1985 Ebdon 135.

British teenagers have been reported by Anna-Brita Stenström (1997) as using *yeah* and *innit* as invariable tags. Examples she cites include these: *And they're not gonna stay with me,* ***yeah?*** *Just gonna go off.* ***Yeah? I was talking to you earlier on innit***. Also (*LGSWE* 1122–3), *Teachers are very unfair in this school* ***innit?*** These examples do not show subject or tense concord and so are indeed instances of invariant use, although negative *innit* seems to follow the principle of reverse polarity in occurring after positive statements. Invariable *innit* is nonstandard but not restricted to teenager use. In CIC British texts, 38 percent of the tokens of *innit* (most of which are in nonstandard contexts) are invariable.

innit <These trainers cost me £70. If I mash them, I'll get another pair, **innit** Miss? > 1990 Sept. *Evening Standard* magazine 72/4.

A number of other expressions can be pressed into service as invariable tag questions, of which the following are examples:

don't you think? <There's a terrible tendency to think of the Jacobean dramatists as parochial and elitist, **don't you think?**> 1985 Taylor 199.
hm <Perhaps you might suggest to Lord Chandler that he keeps in touch, **hm?**> 1989 Dickinson 28.
right <I'm unemployed, **right?** And it's free here, **right?**> 1987 Fraser, *Your* 29.

17 Miscellaneous

17.1 Focus

A number of patterns are available for focusing information in a sentence, and of those patterns, several seem to be particularly characteristic of British English.

1. The specific subject of the sentence may be stated first as an isolated noun phrase, followed by the sentence with a pronoun representing that subject in its normal position. This pattern emphasizes the subject as the topic of discourse. In effect this pattern says, "Here's what I'm talking about, and this is what I'm saying about it."

<**Doreen, she** only works part time down the betting shop.> 1995 Jones 132.

2. The specific subject of the sentence may be shifted to the end of the sentence as a tag, leaving a pronoun in its normal place at the beginning of the sentence. This pattern also focuses an item (the subject) that is normally old information. In effect it says, "Here's what I'm saying, and this is what I'm saying it about." Cf. *CGEL* 18.59.

<**She** was a right old so-and-so, **his mum**.> 1992 Charles 128.

This pattern is also used in questions.

<Will **it** take long, **the tea**?> 1986 Oct. Peter Barnes's adaptation of G. Feydeau's *Scenes from a Marriage*, Barbican, London.

If the subject that is extraposed as a tag is a pronoun identical with the one in the subject position, the effect is one of emphasis and perhaps annoyance.

<**You** hauled me out to come here at very short notice, **you**.> 1985 Clark 102.

3. A variation on pattern (2) is to repeat the operator after the subject in the tag. The effect is emphasis, especially when the extraposed subject is a pronoun identical with the pronoun in the subject position.

<**That's** rubbish **that is**.> 1985 Ebdon 174. <**It's** usually a better motive than sex, **money is**.> 1993 Neel 233.

Alternatively, the operator may be repeated before the subject in the tag.

<**It's** right tasty, **is Websters.**> 1986 Nov. 15 TV ad.

If the main clause contains no operator, dummy *do* is used in the tag, either after or before the extraposed subject.

<. . . **she** likes her mince, **Mrs H does.**> 1985 Ebdon 103. <. . . **she** got about a bit, **did the duchess.**> 1999 Mar. 14 *Sunday Times* 10 54/4.

4. Instead of repeating the subject and a linking-verb *be* as a tag, they may both simply be shifted to the end of the subject complement.

<Six days in an open boat, **my dad was.**> 1985 Mortimer 31–2. <Fifty-eight, **he is.**> 1989 Drabble 9.

This shift occurs also in questions, in which the operator therefore precedes the subject.

<Bad on the motorway **was it** this morning, Brian?> 1988 Lodge 192. <In there, **is she**?> 1993 Smith 285.

5. A combination of the question versions of patterns (4) and (2) produces a sequence of subject complement (with the omission of *a* before an indefinite nominal), followed by operator and subject pronoun, followed by the extraposed subject noun phrase.

<Ypres 1915, **is it, this one**?> 1985 Price 109. <Good writer, **is he, this Eliot bloke**?> 1988 Lodge 340.

6. A variation on pattern (4) is to shift the subject, but omit the linking verb altogether, producing a pattern consisting of a subject complement followed by its verbless subject.

<. . . after the war he couldn't get into Raffles Hotel. **Sad**, that.> 1989 July 22 *Spectator* 41/1. <Comforting thought, **that**, isn't it?> (with a tag question) 1995 Sept. tube train poster ad for an insurance company.

This pattern occurs also for questions.

<Certain to have scarpered to the capital, don't you reckon, **the lad**?> 1992 Dexter 276.

7. A combination of patterns (6) and (2) produces a sequence of subject complement, followed by subject pronoun, followed by the extraposed subject noun phrase.

<Good for trade, **that, a good-looking barmaid.**> 1987 Hart 22.

8. The subject may be extraposed as a tag, leaving the verb in initial position.

<The old Porky Porsche? Yes. Goes all right, **this one.**> 1986 Brett 151.

9. In a pattern related to (8), the extraposed tag subject is accompanied by the operator and sometimes other auxiliaries. The result has a Star-Wars Yoda-speak quality.

<Fair kicking himself **he'll be**.> 1940 Shute 52. <Turned his mind for life, **you have**.> 1986 Bradbury 44. <Always contradicting me, **my sergeant is**!> 1992 Dexter 121.

The accompanying operator may be dummy *do*.

<Like to be noticed, **girls do**.> 1987 Oct. *Illustrated London News* 57/2. <Hated it, **I did**.> 1988 Lodge 114.

In the following imperative, the implicit subject *you* is lacking, as expected.

<Sit down, **do**.> 1986 Sherwood 113.

Did occurs in nonstandard use as an operator with *ought*, especially in the negative *didn't ought to* for "ought not to have," but also in the following example of this pattern.

<Ought to be grateful for the way he stood by her, **she did**.> 1993 Mason 134.

In questions, the extraposed operator and subject resemble a tag question.

<Got any bits about girls in it [a novel], **has it**?> 1985 Mortimer 27. <Go on the canal much, **do you**?> 1993 Smith 23.

In the following negative, the negation has been replicated by *n't* in the tag.

<Never wanted to mix, **he didn't**.> 2000 Rowling 8.

10. A combination of the question versions of patterns (9) and (2) produces a sequence of main verb and complement, followed by operator and subject pronoun, followed by the extraposed subject noun phrase.

<Got his own stormtroopers, now, **has he, the VC**?> 1988 Lodge 85.

11. A variety of other exceptional patterns are illustrated by the following. The subject is extraposed, and the verb (*have* or the like) is omitted altogether.

<No ties, **most of 'em**. And look at the bloke over there, he's got his shirt hanging out.> 1988 Lodge 343.

The object of a preposition is extraposed to initial position as a topic.

<**The selling of council houses**, the party couldn't wait to get on with.> 1989 Sept. 9 *Times* 33/3.

There's (adjective) I am in the sense "I'm glad that" is doubtless a regionalism. Neither CIC nor the *OED* has examples.

<. . . but **there's** glad **I am** I remembered.> 1987 Oliver 217.

17.2 Phatic language

Phatic language consists of expressions used as a basis for social intercommunication. Phatic expressions are not intended to be and, when correctly perceived, are not taken to be literal statements, but are merely conventional formulas of etiquette. For example, the greeting on meeting someone *How do you do?* is not a question about how one does anything or even how one is, but is a formal acknowledgment of an introduction.

Many phatic expressions are common-core English, but British and American differ in their choice of some others. The following is a list of samples, far from extensive. Many such items are treated by Michael Swan (1995, e.g., 82, 539, 543–6, 581).

What one says to ask another speaker to repeat or explain something varies, and may involve questions of propriety. British options include *(I beg your) pardon? Sorry?* and *What (did you say)?* American options are *Excuse me?* and *Pardon me?* (*CGEL* 11.34n). As some of the following citations make evident, Britons disagree about the proper thing to say.

Pardon? (I beg your) <"James p'd the old q." [¶] "I beg your **pardon?**" [¶] "Popped the question. Proposed."> 1984 Brett 174. <'There are lots of examples, fact and fiction, of upper-class siblings having it off. . . . Just like poor Annabella' [¶] 'What?' said Barnaby. . . . [¶] '**Pardon** dear, not what.' [¶] 'Annabella. You know . . . in *Tis Pity*.'> 1987 Graham 249.

Sorry? <"I'll take a shaft [var. of *shufti* "look"] at this lot. You go and see what's in the Max." [¶] "**Sorry?**" [¶] Stan Fogden grinned triumphantly. "Maximum Headroom – Bedroom."> 1984 Brett 38. <Dermot taught me to say 'What?' instead 'Pardon?' (although David Rocksavage, heir to the Marquess of Cholmondeley, said it was probably better to say 'I'm **sorry** . . . ?')> 1990 Sept. *Evening Standard* magazine 22/2.

What? <Samantha Upward's *au pair* comes in very red in the face, saying, 'Zacharias refuses to say "Pardon".' [¶] Whereupon Samantha goes even redder and stands on one leg, saying, 'Well actually we always say "**What**". I don't know why.'> 1979 Cooper 79. <"Did you give him a glass of that malt?" [¶] "**What?**" [¶] "You didn't give him a *drink*?"> 1992 Dexter 210.

A British advance apology is *excuse me* and a retroactive apology is *sorry*, whereas Americans use the former also for an apology after the fact (Swan 1995, 544).

excuse me <Then there were the pompous Beeb cameramen who frantically ran around shouting things like: "**Excuse me**, there's a crew coming through."> 1987 Mar. 23 *Evening Standard* 27/6. <"**Excuse me**, lads!" A middle-aged woman . . . pushed by them.> 1991 Lodge 62.

sorry <Americans . . . say 'Excuse me' when they mean '**Sorry**'.> 1982 Trudgill 134. <. . . inadvertent bodily contact is a moral gaffe and a squashed restaurant in London where neighbouring tables brushed arms would resound with the perpetual echo of "**sorree**".> 1999 Mar. 13 *Times Magazine* 89/2–3.

Agreeing with a request that one do something is also signaled variably and differs between varieties (*CGEL* 8.100, 19.48). Characteristic British responses are *Righto* and *Will do* with pitch falling on the first syllable and rising on the second, compared to an American *Sure* with falling pitch (405.8 iptmw of *sure* in CIC American texts, 147.6 in British). Another response option, *Right*, is sometimes thought of as American, but is nearly 1.7 times more frequent in British texts. Other characteristically British responses of agreement are *Quite* and *Quite so*, with falling pitch, and *Rather* with falling-rising pitch (*CGEL* 8.130n). For these as well as *Righto* and its variants, cf. § 10.

Will do (about 10 times more frequent in CIC British texts than in American) <'I want you to call the public health people.' . . . '**Will do**,' said Fielding.> 1997 fiction CIC.

Thank you and *Thanks* are the principal expressions in common-core English. A British form is *Ta*, occurring initially in 15.7 iptmw of CIC British texts and in 0.5 of American.

A favored British response to *Thank you* or its equivalents is *Not at all*, which is 2 times more frequent in CIC British texts than in American; a favored American response is *You're welcome*, which is 2.7 times as frequent in CIC American texts as in British.

On being introduced to someone, a British response is *How do you do*, which is nearly 4 times more frequent in CIC British texts than in American, where it would be considered formal, a more usual response being *Nice to meet you*, which is 1.7 times more frequent in American texts than in British.

On meeting someone whom one knows, a British greeting is *How are you*, which is 1.74 times more frequent in CIC British texts than in American, whereas the response *How (are) you doing* is 1.4 times more frequent in American texts than in British.

For bidding farewell, the common-core English forms are *goodbye*, its minor spelling variation *goodby* (9.5 times more frequent in American than in British CIC texts), and its short form *bye* (about a quarter more frequent in British than in American). Distinctively British forms with little or no American use are *cheers* and *ta ta*, with the spelling variant *ta ra*.

The salutation in a letter is normally followed by a comma in British use, but by either a comma or a colon in American use. The latter is often said to be more formal (*CGEL* III.11), but it predominates, even after given names, in CIC American texts (which consist, however, not of letters directly but of published versions of letters in periodicals or fiction). The British complementary close to a letter is said to be typically *Yours faithfully/sincerely/truly/ever*, in contrast with the American reverse order of *Cordially/Sincerely/Truly yours* (*CGEL* 8.91n, III.30). The published versions of American letters in CIC have very few complementary closes, probably partly because letters published in periodicals generally do not use them; but among the few examples, *Sincerely yours* and *Yours truly* are equal in representation and both are outnumbered by *Yours forever*. The comparative paucity of evidence and its secondary nature do not allow firm conclusions.

17.3 Numbers

In names for numbers, British and American differ in several respects. In CIC texts, British uses *nought* nearly 30 times more often than American does, and a good many of those uses are for the number *0*. American prefers the spelling *naught*, but uses it mainly as a pronoun synonym of *nothing* rather than as a number. American uses *zero* about 1.6 times more often than British does. British uses *nil* 8 times more often than American does, notably in reporting the scores of sporting events.

CIC British texts have nearly 20 times as many tokens of *double* plus a number as American texts do, thus 5644 might be *five six double four*.

Terms for major units above a million formerly differed between British and American, but the American system has now been generally adopted in England. The more frequent older uses are as follows:

milliard 1,000,000,000, now one billion.
billion 1,000,000,000,000, now one trillion.

For higher numbers and their history, see the *MW* Table of Numbers.

17.3.1 Time of day

In telling time, for minutes under ten after an hour, the number *oh* has been omitted in the following so that *seven five* appears for *seven oh five* or *five after seven*.

<It appears she stayed in the bus station until the Larking bus left at **seven-five**.> 1968 Aird 100.

A matter of punctuation only, hours are separated from minutes by a period or dot in British use, but by a colon in American. Thus British *10.30* would be American *10:30*.

<This Sunday at **3.00** the film is appropriately HG Wells' 'Things To Come'.> 1989 Aug. 30 *Metropolitan* 21/1–2.

Cf. also § 8.1 GONE for constructions like *gone six* for *after/past six* and § 8.2 for constructions like *half five* for *half past five*.

17.4 Dates

For a day that is a week after a specified day, British uses the following patterns:

day **week** A week from *day*: CIC has 18.8 iptmw in British texts and none in American texts, but the construction also exists in some American dialects. <Tony Adams could . . . captain England in the friendly against Romania at Wembley on **Wednesday week**.> 1994 Oct. 3 *Evening Standard* 80/3. <Barnsley's postponed quarter-final tie with Tottenham will now take place **tomorrow week**.> 1999 newspaper CIC. Cf. § 8.2.2 WEEK *DAY*.

To express a time in the past, British can use the formula *year(s) last (month/week)*, in the sense "year(s) ago last (month/week)": <McGuigan relieved Eusebio Pedroza, from Panama, of his World Boxing Association title in London a **year last** June.> 1986 Oct. 1 *Times* 42/7. And it uses the same formula to express a period of time up to some point in the past, in the sense "year(s) as of last (month/week)": <I've been there a **year last** week.> 1998 spoken text CIC.

British uses several patterns for specifying dates. The most frequent is exemplified by *1/1st/first September*, which is 12 times more frequent than in American. The most frequent in American is *September 1/1st/first*, which is about 1.3 times more frequent than in British. If a year follows in the second pattern, it is set off by commas, but not in the first pattern. This difference in order creates ambiguity when numbers are also used for months: *9-11* is September 11 in America but *9 November* in Britain (*CGEL* 6.66). British forms are illustrated below.

< . . . the church would be closed from **27 July** to **1 September**.> 1982 Pym 240. <The next counterfoil after these recorded a withdrawal from a bank in St. Malo on **the first of May**.> 1989 Caudwell 276. < . . . term starts on **September the first**.> 1998 Rowling 17 (*US ed.* September first). <During the Westland affair, back on **the February 15**, 1986, she had held the first of a number of secret meetings at Chequers.> 1987 June 13 *Times* 28/3.

Common-core English can use cardinal numbers for days either before or after months: *9 November* or *November 9*. It also can use ordinal numbers with or without *the* after months: *November (the) 9th* or before in the formula *the 9th of November*. British may, in addition, use a simple ordinal number before the month: *9th November*; this is rare in American.

ordinal month The *ordinal* of *month*; *month* (the) *ordinal* <Born **third October** 1955.> 2003 James 356. <As recently as **30th August** . . . > 2003 Rowling 275 (*US ed.* August 30th).

Bibliography of British book citation sources

Aird, Catherine. 1968. *Henrietta Who?* London: Corgi, 1988.

1977. *Parting Breath.* London: Corgi, 1988.

2000. *Little Knell.* London: Macmillan, Pan Books, 2002.

2002. *Amendment of Life.* London: Macmillan, Pan Books.

Amis, Kingsley. 1969. *The Green Man.* Chicago: Academy Chicago, 1986.

1987. *The Old Devils.* New York: Summit Books.

1988. *Difficulties with Girls.* New York: Summit Books.

Archer, Jeffrey. 1976. *Not a Penny More, Not a Penny Less.* Garden City, NY: Doubleday.

1980. *A Quiver Full of Arrows.* London: Hodder & Stoughton, 1987.

1984. *First among Equals.* New York: Simon & Schuster, Pocket Books.

Ashford, Jeffrey [pseudonym of Roderic Jeffries]. 1963. *Will Anyone Who Saw The Accident . . .* New York: Harper & Row.

1988. *The Honourable Detective.* Roslyn, NY: Detective Book Club, 1989.

Bainbridge, Beryl. 1989. *An Awfully Big Adventure.* New York: Carroll & Graf, 1995.

Barnard, Robert. 1977. *Blood Brotherhood.* New York: Penguin, 1985.

1985. *Fête Fatale* [orig. *Disposal of the Living*]. New York: Dell, 1987.

1986. *Political Suicide.* New York: Dell, 1989.

1991. *A Scandal in Belgravia.* London: Transworld, Corgi, 1992.

Bawden, Nina. 1987. *Circles of Deceit.* New York: St. Martins.

Benedictus, David. 1985. *Floating Down to Camelot.* London: Futura.

Benson, Edward Frederic. 1931. *Mapp and Lucia.* New York: Harper and Row, 1986.

Bingham, Stella. 1985. *Charters & Caldicott.* [Based on the BBC TV serial by Keith Waterhouse] New York: Penguin, 1986.

Bishop, Paul. 1991. *Chapel of the Ravens.* New York: TOR Books, 1992.

Bowker, David. 1995. *The Death Prayer.* London: Vista, 1996.

Bradbury, Malcolm. 1976. *Who Do You Think You Are?* London: Arrow/Arena, 1986.

1987. *Cuts.* New York: Harper & Row.

Brett, Simon. 1982. *Murder Unprompted.* New York: Scribner's.

1984. *Not Dead, Only Resting.* New York: Dell, 1986.

1986. *A Nice Class of Corpse.* New York: Dell, 1990.

1992. *Mrs. Pargeter's Pound of Flesh.* New York: Macmillan, 1993.

Brookes, H. F., and C. E. Fraenkel. 1988. *Life in Britain.* Rev. ed. Oxford: Heinemann, 1989.

Brooke-Taylor, Tim. 1983. *Rule Britannia*. London: Dent.
Brookner, Anita. 1982. *Providence*. London: Triad Grafton, 1988.
Burden, Pat. 1989. *Screaming Bones*. London: Headline, 1991.
Burton-Roberts, Noel. 1986. *Analysing Sentences*. London: Longman.
Byatt, A. S. 1985. *Still Life*. New York: Collier, 1991.
1990. *Possession*. London: Vintage, 1991.
Cannell, Dorothy. 1985. *Down the Garden Path*. New York: Bantam, 1989.
1988. *The Widows Club*. New York: Bantam, 1989.
Carter, Ronald. 1987. *Vocabulary*. London: Allen & Unwin.
Caudwell, Sarah. 1984. *The Shortest Way to Hades*. New York: Penguin Books, 1986.
1989. *The Sirens Sang of Murder*. New York: Dell, 1990.
2000. *The Sibyl in Her Grave*. New York: Dell, 2001.
Charles, Kate. 1991. *A Drink of Deadly Wine*. London: Headline, 1992.
1992. *The Snares of Death*. London: Headline Book Publishing.
1995. *Evil Angels among Them*. London: Headline Book Publishing, 1996.
Clark, Douglas. 1985. *Jewelled Eye*. New York: Harper & Row, Perennial, 1988.
1986. *The Big Grouse*. New York: Perennial Library, 1988.
Cleeves, Ann. 1991. *Murder in My Backyard*. New York: Fawcett.
1993. *Another Man's Poison*. New York: Ballantine, Fawcett Gold Medal.
Cooper, Jilly. 1979. *Class*. London: Corgi, 1989.
Crawford, Phyllis. 1938. *In England Still*. London: n.p.
Critchfield, Richard. 1990. *An American Looks at Britain*. New York: Doubleday, Anchor, 1991.
Critchley, Julian. 1991. *Hung Parliament*. London: Headline, 1992.
1992. *Floating Voter*. London: Headline, 1993.
Daniel, Mark. 1989. *Unbridled* [orig. *Under Orders*]. New York: Avon, 1992.
Department of Transport and Central Office of Information. See *Highway Code*.
Dexter, Colin. 1975. *Last Bus to Woodstock*. Toronto: Bantam, 1989.
1977. *The Silent World of Nicholas Quinn*. New York: Bantam, 1988.
1979. *Service of All the Dead*. New York: Bantam, 1988.
1981. *The Dead of Jericho*. New York: Bantam, 1988.
1983. *The Riddle of the Third Mile*. New York: Bantam, 1988.
1992. *The Way through the Woods*. New York: Ballantine, Ivy Books, 1994.
1993. *Morse's Greatest Mystery and Other Stories Including As Good As Gold*. London: Macmillan/Pan, 1995.
1994. *The Daughters of Cain*. New York: Ivy Books.
1996. *Death Is Now My Neighbour*. London: Pan Books, 1997.
1999. *The Remorseful Day*. London: Pan Books, 2000.
Dickinson, Peter. 1983. *Hindsight*. London: Arrow, 1987.
1986. *Tefuga*. London: Arrow Books, 1987.
1989. *Skeleton-in-Waiting*. London: Arrow, 1990.
1991. *Play Dead*. New York: Mysterious Press, 1993.
1994. *The Yellow Room Conspiracy*. New York: Mysterious Press, 1995.
Drabble, Margaret. 1972. *The Needle's Eye*. Harmondsworth, Middlesex: Penguin, 1984.
1980. *The Middle Ground*. New York: Knopf.
1989. *A Natural Curiosity*. New York: Viking Penguin.
2001. *The Peppered Moth*. San Diego: Harcourt, Harvest Book, 2002.
Ebdon, John. 1985. *Ebdon's England*. London: Sphere, 1987.

Edwards, Ruth Dudley. 1998. *Publish and Be Murdered*. London: HarperCollins, 1999.
Ellis, Arthur Edward. 1954. *Refereeing round the World*. London: n.p.
Firth, Violet Mary [pseudonym Dion Fortune]. 1927. *The Demon Lover*. London: Aquarian, 1957.
1935. *The Winged Bull*. New York: Weiser, 1971.
Fraser, Antonia. 1987. *Your Royal Hostage*. London: Methuen, 1988.
Freeling, Nicolas. 1994. *You Who Know*. New York: Warner, Mysterious Press, 1995.
Frost, David, and Antony Jay. 1967. *The English*. New York: Stein and Day, 1968.
Fyfield, Frances. 1994. *Clear Conscience*. London: Corgi, 1995.
Gash, Jonathan. 1986. *The Tartan Sell*. New York: Penguin, 1987.
Gilbert, Michael. 1984. *The Black Seraphim*. New York: Penguin, 1985.
Gill, Christopher. 1980. *Plato: The Atlantis Story*. Bristol: Bristol Classical Press.
Glaister, Lesley. 1991. *Trick or Treat*. London: Secker and Warburg.
Graham, Caroline. 1987. *The Killings at Badger's Drift*. New York: Avon, 1989.
1989. *Death of a Hollow Man*. New York: Avon, 1991.
1991. *Murder at Madingley Grange*. New York: Avon, 1992.
1993. *Death in Disguise*. New York: Avon, 1994.
1996. *Faithful unto Death*. London: Hodder Headline.
Granger, Ann. 1992. *Cold in the Earth*. New York: Avon.
2000. *Shades of Murder*. London: Headline, 2001.
Grant-Adamson, Lesley. 1991. *Too Many Questions*. New York: Fawcett Crest, 1993.
Green, Christine. 1991. *Deadly Errand*. London: Headline, 1993.
1992. *Deadly Admirer*. London: Headline, 1994.
Greenwood, Diane M. 1991. *Unholy Ghosts*. London: Headline, 1992.
1993. *Idol Bones*. London: Headline.
Grotta-Kurska, Daniel. 1976. *J. R. R. Tolkien: Architect of Middle Earth*. Ed. Frank Wilson. Philadelphia: Running Press.
Hardwick, Mollie. 1986. *Malice Domestic*. New York: Fawcett Crest, 1992.
1990. *The Dreaming Damozel*. New York: Fawcett Crest, 1995.
Harris, Robert. 1995. *Enigma*. London: Arrow Books, 1996.
Hart, Roy. 1987. *A Pretty Place for a Murder*. Roslyn, NY: Detective Book Club.
Hartmann, R. R. K., ed. 1986. *The History of Lexicography*. Amsterdam: Benjamins.
Hazleton, Lesley. 1990. *England, Bloody England*. New York: Atlantic Monthly Press.
Highway Code = Department of Transport and Central Office of Information. 1996. *The Highway Code*. London: HMSO.
Hill, Reginald. 1976. *Another Death in Venice*. New York: Signet, 1987.
Holroyd, Michael. 1988. *Bernard Shaw*. New York: Random House.
Honey, John. 1989. *Does Accent Matter? The Pygmalion Factor*. London: Faber and Faber.
Household, Geoffrey. 1980. *The Sending*. Harmondsworth, Middlesex: Penguin.
How to Speak EastEnders: A Brief Glossary of Cockney Expressions. 1988. N.p.: Lionheart Television.
Howard, Philip. 1990. *A Word in Time*. London: Sinclair-Stevenson.
Innes, Michael. 1937. *Hamlet, Revenge!* Harmondsworth, Middlesex: Penguin, 1979.
1937. *Seven Suspects*. New York: Penguin, 1984.
1945. *Appleby's End*. New York: Harper & Row, Perennial, 1983.
1959. *Hare Sitting Up*. New York: Harper & Row, Perennial, 1982.
1973. *Appleby's Answer*. Harmondsworth, Middlesex: Penguin, 1985.
1974. *The Mysterious Commission*. Harmondsworth, Middlesex: Penguin, 1985.

1981. *Lord Mullion's Secret*. Harmondsworth, Middlesex: Penguin, 1983.
1983. *Appleby and Honeybath*. Harmondsworth, Middlesex: Penguin, 1984.
James, P. D. 1986. *A Taste for Death*. New York: Warner, 1987.
1990. *Devices and Desires*. New York: Knopf.
1997. *A Certain Justice*. London: Faber and Faber, 1998.
2001. *Death in Holy Orders*. New York: Ballantine, 2002.
2003. *The Murder Room*. New York: Random House, Vintage, 2004.
Johnson, Pamela Hansford. 1970. *The Honours Board*. New York: Scribner's.
Jones, Tanya. 1995. *Ophelia O. and the Mortgage Bandits*. London: Headline.
Joss, Morag. 1998. *Funeral Music*. London: Hodder and Stoughton, 1999.
Kavanagh, Dan. 1980. *Duffy*. New York: Perennial Library, 1989.
Knight, Christopher, and Robert Lomas. 1996. *The Hiram Key*. London: Century.
Knox, Bill. 1986. *The Crossfire Killings*. New York: Doubleday.
Lawrence, Thomas Edward. 1938. *The Letters of T. E. Lawrence*. Ed. David Garnett. London: Cape.
Leadbeater, Charles W. 1925. *The Masters and the Path*. Adyar, Madras, India: Theosophical Publishing House, 1983.
Lemarchand, Elizabeth. 1981. *Nothing to Do with the Case*. New York: Walker.
Lessing, Doris. 2001. *The Sweetest Dream*. London: HarperCollins, Flamingo, 2002.
Levi, Peter. 1985. *Grave Witness*. New York: St. Martin's.
Lewis, C. S. 1956. *The Dark Tower*. London: Collins, 1985.
Lodge, David. 1962. *Ginger, You're Barmy*. Harmondsworth, Middlesex: Penguin, 1985.
1975. *Changing Places*. London: Penguin, 1978.
1984. *Small World: An Academic Romance*. London: Penguin, 1985.
1988. *Nice Work*. London: Penguin, 1989.
1991. *Paradise News*. London: Penguin, 1992.
1995. *Therapy*. London: Penguin Books, 1996.
2001. *Thinks. . . .* London: Penguin, 2002.
Lynn, Jonathan, and Antony Jay. 1981. *Yes Minister: The Diaries of a Cabinet Minister*. Vol. 1. London: British Broadcasting Corp.
1982. *Yes Minister: The Diaries of a Cabinet Minister*. Vol. 2. London: British Broadcasting Corp.
Mann, Jessica. 1983. *No Man's Island*. New York: Vintage, 1985.
Mason, Sarah J. 1993. *Frozen Stiff*. New York: Berkeley Books.
Mead, G. R. S. 1908. *The Wedding-Song of Wisdom*. London: Theosophical Publishing Society.
Mort, Simon. 1986. *Longman Guardian New Words*. Harlow, Essex: Longman.
Mortimer, John. 1953. *Like Men Betrayed*. London: Penguin, 1990.
1984. *A Voyage round My Father; The Dock Brief; What Shall We Tell Caroline*. [3 plays copyright 1971, 1958, 1958, respectively.] London: Penguin Books, television edition.
1985. *Paradise Postponed*. New York: Viking Penguin, 1986.
1988. *Summer's Lease*. London: Penguin.
2001. *Rumpole Rests His Case*. London: Penguin, 2002.
Neel, Janet. 1991. *Death of a Partner*. New York: Pocket Books, 1994.
1993. *Death among the Dons*. London: Penguin, 1994.
1996. *A Timely Death*. Harmondsworth, England: Penguin, 1997.
Nicholson, Geoff. 1989. *The Knot Garden*. London: Sceptre, 1990.

Oliver, Anthony. 1987. *Cover-Up*. New York: Fawcett Crest, 1988.
Opie, Iona, and Peter Opie. 1959. *The Lore and Language of Schoolchildren*. Oxford: Clarendon.
Pettigrew, Jane. 1986. *Tea Time*. London: Dorling Kindersley, 1989.
Porter, Joyce. 1968. *Dover Goes to Pott*. Woodstock, VT: Foul Play Press, 1990.
Potter, Dennis. 1974. *Waiting for the Boat*. London: Faber and Faber, 1984.
Price, Anthony. 1972. *Colonel Butler's Wolf*. London: Futura, 1983.
1974. *Other Paths to Glory*. London: Futura, 1985.
1975. *Our Man in Camelot*. London: Futura, 1984.
1979. *Tomorrow's Ghost*. London: Futura, 1984.
1984. *Sion Crossing*. New York: Mysterious Press, 1986.
1985. *Here Be Monsters*. London: Collins, Grafton, 1986.
1986. *For the Good of the State*. London: Collins, Grafton, 1987.
Priestley, J. B. 1966. *Salt Is Leaving*. New York: Carroll & Graf, 1986.
Pym, Barbara. 1982. *An Unsuitable Attachment*. London: Grafton, Collins, 1988.
1985. *Crampton Hodnet*. New York: Dutton.
Quinton, Ann. 1989. *To Mourn a Mischief*. London: Headline, 1990.
Radley, Sheila. 1983. *The Quiet Road to Death*. New York: Penguin, 1985.
Raphael, Frederic. 1976. *The Glittering Prizes*. London: Penguin, 1988.
Rendell, Ruth. 1969. *The Best Man to Die*. London: Arrow, 1994.
1972. *No More Dying Then*. New York: Bantam Books, 1986.
1989. *The Bridesmaid*. London: Arrow, 1990.
Richardson, Alan. 1985. *Dancers to the Gods*. Wellingborough, Northants: Aquarian Press.
Robinson, Robert. 1956. *Landscape with Dead Dons*. London: Penguin, 1983.
Rowlands, Betty. 1990. *A Little Gentle Sleuthing*. New York: Berkley, Jove, 1992.
Rowling, Joanne K. 1997. *Harry Potter and the Philosopher's Stone*. London: Bloomsbury.
1998. *Harry Potter and the Chamber of Secrets*. London: Bloomsbury.
1999. *Harry Potter and the Prisoner of Azkaban*. London: Bloomsbury.
2000. *Harry Potter and the Goblet of Fire*. London: Bloomsbury.
2003. *Harry Potter and the Order of the Phoenix*. London: Bloomsbury, 2004.
Rutherfurd, Edward. 1987. *Sarum: The Novel of England*. New York: Crown.
Sayers, Dorothy L., and Jill Paton Walsh. 1998. *Thrones, Dominations*. New York: St. Martin's, 1999.
Sharpe, Tom. 1980. *Ancestral Vices*. London: Pan, 1982.
1982. *Vintage Stuff*. London: Pan, 1983.
Sherwood, John. 1986. *The Mantrap Garden*. New York: Ballantine, 1987.
Shute, Nevil. 1940. *Landfall*. London: Pan Books, 1962.
Simpson, Dorothy. 1982. *Six Feet Under*. New York: Bantam, 1985.
1986. *Dead on Arrival*. New York: Bantam Books, 1989.
Smith, Godfrey. 1984. *The English Companion*. New York: Potter.
Smith, Joan. 1987. *A Masculine Ending*. London: Faber, 1989.
1993. *What Men Say*. London: Chatto & Windus.
Smith, Sean. 2002. *J. K. Rowling: A Biography*. London: Random House, Arrow Books.
Snow, C. P. 1974. *In Their Wisdom*. New York: Scribner's.
1979. *A Coat of Varnish*. New York: Scribner's, 1988.
Stallwood, Veronica. 1993. *Death and the Oxford Box*. London: Headline, 1994.
Stoppard, Tom. 1988. *Hapgood*. London: Faber and Faber.
1995. *Indian Ink*. London: Faber and Faber.

Symons, Julian. 1982. *The Detling Secret*. Harmondsworth: Penguin, 1984.
1994. *Playing Happy Families*. New York: Mysterious Press, 1995.
Taylor, Alison G. 1998. *The House of Women*. London: Heinemann.
Taylor, Andrew. 1985. *Our Fathers' Lies*. New York: Penguin, 1986.
1988. *Freelance Death*. New York: Penguin, 1989.
Tey, Josephine. 1949. *The Franchise Affair*. New York: Pocket Books, 1977.
Thirkell, Angela. 1942. *Marling Hall*. New York: Knopf.
Tolkien, J. R. R. 1954. *The Fellowship of the Ring*. 2nd ed. London: Allen & Unwin, 1965.
1955. *The Return of the King*. 2nd ed. London: Allen & Unwin, 1966.
Townsend, Sue. 1985. *The Adrian Mole Diaries*. London: Methuen.
Travers, Pamela L. 1934. *Mary Poppins*. London: HarperCollins, 1998.
Trollope, Joanna. 1988. *The Choir*. London: Black Swan, 1995.
1989. *A Village Affair*. London: Black Swan, 1995.
1991. *The Rector's Wife*. London: Transworld, 1992.
1993. *A Spanish Lover*. London: Black Swan, 1994.
1998. *Other People's Children*. London: Black Swan, 1999.
Trudgill, Peter. 1982. *Coping with America*. Oxford: Blackwell, 1988.
Turnbull, Peter. 1989. *Condition Purple*. Roslyn, NY: Detective Book Club.
Underwood, Michael. 1978. *Anything but the Truth*. New York: St Martin's.
1989. *A Compelling Case*. New York: St Martin's.
Wainwright, John. 1989. *The Man Who Wasn't There*. Roslyn, NY: Detective Book Club.
Walters, Minette. 1992. *The Ice House*. London: St. Martin's, 1993.
1994. *The Scold's Bridle*. London: St. Martin's, 1995.
Williams, David. 1989. *Holy Treasure!* Roslyn, NY: Detective Book Club.
Wilson, Derek. 1995. *The Hellfire Papers*. London: Headline.
Winchester, Simon. 1998. *The Professor and the Madman: A Tale of Murder, Insanity, and the Making of the "Oxford English Dictionary."* New York: HarperCollins.

Bibliography of studies, dictionaries, and corpora

AHD = *The American Heritage Dictionary of the English Language*. 2000. 4th ed. Ed. Joseph P. Pickett. Boston: Houghton Mifflin.

Algeo, John. 1988. "British and American Grammatical Differences." *International Journal of Lexicography* 1:1–31.

1988a. "The Tag Question in British English: It's Different, I'n't?" *English World Wide* 9:171–91.

1989. "Queuing and Other Idiosyncrasies." *World Englishes* 8.2:157–63.

1992. "British and American Mandative Constructions." In *Language and Civilization*, ed. Claudia Blank, 2:599–617. Frankfurt-on-Main: Peter Lang.

1995. "Having a Look at the Expanded Predicate." In *The Verb in Contemporary English: Theory and Description*, ed. Bas Aarts and Charles F. Meyer, 203–17. Cambridge: Cambridge University Press.

Algeo, John, and Adele Algeo. Corpus of contemporary citations of British lexical and grammatical items.

Algeo, John, and Thomas Pyles. 2004. *The Origins and Development of the English Language*. 5th ed. rev. Boston: Thomson, Wadsworth.

Allerton, David John. 2002. *Stretched Verb Constructions in English*. London: Routledge.

Andersen, Stan. 1972. "The British-American Differences: Processes of Change." *Neuphilologische Mitteilungen* 73:855–65.

BBI = *The BBI Combinatory Dictionary of English: A Guide to Word Combinations*. 1986. By Morton Benson, Evelyn Benson, and Robert Ilson. Amsterdam: Benjamins.

BBI-97 = *The BBI Dictionary of English Word Combinations*. 1997. Rev. ed. By Morton Benson, Evelyn Benson, and Robert Ilson. Amsterdam: Benjamins.

Benson, Morton, Evelyn Benson, and Robert Ilson. See *BBI* and *BBI*-97.

Biber, Douglas. 1987. "A Textual Comparison between British and American Writing." *American Speech* 62:99–119.

Biber, Douglas, Stig Johansson, Geoffrey Leech, Susan Conrad, and Edward Finegan. See *LGSWE*.

BNC = British National Corpus. A computerized database of more than a hundred million words compiled by several publishers and educational institutions. http://info.ox.ac.uk/bnc/. http://www.hcu.ox.ac.uk/BNC/.

Brinton, Laurel J., and Minoji Akimoto, eds. 1999. *Collocational and Idiomatic Aspects of Composite Predicates in the History of English*. Amsterdam: Benjamins.

British National Corpus. See BNC.

Brown, Lesley. See *NSOED*.

Brown Corpus of edited American English, 1961. ICAME CD-Rom. http://helmer.hit.uib.no/icame/cd/.

Burchfield, Robert W., ed. 1996. *The New Fowler's Modern English Usage*. 3rd ed. Oxford: Clarendon.

Burgess, Anthony. 1992. *A Mouthful of Air: Language, Languages . . . Especially English*. New York: Morrow.

Butcher, Judith. 1992. *Copy-Editing: The Cambridge Handbook for Editors, Authors and Publishers*. 3rd ed. Cambridge: Cambridge University Press.

Butters, Ronald R. 1983. "Syntactic Change in British English Propredicates." *Journal of English Linguistics* 16:1–7.

1989. "Cisatlantic *Have Done*." *American Speech* 64:96.

Cambridge International Corpus. See CIC.

CamGEL = *The Cambridge Grammar of the English Language*. 2002. By Rodney Huddleston and Geoffrey K. Pullum. Cambridge: Cambridge University Press.

Cassidy, Frederic G., and Joan Houston Hall. See *DARE*.

CED = *Collins English Dictionary*. 1991. 3rd ed. Glasgow: HarperCollins.

CGEL = *A Comprehensive Grammar of the English Language*. 1985. By Randolph Quirk, Sidney Greenbaum, Geoffrey Leech, and Jan Svartvik. London: Longman. Cited by section numbers rather than pages.

Chapman, Robert L. 1989. *Thesaurus of American Slang*. New York: Harper & Row.

Chicago Manual of Style. 2003. 15th ed. Chicago: University of Chicago Press.

CIC = Cambridge International Corpus. 198 million words of spoken and edited British and American English. Cambridge: Cambridge University Press.

CIDE = *Cambridge International Dictionary of English*. 1995. Ed. Paul Procter. Cambridge: Cambridge University Press.

Claridge, Claudia. 1997. "A Century in the Life of Multi-Word Verbs." In *Corpus-based Studies in English: Papers from the Seventeenth International Conference on English Language Research on Computerized Corpora (ICAME 17), Stockholm, May 15–19, 1996*, ed. Magnus Ljung, 69–85. Amsterdam: Rodopi.

Collins English Dictionary. See *CED*.

Concise Oxford = *The Concise Oxford Dictionary of Current English*. 1995. 9th ed. Ed. Della Thompson. Oxford: Clarendon.

Connell, Tim. 2001. "*In* versus *On* Revisited." *English Today* 66 17:29–31.

Curzan, Anne. 2003. *Gender Shifts in the History of English*. Cambridge: Cambridge University Press.

DARE = *Dictionary of American Regional English*. 1985–. Vols. 1–. Ed. Frederic G. Cassidy and Joan Houston Hall. Cambridge, MA: Belknap Press of Harvard University Press.

Di Paolo, Marianna. 1993. "Propredicate *Do* in the English of the Intermountain West." *American Speech* 68:339–56.

Estling, Maria. 1999. "Going out (of) the Window?" *English Today* 59 15.3:22–7.

Flexner, Stuart Berg, ed. 1987. *The Random House Dictionary of the English Language*. 2nd ed. New York: Random House.

FLOB Corpus of edited British English, 1991. A parallel to the LOB (Lancaster-Oslo-Bergen) Corpus prepared at the University of Freiburg. ICAME CD-Rom. http://helmer.hit.uib.no/icame/cd/.

Francis, W. Nelson, and Henry Kučera. 1982. *Frequency Analysis of English Usage: Lexicon and Grammar*. Boston: Houghton Mifflin.

Fries, Udo. 1993. "Periphrastic Comparison of Monosyllabic Adjectives." In *The Noun Phrase in English: Its Structure and Variability*, ed. Andreas H. Jucker, 25–44. Anglistik & Englischunterricht 49. Heidelberg: Winter.

Frown Corpus of edited American English. 1992. A parallel to the Brown Corpus prepared at the University of Freiburg. ICAME CD-Rom. http://helmer.hit.uib.no/icame/cd/.

Gilman, E. Ward, ed. 1994. *Merriam-Webster's Dictionary of English Usage*. Springfield, MA: Merriam-Webster, first pub. 1989.

Gowers, Sir Ernest. 1986. *The Complete Plain Words*. Rev. ed. Sidney Greenbaum and Janet Whitcut. London: Her Majesty's Stationery Office.

Green, Jonathon. 1998. *The Cassell Dictionary of Slang*. London: Cassell, 1999.

Greenbaum, Sidney. 1986. "The *Grammar of Contemporary English* and the *Comprehensive Grammar of the English Language*." In *The English Reference Grammar: Language and Linguistics, Writers and Readers*, ed. Gerhard Leitner, 6–14. Tübingen: Niemeyer.

1988. *Good English and the Grammarian*. London: Longman.

Hargraves, Orin. 2003. *Mighty Fine Words and Smashing Expressions: Making Sense of Transatlantic English*. Oxford: Oxford University Press.

Heacock, Paul, and Carol-June Cassidy. 1998. "Translating a Dictionary from British to American." In *The Major Varieties of English: Papers from MAVEN 97*, ed. Hans Lindquist, Staffan Klintborg, Magnus Levin, and Maria Estling, 93–9. Växjö, Sweden: University of Växjö.

Hofland, Knut, and Stig Johansson. 1982. *Word Frequencies in British and American English*. Bergen: Norwegian Computing Centre for the Humanities.

Horwill, Herbert W. 1935. *A Dictionary of Modern American Usage*. Oxford: Clarendon.

Huddleston, Rodney. 1970. "Two Approaches to the Analysis of Tags." *Journal of Linguistics* 6:215–22.

Huddleston, Rodney, and Geoffrey K. Pullum. See *CamGEL*.

Hundt, Marianne. 1997. "Has BrE Been Catching Up with AmE over the Past Thirty Years?" In *Corpus-based Studies in English: Papers from the Seventeenth International Conference on English Language Research on Computerized Corpora (ICAME 17), Stockholm, May 15–19, 1996*, ed. Magnus Ljung, 135–51. Amsterdam: Rodopi.

1998. *New Zealand English Grammar: Fact or Fiction? A Corpus-based Study in Morphosyntactic Variation*. Amsterdam: Benjamins.

1998a. "It Is Important That This Study (*Should*) *Be* Based on the Analysis of Parallel Corpora: On the Use of the Mandative Subjunctive in Four Major Varieties of English." In *The Major Varieties of English: Papers from MAVEN 97*, ed. Hans Lindquist, Staffan Klintborg, Magnus Levin, and Maria Estling, 159–75. Växjö, Sweden: University of Växjö.

ICE-GB = The International Corpus of English: The British Component. CD-Rom. http://www.ucl.ac.uk/english-usage/ice-gb/index.htm.

International Corpus of English. See ICE-GB.

Iyeiri, Yoko, Michiko Yaguchi, and Hiroko Okabe. 2004. "*To Be Different From* or *To Be Different Than* in Present-Day American English?" *English Today* 79 20.3:29–33.

Jespersen, Otto. 1940. *A Modern English Grammar on Historical Principles*. 7 vols. London: Allen & Unwin, 1961, 1965.

Johansson, Stig. 1979. "American and British English Grammar: An Elicitation Experiment." *English Studies* 60:195–215.

Johansson, Stig, and Knut Hofland. 1989. *Frequency Analysis of English Vocabulary and Grammar, Based on the LOB Corpus*. Vol. 2: *Tag Combinations and Word Combinations*. Oxford: Clarendon.

Kahn, John Ellison, and Robert Ilson. 1985. *The Right Word at the Right Time*. London: Reader's Digest Association.

Kjellmer, Göran. 1997. "The Conjunction *Once*." In *From Ælfric to the New York Times: Studies in English Corpus Linguistics*, ed. Udo Fries, Viviane Müller, and Peter Schneider, 173–81. Amsterdam: Rodopi.

Lancaster-Oslo-Bergen Corpus. See LOB.

Lavelle, Thomas, and David Minugh. 1998. "And High Time Too: A Corpus-based Study of One English Construction." In *The Major Varieties of English: Papers from MAVEN 97*, ed. Hans Lindquist, Staffan Klintborg, Magnus Levin, and Maria Estling, 213–26. Växjö, Sweden: University of Växjö.

LDEL = *Longman Dictionary of the English Language*. 1991. New ed. Harlow, Essex: Longman.

LDOCE = *Longman Dictionary of Contemporary English*. 1995. 3rd ed. Harlow, Essex: Longman.

LDOCE 1978 = *Longman Dictionary of Contemporary English*. 1978. Harlow, Essex: Longman.

LGSWE = *Longman Grammar of Spoken and Written English*. 1999. By Douglas Biber, Stig Johansson, Geoffrey Leech, Susan Conrad, and Edward Finegan. Harlow, Essex: Pearson.

Levin, Magnus. 1998. "Concord with Collective Nouns in British and American English." In *The Major Varieties of English: Papers from MAVEN 97*, ed. Hans Lindquist, Staffan Klintborg, Magnus Levin, and Maria Estling, 193–204. Växjö, Sweden: University of Växjö.

2001. *Agreement with Collective Nouns in English*. Lund Studies in English 103. Lund, Sweden: Lund University.

Lindquist, Hans. 1998. "The Comparison of Disyllabic Adjectives in *-y* and *-ly* in Present-day British and American English." In *The Major Varieties of English: Papers from MAVEN 97*, ed. Hans Lindquist, Staffan Klintborg, Magnus Levin, and Maria Estling, 205–12. Växjö, Sweden: University of Växjö.

Ljung, Magnus. 1997. "The *S*-genitive and the *Of*-construction in Different Types of English Texts." In *From Ælfric to the New York Times: Studies in English Corpus Linguistics*, ed. Udo Fries, Viviane Müller, and Peter Schneider, 21–32. Amsterdam: Rodopi.

LOB = Lancaster-Oslo-Bergen Corpus of edited British English, 1961. A parallel to the Brown Corpus. ICAME CD-Rom. http://helmer.hit.uib.no/icame/cd/.

Longman Dictionary of Contemporary English. See *LDOCE* and *LDOCE* 1978.

Longman Dictionary of the English Language. See *LDEL*.

Mair, Christian. 1997. "The Spread of the *Going-to*-Future in Written English: A Corpus-based Investigation into Language Change in Progress." *Language History and Linguistic Modelling: A Festschrift for Jacek Fisiak on His 60th Birthday*, ed. Raymond Hickey and Stanislaw Puppel, 1537–43. Berlin: Mouton de Gruyter.

1998. "Corpora and the Study of the Major Varieties of English: Issues and Results." In *The Major Varieties of English: Papers from MAVEN 97*, ed. Hans Lindquist, Staffan Klintborg, Magnus Levin, and Maria Estling, 139–57. Växjö, Sweden: University of Växjö.

McMillan, James B. "Infixing and Interposing in English." *American Speech* 55 (1980): 163–83.

McMillion, Alan. 1998. "Ergative Verb Variation in British and American English." In *The Major Varieties of English: Papers from MAVEN 97*, ed. Hans Lindquist, Staffan Klintborg, Magnus Levin, and Maria Estling, 227–37. Växjö, Sweden: University of Växjö.

MICASE = Michigan Corpus of Academic Spoken English. http://www.hti.umich.edu/m/micase/.

Michigan Corpus of Academic Spoken English. See MICASE.

Millar, Martin, and Keith Brown. 1979. "Tag Questions in Edinburgh Speech." *Linguistische Berichte* 60:24–45.

Mindt, Dieter, and Christel Weber. 1989. "Prepositions in American and British English." *World Englishes* 8:229–38.

Mish, Frederick C. See *MW*.

MW = *Merriam-Webster's Collegiate Dictionary*. 2003. 11th ed. Ed. Frederick C. Mish. Springfield, MA: Merriam-Webster.

Nässlin, Siv. 1984. *The English Tag Question: A Study of Sentences Containing Tags of the Type "Isn't It?" "Is It?"* Stockholm: University of Stockholm.

Nichols, Ann Eljenholm. 1987. "The Suasive Subjunctive: Alive and Well in the Upper Midwest." *American Speech* 62:140–52.

NODE = *The New Oxford Dictionary of English*. 1998. Ed. Judy Pearsall and Patrick Hanks. Oxford: Clarendon.

NSOED = *The New Shorter Oxford English Dictionary on Historical Principles*. 1993. Ed. Lesley Brown. Oxford: Clarendon.

O'Connor, J. D. 1955. "The Intonation of Tag Questions in English." *English Studies* 36:97–105.

OED = *The Oxford English Dictionary*. 1992. 2nd ed. on Compact Disc. Oxford: Oxford University Press, 1992.

Övergaard, Gerd. 1995. *The Mandative Subjunctive in American and British English in the 20th Century*. Studia Anglistica Upsaliensia 94. Uppsala: Acta Universitatis Upsaliensis.

Oxford English Dictionary. See *OED*.

Palmer, Frank R. 1968. *A Linguistic Study of the English Verb*. Coral Gables, FL: University of Miami Press.

Partridge, Eric, and John W. Clark. 1951. *British and American English since 1900*. London: Andrew Dakers.

Pearsall, Judy, and Patrick Hanks. See *NODE*.

Peters, Pam. 1999. "Plurals of Latin Loanwords: A Report on LANGSCAPE 4." *English Today* 59 15.3:28–32.

2004. *The Cambridge Guide to English Usage*. Cambridge: Cambridge University Press.

Pickett, Joseph P. See *AHD*.

Procter, Paul. See *CIDE*.

Quirk, Randolph, Sidney Greenbaum, Geoffrey Leech, and Jan Svartvik. See *CGEL*.

Read, Allen Walker. Corpus of historical citations of British lexical items.

Ritter, Robert M. 2002. *The Oxford Guide to Style*. Oxford: Oxford University Press.

Rosenbach, Anette. 2002. *Genitive Variation in English: Conceptual Factors in Synchronic and Diachronic Studies*. Berlin: Mouton de Gruyter.

Safire, William. 2004. "On Language." *New York Times Magazine* (June 27): 21.

Seaton, Anne. 2005. "Explaining *Oneself*." *English Today* 83 21.3:8–15.

SEU = Survey of English Usage. University College London corpus of contemporary British texts.

Stein, Gabriele. 1991. "The Phrasal Verb Type 'To Have a Look' in Modern English." *International Review of Applied Linguistics* 29:1–29.

Stein, Gabriele, and Randolph Quirk. 1991. "On Having a Look in a Corpus." In *English Corpus Linguistics: Studies in Honour of Jan Svartvik*, ed. Karin Aijmer and Bengt Altenberg, 197–203. London: Longman.

Stenström, Anna-Brita. 1997. "Tags in Teenage Talk." In *From Ælfric to the New York Times: Studies in English Corpus Linguistics*, ed. Udo Fries, Viviane Müller, and Peter Schneider, 139–47. Amsterdam: Rodopi.

Survey of English Usage. See SEU.

Swan, Michael. 1995. *Practical English Usage*. 2nd ed. Oxford: Oxford University Press.

Szmrecsanyi, Benedikt. 2003. "BE GOING TO versus WILL/SHALL." *Journal of English Linguistics* 31:295–323.

Thompson, Della. See *Concise Oxford*.

Thumboo, Edwin, ed. 2001. *The Three Circles of English: Language Specialists Talk about the English Language*. Singapore: UniPress, Centre for the Arts, National University of Singapore.

Tottie, Gunnel. 1991. "Conversational Style in British and American English: The Case of Backchannels." In *English Corpus Linguistics: Studies in Honour of Jan Svartvik*, ed. Karin Aijmer and Bengt Altenberg, 254–71. London: Longman.

2002. *An Introduction to American English*. Oxford: Blackwell.

Trudgill, Peter. 1988. *Coping with America*. 2nd ed. Oxford: Blackwell.

Trudgill, Peter, and Jean Hannah. 2002. *International English: A Guide to Varieties of Standard English*. 4th ed. London: Arnold. 1st ed. 1982.

Turner, John F. 1980. "The Marked Subjunctive in Contemporary English." *Studia Neophilologica* 52:271–7.

Wales, Katie. 1996. *Personal Pronouns in Present-Day English*. Cambridge: Cambridge University Press.

Weiner, E. S. C. 1983. *The Oxford Guide to English Usage*. Oxford: Clarendon.

Weiner, E.S.C., and Andrew Delahunty. 1994. *The Oxford Guide to English Usage*. 2nd ed. Oxford: Clarendon.

Wierzbicka, Anna. 1982. "Why Can You *Have a Drink* When You Can't **Have an Eat*?" *Language* 58:753–99.

Index